Major-General Oliver Nugent

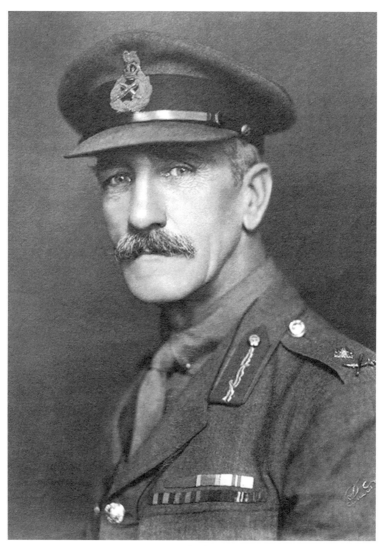

Major-General Oliver Nugent

Major-General Oliver Nugent

The Irishman who led
the Ulster Division in the Great War

NICHOLAS PERRY

ULSTER HISTORICAL FOUNDATION

DUSTJACKET
Front cover – Major-General Sir Oliver Nugent (William Conor)
This portrait is reproduced by the kind permission of Belfast City Council.
The original can be viewed at City Hall, Belfast
Rear – Nugent at the unveiling of the Lisburn war memorial,1923 (PRONI)
Inside front flap – British troops in the Boer war (Nugent family)
Inside rear flap – Ulster Division training, 1915 (PRONI)

ENDPAPERS
Front – The officers of 1st KRRC, India, 1895:
Nugent seated 4th from right (Nugent family)

Back – The officers of 1st KRRC at the Malakand Pass, 1895:
Nugent seated at the front, 2nd from left (Nugent family)

Published 2020
by Ulster Historical Foundation
www.ancestryireland.com
www.booksireland.org.uk

ISBN: 978-1-909556-82-9

DESIGN AND FORMATTING
FPM Publishing

COVER DESIGN
Jill Morrison

PRINTED BY
Gráficas Castuera

Contents

INTRODUCTION   vii

ACKNOWLEDGEMENTS   ix

NOTE ON OLIVER NUGENT'S PAPERS   xi

GLOSSARY   xii

1   Imperial Warrior: The Nugents, the Irish gentry   1
    and the British army, 1860–1900

2   Conflicted Soldier: Defending Cavan and protecting Hull,   34
    1901–April 1915

3   Learning the Ropes: Integrating the New Armies,   55
    May–August 1915

4   Divisional Commander: Politics and professionalism   81
    in the Ulster Division, September 1915–June 1916

5   Sacrifice on the Somme: Operational failure,   110
    reputational triumph, July 1916

6   Manpower and Politics: Recruitment and trench warfare,   135
    August 1916–March 1917

7   Wearing Out: The Irish Divisions, attrition and the   163
    limits of partnership, April–August 1917

8   New Ways of War: Cambrai and the birth of military   197
    modernity, September 1917–February 1918

9   Kaiserschlacht: The German spring offensive and the   227
    crisis in command, March–May 1918

10 Staying On: India, Ireland and the crisis of empire,   259
      June 1918–May 1926

11 Conclusion   281

    ANNEX A: ORDER OF BATTLE   283

    BIBLIOGRAPHY   285

    INDEX   298

Introduction

On the morning of 27 March 1918 the commander of the 36th (Ulster) Division, Oliver Nugent, and one of his brigadiers, William Hessey, met in a small French village near Montdidier to discuss how to stop, with the handful of exhausted troops they had left, the two German divisions bearing down on them. Both men knew that the next few hours were critical, because the Ulster Division, which had been fighting for its life for six days in the teeth of Germany's largest offensive of the war, was facing annihilation. At the same time in London, in the very different surroundings of 10 Downing Street, members of Lloyd George's cabinet were assembling to consider extending conscription to Ireland. Their decision the following day to do so would have far-reaching consequences for Ireland's political future and accelerate the collapse of support for the war across much of the island.

This coincidence of military and political events, with Irish soldiers fighting desperately at the front while political decisions were taken at home that would impact directly on the levels of support they received, was not a new experience for Nugent; he had encountered similar situations in both 1916 and 1917. It illustrated once again, however, the tensions inherent in his command of a unique division and the interconnectedness of the military and political factors he had to manage. The dilemmas were personal as well as professional. As a regular soldier he wanted compulsory service as a means of keeping his division up to strength and in action, but as a Cavan landowner he had also hoped for an Irish political settlement based on devolved government for the entire island within the United Kingdom (not a view shared by the division's political patrons, Edward Carson and James Craig), a possibility that the conscription crisis would end forever. While highly-regarded by many senior officers, especially Herbert Plumer, his relations with his commander-in-chief, Douglas Haig, were by 1918 very strained, in part at least because of disagreements over the division's response to the falling numbers of Irishmen in its ranks, and Nugent went into the March fighting knowing that Haig intended to remove him at the next opportunity. And his relationship with James Craig, the Ulster unionist leader, with whom he might have expected to make common cause on conscription, had by now so completely broken down – fundamentally over their very different views on Ireland's future, but also over Ulster's recruiting performance – that they were scarcely on speaking terms.

How it came about that Nugent, an Irish unionist, ended up commanding an Ulster unionist formation and how this affected his approach to leading the Ulster Division in action are amongst the aspects of his career that this book seeks to explore. Others are how his previous experiences as an Irish landlord, colonial soldier and UVF organiser had shaped his views; how he turned his division of citizen-soldiers into an effective military formation; how he exercised command in their five biggest battles (the Somme, Messines, Third Ypres, Cambrai and the German spring 1918 offensive); and how he adapted to the revolutionary upheavals of post-war Ireland. His career reflects in many ways the broader fortunes of the Irish landed class between the mid-nineteenth century and partition, and also their relationship with the British army, on which I hope this study may shed some light.

Acknowledgements

I owe a great debt to the many people without whose help and support this book would never have seen the light of day.

It was Dr William Roulston of the Ulster Historical Foundation who first suggested it, and who has been unfailingly helpful (and patient) during its lengthy genesis.

Oliver Nugent's family have been hugely supportive: his daughter, Alison Hirschberg, who before her death in 2009 discussed her father with me on a number of occasions; his grandson, the late Myles Stoney, Myles's wife Susie and her son, Richard Moeran, both for their unstinting hospitality at Farren Connell and for providing much information and allowing me access to papers and photographs still in the family's possession; and his granddaughter Theffania Everett, great-granddaughter Benita Stoney and other members of the family for their support and interest.

The families of several senior officers connected with Nugent and the Ulster Division have been kind enough to provide information and share papers or photographs: Sarah Baker, who allowed me access to the correspondence of her grandfather William Hessey; A. G. Hickie and Sarah O'Connell, in connection with their ancestor William Hickie; Michael Pakenham regarding H. A. Pakenham; and Charles Comyn, in relation to his grandfather Lewis Comyn.

I am grateful to the staff of the Public Record Office of Northern Ireland, where Oliver Nugent's papers form part of the outstanding Farren Connell collection, for their help, especially Ian Montgomery, himself an historian of the Great War, and Dr Anthony Malcomson, who was Deputy Keeper of the Records when I first started working on Nugent's papers; I thank the current Deputy Keeper for permission to use material from the Farren Connell and other PRONI collections, identified in the bibliography. I am grateful similarly to the trustees of the Imperial War Museum and the National Library of Scotland for permission to use papers in their possession. Joanna Badrock, archivist at Harrow School, kindly provided details of Nugent's school career.

Dr Tim Bowman, Professor John Bourne and Chris McCarthy were heroic enough to read the entire manuscript in draft, and I have benefitted enormously from their perceptive comments. Professor Ian Beckett, Dr Terry Denman, and Robin Brodhurst kindly reviewed individual chapters, and Professor Sir Hew Strachan, Professor Christopher Tyerman, Dr

Jonathan Cherry, Dr Simon Jones, Dr Gyanesh Kudaisya, Dr Brendan Scott, Dr Tim Wilson, Alan Jeffreys and Nick Metcalfe helpfully provided information on specific issues. Their advice has been invaluable.

Other historians of Ireland and the First World War from whom I have learned an enormous amount include two outstanding and much missed scholars, Professors Keith Jeffery and David Fitzpatrick, along with Jane Leonard, Professor Richard Grayson, Philip Orr and Martin Staunton. Other historian friends, many of them fellow members of the British Commission for Military History, who have provided advice and information over the years include Will Bennett, Gordon Corrigan, Dr Tony Cowan, Dr Doug Delaney, Andy Grainger, Dr Paul Harris, John Lee, Kate Mazur, Major-General Mungo Melvin, the late Charles Messenger, Michael Orr, Dr John Peaty, Professor Bill Philpott, Dr Chris Pugsley, Peter Robinson, Professor Gary Sheffield, Professor Peter Simkins, Dr Andy Simpson, Kathy Stevenson, and Martin Windrow. In Northern Ireland I have been lucky enough to draw on the expertise of, amongst others, Robert Corbett, Richard Doherty, Dr Chris Manson, Amanda Moreno, Michael Nugent, Dr Stephen Sandford, Stephen Scarth, Alan Skelton, Dr Tom Thorpe, and Carol Walker and Alan McFarland (Somme Association), and in the Military History Society of Ireland Dr Harman Murtagh, Dr Pat McCarthy, Dr Kenneth Ferguson, Colonel Donal Carroll, Kevin Myers and Tom Burke.

Amongst military experts from whose practical knowledge I have profited over the years – including colleagues in an enjoyable 12-year spell as a reserve officer in the Royal Irish Rangers, which provided at least some insight into military life – are Major-Generals Anthony Leask and Colin Weir; Brigadiers Jeremy Mooney, Joe O'Sullivan, Andrew Roe and Rob Thompson; and Lieutenant-Colonels Andy Hart, Arthur Reid and Mark Scott.

Fintan Mullan, Dr William Roulston, Jill Morrison and the rest of Ulster Historical Foundation's production team have been both thoroughly professional and a pleasure to work with throughout the book's preparation.

And last, but most definitely not least, there is my wonderful family – Linda and Richard, Caroline and David, and Wendy (without whose tireless help this book would definitely not have been completed): they have all my love, and my gratitude.

It goes without saying that responsibility for any remaining errors, despite having had the benefit of so much assistance, is entirely mine.

Note on Oliver Nugent's papers

In 2007 the Army Records Society published an edition of Nugent's wartime correspondence, *Major General Oliver Nugent and the Ulster Division 1915–1918*, edited by myself. When letters reproduced there are cited in this volume, the references are (for reasons of accessibility) to the Army Records Society edition; where documents have not previously been published, references are to PRONI's Farren Connell (D3835) collection; and where papers and photographs remain in the possession of the family, they are identified here as the 'Nugent family papers'.

The name of the Cavan village where the Nugent estate was has two forms, Mount Nugent and Mountnugent. Oliver Nugent used the second, which is the one used here.

Glossary

AA&QMG	Assistant Adjutant & Quartermaster General
ADC	Aide de Camp
ADRIC	Auxiliary Division Royal Irish Constabulary
ANZAC	Australian and New Zealand Army Corps
BLSI	British Legion Southern Ireland branch
C in C	Commander-in-Chief
BEF	British Expeditionary Force
CIGS	Chief of the Imperial General Staff
CO	Commanding Officer
CRA	Commander Royal Artillery
CVF	Cavan Volunteer Force
DCLI	Duke of Cornwall's Light Infantry
DORA	Defence of the Realm Act
DSO	Distinguished Service Order
FSR	Field Service Regulations
GHQ	General Headquarters
GOC	General Officer Commanding
GSO	General Staff Officer
HQ	Headquarters
IRA	Irish Republican Army
IWA	Irish Women's Association
KOSB	King's Own Scottish Borderers
KOYLI	King's Own Yorkshire Light Infantry
KRRC	King's Royal Rifle Corps
MP	Member of Parliament
NCO	Non-Commissioned Officer
OP	Observation Post
OTC	Officer Training Corps
RFA	Royal Field Artillery
RIC	Royal Irish Constabulary
TF	Territorial Force
USC	Ulster Special Constabulary
UUC	Ulster Unionist Council
UVF	Ulster Volunteer Force

1

Imperial Warrior

The Nugents, the Irish gentry
and the British army, 1860–1900

Introduction

Oliver Nugent was born in 1860 into an important if not especially wealthy Irish landed family, and inherited a complex sense of identity in which Irish and British traditions were entwined: like his near-contemporary Henry Wilson, he 'grew up when the definition of 'Irishness' was by no means clear-cut'.[1] On his father's side the family's Hiberno-Norman origins went back to the twelfth century and on his mother's to British settlers of the seventeenth; his home in County Cavan lay in a part of Ireland where, as one historian has written, 'Britishness and Irishness met', too Catholic to be part of unionist Ulster but too Protestant to be completely part either of the nationalist heartland.[2] Nugent himself was a unionist, a regular British officer and a committed member of the Anglican Church of Ireland, and he had no difficulty in seeing himself as both Irish and British, in serving the crown and in supporting wholeheartedly Britain's imperial mission, but he was always very conscious, and proud, of his deep Irish roots. His awareness of his family's heritage and its long connection with the Irish midlands is of more than merely antiquarian interest when considering his career, because this profound sense of belonging influenced key decisions he would make, at home and on active service, during the Great War and Irish revolutionary period between 1912 and 1923.

The Nugents had lived on the Farren Connell estate, at Mountnugent in south Cavan, since the seventeenth century and as members of the Catholic gentry had fought for the Irish Confederation in the 1640s and the Jacobites in the 1690s. Those wars brought ruin for the Catholic landed interest but some families chose as a survival strategy to convert to Protestantism to keep their lands. The senior branch of the Nugents, the earls of Westmeath, did so and so did their cousins, the Nugents of Farren

---

[1] Keith Jeffery, *Field Marshal Sir Henry Wilson: A Political Soldier* (2006), p. 5.
[2] Alvin Jackson, *Colonel Edward Saunderson: Land and Loyalty in Victorian Ireland* (1995), p. 7.

Connell, who by the second half of the eighteenth century were fully integrated into the Protestant Irish ascendancy. They had also established a close association with the British army that would last well into the twentieth century.

The Nugents and the army

The Nugents' links with the British army began in the 1760s. While some landed Irish families (which until the Catholic relief acts of the 1790s almost invariably meant Protestant families) could trace their military origins back to service in the Elizabethan, Cromwellian and Williamite armies, for many their continuous connection with the army as an institution dated back to the middle decades of the eighteenth century. This period in effect saw the origin of Irish 'military' families, in the sense of long-term, multi-generational links with the British armed forces. Successive expansions of the officer corps between the 1740s and 1780s – followed rapidly by contractions, but each one leaving it somewhat larger than before – to meet the demands of the War of the Austrian Succession, the Seven Years War and the American War of Independence, provided opportunities eagerly sought by an ascendancy class feeling more secure in their property and domestic political position as the upheavals of the late seventeenth century receded, and keen to pursue military careers at a time when changing social attitudes were limiting the occupations open to gentlemen.[3] From then on the Irish landed class was a major source of officers for the army, and by the late nineteenth century the military tradition had become deeply embedded in the Protestant gentry's sense of identity (and amongst many Catholic landed families also). As the Anglo-Irish writer Elizabeth Bowen put it, 'Not a family had not put out, like Bowen's Court, its generations of military brothers – tablets in Protestant churches recorded deaths in remote battles; swords hung in halls'.[4]

The description accurately fitted the Nugents of Farren Connell, who sent five generations of officers into the army between 1760 and 1920. Two of Oliver Nugent's great-great uncles served in the early years of George III's reign, one fighting in the American war and the other, after leaving the British army, going on to spend 20 years in the Russian service. His

[3] For a similar process in Scotland, see Stana Nenadic, 'The Impact of the Military Profession on Highland Gentry Families, *c.* 1730–1830', *The Scottish Historical Review*, 85:1 (2006), pp 75–99.

[4] J. A. Houlding, *Fit for Service: the Training of the British Army, 1715–1795* (1981), pp 99–116; Stephen Conway, *War, State, and Society in Mid-Eighteenth-Century Britain and Ireland* (2006), pp 67–9; idem, *The British Isles and the War of American Independence* (2000), pp 30–32; Elizabeth Bowen, *Bowen's Court* (1942), p. 465.

grandfather, Christopher Edmond Nugent (1771–1853), was an officer of dragoons during the Napoleonic wars, during which three great-uncles also held commissions. His father, St George (1825–84), had served in the first Sikh War as an ensign in the 29th Regiment and been seriously wounded at Sobraon in 1846, subsequently holding appointments in Aldershot, Nova Scotia, Ireland and Malta before retiring as a major-general in 1880, while an uncle was an officer in the East India Company's Madras army. Oliver's son, also St George, was commissioned into his own regiment, the King's Royal Rifle Corps, in 1919. His mother's family too had military connections – Emily Litton, daughter of a senior judge who was Conservative MP for Coleraine, had a grandfather who had fought at Bunker Hill in 1775, while her brother Richard served in the Crimea and two of her sisters also married officers.[5] The apogee of the Irish landed class's commitment to service in the British military was perhaps the period between the mid-nineteenth century and the mid-twentieth, when around half the males from landed families to reach adulthood, including Nugent, his father and son, served as officers (regular, reserve or wartime) in the armed forces.[6] Although driven to a considerable extent by the two world wars their levels of military participation also reflected a search, considered further below, for collective purpose in military and imperial service at a time of political and socio-economic upheaval for them at home.

Early years

Nugent's career would be shaped by, along with his devotion to his family and dedication to the army, his commitment to the family estate, but when he was born on 9 November 1860 in Aldershot the chances of him inheriting Farren Connell seemed remote. His father was the youngest of six brothers, two of whom had sons ahead of Oliver in line of inheritance, while he himself had an older brother. By the 1880s, however, the accidents of mortality and the terms of his grandfather's will had transformed the situation. In 1865 his brother St George died, aged just six, and in 1876 his only surviving male cousin, Edmond, who had inherited Farren Connell,

---

[5] Family details from Burke's *Landed Gentry of Ireland* (1912). See also Brian Nugent, *A Guide to the 18th-Century Land Records in the Irish Registry of Deeds* (2012), pp 174–268.

[6] Nicholas Perry, 'The Irish Landed Class and the British Army, 1850–1950', *War in History*, 18:3 (2011), pp 304–32. Of 4,865 males aged 18 or over, from families with 1,000 acres or more in 1878, at least 2,412 (50%) were commissioned into the armed forces: 1,563 (32%) as regulars; 333 (7%) as militia officers; and 516 (11%) in the two world wars, of whom perhaps a third might have sought regular commissions in any event (ibid., p. 310).

died childless at the age of 37. On Oliver's 21st birthday in 1881 the estate passed to him as Christopher Nugent's eldest surviving grandson, though for the time being his father ran it on his behalf. Part of Oliver Nugent's lifelong commitment to Farren Connell may have stemmed from the fortuitous circumstances in which he succeeded to it. With the property, though, came significant financial burdens that in turn influenced his military career.

Nugent's early years had been spent in Halifax, Nova Scotia, where his father was stationed, but on the family's return to the United Kingdom he was sent to Harrow, staying at the school from 1874 to 1877. He was the first member of his immediate family to go to public school. Although aristocratic and wealthy Irish families had long sent their sons to schools like Harrow and Eton, it was not until the expansion of the public school movement in the middle of the nineteenth century, along with improved transport links, that Irish gentry families began sending their sons in large numbers to England and Scotland to be educated. By the early twentieth century most who could afford it did so, and the daughter of an Irish general later recalled that it 'had become obligatory to look and speak like an English public school man and, therefore, anyone who could scrape together the necessary cash sent his son to an English public school'.[7] This was not simply a matter of snobbery. The focus of the Irish landed class, as their privileged position at home was eroded, remained firmly on monarchy, military service and empire as embodying ideals (and offering opportunities) transcending the 'sordidness' of domestic politics. Indeed, a Protestant Irish observer, Canon Hannay, believed the Irish gentry lost touch with the bulk of their fellow countrymen precisely because their obsession with military and imperial service took so many of them overseas – they were 'dazzled with England's greatness and the prospect of Imperial power'.[8] Public schools, with their strong military and imperial ethos, served the dual purpose for aspiring parents of helping their sons establish the social connections they would later need while reinforcing their sense of belonging to a shared British identity.

Montagu Butler, Harrow's headmaster throughout Nugent's time, presided over 'one of the great powerhouses of the late nineteenth-century British Establishment'. Of 4,000 boys to pass through the school during Butler's tenure between 1860 and 1885, over 100 became MPs and one, Baldwin, Prime Minister, four were viceroys of India and one became

[7] Nora Robertson, *Crowned Harp* (1960), p. 101. She was the daughter of Sir Lawrence Parsons, commander of the 16th (Irish) Division in 1914–15.
[8] Quoted in Mark Bence-Jones, *Twilight of the Ascendancy* (1987), p. 154.

archbishop of Canterbury, while during the Great War the school produced no fewer than 64 generals, including Nugent.[9] At the school he demonstrated an aptitude for languages and English (family tradition says he and Winston Churchill shared the same English master) and a weakness in mathematics. Nineteenth-century public schools were tough environments and like Churchill in the 1890s Nugent did not look back on his school career with affection – so much so, indeed, that he sent his own son to Eton. The fault may not have been entirely Harrow's. The indications are that the young Nugent was difficult, clashing with a strict father and prone, as his early days with successive regiments would demonstrate, to alienating his peers by his quick temper and brashness. He left the school with a good education but few particular friends.[10]

Royal Munster Fusiliers

In October 1879 he was commissioned into the Cavan militia as a second-lieutenant, and from there he followed a route into the regular army used by many others, including John French, Henry Wilson and Bryan Mahon. Qualified militia officers (in the late 1870s the requirement was to be aged 19 to 22, have attended at least two annual trainings and passed an examination) could be recommended by their regiment for a regular commission and in this way Nugent secured a commission in the Royal Munster Fusiliers in July 1882, joining the 2nd Battalion in Malta that autumn.[11] The regiment had been in existence in its current form for little over a year, following the territorialisation of the infantry under the Liberal Secretary of State for War, Hugh Childers. Before that the 2nd Battalion had been the 104th Regiment, a title many of its members continued to use, but its origins lay in the East India Company's army as the 2nd Bengal European Regiment. It had been absorbed into the Queen's forces in 1861, one of the few European regiments not to mutiny during the transfer process, and had come to the British Isles for the first time in 1871. Its

[9] Christopher Tyerman, *A History of Harrow School 1324–1991* (2000), pp 303–04. I am grateful to Professor Tyerman for elucidating for me the Irish Harrovian connection. See also Geoffrey Best, 'Militarism and the Victorian Public School', in B. Simon and I. Bradley (eds), *The Victorian Public School* (1975), pp 129–46.

[10] I am indebted to Joanna Badrock, Harrow's archivist, for details of Nugent's school career.

[11] William Butler, *The Irish Amateur Tradition in the British Army 1854–1992* (2016), pp 58–60. Nugent may have been deterred from the alternative entry route, via the Royal Military College, Sandhurst, because of the expense.

move to Malta in August 1882 arose from the British intervention in Egypt that summer, though the battalion in the end was not deployed there.[12]

Nugent served with the Munsters for only nine months and it was not a positive experience. He found many of his fellow officers boorish and uncouth and his disapproval of them was cordially reciprocated. He disliked the rough horseplay that characterised life in the mess: following a fight with three drunken subalterns trying to dump him into a bath in the middle of the night, for example, he was left not only badly bruised but feeling 'awfully miserable'.[13] This sort of bullying heartiness was common and had he reacted better he might have been picked on less, his diary revealing an immature and self-centred young man, alternating spells of over-confidence with bursts of self-pity. Disastrously he let it be known that his father and uncle were working to secure his transfer to a more prestigious regiment, the King's Royal Rifle Corps, with the result that his popularity with his comrades plummeted, and in February 1883 he bemoaned his lot – 'what a terrible mistake I have made since I came out to Malta, boasting of my own prospects and family ... swaggering, extravagant when almost penniless, abusing my regiment all over the town in public. How can it have avoided coming to someone's ears in the regt'.[14] He did little to help himself, attracting the irritation of his superiors by being cavalier about his duties and constantly late, for drill, for gym, for inspections. When a popular officer left Nugent noted mournfully, 'I don't think anyone in the regt would weep at my leaving. I have not succeeded in making myself very popular. I hate them except Benson and Titus and they hate me'.[15] Despite this he was learning the basics of army life, including drill, musketry and at least some tactical training, where there were signs of him starting to take an interest in his profession. On a field day in March 1883, for example, he carried the regimental colours, still thought indispensable on the battlefield, during a practice attack but had doubts about the tactics:

> We did an attack and fired blank cartridge, so what colours were wanted for heaven only knows. The General muddled everything as

---

[12] Capt. S. McCance, *History of the Royal Munster Fusiliers* (1927), ii, pp 92–8; Peter Stanley, *White Mutiny: British Military Culture in India 1825–1875* (1998), pp 185–90.

[13] 9 Mar. 1883 (Nugent family papers, 1883 diary).

[14] 14 Feb. 1883 (Nugent family papers, 1883 diary).

[15] 12 Mar. 1883 (Nugent family papers, 1883 diary).

> usual. Wheeled the Brigade to a flank to prepare for Cavalry, thereby
> of course exposing them to a heavy enfilade from the enemy in our
> front, at least so it seemed to me.[16]

Illustrating the military revolution that occurred during his lifetime, 35
years later almost to the day, in March 1918, Nugent would be fighting a
battle involving tanks, aircraft, heavy artillery, gas, machine-guns and
flamethrowers – but, perhaps surprisingly, still mounted cavalry also.[17] At
last came the news that his transfer to the King's Royal Rifle Corps had
been approved and on 28 April 1883 he set sail for home. His assessment
of his time with the Munsters was candid: 'I began lonely enough in a
regiment I hated, and where I was hated. I had no friends in Malta, I made
none'.[18] He could now, at least, look forward to a fresh start in a sought-
after regiment.

The economics of soldiering

The 1st Battalion of the King's Royal Rifle Corps (KRRC) – also known as
the 60th Rifles, the title Nugent generally used – were stationed in the
Royal Barracks in Dublin, where he joined them in June 1883.[19] Although
he settled in better than he had with the Munster Fusiliers he still early on
managed to rub his fellow subalterns up the wrong way. More seriously, it
also quickly became clear that the £120 annual allowance his father had
given him on top of his yearly pay of £95 was quite insufficient to support
his extravagant lifestyle in an expensive regiment on a home posting.

The financial difficulties he faced illustrate some broader aspects of the
economics of soldiering for the Irish landed class in the late nineteenth
century. A key determinant of the viability of military careers, in an era
when army officers could not live on their pay, was self-evidently money,
the abolition of the purchase of commissions in 1871 notwithstanding.[20]
Irish landed officers, with their smaller and frequently under-capitalised
estates, were generally less well-off than their English counterparts, but the
most prominent Irish military families, like the Brookes and Pakenhams,
while lacking the significant wealth of families such as the Londonderrys,
were by Irish standards at least moderately prosperous (it was difficult
otherwise to sustain multiple members of a family in military careers over

[16] 15 Mar. 1883 (Nugent family papers, 1883 diary). Colours were carried in action
   by the British army for the last time at Tel-el-Kebir in 1882.
[17] See Chapter 9.
[18] 31 Dec. 1883 (Nugent family papers, 1883 diary).
[19] Now Collins Barracks. Maj.-Gen. Sir Steuart Hare, *The Annals of The King's Royal
   Rifle Corps* [henceforth *KRRC*] (1929), iv, pp 112–13.
[20] Edward M Spiers, *The Late Victorian Army 1868–1902* (1992), pp 103–05.

more than a generation). To generalise, poor Irish landowners often could not afford military careers; rich landowners could but frequently did not remain in the army for long; and so the majority of Irish landed career officers came from those middling-sized families whose incomes ranged from adequate to comfortable.[21]

The Nugents of Farren Connell fell into this third category. Although a distinguished county family they were not by the 1880s a rich one – the estate rental of around £1,500 was not large and for reasons to be discussed their disposable income was considerably less than that – and so they came from what economically might be called the 'lesser gentry', which provided around half of all Irish landed regular officers in the period from 1850 to 1950. Eight out of ten of these lesser gentry officers served in more affordable units such as the line infantry, artillery and engineers or the Indian army, and these economic realities were in turn reflected in the geography of officer recruitment.[22] Ulster and Leinster, the most prosperous provinces, were also the most militarised, with over half the males aged 18 and over from their landed families being commissioned; but there were regional variations within this overall pattern, and it was in the agriculturally mixed areas of central and south Ulster, south Leinster and north Munster, where lesser gentry families were common, that the levels of landed regular military service were highest.[23] Some historians have seen in the Anglo-Irish 'the nearest thing Britain ever possessed to the Prussian Junker class'; if there were Irish Junkers this was where they were to be found. Cavan and the surrounding counties were for structural as well as other reasons particularly fruitful recruiting areas for the officer corps.[24]

In deciding to pursue a military career, then, Nugent was typical of the Irish gentry as a whole, but he was unusual in joining an exclusive regiment

---

[21] Perry, 'Irish landed class', pp 319–24.

[22] Perry, 'Irish landed class', pp 323–4. 'Lesser gentry' for this purpose means landed families worth less than £3,000 per annum in the 1870s.

[23] The percentages of those commissioned between 1850 and 1950 were: Ulster, including Cavan, 55%; Leinster 51%; Munster and Connacht 42% apiece. The figures include wartime and militia as well as regular commissions (Perry, 'Irish landed class', p. 321).

[24] Correlli Barnett, *Britain and Her Army, 1509–1970* (1970), pp 314–15. To illustrate the point, if a rectangle 90 miles long by 40 miles wide, an area about twice the size of Cornwall, was placed on Cavan town, it would cover that part of north central Ireland where Ulster, Leinster and Connacht meet. In the late nineteenth and early twentieth centuries it was a relatively under-populated region but between 1914 and 1945 it nevertheless produced six field marshals, four generals, three lieutenant-generals, eight major-generals, 11 brigadiers, five admirals, two vice-admirals, an air marshal, an air vice-marshal and an air commodore (Perry, 'Irish Landed Class', pp 305–07, 331–2).

like the KRRC with so little family money behind him and from the start he struggled. Some of it was his own fault, as within weeks of joining, and despite being scarcely able to pay his mess bills, he had bought a horse, a hunting rifle and a number of expensive outfits; despite bouts of fierce self-criticism – 'I am selfish, ignorant, stupid and overbearing', he reproached himself at the end of 1883 – he was unable to help himself.[25] For wealthy families capable of supporting sons largely or entirely from their own resources an officer's pay, inadequate though it was, might represent a useful supplement to the family's income, but for those like the Nugents who could not, service in an elite regiment represented a considerable and potentially dangerous financial drain. Within a year his personal debts had risen to over £400 (the equivalent of £35–40,000 in modern spending power), and he owed money not just to the bank but also to a Farren Connell tenant, John Lord, from whom he had borrowed money without telling his father.

In May 1884 St George Nugent died, aged 59 – he had been in poor health for several years – and though he had not always been an easy man his son mourned the death of his 'best and truest friend'. Responsibility for Farren Connell now rested solely on Nugent's shoulders as one of 90 or so Cavan landowners with 1,000 acres or more, though his 1,800 acres was a long way behind the county's largest landlord, Lord Farnham, and his 29,000-acre estate. Unlike many contemporaries Nugent did not immediately resign his commission to concentrate on running Farren Connell: he enjoyed soldiering and wanted to continue to serve, if he could.[26] The timing, however, could scarcely have been worse. The estate, saddled with over £1,000 of debt, was in crisis.[27] In addition to his own debts, which in other circumstances might have been manageable, there were other major calls on its income. His father's will made the usual financial provision for both his mother and his younger brother Cyril (whose ill-health – he suffered from violent epileptic fits – would lead to his premature death, aged 28, in 1889), and for payments to several of Nugent's female cousins, the owner of Farren Connell having responsibilities to the wider family. The estate had, however, an additional crippling liability, and that was the annual payment due to Ida Wiseman, widow of Nugent's cousin Edmond, now re-married to a cavalry officer in

[25] 31 Dec. 1883 (Nugent family papers, 1883 diary).
[26] 29 May 1884 (PRONI, D3835/E/3/1, 1884 diary); Jonathan Cherry, 'The structure, demise and legacy of landowners in County Cavan, c. 1870–c. 1970', in Jonathan Cherry and Brendan Scott (eds), *Cavan: History and Society* (2014), pp 448–51.
[27] 29 May, 6 June 1884 (PRONI, D3835/E/3/1, 1884 diary).

England. This came to over £500 a year, comprising a generous jointure, effectively a widow's allowance, of £300 and mortgage payments of around £200 relating to money invested in the estate before Edmond's death. The estate was already struggling to maintain these payments when Nugent inherited and would soon fall further behind, and the next 12 years would be dominated by a bitter struggle in the courts as Mrs Wiseman attempted to force the sale of Farren Connell to get her money.

There were also wider political and social factors at play. By the mid-1880s the combination of an agricultural depression and shifting political attitudes had reignited the land war of the late 1870s, when tenants across Ireland, organised by the Land League, had successfully fought landlords for greater rights. The resumed agrarian protest from 1885 on, allied as it was to Charles Stewart Parnell's growing Home Rule movement, posed an even greater economic and political threat to the Irish landed class, and the tenants' campaign was accompanied by a rise in anti-landlord rhetoric and a decline in the deference (and sometimes an increase in the violence) shown towards them. In 1882 an elderly but fiery priest, Father Briody, had made national headlines by announcing from the pulpit in Mountnugent chapel that 'it would serve the Irish landlords right if the people rose and cut their throats, as the French did with their landlords 100 years ago', while on his return from Malta in 1883 Nugent had been warned by a Cavan neighbour that 'the whole character of the people is changed, surly and insolent, and that the money that has been taken from the landlords has gone to the publicans'. In February 1885, after Nugent had as a matter of course been appointed to the magistracy, one of the county's MPs, Home Rule-supporting Joe Biggar, asked the Chief Secretary about Nugent's qualifications for the role. The government's justification was simply that Nugent was 'a gentleman of property and had a residence in the county', but it was another example of the growing challenge to the authority of his class across a range of spheres.[28]

Matters became worse with Gladstone's election victory in November 1885 and his espousal of Home Rule. Nugent and his peers were deeply alarmed: 'Ireland is once more to be handed over to the tender mercies of the radical party', he wrote in January 1886, 'Heaven help us in this unfortunate country'; he also predicted that, in the event of Home Rule, 'we shall be murdered if we live in the country' and denounced a prime minister who 'proposes to abolish the Union of the Kingdom'.[29] The

[28] *Freeman's Journal*, 21 Nov. 1882, 28 Feb. 1885; 23 May 1883 (Nugent family papers, 1883 diary).
[29] Terence Dooley, *The Decline of the Big House in Ireland* (2001), pp 96–9; 26 Jan., 18 Mar. and 9 Apr. 1886 (PRONI, D3835/E/3/3, 1886 diary).

political response to the growing momentum of Home Rule (Parnell's party won 85 of 103 Irish seats in the 1885 election) was the emergence of Irish unionism in its modern form, led by another Cavan landowner, Colonel Edward Saunderson, and the development of nationalist/unionist politics would in due course have profound personal consequences for Nugent.[30] His anxiety about the political future did not, however, translate in 1885 into any practical support for the anti-Home Rule cause; he could not afford to make a financial contribution to the Protestant candidate's election campaign, and he failed to vote simply through being too disorganised. His overriding concern at this point was not politics but the impact of the land war on his finances.

In late 1885 the Farren Connell tenants, like their counterparts across much of Ireland, refused to pay their rents without reductions of at least 25%. On 11 November, the day the rents were due, Nugent told his recently-appointed land agent Garnett Tatlow, whose Dublin-based firm would remain in the role until after the Great War, that he could not rejoin the regiment unless he could borrow at least £400, which Tatlow warned was impossible. Later that day Nugent informed his assembled tenants that he 'could not give either time or abatement' and in consequence almost no rents were paid. To his debt burden was now added a chronic cash-flow problem. He was not alone: landlords all over Ireland were being forced to sell up or slipping into bankruptcy.[31] Yet that evening, to keep up appearances, he joined a well-heeled shooting party at a neighbouring country house that included Lords Headfort and Kilmorey and Prince Edward Saxe-Weimar, while on his return to the battalion, now in Cork, he quickly returned to his previous habits, not least losing money almost nightly at cards.[32]

Matters came to a head in early 1886 when, as he dodged tradesmen attempting to serve writs for outstanding debts, he concluded that he must transfer to the regiment's 4th Battalion, stationed in India, to live more cheaply. He calculated that even there, however, he would need £150 a year on top of his pay. When Tatlow told him that the estate could provide nothing like that sum, breaking point had been reached. Approaches to various relatives and friends secured no offers of financial assistance and he had a frosty reception from his commanding officer when he explained his

---

[30] Jackson, *Saunderson*, pp 60–72; Terence Dooley, 'The Organisation of Unionist Opposition to Home Rule in Counties Monaghan, Cavan and Donegal, 1885–1914', *Clogher Record*, 16:1 (1997), pp 46–70. Nugent had served with Saunderson in the Cavan militia.

[31] Dooley, *Decline of the Big House*, pp 90–102.

[32] 11 Nov. 1885 (PRONI, D3835/E/3/2, 1885 diary).

predicament. In May 1886 he concluded, deeply depressed, that he would have both to resign his commission and to sell Farren Connell. He advised the regiment of his intentions – 'God knows it cost me a heavy blow and great grief', he recalled, 'but when I wrote I did not see how I was to remain in the Service, owing over £400, a ruined estate, extravagant and selfish tastes and an expensive regiment'. He looked desperately at options like entering the Indian Staff Corps, for which he was ineligible, and emigrating to Texas but got little sympathy from his infuriated mother, a formidable personality in her own right, who blamed his fecklessness for the impending loss of the family home and who advised him to enlist as a private soldier after sending in his papers. 'Very feeling!', he noted sourly.[33]

After much heart-searching, however, in July 1886 he changed his mind, one of the turning-points of his life. He withdrew his resignation and decided to go to India and fight to keep the estate, writing in his diary: 'Have fully resolved to go out to India to try and get on on £60 a year, it appears to be possible but whether I shall have self-denial or not sufficient I do not know. I should have hated to leave the regiment … I trust that everything will be for the best, God grant it may. I will try it anyhow'. He agreed with his mother, with whom he was reconciled, and Tatlow that they would keep Farren Connell going as best they could – a temporary accommodation had been reached with the tenants, based on a 10% reduction in rents – and on 5 September he said 'a long goodbye to my dear old home [which] I may never see again. God protect it in my absence and send it and us better days'. At the end of the month, now a 25-year-old lieutenant, he left Portsmouth for India on the 'Serapis', the ship that had taken the 4th Battalion to the sub-continent ten years previously.[34]

India

He arrived at Bombay on 20 October 1886 after almost a month at sea, and joined the 4th Battalion at Peshawar, on the north-west frontier, eight days later. The four-and-a-half years he would spend with it proved crucial for him, because during that time Oliver Nugent grew up. Unsurprisingly he found his new surroundings 'most interesting, everything so novel and strange'; the subaltern who showed him around, Charles Markham, would in 1915 be his fellow brigadier in the 14th Division in the Ypres Salient. The 4th, after a decade in India, had a reputation as an efficient but hard-bitten battalion, with more than one annual inspection report commenting caustically on their behaviour; not long after his arrival Nugent was on parade when the brigade commander 'gave the men a frightful wigging on

[33] 21 and 26 May, 31 Dec. 1886 (PRONI, D3835/E/3/3, 1886 diary).
[34] 18 July, 5 Sep. 1886 (PRONI, D3835/E/3/3, 1886 diary).

account of the crime: 58 C[ourt]s M[artial] in 6 months, threatened to make a special report if this continued, which would mean that we should never go on service if there was any'.[35]

He rapidly adjusted to the routine of garrison life in India. Much time was devoted to big game-hunting (he was always a passionate pursuer of wildlife, at home and abroad), cricket and other sports, and only part of each year was spent on military training. What training there was, though, was more intensive and realistic than anything he had experienced in Malta or Ireland, helped by the fact that battalions in India were generally better manned than their counterparts at home. The 4th KRRC's skirmishing drills were new to him and during his first practice he 'was not very smart at it and got cursed in consequence, in a most nasty snapping way by [Lieutenant-Colonel] Kinloch whom I begin to dislike as a CO very much'.[36] Overall, though, he settled in better than he had with either the Munsters or the 1st Battalion. Fortunately, he early on found a project that both caught his imagination and widened his circle of friends, the rejuvenation of the Peshawar Vale Hounds, hunting jackals instead of foxes.

He quickly realised, however, that his hopes of getting by on an additional £60 a year were unrealistic: even 'though I starve', he noted anxiously, and with 'the strictest economy', he needed at least £160. This was very high for an Indian-based unit and the 4th Battalion would be criticised by the regimental colonel in the 1890s for its excessive mess bills, the result of mismanagement as well as indulgence.[37] Yet again Nugent turned to his mother for help, who provided support from money left to her by her father and by foregoing income she was entitled to from the estate. Nugent tried also, however, to help himself. Where possible he took up appointments that attracted allowances and he regularly volunteered to command detachments away from the expenses of the main garrison. When in December 1887 the battalion moved from Peshawar to Chakrata, the Meerut garrison's hill station 7,000 feet up in the Himalayan foot-hills – marching 400 miles over 88 days to do so – he secured the post of station staff officer, which brought with it extra pay. He also learned Hindustani and acted as interpreter at court hearings and other official events, for which he received small sums.[38] Most of these years, however, were spent on regimental duty and the annual cycle of individual, company, battalion and brigade training. Nugent spent a lengthy period as acting company

[35] 20 and 30 Oct., 19 Nov. 1886 (PRONI, D3835/E/3/3, 1886 diary); Hare, *KRRC*, iv, p. 138.
[36] 24 Nov. 1886 (PRONI, D3835/E/3/3, 1886 diary).
[37] 5 Nov. 1886 (PRONI, D3835/E/3/3, 1886 diary); Hare, *KRRC*, iv, p. 136.
[38] 27 Oct. 1887 (PRONI, D3835/E/3/4, 1887 diary).

commander and with experience added to his assertive personality he became acknowledged as a capable leader.

In early 1891 he secured the post of temporary private secretary to Sir Auckland Colvin, a distinguished colonial administrator recently returned from Egypt and now deputy governor of the Punjab. Sir Auckland did not realise, perhaps fortunately, that Nugent was besotted with his daughter Amy, one of a series of infatuations the young officer had during these years, though nothing came of them; of more lasting importance was his introduction to another of Colvin's daughters, Charlotte, and her husband Colonel (later General Sir) Bindon Blood, an engineer officer from County Clare and one of the north-west frontier's rising stars, who would later act as an important patron for him. In the event Nugent's period as a private secretary was cut short. Now promoted to captain, he had successfully requested a transfer back to the 1st KRRC, recently arrived in India from the United Kingdom, but had intended deferring joining until his spell with Colvin was over. Almost as soon as it arrived, however, the battalion was warned off for operations on the north-west frontier and on 27 March 1891 Nugent noted in his diary, 'I am very anxious about the 1st Battn, if they cross the frontier I must go up, it would be discreditable not to'. Colvin agreed to release him, and though Nugent was sorry to leave – he had enjoyed his brief insight into the workings of the Indian government and the opportunity to be noticed by influential people like the Viceroy, Lord Lansdowne – his main concern as he hurried north was that he might miss the fighting: 'if I am only in time I shan't mind. It will be an awful disappointment if I am too late'.[39]

North-west frontier

On 6 April Nugent arrived at the 1st Battalion's encampment at Durband, 70 miles north of Rawalpindi, in the valley of the Indus river where it winds through the mountainous Hazara region. He was warmly greeted by those officers he had served with previously, 'all looking ruffians with a week's growth of beard', and those who had known him in Ireland immediately saw the change in him:

> To those who had known him from before in the 1st Battalion the new Oliver who came back from the 4th Battalion was a surprise and a revelation. He had left them an undeveloped boy, with no more serious interest in life than sport. He returned a keen and level-headed soldier and a strong character, and was soon recognized

---

[39] 27 Mar., 1 Apr. 1891 (PRONI, D3835/E/3/8, 1891 diary).

as a coming leader of men; but there remained to him then and all through his life his innate humour.[40]

If the period from 1886 to 1890 had helped shape Nugent's personality, that from 1891 to 1895 gave momentum to his career. During those years he would take part in a series of operations against Pathan (Pashtun) tribes which gave him experience of both regimental and staff duties on operations and the opportunity to demonstrate the physical courage so important to advancement in the Victorian army. They also provided him with a network of senior officer patrons which would prove invaluable.

The north-west frontier had been turbulent ever since the boundary of British India first pushed up against it in 1849, following the annexation of the Punjab. The background to the campaigns of the 1890s was the intensification of the so-called 'forward policy', first formulated in the late 1870s and whose purpose was to halt in Afghanistan any Russian advance on India. This involved creating permanent garrisons at strategic points along the frontier, accompanied by efforts to extend British influence and political control into tribal territory, which unsurprisingly drew a hostile reaction from the tribes.[41]

At first Nugent's prospects of seeing action appeared slim. The 1st Battalion formed part of the reserve brigade for Major-General Elles's punitive expedition against the Hassanzai and Asazai tribes in the Black Mountain area, but to the officers' frustration they had spent a week watching the campaign winding down without being employed. 'Elles has had the funks ever since he got up and the Hassanzais at Baio having eaten all their grub are scattering and will not show in force again', Nugent wrote furiously on 6 April, 'Everyone disgusted with it'. It was, though, as well the 1st KRRC had not been sent straight into action. Having arrived in India only in December it was still relatively unacclimatised and its 70-mile march over five days, in considerable heat, from Rawalpindi to Durband had degenerated into a shambles. By the time it arrived on 31 March 'a great number of men had fallen out (some with heat apoplexy), the transport was all over the place, and the rearguard was miles behind', and a respite was needed to pull things together. On 7 April, however, Nugent noted excitedly that there was '[g]reat news – orders received last night that we were to march at once for Kohat with the rest of the Brigade. There is

---

[40] Obituary, *The King's Royal Rifle Corps Chronicle* (1927), p. 242.

[41] Andrew Porter, 'Introduction', in A Porter (ed.), *The Oxford History of the British Empire, Volume III: The Nineteenth Century* (1999), pp 11–14; Andrew Roe, *Waging War in Waziristan: The British Struggle in the Land of Bin Laden, 1849–1947* (2010), p. 83; Victoria Schofield, *Every Rock, Every Hill: The Plain Tale of the North-West Frontier and Afghanistan* (1984), pp 102–05.

no knowing how big the affair will be, but it may be very big and with Lockhart in command instead of old Elles we are sure to see fighting'.[42]

The new orders were the result of a rising on a different part of the frontier, the Miranzai valley in the Tirah region about 40 miles south-west of Peshawar. The trouble centred on the Samana ridge near Kohat, along which the British had been building roads. This lay on the edge of the territory of the Orakzai tribe who regarded the work as an unacceptable intrusion and on 4 April attacks began on the construction parties. The government hurriedly assembled a force to restore order under Brigadier-General William Lockhart, another officer who would play an important part in Nugent's career. In addition to the 1st KRRC, the expedition comprised nine Indian infantry battalions and two cavalry regiments, organised into three columns and totalling some 7,400 men. On 12 April Nugent and the rest of the battalion reached Kohat, 'a curious little place … all made of mud and right under the hills which are beyond our border', and on 16 April Lockhart's force crossed a steep ridge to its front and entered tribal territory. There were rumours that the Orakzai had dispersed and Nugent feared that 'all we have in prospect is an infernal climb, and nothing to show for it'.[43] He was wrong.

On 17 April the 1st KRRC took over as the lead battalion, advancing west along Samana ridge, and after a few miles it came under fire from tribal snipers. Nugent's 'F' Company passed through the advance guard to clear them out:

> As we came over the hill, a volley was fired from a tower 700 yds to our front. 'F' Co were a little scared and I had to shout at them to get them forward. We lay down and fired a couple of volleys and then the guns came up. After a few rounds the battn advanced[,] 'F' and 'C' in the first line. We were enfiladed from a hill to the right. The Col[onel] was shot through the wrist.

The tribesmen withdrew as the British approached and the 1st Battalion's losses in the day's fighting, in addition to the CO, Colonel Cramer, were just three men wounded: the regimental history referred to the tribesmen's 'smart but ill-aimed fire' while a later study described the fighting as 'desultory'. Understandably that was not how it seemed to Nugent, who wrote that night: 'Thus ended the first day under which I have been under

---

[42] 6 and 7 Apr 1891 (PRONI, D3835/E/3/7, 1891 diary); Capt. H. L. Nevill, *North-West Frontier: British and Indian Army Campaigns on the North-West Frontier of India 1849–1908* (1992), pp 118–24; Hare, *KRRC*, iv, p. 117.

[43] Hare, *KRRC*, iv, p. 121; Nevill, *North-West Frontier*, pp 126–9; 12 and 16 Apr. 1891 (PRONI, D3835/E/3/8, 1891 diary).

fire. I must say I did not like it, but I hope I did not show any sign of it'. The advance resumed next day and though Nugent's company was not directly engaged it, like the rest of the force, suffered from the intense heat and lack of water. He was not impressed by his men's performance: 'Lots of them showed great want of grit and fell out all over the place … The men are very helpless. They have not learnt to do anything for themselves and some of them are awful cads'. His frustration increased when, on 20 April, his company missed the biggest clash of the campaign when a joint attack by the 1st KRRC and the 5th Gurkhas succeeded, unusually, in inflicting heavy casualties on a tribal force before they could escape. 'The Gurkhas', he heard, 'spoiled our fun by spreading over our front and they cut up everyone they found with their kukries'. (A few days later, riding through the area, he came across some of the dead Pathans, who 'were nasty sights, especially one who had his thigh blown away by a shell and whom the Gurkhas had set on fire'.)[44]

On 21 April he was given the opportunity to join Lockhart's personal staff as an extra orderly officer, a position he held until the end of the campaign. It proved a valuable experience, allowing him to observe first-hand the handling of the campaign by a leading practitioner of frontier fighting. On 22 April, for example, he watched Lockhart manoeuvring his units to cover the burning of villages and crops in the valley: 'The General sent the 2nd P[unjab] I[nfantry] and 3rd Sikhs down below [the tribesmen] and the 1st P.I. above them into the valley to try and cut them off, they were too quick for us and most of them got away … We had a splendid view of the whole game'. Lockhart was careful to prevent his units clashing with the neighbouring Afridis – 'the govt would go to any lengths to avoid a fight with them', noted Nugent, 'as so many of them are in our pay and they are very powerful' – and was cautious about advancing too far into Orakzai territory without political clearance. On 5 May the senior Indian political service officer in the region, Richard Udny, joined the expedition and agreed to extend the operation, but Nugent like other officers still thought the 'politicals' too conciliatory towards the tribesmen. 'Leigh [the political agent attached to the column] I fear is an old woman as a political', he grumbled on 12 May, 'he is too anxious for peace and deprecates anything calculated as he thinks to make them nervous'; the next day he heard that a nearby tribe would not be attacked 'as Leigh and Udny are both against it. Confound all politicals and funks'. Orders for restraint were not always obeyed; advancing down one valley Nugent noted that '[w]e have been

---

44 17, 18, 20 and 21 Apr. 1891 (PRONI, D3835/E/3/8, 1891 diary); Hare, *KRRC*, p. 121; Nevill, *North-West Frontier*, p. 129.

ordered not to burn their villages, but strange to say they most of them catch fire as we pass'.[45] The tribesmen by now had had enough and began submitting in a series of meetings (jirgahs) with British officials – Nugent watched one delegation come in, 'a most truculent looking lot of scoundrels' – and by late May large-scale operations had ended. Total British casualties had been just over a hundred and the 1st KRRC's fewer than ten, but though the fighting had not been severe the battalion had gained useful experience, and when Lockhart's despatch was published Nugent was mentioned as a 'keen and excellent officer'. His first experience of operational service had been a success.[46]

That summer he returned to Ireland on leave, his first home visit for almost five years. He found his mother little changed and Farren Connell 'looking lovely, but sadly neglected'. The estate's finances were still precarious and rental income had fallen further, but straitened circumstances did not prevent a display of traditional tenant deference on the evening of his arrival – 'there was a bonfire on Tally-ho Hill and a lot of tenants had collected. I sent up some whisky and porter and went up and made a speech. I think they were glad to see me'. (He had a less rosy-eyed view when he next returned home, in 1896, warning his mother in advance 'not to let people know when I arrived as I did not want a lot of blackguards to come drinking at my expense as they did last time out of no love for me'.) His leave went in quickly, and by July 1892 he was back with the battalion in Rawalpindi.[47]

In October 1892 the 1st KRRC was once again deployed in the Black Mountain area, against the Isazai. The two-brigade force, again commanded by Lockhart, saw no fighting, the Isazais having melted into the hills, so the columns had to content themselves with burning some villages and destroying crops, to Nugent's frustration – 'The expedition was a fiasco', he complained afterwards, 'heat was terrible and altogether we had a very poor time'. The aftermath was worse. Half the battalion was struck down by malaria on the return march to Rawalpindi, including Nugent, to be followed immediately by an outbreak of cholera that forced it to spend ten days in a quarantine camp.[48] His circle of senior contacts had, however,

---

[45] 21, 22, 25 and 30 Apr., 12/13 May 1891 (PRONI, D3835/E/3/8, 1891 diary).

[46] 24 Apr., 10 June, 7 July 1891 (PRONI, D3835/E/3/8, 1891 diary); Hare, *KRRC*, iv, p. 123. For political officers on the frontier in the 1890s, see Christian Tripodi, *Edge of Empire: The Political Officer and British Tribal Control on the North-West Frontier 1849–1947* (2011), pp 49–90.

[47] 14 Aug. 1891, 26 Feb. 1896 (PRONI, D3835/E/3/8 and 12, 1891 and 1896 diaries).

[48] Nevill, *North-West Frontier*, p. 124; 28/29 Sep. 1892 (PRONI, D3835/E/3/9, 1892 diary); Hare, *KRRC*, iv, p. 124.

continued to grow. Freddie Roberts, son of Lord Roberts of Kandahar, was now in the battalion and Nugent took him under his wing: as a result he met 'Bobs' and Lady Roberts several times and became close to them. Friends also recommended him to Sir George White, Roberts's successor as commander-in-chief and also an Irishman (from County Antrim), and when White visited Rawalpindi in November 1893 Nugent lobbied Ian Hamilton, his military secretary and later the British commander at Gallipoli, for a staff appointment. He was unsuccessful because as, Hamilton pointed out, he had yet to obtain the necessary qualifications, which caused him to think seriously about the future direction of his career.[49]

Chitral

Early in 1895 came an opportunity for active service on a larger scale than he had yet experienced. Chitral, a small and isolated independent Indian state in the Hindu Kush mountains between Kashmir and Afghanistan, was undergoing a leadership crisis and in March 1895 one of the pretenders, Sher Afzul, besieged Chitral fort, inside which was the British Agent, Surgeon-Major Robertson, and a small garrison.[50] The fort's defence, and its relief on 20 April by a column from Gilgit under Colonel Kelly after a hazardous march through mountainous terrain, became a Victorian epic. The main relief expedition, under Lieutenant-General Sir Robert Low, took the only practicable but still difficult route for a large force, from Nowshera north through the Malakand Pass into the Swat valley, and then over the Lowarai pass to Chitral. Low's command consisted of three brigades and divisional troops, totalling some 15,000 men and over 30,000 pack-animals. Its 1st Brigade included, in addition to the 1st KRRC, the 1st Bedfordshire Regiment, 15th Sikhs and 37th Dogras, and was commanded by Brigadier-General Kinloch, Nugent's CO when he first joined the 4th Battalion and a famous big-game hunter – a rather better hunter, it would prove, than brigade commander.

Nugent and the battalion, 18 officers and 801 other ranks strong, left Nowshera on 31 March 1895, and by the morning of 3 April Low, after making feints to confuse the enemy, had concentrated his three brigades at the foot of the Malakand Pass, held by up to 12,000 tribesmen (though

---

[49] 18 Jan., 20 Feb., 13 and 16 Nov. 1893 (PRONI, D3835/E/3/10, 1893 diary).
[50] Tim Moreman, *The Army of India and the Development of Frontier Warfare, 1849–1947* (1998), pp 42–53; Nevil, *North-West Frontier*, pp 164–96; Hare, *KRRC*, iv, pp 126–34.

only around a third had firearms). Low's plan was to use the 2nd Brigade to occupy both the steep ridge overlooking the approach to the pass and the pass itself, following which the 1st Brigade would advance into the Swat valley beyond, but when the attack began the British found the ridge so strongly held that Low had to commit both brigades to secure it.

Shortly after noon on 3 April, therefore, the 1st KRRC were inserted between the Guides and the King's Own Scottish Borderers (KOSB) of the 2nd Brigade and began advancing up the precipitous slopes of the ridge. Nugent afterwards thought it 'about the worst climb I ever did', in several places having to use both hands to pull himself up. He could see 'far above up among the rocks, the Guides ... working up to the top of the hill'; the KOSB, just above him, were pinned down and 'apparently making no headway at all'; over to the right, close to the entrance to the pass, the Gordon Highlanders were also making limited progress despite covering fire from the mountain batteries below. The tribesmen were defiant – he described how 'from every knoll and ridge and crestline came the yells of the Swatis; each knoll and any commanding point had a sangar on it from which came a heavy irregular fire, and banners were waving over the whole hill side' – and the KRRC's advance initially was slow. Frustrated by this, Nugent took over the lead and, moving fast, led his company up a spur leading to the top. Half way up

> a fanatic appeared on the hill about 500yds above us and began to rally the true believers who were now falling back before us up the hill. He also scorned cover but stood like a brave man on a rock and called down the vengeance of Allah on our heads ... I took a rifle from one of my men and got onto a rock above the old Buddhist road and fired a shot at him with 500yds sight, he took no notice so I gave him another shot aiming a little higher up his body, he fell like a stone and in revenge I suppose for his fall, a shower of bullets came whistling about my ears.

Closer to the summit he and his men found themselves in a defile which threatened to become a death-trap, as 'there were Swatis on our left and front all firing at us from the sangars and there was a regular pandemonium of yells all round, increased many times by the echoes among the rocks and ravines'. Nugent managed to scramble onto higher ground with a dozen men and drive the enemy back and then, with his CO, Colonel McCall, just behind, he led his company onto the next rise, where they were met by intense fire. Four men were killed and four seriously wounded almost immediately. One, Private Gardner, crouching beside him, had a bullet go through his helmet: 'he took it off and said 'Well that's a lucky one'; as he spoke another bullet went through his brain'. Another, Private Palmer, was badly hit in the leg and lying out in the open, and Nugent and a signaller dashed out under fire and carried him to safety (Palmer's leg was amputated next day). Nugent was hit painfully in the leg by a ricochet but was still able to move, and with the British now almost at the top the tribesmen retreated, the crest being occupied without further fighting.[51]

The battle had lasted five hours. Total British casualties were 11 killed and 51 wounded, the tribesmen's losses an estimated 500. British technological superiority in the end had been crucial, a newspaper account describing how '[t]he Maxims playing from right and left of the gorge created an ideal picture of a civilised attack on a savage enemy'. Nugent was delighted with 'a very good fight, the best there has been this side of the world since the Afghan War', but he and the rest of the battalion were frustrated by the lack of recognition they received in initial newspaper accounts. McCall complained to Bindon Blood, Low's chief of staff, and the omission was corrected in Low's final despatch. Blood also sent a message which, Nugent wrote, 'made me as proud as a dog with a new bone, which was that I had been specially mentioned for gallantry on the Malakand'.[52]

The rest of the campaign was, however, an anti-climax for the 1st KRRC. Kinloch was a poor brigadier, both tactically and administratively, and Nugent did not hold him in high regard. He was also a notoriously awkward individual and fell out badly with both Low and Blood, and as a result the 1st Brigade was largely side-lined in future operations. On 8 April Nugent heard that the brigade was to be left behind to guard the lines of communication, 'an awful blow', and went to Blood to remonstrate, but got nowhere: 'Blood said it was to be so, that he was very sorry but circumstances he could not discuss made it necessary; of course we all knew pretty well the reason why and that it was due to Kinloch'. By the end of April the active phase of the campaign had ended with Chitral's relief, but the battalion remained on garrison duties until September before returning to India. Nugent had one unpleasant duty to perform before the withdrawal, when he oversaw an execution: 'A native had tried to cut down a sepoy in broad daylight and was sentenced to be shot; we tied him to a tree and a party of 6 of our men shot him; the Lee-Metford bullets made a very slight mark, the body was burnt afterwards'.[53]

[51] Quotations in these two paragraphs from Nugent's 'Account of the Chitral Expedition' (Nugent family papers, 1895 diary).

[52] Moreman, *The Army in India*, p. 51; 'Account of Chitral'.

[53] 29 May 1895 (Nugent family papers, 1895 diary). The Lee-Metford rifle had recently been issued to the battalion.

Nugent had had a good campaign and he recognised at once that it could be the launch pad for an attempt at a place at the Staff College at Camberley which, in a sign of the college's increasing status, he regarded as the key to his professional future.[54] The majority of each annual intake, usually around 34 students, secured their places through competitive examination but by the mid-1890s about a third were nominated – subject to achieving a sufficient standard in the exams – by the commanders-in-chief at home and in India. Nugent set out to secure one of these nominations, and in October he asked Lockhart and Blood to recommend him to Lord Wolseley, commander-in-chief in the United Kingdom, and to request Sir George White to do the same. Lockhart undertook to write immediately to the War Office, and Blood too wrote to both Wolseley and General Sir Redvers Buller, the Adjutant General, on his behalf.[55] The late Victorian army was famously riven by personal rivalries, centred on the 'rings' or networks of supporters around Wolseley, Roberts and the Duke of Cambridge, and Nugent's patrons were all closely associated with Roberts's Indian ring. It is striking, therefore, that Lockhart and Blood were confident, as was Nugent himself, that their representations to Wolseley and Buller, who was still in Wolseley's camp despite their strained personal relations by 1895, would not be counter-productive.[56] While Nugent had the advantage that Buller was himself a former KRRC officer and also that as a captain he was too junior to be caught up in the manoeuvrings over strategy and senior appointments that divided the rings, the application of patronage in his case is a reminder that the divisions between the groupings were not absolute.[57]

Nugent began studying for the Camberley entrance exam immediately but was soon struggling with the mathematics syllabus, despite working up to seven hours a day with a tutor. He had obtained the prospectus for Captain James's well-known crammer in London, later attended by Churchill, but was doubtful whether the cost (£20 per month living in, £10 if not) was worth it unless he knew for sure he was on the nominated list. He became more confident when in January 1896 the award of his Distinguished Service Order (DSO) for the Malakand was gazetted – 'a

[54] Brian Bond, *The Victorian Army and the Staff College, 1854–1914* (1972), p. 153.
[55] 13, 15 and 28 Oct., 17 Dec. 1895 (Nugent family papers, 1895 diary).
[56] Halik Kochanski, *Sir Garnet Wolseley: Victorian Hero* (1999), pp 213–14.
[57] I am indebted to Professor Ian Beckett for his advice on the operation of the rings; see also his *The Politics of Command: The Late Victorian Army, 1872–1902* (2018), pp 74–108.

proud day for Ireland, at any rate for me', he noted, 'I think I can say that mine is the best DSO of the lot, for it is the only one awarded for actual gallantry'.[58]

Home

In March 1896 Nugent left for home after almost ten years in India. On arriving in London he lunched with Lord and Lady Roberts before crossing to Ireland, but while glad to see his family and Farren Connell again he was soon back in the capital, having decided after all to attend James's crammer. He quickly felt discouraged by the scale of the challenge: 'The more I see of it the more hopeless it seems to me to get in without a nom[ination], indeed I feel very doubtful if I shall even qualify. I am working over 10 hours a day but it is not even half enough to teach me all I have to know'. He was not the only one working anxiously for a place. Back in India Captain William Robertson of the 3rd Dragoon Guards, also a DSO winner from the Chitral campaign and a future field-marshal, was studying intensively in his spare time, getting up every morning between 4am and 5am to work before going into the office: 'I was oppressed with the thought that I had but the one chance of getting into the college', he recalled, 'because by the time the next examination came round I would be over the regulation age for admission'. George Barrow of the Indian cavalry was also hard at work, using his year's study leave to spend the winter in Brussels learning French before attending a crammer for six months, despite knowing that he was on the commander-in-chief India's list for a nomination.[59] Nugent eventually decided to go and see Buller in person at the War Office: 'I may as well know what my fate as regards selection is likely to be', he wrote, 'and try for Egypt as well' (there were rumours of a campaign to re-conquer the Sudan). The meeting went better than Nugent had dared hope:

> Went to Buller's levee today with my heart in my mouth, told him I was very anxious about getting into S[taff] C[ollege], that my future was in it and that I had only the one chance as I was too old for 2 shots and hoped he would give me one of the nominations next Aug. He was most affable, said he quite understood and that none of the selections were filled up and that he saw no reason why

[58] 21 and 23 Jan., 5 Mar. 1896 (PRONI, D3835/E/3/12, 1896 diary).
[59] 25 Apr. 1896 (PRONI, D3835/E/3/12, 1896 diary); Field-Marshal Sir William Robertson, *From Private to Field-Marshal* (1921), p. 79; Gen. Sir George Barrow, *The Fire of Life* (1942), p. 41.

I should not have one; nothing could have been better; considering he is the man who gives them, I look upon it as tantamount to a promise; asked him then to let me go to Egypt, he said he thought there would be nothing there and recommended me to do one thing at a time and mind about the S.C. Came away absolutely on air; I never anticipated anything so good.[60]

This piece of encouraging news was soon followed by another. On 6 May 1896 word came of the death of Ida Wiseman. 'Thank God, my troubles are over at last', Nugent rejoiced, 'I need never more go to India and I can at last pay my debts … I can hardly realise that the awful burden which has weighed on me and my home for so many years is gone at last'. In fact he had finished with neither India nor financial worries, but the threat hanging over Farren Connell for the past 12 years had receded. His good mood was dented a few days later, however, when to his chagrin he was stopped in a London street by a woman accompanied by a police officer:

The female identified me as James Watson and charged me with being the father of her baby and served me with a Bastardy Summons to attend at W[est] London P[olice] C[ourt] at 2pm on Tuesday 2 June. Devilish funny for everyone but me, too annoyed for words. I believe she says the baby was born 3 years ago when of course I was in India but having to appear in a London P.C. to answer a woman I have never seen and be badgered by some duty attorney, find my name in the newspapers and be credited with knowing more than appears about it, the whole thing is too bad.

In the event matters were resolved without a court appearance, though as he predicted his friends were much amused.[61] When the college exams took place George Barrow's preparation had paid off; he passed in fifth on the merit list and did not require the nomination he had been offered. Robertson also did well, qualifying in all subjects and only just missing out on a competitive place: Sir George White stepped in to nominate him for a selection vacancy. On 3 October Nugent was disappointed though not surprised to learn that he had not passed high enough for an automatic place – he had done well in eight of the nine topics but had been brought down by his weakness in maths (as Douglas Haig had been the previous year) – but next day he heard with relief that he too had been nominated.

[60] 29 Apr. 1896 (PRONI, D3835/E/3/12, 1896 diary).
[61] 6 and 21 May 1896 (PRONI, D3835/E/3/12, 1896 diary).

'Thank God for that', he exulted, 'I worked hard for it and gave up the best of my leave and I have my future before me'.[62]

Staff College

Nugent left no account of his time at Staff College but appears, like Robertson and Barrow, to have enjoyed it. 'The two years at the Staff College were some of my happiest', Barrow wrote later, 'Most of the work was of great interest and all of it accompanied by the satisfactory feeling that it was useful'.[63] The course was important not just for the professional knowledge it imparted but for the personal contacts it provided. Amongst Nugent's fellow students were some of the most important British military leaders of the Great War: future field-marshals and generals in his own year included, in addition to Robertson and Barrow, Archie Murray and Colin Mackenzie; in the year ahead Douglas Haig, Edmund Allenby, George Macdonogh, Richard Haking, Thomas Capper and William Furse (as well as James Edmonds and Reginald Dyer, who for different reasons became famous as brigadiers); and in the year behind George Milne, Aylmer Hunter-Weston, John Fowler, Arthur Lynden-Bell and Walter Braithwaite. At Camberley he established contrasting relationships with two fellow students which would have an important influence on his career – his close friendship with Archie Murray, who was Deputy CIGS at the time of his appointment to command the 36th (Ulster) Division in 1915, and the mutual antipathy that developed, for reasons which are obscure, with Douglas Haig.

In addition to classroom work there were tactical exercises and, in the summer of the second year, 1898, a visit to the battlefields of the Franco-Prussian war. Like many others Nugent especially valued the lectures of Colonel G. F. R. Henderson, an inspirational teacher and one of the army's foremost thinkers. Nugent kept his essays with Henderson's annotations and comments, which confirm the recollections of other students about the care and insight Henderson brought to his role. On a paper Nugent did on Stonewall Jackson's 1862 Valley campaign, for example – where he was acting the part of chief of staff to one of the Union generals, a typical Henderson teaching technique – Henderson wrote, 'This is undoubtedly a very able paper, of course much assisted by knowledge of what actually happened … For the course proposed, I think your force insufficient … Prudence is as valuable as dash. Nevertheless, your plan, worked out as it is,

---

[62] Barrow, *Fire of Life*, p. 41; Robertson, *Private to Field-Marshal*, p. 79; 4 Oct. 1896 (PRONI, D3835/E/3/12, 1896 diary). In Nugent's year 10 of 32 students were nominated (*Army List*, July–Sep. 1898).

[63] Barrow, *Fire of Life*, p. 45.

has much to recommend it'. On Nugent's appreciation of the strategic situation facing the Duke of Wellington in June 1815, Henderson interjected, alongside a critique of Wellington's delayed decision to concentrate his forces, a contemporary comment relevant to Nugent's own experience: 'If you read Lord Roberts's confidential paper on the NW Frontier you will see how strongly he brings out the dangers to which we are there exposed, and how carefully he works out the way in which they should be provided against'.[64]

Marriage

In 1897, while still at Camberley, Nugent met, through a brother officer, Catherine Lees. Kitty, as she was always known, was intelligent, attractive and vivacious, one of the six children (five of them daughters) of Thomas Evans Lees, a rich Cheshire cotton mill owner-turned-landowner. The family home at South Lytchett in Dorset was now owned by Kitty's brother Elliott, a Conservative MP who had been knighted in 1897. Nugent was an ardent suitor and on 7 February 1899 they were married in Wimborne, Dorset, the beginning of an extremely happy partnership. Nugent was absolutely devoted both to her and, in due course, to their son and two daughters; with his family, indeed, he displayed a sentimental and affectionate side of his nature which would have astonished his military colleagues had they known of it. Kitty also brought with her a substantial dowry, a valuable injection of capital at a time when the estate was still struggling financially. She became deeply attached to Farren Connell and to Cavan and Ireland more generally. She was also, importantly, Nugent's confidante: his letters to her were both accounts of his doings and a way of relieving his feelings. They went on honeymoon to Canada, and their first child arrived quickly, in November 1899. Nugent was not present for St George's birth, however; he was by then several thousand miles away, seriously wounded and a prisoner of war.

Boer War

In September 1899, a few weeks after returning from honeymoon, he re-joined the 1st KRRC, now in South Africa. On 25 September he and the rest of the battalion, under Lieutenant-Colonel Gunning and consisting of 17 officers and 767 other ranks, left Durban in Natal for Ladysmith, 150 miles to the north. Tensions between the British Empire and the Boer republics of Transvaal and the Orange Free State, simmering since the

---

[64] Bond, *Army and the Staff College*, pp 153–80; Nugent's Staff College papers (PRONI, D3835/E/12/1).

Jameson raid almost four years earlier, looked set to spill over into hostilities, and the British faced a difficult military situation. While the Boers could put at least 50,000 men into the field the British garrison in South Africa was only around 10,000, and although reinforcements were being hurriedly assembled in the United Kingdom and India they could not arrive for several weeks. Nugent, like many of his brother officers, was unconcerned. 'Nearly everyone who knows the Boers say we shall have no fighting', he wrote, because 'the Boers who are quite ignorant of what they are taking on in challenging us, will never stand our artillery'. But as the Rifles left Durban with cheering crowds lining the railway tracks there were, as Nugent noted, 'sadder scenes also: several wives were weeping … [Mrs Gunning] was looking very white and wan'.[65]

War was declared on 11 October. The British leadership had debated the wisdom of trying to hold northern Natal, surrounded on three sides by the Boer republics. Sir George White, now commanding in Natal, opposed the idea but relented in the face of political pressure and the result was an unfortunate compromise, the main British force concentrating at Ladysmith while a brigade under Major-General William Penn Symons remained forward at Dundee, 45 miles to the north, to cover the coalfields there. Symons's force of four infantry battalions, including the 1st KRRC, a cavalry regiment and 18 guns, totalled almost 3,300 infantry and just under 500 cavalry, and despite their exposed position Nugent and his comrades were spoiling for a fight.[66] On 19 October he wrote to Kitty describing the possibility of an attack by 'those dirty Boers', denouncing 'Sir G White's pusillanimity' for pulling troops back to Ladysmith because of rumours of a Boer advance and declaring '[w]e don't understand Generals of this sort and all we hear from Ladysmith is that Sir G W has got the jumps badly. We sadly want a man and are already looking out for Sir Redvers' arrival'.[67] His high hopes of Buller would be disappointed, but even before the new commander arrived at the end of October Nugent's active part in the war was over. The Boers had indeed concentrated their forces against Symons, sending one commando to cut the Ladysmith railway and two others directly against Dundee. The latter force, 3,500 men and seven guns under Lucas Meyer, arrived on the night of 19/20 October and occupied two prominent heights, Talana Hill and Lennox Hill, about a mile north-east of the town. The British did not realise they were there until the morning mist

[65] Oliver Nugent [ON] to Catherine (Kitty) Nugent [CN], 26 Sep. 1899 (PRONI, D3835/E/1/11 (MIC591/1)).

[66] Maj.-Gen. Sir Frederick Maurice, *History of the War in South Africa*, i, (1906), p. 123.

[67] ON to CN, 19 Oct. 1899 (PRONI, D3835/E/1/2/4).

cleared at 5.30am on the 20th and they saw hundreds of Boers on the high ground above them; minutes later Boer shells began dropping into their camp. Symons immediately decided to clear Meyer's men off Talana Hill, and, covered by the fire of two artillery batteries, three of his infantry battalions began moving into position.

Talana was a flat-topped hill about 600 feet high with commanding views over Dundee. About 150 feet below the summit was a flat terrace 80 yards wide, bounded on the downward slope side by a stone wall, from where the gradient fell away to level ground. The only part of the slope not in direct view and therefore the field of fire of observers at the top was the area immediately in front of the stone wall, though even that could be partially enfiladed from Lennox Hill. Near the bottom was a farm – Smith's Farm – and a small wood. To reach the hill the British had to cross 800 yards of open ground from the nearest substantial cover, a stream bed called Sand Spruit. By 7am Symons's three battalions, the 2nd Royal Dublin Fusiliers, the 1st KRRC and the 1st Royal Irish Fusiliers, were lining the spruit waiting for the order to attack, while his mounted troops, the 18th Hussars under Colonel Möller, reinforced by the mounted companies of the infantry battalions and an artillery battery, had been sent on a wide outflanking move to get behind the Boers. Symons's orders were straightforward. The infantry would assault up the hill under covering fire from the artillery, the Dublin Fusiliers in the first wave, the Rifles in the second and the Irish Fusiliers in support, and drive the Boers into the arms of the British cavalry.

At 7.20am the Dublin Fusiliers moved forward from the spruit and despite coming under long-range rifle fire reached Smith's Farm with only slight casualties; the Rifles, following up, extended the line to the right and the Irish Fusiliers moved up behind them. After a pause the Dublin Fusiliers advanced up the hill but quickly found themselves pinned down by heavy fire. Symons, who had come forward to observe, was fatally wounded and command devolved to his deputy, Brigadier-General Yule. Yule now ordered the Rifles to advance, but though they managed to reach the lower wall of the terrace with fairly light losses, again heavy Boer fire halted the attack. An inconclusive fire-fight followed, but when the British artillery moved forward to shell the summit more accurately the Boer fire appeared to slacken and at 10am, sensing an opportunity, Colonel Gunning led his men over the wall. The riflemen were met immediately by a hail of fire, as Nugent described:

> The ground in front of me was literally rising in dust from the bullets, and the din echoing between the hill and the wood below and among the rocks from the incessant fire of the Mausers seemed to blend with every other sound into a long drawn-out hideous roar.

> Half way over the terrace I looked round over my shoulder and I
> confess I was rather horrified at what I saw … the whole ground we
> had already covered was strewn with bodies, and no more men were
> coming from over the wall. At that moment I was hit the first time
> … I was hit through the knee. The actual shock was as if someone
> had hit me with their whole strength with a club. I spun round and
> fell, my pistol flying one way and helmet another … I was hit a
> second time by a shot from above; the bullet hit me on the back
> above my right hip and came out in front of my thigh.[68]

At this point the British artillery mistook the attackers for Boers and fired
on them, inflicting further casualties. Nugent wrote later:

> I was just beginning to bandage my leg, when a shrapnel shell burst
> overhead. We both, W[ortley] and I, stared in astonishment. We
> could see our artillery on the plain below us 1500 yards off … It
> seemed impossible that they should not have seen our advance from
> the wall … I felt rather beat then … It seemed so hard, after
> escaping the Boers to be killed by our own people.

Colonel Gunning, signalling urgently to the gunners to cease firing, was
killed by a Boer marksman. By now, however, with the British almost upon
them, the defenders began retiring down the reverse slope and, picking up
their ponies, made off across the plain beyond. Möller's mounted
outflanking move had been intended for precisely this moment, but
through a misjudgement he had managed to get cut off by superior forces
and was forced to surrender with over 240 men. When the fighting ended
British losses stood at over 500: 52 dead, including 10 officers (amongst
them the brigade commander and a battalion CO); 203 wounded, 20 of
them officers; and 246 prisoners, including 9 officers, the result of Möller's
debacle. The 1st KRRC's casualties were five officers and 23 men killed or
died of wounds, seven officers and 73 men wounded, and one man missing.
Boer losses, by their own count, amounted to 31 fatalities, 66 wounded and
20 captured. The British had driven the Boers off the hill but their losses
had been disproportionate.[69] Gravely injured though he was, Nugent
managed to write to Kitty the next day, describing the battle as 'perhaps as
hard a fight as we have had since the Crimea':

---

[68] Quoted in Thomas Pakenham, *The Boer War* (1997), pp 131–2.
[69] Hare, *KRRC*, iv, pp 183–96; Pakenham, *Boer War*, pp 125–32; Maurice, *War in South Africa*, i, pp 123–41.

> We assaulted a position almost impregnable, held by between 5000 and 6000 Boers, our own strength being about 2200. We did as we were told to do but at a frightful cost of valuable lives thrown away. We could have gone round the hill out in the veldt and turned them out at a loss of probably under a quarter what we actually suffered. However the General poor man has paid for his mistake so it is no use saying more.[70]

His assessment of the relative strengths of the two sides was wide of the mark but his judgement about the conduct of the battle was not. When the British evacuated Dundee two days later they left without the seriously wounded, Nugent amongst them, who were too ill to be moved.[71]

Prisoner of War

Nugent, now a prisoner, was later convinced that his initial treatment by an army doctor nearly killed him and that, as a minimum, had he been left in Dr Daly's care his leg would have been amputated. Fortunately he and the other wounded (including Maurice Crum, a KRRC subaltern who became a good friend) were transferred to the charge of Dr Galbraith, Dundee's principal medical practitioner and a capable physician. Nugent's leg was saved but his injuries were serious. The bullet that hit him in the back, fragments of which remained there for the rest of his life, only narrowly missed his spine and injured a lung; the others had passed through his thigh and knee, the last extremely painful but amazingly causing no permanent damage. When fit enough he was moved to Pretoria, where he was held initially in the Bourke hospital, a well-run Red Cross facility, and then, when sufficiently recovered, in the main officers' prisoner of war compound in the neighbouring States Schools building. His view of the Boers, whom he acknowledged he had underestimated as fighters, had changed: 'I shall never have anything but a warm feeling for the Boers after the way they have treated me', he wrote. He was particularly grateful to a Transvaal artillery officer, Lieutenant du Toit, nephew of the Transvaal state secretary for war, who had been wounded at Talana (where he had been directing a quick-firing 'pom-pom' gun against Nugent's battalion) and who helped secure the release from the censor's office of Kitty's letters.[72]

---

[70] ON to CN, 21 Oct. 1899 (PRONI, D3835/E/1/2/5A).

[71] For Talana and its significance, see Denis Judd and Keith Surridge, *The Boer War: A History* (2013), pp 106–08; Bill Nasson, *The South African War 1899–1902* (1999), pp 85–8.

[72] ON to CN, 31 Oct. 1899, 11 Jan. 1900 (PRONI, D3835/E/1/3/1 and 1/3/3).

The next few months passed slowly, with news from both the front and home sporadic: he did not learn of St George's birth for several weeks and not until after his release that Kitty had been dangerously ill during the pregnancy. Information was provided by new prisoner arrivals, often of its nature involving tales of setbacks: he met Colonel Möller, captured at Talana, 'who did not seem in the least depressed as, if all the accounts of his manoeuvres which I have heard are true, he certainly ought to be'; the survivors of the summit of Spion Kop described their 'terrible experience'; Colonel Carleton of the Irish Fusiliers, cut off with most of his battalion at Nicholson's Nek on 30 October 1899, felt they had been 'sacrificed by the incompetence' of Sir George White's staff. There were occasional excitements, including the escape of three officers who hid for several days under the floorboards of the building; one of them, Captain Aylmer Haldane of the Gordon Highlanders, would have a fraught relationship with Nugent in Flanders in 1915.[73] The experience of captivity did not undermine Nugent's belief in the imperial cause, however. The war was a divisive issue in Ireland, with many nationalists sympathetic to the Boers, but Nugent himself had no doubts. 'It is a great day for the Empire that has brought Englishmen, Australians, Canadians and our own colonials out here into line on the battlefield', he told Kitty. 'It is the real federation of the Empire and worth many federations on paper. Though I am a prisoner of war, I'm Irish and so British'.[74] The war had reinforced imperial sentiment amongst Irish unionists of all classes, and Nugent was not the only one to end up in Boer hands. At Lindley in May 1900, for example, over 400 members of the 13th Imperial Yeomanry, including a large Irish contingent, were captured.[75] Some, like Lord Longford, he knew personally but one he did not was James Craig, the future Ulster unionist leader. Their shared experience of Boer captivity (they were in different camps and did not meet) would not noticeably help their relationship during the Great War.

At last, in late May 1900, the sound of artillery indicated that Lord Roberts's army was drawing closer and on 1 June, with news that the

[73] ON to CN, 16 Jan., 2 and 27 Feb., 3 Apr. 1900 (PRONI, D3835/E/1/3/3, 1/3/8, 1/3/14 and 1/4/1); Gen. Sir Aylmer Haldane, *A Soldier's Saga* (1948), pp 161–83.
[74] ON to CN, 5 May 1900 (PRONI, D3835/E/1/4/6); Alvin Jackson, 'Irish Unionists and the Empire, 1880–1920: Classes and Masses', in Keith Jeffery (ed.), *'An Irish Empire'? Aspects of Ireland and the British Empire* (1996), pp 132–3; Keith Jeffery, 'The Irish soldier in the Boer War', in John Gooch (ed.), *The Boer War: Direction, Experience and Image* (2000), pp 146–8.
[75] Pakenham, *Boer War*, pp 436–7; Will Bennett, *Absent-Minded Beggars: Yeomanry and Volunteers in the Boer War* (1999), pp 110–22.

Transvaal government had fled, the prisoners were jubilant. Yet four days later British troops had still to arrive and there were worrying rumours that the Boers might move the prisoners out of Pretoria (they had already been relocated to a camp on the outskirts of the city). On 6 June, however, Nugent and the others saw three horsemen approaching:

> While we were looking, 3 men on horses came out from among the trees and came galloping towards us. As they came closer, 2 of them seemed to be in khaki … but we still doubted until one of them took off his hat and waved it to us. Then we knew it was all right at last, that the day we had waited for, for so many weary hours, was come at last. As they came up they were recognised as Winston Churchill and the Duke of Marlborough.[76]

Churchill later left his own account of the same encounter:

> [A]s we rounded a corner, there was the prison camp, a long tin building surrounded by a dense wire entanglement. I raised my hat and cheered. The cry was instantly answered from within … The prisoners rushed out of the house into the yard, some in uniform, some in flannels, hatless or coatless, but all violently excited. The sentries threw down their rifles, the gates were flung open, and while the last of the guard (they numbered 52 in all) stood uncertain what to do, the long-penned-up officers surrounded them and seized their weapons. Someone produced a Union Jack, the Transvaal emblem was torn down, and amidst wild cheers from our captive friends, the first British flag was hoisted over Pretoria.[77]

Serving with Roberts's force were Kitty's brother Elliott and her brother-in-law Percy Browne, both with the Imperial Yeomanry, and the three of them met for dinner in Pretoria and had their photographs taken (another brother-in-law, Colonel Lawrence Parke, was on the staff of General Clery, operating under Buller in Natal). Nugent was now desperate to get home, despite an offer from Ian Hamilton to join his staff for operations against the Boer guerrillas. He had been placed temporarily in charge of the police in Pretoria, where he deliberately adopted a conciliatory approach to the civilian population – 'I feel sure that a great deal will depend on the tone adopted towards them now' – but on 23 June he met Roberts, who after inquiring about his health ordered him home.[78]

[76] ON to CN, 5 June 1900 (PRONI, D3835/E/1/4/10) – this seems to be a copy in Kitty's handwriting of Nugent's original letter.
[77] Winston Churchill, *My Early Life* (1949), p. 347.
[78] ON to Cn, 12 and 25 June 1900 (PRONI, D3835/E/1/4/14 and 15).

On 11 July 1900 Nugent left the Cape for England, having spent eleven of the previous 14 years overseas. With a DSO and several campaign medals, a Staff College qualification, an attractive wife and a son and, temporarily at least, a degree of financial stability, things seemed set fair for the next phase of his career. The thought that 14 years later Europe would be on the verge of a major war would not have surprised him; the idea that before then he would be leading an armed paramilitary force in Ireland, apparently ready to fight the British army, most certainly would.

2

Conflicted Soldier

Defending Cavan and protecting Hull, 1901–April 1915

Introduction

Between 1901 and 1914 Nugent's military career developed along conventional lines. In the spring of 1914, however, his two worlds as an Irish unionist landowner and a serving British officer collided dramatically when he assumed command of the Ulster Volunteer Force (UVF) in Cavan. As he described it that December: 'What a year. It began with my turning a rebel, then with my being in danger of arrest as one, or of being shot by the British Army and ends with my being in command of a most important fortress. It's a funny world'.[1]

The first half of 1914 was a traumatic period, with civil war in Ireland apparently looming. Although the outbreak of the Great War deferred (though it did not in the end prevent) violent conflict on the island, the crisis had not only widened the political gulf between unionists and nationalists, it also brought much of the landed gentry of Ulster into direct confrontation with the British state and divided the army's officer corps, evidenced by events at the Curragh in March. Nugent, as both an Ulster landowner and a serving officer, was deeply conflicted. Although in the end he threw in his lot with his political class, he used his influence to try to ensure there would be no clashes between the Cavan Volunteers and the army and police. His experiences in the spring and summer of 1914 also served to crystallise his political views and personal sense of identity in a way that set him apart from mainstream Ulster unionist thinking, views that would later influence his approach to commanding the Ulster Division.

Staff and regimental service

On his return from South Africa it took Major Nugent, as he now was – his promotion had come through in late 1899 – some time to recover from the wounds he had received, and the army helped by giving him successive staff appointments. The first of these was in Dublin in 1901–02, on the

---

[1] ON to CN, 31 Dec. 1914 (PRONI, D3835/E/1/223).

staff of the commander-in-chief in Ireland, which gave him the opportunity both to oversee a major renovation of the house at Farren Connell, made possible by Kitty's dowry, and to re-connect with landed society in Cavan and the surrounding counties after his years overseas – families such as the Maxwells of Fortland, the Burrowes of Lismore and Stradone, the Napers of Loughcrew, the Saundersons of Castle Saunderson, the Godleys of Killegar and the Pakenhams of Pakenham Hall. A close friendship developed between him and Arthur Kenlis Maxwell, the 11th Baron Farnham and Cavan's largest landowner, despite Farnham being ten years his junior. Their shared political and social outlook was reinforced by their mutual interest in sailing – Nugent kept a launch on Lough Sheelin, adjoining the estate – a popular past-time amongst the landed families of the lakeland counties of Cavan and Fermanagh. The Nugents' second child, Theffania, was born in May 1903 and early in 1904 he was posted to the 3rd KRRC as second-in-command, in which role, accompanied for a time by Kitty, he spent a pleasant 18 months in Bermuda. In October 1906, on promotion to lieutenant-colonel, he assumed command of the 4th KRRC at Colchester.

Sale of the estate

Although the events of 1912–14 marked the start of a political revolution in Ireland that would play out over the next decade, that revolution was preceded by a socio-economic one that between 1880 and 1909 dismantled the political and economic power of the Irish landed class, 'a non-violent revolution', as one historian has described it, 'that arguably transformed Irish life and society considerably more than the revolution of the 1912–23 period'.[2] For the Nugents of Farren Connell this entered a decisive phase in the first decade of the twentieth century, when Nugent finally sold off an estate that had been in his family's possession for centuries.

Landed estates were by the early twentieth century increasingly difficult to sustain economically and politically and in 1903 the government enacted new legislation, the Wyndham Act, which offered the most generous terms yet to landlords to sell their estates. The scheme enabled tenants to buy their holdings, often through the Land Commission, at affordable rates but also offered landlords better returns than previously.[3] It was an opportunity that Nugent could not afford to miss but initially he intended to sell only part of the estate, telling his sister-in-law in June 1904 that he would only

---

[2] Terence Dooley, *The Irish Revolution 1912–23: Monaghan* (2017), p. 5.

[3] The equivalent, including a 12% cash bonus, of over 25 years' purchase (i.e. 25 times the land's annual rental value). See Dooley, *Decline of the Big House*, pp 112–15.

dispose of the three townlands, out of eight, most distant from the demesne and that he would 'never sell Farren Connell or the land occupied by tenants immediately adjoining it'. By the end of 1904 around a third of the estate had been sold to 32 occupying tenants.[4] He soon realised, however, that what was left was barely viable and that the Act's advantageous terms were unlikely to be repeated, and so in 1907–08 the rest of the land was sold to the remaining 39 tenants.[5] He was not alone. At least 36 other Cavan landlords sold some or all of their estates in this period and they had made the right decision, because those who failed to avail of the terms of the Wyndham Act came to regret it, subsequent land purchase legislation being much less generous.[6] Although the income Nugent now received from interest payments from the Land Commission, at just under £1,100 per annum, was lower than his nominal rental income in 1903, this was offset by the capital sum he received which, like many of his peers, he invested to a significant extent in overseas concerns like Brazilian railways and Malayan rubber.

Nugent was no longer a landlord but he was still a landowner, the Farren Connell demesne amounting to about 500 acres, and for now at least he had financial stability, reassuring Kitty in 1910 that they had 'just enough to live comfortably on'.[7] Furthermore, with the land question at Farren Connell resolved a long-standing source of friction between the Nugents and the community in which they lived had been removed: as would be seen in Cavan and other areas during the Irish War of Independence and Civil War, unresolved agrarian grievances could be a significant motive for 'political' violence against former landlords. The settlement also enabled Nugent to continue his military service, at a time when a private income remained essential in most regiments, with dignity and a degree of financial certainty. From the perspective of the British armed forces an important if incidental result of the relative generosity of the 1903 Act was that it maintained the goodwill and (at least temporarily) the economic viability of the Irish gentry and therefore a key source of officer recruitment.

[4] ON to Florence Lees, 1 June 1904 (PRONI, D3835/E/1/5/25); 1905 estate accounts (PRONI, D3835/E/14/10/3).

[5] 1907 & 1908 estate accounts (PRONI, D3835/14/10/5 & 6). A section of land adjoining the demesne was retained until 1918.

[6] Cherry, 'The structure, demise and legacy of landlordism in County Cavan, c. 1870–c. 1970', pp 465–9.

[7] ON to CN, 19 Aug. 1910 (PRONI, D3835/E/1/9/11).

Commanding officer

As soon as he took over the 4th KRRC at Colchester in October 1906 Nugent displayed the characteristics that would define all his future command positions. He insisted on high standards and was quick to find fault, his explosive temper, exacerbated by his South African wounds, meaning that subordinates were often in awe of him. Although his appointment came at an important time for the army, during a period of reform begun in the immediate aftermath of the Boer War and continued, from 1906, by the new Liberal Secretary of State for War Richard Haldane (the reforms included the creation of a seven-division expeditionary force, the establishment of the Territorial Force and improvements in doctrine and training), ceremonial duties and sport still dominated the first two years of Nugent's tenure.[8] The Prince of Wales, the regimental colonel-in-chief to whom he had now been appointed ADC (which became an even more valuable connection when the prince succeeded to the throne in 1910 as George V), inspected the 4th KRRC in July 1907 and that autumn it mounted guard at Buckingham Palace and provided a detachment to line streets in London for the visit of the emperor of Japan. It also won the army football cup in 1908, beating the 2nd Lancashire Fusiliers in the final. There were still, though, opportunities for military training and the battalion took part in manoeuvres in 1907 and 1908 on Salisbury plain which attracted large crowds; in 1907, for example, Nugent described the scene for Kitty:

> There was a huge crowd of spectators, foreign attaches and the Duke of Cambridge. We had the luck to be right in the middle of them in making an attack and I made the men run like hares and led them myself! The French military attache was so overcome by emotion at the dash we displayed that he dropped his reins and clapped his hands as we hurled ourselves on the enemy who fled in disorder.[9]

Nugent's admittedly light-hearted description does not suggest a great deal of tactical realism, an accusation that Sir John French later levelled at Sir Horace Smith-Dorrien's conduct of the 1907 manoeuvres (though that may have reflected more the animosity between the two men, given Smith-Dorrien's generally serious approach to training).[10]

---

[8] Edward Spiers, 'The Late Victorian Army 1868–1914', in David Chandler and Ian Beckett (eds), *The Oxford Illustrated History of the British Army* (1994), pp 205–16.

[9] ON to CN, 5 Sep. 1907 (PRONI, D3835/E/1/5/30).

[10] Timothy Bowman and Mark Connelly, *The Edwardian Army: Recruiting, Training, and Deploying the British Army, 1902–1914* (2012), pp 71–4.

The main event of Nugent's period in command was the battalion's move to India in late 1909, a major logistical undertaking. On 1 December 17 officers and 427 other ranks embarked at Southampton on the 'Dongda', a hired transport, arriving at Karachi on 21 December: Kitty and the children (their third child, Alison, had been born in May 1909) remained in England. The battalion went first to Meerut and then on to Chakrata in the Himalayan foothills, both locations where Nugent had served previously. Garrison life in India away from the frontier was still much as it had been in the 1890s – the atmosphere would be different when he returned in 1918 – but already there were signs of changing attitudes. Despite Nugent's efforts to prevent it, for example, one of his officers was formally reprimanded for beating an Indian servant ('a very mild beating', Nugent complained, 'which he richly deserved … Insolence from a native is one of the things I never could stand').[11] He regarded firm discipline as essential. The battalion had been joined on arrival by almost 400 men transferring from the 2nd KRRC, now on its way home, and integrating them proved tricky: 'There are a lot of men who came from the 2nd Battn who give a good deal of trouble', he noted, 'but I am taking them on by degrees. India is a bad country for discipline'.[12] Tragedy struck when a soldier was murdered in barracks by a comrade, the killer then being beaten unconscious by other members of the company. Nugent hoped he would survive to be hanged at a garrison parade as a warning – 'In India it has to be like this, because men out here … become subject to sudden epidemics of crime and examples are essential'.[13] He speculated that when he left some of his officers would be sorry to see him go but that the men would feel differently: 'I have not spared them and I have never failed to give them beans when it is necessary, but men don't really mind that. They like a man who is the same always, who does not preach at them and who downs them impartially'.[14]

While consistency was important his leadership style was undoubtedly hard, demonstrated by an incident towards the end of his tour. A disturbance arose in the battalion's married lines one night when a sergeant visited the wife of a fellow NCO, away on a course, in her quarters; two other sergeants, suspecting impropriety, burst in and a fracas ensued. It seems there was no inappropriate behaviour – also in the quarters was the pregnant wife of another NCO – but the visit was certainly ill-judged. Nugent had both women and the three sergeants up before him next day,

[11] ON to CN, 23 June 2010 (PRONI, D3835/1/9/2).
[12] ON to CN, 3 Aug. 1910 (PRONI, D3835/E/1/9/8).
[13] ON to CN, 6 Aug. 1910 (PRONI, D3835/E/1/9/9).
[14] ON to CN, 30 Aug. 1910 (PRONI, D3835/E/1/9/10).

and having demoted the 'visiting' sergeant he proceeded to berate them so savagely that the sergeant's wife dissolved into hysterics, her pregnant friend collapsed and had to be carried out and one of the sergeants 'was so overcome at my eloquence that he had a trembling fit and had to be supported while I continued to slate him'.[15] Nugent's account to Kitty was couched humorously but more than a decade later a former subordinate recalled the episode as an example of the 'streak of intolerance' that occasionally marred Nugent's leadership qualities.[16]

Although the battalion saw no active service Nugent's period in command was regarded as a success. He was made a brevet colonel and sufficiently impressed the military authorities in India that he was sounded out about a possible brigade command as well as senior staff appointments in Simla and in Burma, which he turned down because he wanted to return home. In October 1910 he handed over command to Dick Montagu-Stuart-Wortley, with whom he had been wounded at Talana. Torrential rain prevented him from saying goodbye to the battalion on parade and he instead bid farewell by means of a special order of the day, but his hopes of slipping away quietly the following morning were thwarted. Despite the rain the entire battalion, whether voluntarily or not, was there to see him off – 'I rode down to the square and found the officers and men there and I said goodbye as well as I could, the band played 'Auld lang syne' and everyone cheered and I galloped off into the fog as hard as I could go'.[17]

Territorial Force

He arrived in England unsure what his next job would be but hoping for a regular brigade. Following a brief period on half-pay, however, he learned that his next appointment would be command, as a colonel, of a Territorial Force (TF) infantry brigade, the Hampshire Brigade, and he took up post in January 1911. There was a certain irony in his appointment to the TF, because in the debate that raged in the Edwardian period between those, like Lord Roberts, who favoured compulsory military service in peacetime to guard against invasion, and those who believed home defence requirements could be met by voluntarily-raised auxiliary forces, Nugent had been firmly in the national service camp.[18] In January 1910, for example, during one of the periodic invasion scares, he had complained

[15] ON to CN, 13 Sep. 1910 (PRONI, D3835/E/1/9/12).
[16] Maurice Crum to ON, 2 Jan. 1922 (PRONI, D3835/E/2/21).
[17] ON to CN, 4 Oct. 1910 (PRONI, D3835/E/1/9/14).
[18] Bowman and Connelly, *Edwardian Army*, pp 47–8, 159–62; Rodney Atwood, *The Life of Field Marshal Lord Roberts* (2015), pp 243–6.

bitterly that British politicians lacked the courage 'to say to the people that there is no chance of getting an army for home defence without national service':

> What makes me so angry is that we poor soldiers who will have to stand in front if ever England is invaded, knowing that we have not a ghost of a chance against the armies Germany could pour in if we lost command of the sea, have no say in the government of our own army ... We know that we shall probably all be killed vainly because the people in England will not face their duty and because no statesman in England will risk the loss of votes by telling them what is their duty.[19]

While disappointed not to be given a regular formation he threw himself into his new role with characteristic energy. His brigade consisted of four battalions of the Hampshire Regiment and formed part of the Wessex Division, one of 14 Territorial infantry divisions established in 1908 as part of Haldane's reforms. He arrived as the initial enthusiasm for the TF was waning. Following an early surge of recruiting, by June 1909 it had reached a strength of 269,000 against an establishment of over 310,000, but by September 1913 numbers had fallen below 246,000.[20] In February 1911, when he carried out his initial inspection of his units, he discovered a mixed picture – with the 4th Hampshires in Winchester he found a '[p]oor turn out. Arms drill good, movement bad'; the 5th Hampshires in Southampton had a fair turnout, but while the men were good he thought the officers were of 'indifferent class' and the adjutant 'a toady'; the 6th Hampshires at Portsmouth were 'quite good'; the 7th at Bournemouth, commanded by his brother-in-law Colonel 'Ponto' Parke, were the most impressive, 'good numbers, men looked well, drilled well for Ponto'.[21] Over the next two years he set about raising standards, and by the summer of 1913 there were clear signs of improvement. The camp that August at Blandford, in Dorset, with over 2,000 of the brigade present, went well both militarily and socially; in addition to the training it was also a civic event with a wide range of activities in surrounding towns and villages, including tattoos, concerts, church parades and displays. The public were allowed to watch part of the manoeuvres and thousands turned up to see the brigade

[19] ON to CN, 30 Jan. 1910 (PRONI, D3835/E/1/7/5).
[20] Edward M. Spiers, *Haldane: An Army Reformer* (1980), pp 172–85; Ian F. W. Beckett, *The Amateur Military Tradition, 1558–1945* (1991), pp 213–22; K. W. Mitchinson, *Defending Albion: Britain's Home Army 1908–1919* (2005), pp 1–33.
[21] Nugent 1911 diary (PRONI, D3835/E/5/13).

conducting an advance to contact and occupying a position near Blandford 'from the Old Cricket Ground on Monckton Down to Feris Plantation': they left apparently well-satisfied with the spectacle, which they had vigorously applauded.[22] The performance masked significant underlying problems with the TF, in terms of recruiting shortfalls, high turnover of soldiers, shortage of officers and difficulties in meeting training commitments. Furthermore, in the summer of 1913, just a year away from war, only 7% of the TF had signed up for overseas service.[23]

Although he took his role seriously Nugent found it less than fulfilling and in February 1912 he had gone to see Launcelot Kiggell, Director of Staff Duties at the War Office, 'reference my getting something better. Told me I should but must wait'.[24] The question was whether command of a reserve formation inevitably indicated a career drawing to a close: Nugent did not believe it did and there were those in the army, like Ian Hamilton, arguing that Territorial commands should go to regular officers capable of further promotion. Nugent came into frequent contact with influential senior officers like Charles Douglas, the CIGS, Jack Cowans, Director General of the Territorial Force and Horace Smith-Dorrien, GOC Southern Command, and in May 1913 he took part in a major four-day command post exercise, under Smith-Dorrien's direction, which involved six major-generals (including Henry Rawlinson) and a considerable number of brigadiers and colonels.[25]

The TF was still too newly-established to be associated with a definite career trajectory and the outbreak of war makes it impossible to judge how many regulars in senior TF positions would have gone on to greater things had peace been maintained. An indication, however, is provided by the number who held front-line commands in the Great War. Excluding the two London Territorial divisions, whose command structures were directly linked to the Brigade of Guards, the other 12 infantry divisions contained 39 infantry brigades (the TF was not raised in Ireland). In 1912–13 a total of 16 officers, all regular major-generals, served as divisional commanders and of these seven would serve at the front, including one future army commander (Byng) and three corps commanders (Woollcombe, Keir and Townshend). At the next level down, of 33 regular colonels commanding brigades (out of 51 in total, the others being reserve/volunteer officers) 17 went on to hold operational commands, including a corps commander

---

[22] *Western Chronicle*, 8 Aug. 1913.
[23] Beckett, *Amateur Tradition*, pp 221–2.
[24] Nugent 1912 diary (PRONI, D3835/E/5/14).
[25] *Gloucestershire Echo*, 6 May 1913.

(Bulfin) and two divisional commanders (Nugent and Hare).[26] These figures do not suggest that a TF appointment was necessarily the end of the road; nevertheless, the fact that 'something better' had not come along by the time Nugent's tour ended in February 1914 and he went on half-pay for a second time, must have concerned him. That anxiety would soon be eclipsed by far greater worries, however, when he arrived back in Ireland. As for the Hampshire Brigade, on mobilisation in 1914 it was sent to India to release regular troops for service elsewhere and languished there for much of the war, despite undertakings that it would be brought back quickly: in September 1916 the 6th Hampshires were still lobbying the county Territorial association to press the War Office to redeem its promise, without success.[27]

Cavan and Home Rule

Nugent returned to Cavan in late February, just as the Home Rule crisis reached a tipping point and Ireland seemed to be slipping towards civil war. The next few months were not only extremely difficult for him personally, they represented a period he looked back on with great distaste.

Tensions had been rising for almost two years, with the introduction in April 1912 by Asquith's Liberal government of the Third Home Rule Bill. Although its two predecessors had been defeated, in 1886 and 1893, the parliamentary arithmetic and the constitutional framework were now different (John Redmond's Irish Parliamentary Party held the balance of power and the 1911 Parliament Act meant that the bill could only be delayed by the Lords and not rejected). This led to massive unionist mobilisation in Ulster, and in September 1912 almost 500,000 Ulster men and women signed the Ulster Covenant or Declaration, its equivalent for women. In Cavan 4,423 men and 3,722 women did so, representing 71% and 65% respectively of the county's non-Catholic population aged over 16.[28] These figures were proportionately lower than for some other counties but still high in absolute terms and they included Kitty, who signed at Farren Connell with two of the domestic staff; Nugent's mother and cousin did so in London.[29] Nugent also signed, in Dublin, the certificate with his signature surviving in his papers, but seems to have done so privately. He had reason to be cautious, since as a serving Territorial brigade commander he was sailing very close to the wind in taking such an

---

[26] Calculated from *Army Lists*, 1912–14.

[27] Ian Beckett, 'The Territorial Force', in Ian F. W. Beckett and Keith Simpson, *A Nation in Arms* (1985), pp 134–5.

[28] David Fitzpatrick, *Descendancy: Irish Protestant Histories since 1795* (2014), p. 243.

[29] List of Ulster Covenant signatories (PRONI website).

overtly political stand.[30] The reality, though, was that however high local levels of unionist participation in anti-Home Rule activities might be, Cavan was not only a mainly Catholic county (81% of its population of 91,000), but its Protestant population was more widely dispersed than those of Monaghan (25% Protestant) and Donegal (22%), which were relatively concentrated in north Monaghan and east Donegal.[31] In a telling illustration of the Nugents' isolation in the Mountnugent area, only one of their 71 former tenants signed the Covenant in 1912.[32]

In January 1913 the Ulster Unionist Council (UUC), Ulster unionism's ruling body, had established the UVF as the resistance movement's military wing and in September the UUC announced plans for a provisional Ulster government if the Home Rule bill was passed without an opt-out clause for Ulster; in November 1913 the nationalist Irish, or National, Volunteers were set up in response. As soon as Nugent returned to Ireland Lord Farnham, now leader of the Cavan unionists, asked him to take command of the UVF in the county. The request placed him in a difficult position. Signing the Covenant was one thing, but involvement as a serving officer, even if on half-pay, in this paramilitary organisation left him open to prosecution under King's Regulations and in extremis could lead him into direct conflict with the army he had served in for 32 years. On the other hand, his home, his family and his friends seemed to be under threat. Across Ulster the landed class was playing a leading role in organising resistance to Home Rule – in Cavan and Monaghan the Farnhams, the Saundersons, the Maddens, the Leslies and a score of other landed families were commanding UVF detachments, storing weapons or allowing their demesnes to be used for training, while a significant part of the UVF's leadership cadre (one estimate, possibly on the high side, suggests over 60% of its leadership at battalion level and above) were former officers, many from landed backgrounds; a few were still serving.[33] Nugent also felt a strong sense of solidarity with ordinary Cavan unionists, shopkeepers, farmers and professional people, who looked to figures like him for leadership, and he detested Asquith's government. He resolved his personal dilemma by becoming involved on his own terms:

[30] He is not listed amongst the 2,000 Dublin signatories on the PRONI website.
[31] Eileen Reilly, 'Cavan in the era of the Great War, 1914–18', in Raymond Gillespie (ed.), *Cavan: Essays on the History of an Irish County* (1995), p. 177; R. B. McDowell, *Crisis and Decline: The Fate of the Southern Unionists* (1997), p. 5.
[32] List of Ulster Covenant signatories (PRONI website).
[33] Hew Strachan, *The Politics of the British Army* (1997), p. 112; Timothy Bowman, *Carson's Army: The Ulster Volunteer Force, 1910–22* (2007), pp 57–60.

I joined the UVF not for the purpose of rebellion or civil war because I disagreed all along on the policy which created the UVF but because I thought I should do more good in my own country by organising a force for defence in case of attack and that I would never consent to leading them in an unprovoked attack on anyone and that I said at the time that those were the conditions on which I would take part and on no other. They were not popular outside of Cavan.[34]

They were not popular within Cavan either, as would soon become apparent. His first task was to run a training camp on Farnham's estate, from 8 to 14 March, for 120 UVF section and squad leaders, and in preparation for it he drew up a set of instructions in his role as commander of the 'Cavan Volunteer Force' (CVF) – a title he preferred to the more military 'Cavan Regiment, UVF'. The instructions were clear that he saw the CVF's role as defensive, to protect local Protestants and unionists in the event of attack. The opening section of the 19-page document was an analysis, in military appreciation style, of why a defensive approach was unavoidable. Cavan was 'geographically and politically isolated from North East Ulster'; with just 1,650 men in the CVF (Nugent's figure was strikingly lower than the police estimate, see below) it could not send men to help other areas and its best contribution to the wider UVF was to be self-sufficient defensively, acting as a police force or 'organization for mutual defence' rather than a military one:

It must not be forgotten that the CVF is formed for defence and not for aggression and that that is the principal reason why its organization has a civil and not a military basis. The CVF is formed for mutual support and for defence against unprovoked attack. It is not intended that it should be used against any of the Armed Forces of the Crown, but on the contrary, to assist them, should occasion arise, in the maintenance of peace and security in the County.[35]

The training camp at Farnham House went well. Instruction covered minor tactics, drill, arms handling and musketry, and amongst those involved were several other members of the local gentry with military experience – Farnham himself, a former lieutenant in the 10th Hussars and a major in the North Irish Horse; Mervyn and Audley Pratt of Cabra Castle; Somerset Saunderson of Castle Saunderson; and Major Head, the CVF's second-in-command. The press took a close interest and predictably reported the

[34] ON to CN, 5 Feb. 1916, in *Nugent*, p. 47.
[35] CVF Instructions (PRONI, D3835/E/10/1/1).

event in line with their political outlooks. The unionist *Northern Whig* described admiringly the good behaviour and keenness of the volunteers and praised them for leaving their farms at a busy time, evidence of 'their determination to take part with their fellow-Unionists of the other Ulster counties in armed resistance to Home Rule'; the nationalist *Anglo-Celt*, by contrast, reported scornfully that 'Colonel Nugent, DSO, an ex-officer of the King's Own Rifles … is now 'Commander' of the Cavan battalion of the Carsonite Volunteers … these men to the full strength of 120 in a county with a population of 91,173, met at Lord Farnham's last week'.[36] The *Anglo-Celt* might scoff, but Cavan was becoming militarised at an alarming rate. By the end of March 1914 the police estimated the UVF's strength in Cavan at 3,406, with 2,767 rifles of various sorts between them, and the number of rifles would increase following the Larne gun-running, consignments from which had started arriving in Cavan by early May. The proportion of adult Protestant males involved in the Cavan Volunteers, an estimated 56%, was the highest in Ulster and reflected the unionist community's sense of isolation.[37] The numbers of the National Volunteers were also building rapidly. By the summer they would have 6,366 members, less well-equipped than the UVF but still with considerable quantities of weapons, primarily shotguns and revolvers. One of the driving forces behind the National Volunteers was Lieutenant R. B. Sheridan of Mountnugent; by coincidence two of the leading figures in the organisation of Cavan paramilitarism came from the same village.[38]

The growing threat of violence worried Nugent. Also present at the Farnham training camp had been a reporter from the pro-Home Rule *Manchester Guardian*, who was touring Ulster assessing the mood of the province. He interviewed Nugent, who had obviously been forewarned because he prepared detailed notes beforehand: these, and the published interview, give a clear insight into the thinking of a leading Cavan unionist at a critical moment, and of his efforts to avoid confrontation.[39] The crisis stemmed, Nugent believed, from the failure of the Liberal government to recognise that Catholic nationalist Ireland and Protestant unionist Ulster were effectively 'two different races'; he thought that belittling the seriousness of unionist opposition to Home Rule was a grave error. He accepted that the political representatives of 80% of the people of Ireland wanted the form of Ireland's government to change but regarded the

---

[36] *Northern Whig*, 14 Mar. 1914; Reilly, 'Cavan in the era of the Great War', p. 182.
[37] Fitzpatrick, *Descendancy*, p. 244.
[38] Reilly, 'Cavan in the era of the Great War', pp 181–2.
[39] The notes are not titled as such, but from internal evidence it is clear that was the document's purpose (PRONI, D3835/E/2/20/3).

current Home Rule bill as fatally flawed and also unenforceable by the civil authorities and 'a few hundred policemen … against half a million men banded together by solemn oath and inflexible resolve'. In a candid assessment of the UVF's military effectiveness, he thought that '[t]o the employment of military force, the Unionists of Ulster have no answer':

> A few machine guns playing on the Protestant masses in the streets of Belfast would soon clear them away. A number of small flying columns to shoot down the Presbyterian farmers of Antrim and Down and the hanging of the leaders would be quite effective.

His point was to underscore the absurdity, in his view, of military coercion – 'The employment of the military forces of the Crown to compel acceptance is inconceivable'.[40] The essentials of a political solution, if Home Rule had to happen, lay he believed in the proposals of Lord MacDonnell (who as Sir Anthony MacDonnell had been Under Secretary at the Irish Office in the early 1900s), who advocated protection for Ulster's position through weighted voting mechanisms within an Irish parliament.

The interview appeared in the *Manchester Guardian* on 18 March and was re-printed by the *Anglo-Celt* three days later.[41] In his introduction the correspondent described Nugent as a moderate, one of the few unionists he had met 'who could discuss Home Rule with even an appearance of dispassionateness'. He noted that Nugent had stressed the defensive purpose of the Cavan Volunteers – 'We should probably have enough to do to protect ourselves without fighting British soldiers and in Cavan I have never considered that a possibility'. Nugent was also clear about his opposition to Home Rule for the entire island and was patronisingly sceptical, typically of many unionists, about the ability of Irish people to govern themselves efficiently, even-handedly and without 'jobbery'. But he was equally frank about his opposition to partition (Asquith had recently suggested that individual Ulster counties could vote to opt out of Home Rule for a period of up to six years, a proposal rejected for opposite reasons by both Carson and Redmond) and his willingness to accept, if all else failed, a bad Home Rule settlement rather than a divided island:

> I am an Irishman, and Home Rule or no Home Rule, there are a lot of us who will have to live in Ireland among our Catholic neighbours. I shall be guided by my leaders, but, subject to what they have to say, my own position would be to make the best of a

---

[40] Ibid.
[41] *Anglo-Celt*, 21 Mar. 1914.

bad job if it is to come to that. It may be that Ulster combining with the moderates of the Nationalist Party would dispel one's fears for an Irish Parliament. I doubt it very much; but if we are to have an Irish Parliament I should much prefer to see Ulster represented in it. Exclusion seems to me to be quite impracticable and quite impolitic too, if the interests of the Protestants who live outside Ulster enters into the question at all. I devoutly hope that the Bill will be killed, but if that cannot be, a scheme of administrative autonomy for Ulster, accompanied by a veto on legislation, strikes me as the most satisfactory settlement.

Although MacDonnell's proposals had already been rejected by both sides, Nugent's position was exactly that of many southern unionists. His opinions were, however, strikingly out of step with Ulster unionist views, including the position (publicly at least) of the Cavan leadership. The *Anglo-Celt* had picked up his interview enthusiastically, putting it on its front page on 21 March under the headline 'Volunteers and Ulster: Col. Nugent Wants Inclusion'. Its editorial, contrasting Nugent's 'words of apparent conciliation' with the bellicose posture of Carson, wondered whether Nugent's emphasis on the CVF's defensive role and opposition to exclusion might cause the 'ordinary Carsonite' to 'wipe his eyes and ask what he has been drilling for when the man in supreme control in the county makes the statement which we have quoted above'. Cavan unionists knew they were vulnerable in the event of conflict but they also feared, with reason, abandonment by their co-religionists and were keen to assert their solidarity with the rest of Ulster and their readiness to fight if they had to. At the annual Orange Order Twelfth celebrations at Belturbet in July 1914, for example, R. H. Johnston, County Grand Master of the Order in Cavan, stressed the strength of the UVF – 'our one hundred thousand Volunteers well disciplined, well armed, staunch and true men … the sons of the men who died at Derry, Aughrim and the Boyne were quite ready to let their red blood flow', while Farnham spoke of Protestants being 'prepared to fight for their civil and religious liberties'.[42] This may simply have been rhetoric but it was very different in tone from Nugent's interview. Kitty was present at Belturbet as part of the platform party along with other county grandees, including the Farnhams and the Saundersons, but Nugent himself was not, despite the presence there of a sizeable CVF detachment. He was not an Orangeman and he may have been unavoidably detained elsewhere, but it may too have been convenient for the Cavan leadership that he be absent; certainly, after the interview, his public profile was much lower for the remainder of the crisis.

[42] *Anglo-Celt*, 18 July 1914.

On the same day, Saturday, 21 March, that Nugent's interview appeared in the *Anglo-Celt*, the Curragh incident was continuing to play out as other serving officers, not all of them Irish, faced a similar conflict of loyalties. (Although he knew several of the principal actors, there is no evidence that Nugent had any contact with them at this time.) The decision by Hubert Gough and the officers of the 3rd Cavalry Brigade to offer to resign rather than serve against the Ulster unionists, following an apparent ultimatum from the politically inept commander-in-chief in Ireland, General Paget, and the concessions made to them by the War Office and subsequently disowned by the cabinet, made the use of the army to compel Ulster virtually impossible.[43] Far from forcing a re-think on Home Rule, however, it now made more likely a partitionist outcome of the sort Nugent opposed.

Nugent also found himself debating political issues directly with nationalist representatives in his own locality. At the end of March he exchanged letters with William Ahern, a neighbour and nationalist district councillor, which Ahern then made public. A successful farmer who owned a stone-cutting business, Ahern was one of the rising Catholic middle-class who had benefited from the reform of local government in the late 1890s and who, until the emergence of Sinn Fein, were the main beneficiaries of the democratisation of Irish politics; he and Nugent knew each other, and their exchanges were courteous.[44] Ahern had criticised the motives of the Cavan Volunteers and their purpose in training, and Nugent had written to him regretting 'that wrong impressions should be about amongst those whose good feeling I have always valued' and offering a meeting. When Ahern declined, on the basis that he would be addressing the council on the topic, Nugent replied that he agreed with him 'that no man ought to be allowed to carry arms for the purpose of fighting his Majesty's troops or of shooting his fellow-countrymen, and so far as I know no one in Cavan is doing so'. Ahern read this out at the council meeting as providing some reassurance, but nevertheless criticised Nugent for heightening tensions in the area.[45]

Local hostility to Nugent's position manifested itself in more pointed ways. 'There never has been any disagreement between us and the country folk', he later told Kitty, 'except the excitement caused by my organisation of the Cavan Volunteers: the excitement that caused is really proof of how much the country people look upon Nugents as their natural leaders, because they considered I had deserted the side I ought by heredity to be in

---

[43] Hew Strachan, *Politics of the British Army*, pp 111–17; Jeffery, *Wilson*, pp 120–25. See also Ian Beckett (ed.), *The Army and the Curragh Incident 1914* (1986) and Sir James Fergusson, *The Curragh Incident* (1964).

[44] Dooley, *Monaghan*, pp 6–8.

[45] *Anglo-Celt*, 4 Apr. 1914.

sympathy with'.[46] A shopkeeper in Mountnugent, Peter Lynch, organised a meeting in April 1914 to demand that the village's name be changed to Daly's Bridge, an earlier title, because it should not be called 'after a family whose representative in Farrenconnell, Colonel Nugent, was to-day an Orange drill master at Cavan'. Ahern, who was present, spoke against the proposal and in defence of Nugent, who, he said, 'had apologised and was sorry for going to drill the Unionist scouts at Cavan', a debatable statement that failed to satisfy Lynch.[47] Nothing came of the suggested name change, however, and a short time later Lynch was seeking Nugent's help to resist eviction from his premises in the village (by a local Catholic auctioneer), and Nugent did what he could to assist.

Events marched on inexorably towards what seemed inevitable conflict. In May the Home Rule bill passed its Third Reading in the Commons and in June an amendment permitting the temporary exclusion of Ulster was introduced in the Lords but was there changed to permanent exclusion, which was unacceptable to nationalists. That month Nugent ordered the CVF to intensify daytime training, which had been scaled back in April to allow farmers to carry out essential work, with a particular emphasis on arms handling and defensive tactics.[48] In July the King convened a conference of the various parties in Buckingham Palace but no agreement was reached – 'I see no hope of peace', said Carson afterwards – and the Howth gun-running and subsequent fatal shooting of four civilians by soldiers in Dublin heightened tensions still further.[49] At this point, events in Europe intervened.

Outbreak of war

The July crisis and the outbreak of hostilities in early August postponed the political crisis in Ireland, and the United Kingdom's declaration of war even for a while brought unionists and nationalists together. The *Anglo-Celt*, in an editorial on 8 August, described John Redmond's call to nationalists to join up as 'magnificent' and hoped that the fact of both traditions working together to 'hold Ireland for the empire against the enemy' would help 'end an age-old quarrel'.[50] On 7 August 400 men, mostly reservists and including many National Volunteers, left Cavan town by train to join their units, some reportedly singing 'A Nation Once Again'. When Home Rule made it onto the statute book in September it was agreed that its operation

---

[46] ON to CN, 10 Aug. 1917, in *Nugent*, pp 165–6.
[47] *Anglo-Celt*, 2 May 1914.
[48] CVF memorandum on training, 5 June 1914 (PRONI, D3835/E/10/1/1).
[49] Bardon, *A History of Ulster* (1992), pp 447–8.
[50] *Anglo-Celt*, 8 Aug. 1914.

would be suspended for the duration of the war, with undertakings given about special (though undefined) provision for Ulster. Also in September Carson offered the government the services of the UVF and CVF members began enlisting.[51] By October 1914 the police estimated that 238 Cavan reservists had been called up, of whom 153 were National volunteers and 55 UVF members, and that 210 new recruits (including 47 National and 71 Ulster Volunteers) had come forward. Enthusiasm for enlistment in Cavan, amongst both Catholics and Protestants, would not last but at this stage only Sinn Fein amongst the political parties struck a discordant note, posting anti-recruitment notices and distributing anti-war leaflets.[52]

Nugent was relieved to end his involvement with the CVF. He had been uncomfortable with it from the start, writing in June 1916 that 'I always maintained that the physical force movement was a mistake and the arming of Ulster a still greater mistake'.[53] He was aware of the damage the political crisis had caused to the army, with the resignations of the Secretary of State for War, CIGS and Adjutant General and the divisions created within the officer corps, something of which he was very conscious when he took over the Ulster Division. He now had to turn his attention back to conventional military concerns, as on 1 August, three days before Britain's declaration of war, a telegram had arrived from the War Office summoning him urgently to London.

Hull

He arrived at Euston station on the morning of 2 August, to be met by a staff officer with orders to report immediately to General Plumer, GOC Northern Command, at York and assume command of the Humber defences, which provided protection for a complex of naval operational and logistic facilities around Hull and Grimsby. Nugent got the next available train and reported to Plumer that afternoon, where he was briefed on his new role. At this stage the threat of invasion was regarded as real, as was the possibility of coastal raids and sabotage. Now a temporary brigadier-general and with six battalions and some artillery under command, he summarised his task for Kitty: 'My job begins if the Germans try to land. The Navy's job is to attack them before they get into the Humber'.[54] His area of responsibility was 14 miles of the River Humber and the coastline for several miles on either side of the estuary.

[51] Falls, *Ulster Division*, p. 4.
[52] Reilly, 'Cavan in the era of the Great War', pp 182–5.
[53] ON to CN, 6 June 1916, in *Nugent*, p. 72.
[54] ON to CN, 2 Aug. 1914 (PRONI, D3835/E/1/156).

On 4 August the expected but still momentous news of the outbreak of war arrived, and Nugent wrote to Kitty

> I have just this moment got a telegram announcing the declaration of war between Germany and ourselves and at [the] same time your wire that Walters [the chauffeur at Farren Connell and an army reservist] has had to go … I don't know what may happen in the near future but I am as I hope we all are confident in our Navy, but oh my dearest how appalling it is.[55]

For the next few weeks Nugent was intensely busy, arranging for the protection of key installations, agreeing with the navy procedures for searching vessels entering the Humber estuary and the circumstances in which shore batteries could open fire, and discussing with the municipal authorities in Hull practical arrangements such as finding billets for the 14,000 troops who by 9 August were under his command. He also had the task of interning German sailors and other German nationals in the area and by 13 August had six German merchant vessels under guard and around 200 of their crewmen imprisoned on a ship on the river: these he found, on inspecting their quarters, to be 'a truculent looking crowd many of them and mostly inclined to be insolent'. Some internees were long-time Hull residents and their distraught wives frequently asked to see him to try to secure their release: 'I am very sorry for them and don't see them for fear I should be weak. I send one of my staff to explain that much as I should like to let him go I must do my duty'.[56]

A striking feature of his new command was the sweeping powers he had available. On 8 August the government had rushed through parliament the Defence of the Realm Act (DORA) which provided the basis for a range of measures including press censorship, restricted opening hours for public houses and constraints on owning wireless transmitters, lighting bonfires or flying kites (as possible methods of signalling). It also provided for trial by court martial for contravention of regulations made under the Act, and as he told Kitty, 'I seem to have very extensive powers when I come to think of it, as governor of a fortress in wartime. I can really almost order anything to be done that I think is right and it is done. However I am pretty merciful'.[57] He was soon using the powers to close roads and restrict access to military and naval installations, curtail opening hours and requisition accommodation (including two large schools in Hull) for his troops. He

55 ON to CN, 4 Aug. 1914 (PRONI, D3835/E/1/168).
56 ON to CN, 3 and 8 Aug. 1914 (PRONI, D3835/E/1/157 & 161).
57 ON to CN, 11 Aug. 1914 (PRONI, D3835/E/1/162).

went out of his way, nevertheless, to maintain good relations with the local authorities; he also persuaded them to convert Hull's swimming baths into a soldiers' club, which proved extremely successful.

Plumer remained at Northern Command until January 1915, when he left to command a corps on the western front. Nugent would later have a highly successful relationship with him but on occasions at Hull he found him less than helpful; in mid-September he fumed that Plumer was 'a terrible obstructionist. Whenever after endless labour I have made out a plan for housing 300 or 400 men he objects to it on some very trivial grounds and I have to begin all over again. It is really most heartbreaking'.[58]

Nugent naturally followed closely the course of the fighting in France. 'We must expect to hear of awful losses', he had warned Kitty on 17 August, and could not contain his true feelings: 'It is no good pretending I am contented to be here. I can't bear to think I may not get a chance of taking my share in what the Army is doing. I have been getting restless and want to be doing something. I fear I may be forgotten here'.[59] While anxious to obtain an operational posting, however, there were some jobs he was not keen on. In September 1914, just after Carson's announcement about the UVF, he told Kitty, 'I hope they won't ask me to command a brigade of the Ulster Volunteers. I don't much believe in them and especially their officers'.[60] The realities of war were brought home early on with the death in action in France on 13 October of Kitty's nephew, 23-year-old Lieutenant Walter ('Bob') Parke of the 2nd Durham Light Infantry, son of her sister Evie.

Fear of invasion had now been replaced by fear of espionage, with a succession of spy scares, and in mid-October, acting on a Home Office directive, Nugent ordered all Belgian refugees to leave Hull and Grimsby (the fear being that enemy agents were concealed amongst them). Despite protests – there were over 200 Belgian refugees in Hull being looked after by various charitable groups – the order was carried out.[61] Under DORA he could in certain circumstances direct the local police and in December a civilian, Archibald Cocks, was court-martialled for illegal possession of wireless equipment and sentenced to six months' hard labour (reduced by Nugent to two months to reflect time spent on remand); and in February 1915 a fruit merchant, Joseph Smith, was convicted of 'making statements likely to prejudice recruiting in the Army' – he had declared that men

[58] ON to CN 19 Sep. 1914 (PRONI, D3835/E/1/180).
[59] ON to CN 17 Aug. 1914 (PRONI, D3835/E/ 1/166).
[60] ON to CN 5 Sep. 1914 (PRONI, D3835/E/1/177).
[61] *Hull Daily Mail*, 23 Oct. 1914.

joining the army were 'bloody fools' – and was released only after apologising.[62] On some matters Nugent felt unable to intervene. In October 1914 the Bishop of Hull and the YWCA suggested that girls under the age of 18 'should not be permitted to loiter in the streets after 9pm without a permit'. The Hull Watch Committee put this proposal to Nugent who told them he had no power to make such an order, and the committee decided instead to create four 'women patrols' to address the problem.[63]

The naval war had been underway intensively since the opening day of the war and in October, following a meeting with city councillors and local businesses, Nugent imposed a night-time black out against the possibility of a German naval attack. The measure was highly unpopular but following the shelling of nearby Hartlepool by part of the German High Seas Fleet in December, which killed 130 people, opposition unsurprisingly disappeared.[64] A new threat would materialise in May 1915, when a Zeppelin bombed Hull, but by then Nugent was in France.

The final element of his duties was supporting recruitment. He spoke at corporation events, inspected parades, presented medals and attended recruiting drives. His speeches were reported in the local press, and in April 1915 he published a lengthy letter in the *Hull Daily Mail* appealing for more recruits to come forward: 'There are tens of thousands of young, able-bodied men in Great Britain today, to whom the thousands of our countrymen in France and Belgium are calling to come over to help them … Sooner or later, I believe every able bodied man will be forced, by public opinion, and by the pressure of circumstances, to drop everything else and work solely for the State'.[65] Local politicians, the Lord Lieutenant (Lord Nunburnholme) and the press rallied behind him, the *Mail* hoping his words would not 'fall on heedless ears'. When 20 months later he made a similarly blunt call in the Belfast press, the political reaction would be quite different.

He had continued to lobby hard for a more operational posting, his anxiety intensifying as news from the front came in. In early April he heard of the serious setback the previous month at Neuve Chapelle:

> It is a breakdown all round, but neither Haig nor Smith-Dorrien have been sent home. Some Brigadiers have I am told. One or two Divisional Generals were very near it but survived. Harry Rawlinson

---

[62] *Hull Daily Mail*, 10 Dec. 1914 and 24 Feb. 1915.
[63] *Hull Daily Mail*, 23 Oct., 10 Dec. 1914; *Yorkshire Post*, 20 Oct. 1914.
[64] *Hull Daily Mail*, 19 Oct. 1914.
[65] *Hull Daily Mail*, 23 Apr. 1915.

was nearly sent home but saved himself and is now looked upon as an unlucky General more than a bad one. It is a bad reputation to have all the same.[66]

On 14 April he went to London 'to see Sir J. W. Murray, the Chief of the General Staff, on my future prospects … I am afraid it will only be to hear that the Army Council would like to give me a command but that Lord K[itchener] won't let me move from here'. He was unsure whether this was a compliment or not.[67] His meetings in the War Office seemed to confirm his fears:

> I saw Sir James Wolfe Murray, Robb [Military Secretary] and Archie Murray [Deputy CIGS] today and from each heard the same thing, that the Army Council wants me to have a command but Lord K has blocked me. Both Robb and Archie Murray assured me that they would not let my claim drop and Archie Murray told me I might be sure of getting a command. He told me that he wanted me to have a Division but that I must first have a Brigade and he wants me to have a Division of the New Army. It might be some time before they go out and I sometimes think that after all they may never go to Belgium.[68]

Just four days later, however, came welcome news:

> I have just got a wire from the WO telling me that I am appointed to the command of the 41st Brigade [14th Division]. That's one of K[itchener]'s 1st Army. They will probably go to France next month. I do not yet know when I shall leave here as I must hand over to my successor. Well, I hope that I shall do my duties in the way they should be done and that I shall not disgrace my name when the opportunity comes.[69]

Murray had delivered for his friend from Staff College, not for the last time. Nugent's successor, Major-General Ferrier (the step-up in rank an indication of how big Nugent's job had become), arrived in early May and on 5 May Nugent took the train south to Aldershot.

[66] ON to CN, 8 Apr. 1915 (PRONI, D3835/E/2/1/27).
[67] ON to CN, 13 Apr. 1915 (PRONI, D3835/E/2/1/30).
[68] ON to CN, 13 Apr. 1915 (PRONI, D3835/E/2/1/31).
[69] ON to CN, 13 Apr. 1915 (PRONI, D3835/E/2/1/31).

3

Learning the Ropes

Integrating the New Armies, May–August 1915

Introduction

Nugent spent only four months with the 14th Division, but it was a defining experience. It gave him both his first taste of commanding New Army troops in action (though he had commanded 'citizen soldiers' in both the Hampshire Brigade and at Hull and, in a sense, with the CVF) and his first exposure, in particularly intense form, to trench warfare on the western front. He experienced directly the BEF's inferiority to the Germans at this stage of the war in tactics and technology, and witnessed weaknesses in British operational performance resulting not only from organisational and doctrinal deficiencies but also from incompetence. And he came close to losing his own command as a result of a major operational setback, his career being salvaged in part because of his ability to mobilise key military patrons on his behalf. He learned a great deal operationally and at the same time acquired a deep and enduring dislike of the Ypres Salient.

Unlike some others, the 14th Division's baptism of fire did not come in a large-scale action but simply in holding trenches. Because those trenches were in the Salient, however, where the reverberations of the recent intense fighting rumbled on and German domination in terms of artillery, other trench-fighting equipment and observation over the British lines was especially marked, the cost proved extremely high. The 14th suffered over 4,000 casualties in its first eight weeks in the line, and while inexperience and inferior weaponry played a large part so too did British generalship that at times was startlingly callous. The unsympathetic attitude shown by senior officers and regular formations to this New Army division trying to find its feet, and their readiness to criticise and find fault, says something about both the command culture of Second Army that summer – despite the fact that Herbert Plumer, the general whom Nugent would come to regard as the best he served under, had recently assumed command – and the continuing adjustment of the BEF's leadership to commanding a mass volunteer army.

Active Service

The 14th (Light) Division, as part of the first of Kitchener's New Armies, had begun forming in August 1914. It comprised, as its title suggested, rifle and light infantry battalions from across the army, mainly from the KRRC and Rifle Brigade with three battalions apiece but also one each from the English light infantry regiments.[1] The division's senior appointments were dominated by Riflemen. The divisional commander, Major-General Victor Couper, a Rifle Brigade officer with whom Nugent got on well, was a capable leader with an engaging sense of humour; he ended up as one of the longest-serving New Army divisional commanders, remaining in post until March 1918. Nugent's fellow infantry brigadiers, George Cockburn and Charles Markham, were from the Rifle Brigade and KRRC respectively, Markham an old friend from India in the 1880s, while the officer Nugent replaced as commander of 41 Brigade, Sandie Fortescue, had preceded him in command of the 4th KRRC, which made the supersession even more difficult: 'I am pretty sure he has been found not suitable and it will be horribly unpleasant taking it from him', Nugent told Kitty, 'but of course I can't help myself only I know he will feel it most terribly'.[2]

Nugent also knew a number of officers at lower levels. The four commanding officers of 41 Brigade were regulars who had been on the active list in 1914 – George Rennie and 'Verdant' Green of the 7th and 8th KRRC respectively, with both of whom he had served previously, and James Heriot-Maitland and Ronnie Maclachlan of the 7th and 8th Rifle Brigade. Rennie and Maitland had DSOs from South Africa while Maclachlan had commanded the Oxford University OTC in 1914. Also in the brigade was his old companion from Pretoria, Maurice Crum, now second-in-command (2ic) of the 8th KRRC, as well as a scattering of other current and former regulars across the battalions. This represented relative riches, in terms of experience and ability, that later New Army formations did not enjoy. The fact that the 14th Division was one of the first to be raised, the prestige of its regiments and the influence they could wield – an Indian army officer seconded to the division commented on 'the regimental nepotism in the KRRC and the RB, which I found to be worse than anything I had experienced in India' – and the practical advantage that, with eight regular battalions between them in the pre-war army, the KRRC and Rifle Brigade had a bigger reservoir of officers from which to draw,

[1] The Oxfordshire & Buckinghamshire, King's Shropshire, Somerset, Duke of Cornwall's, King's Own Yorkshire and Durham Light Infantry. The other divisions in the First New Army were the 9th (Scottish), 10th (Irish), 11th, 12th & 13th.
[2] ON to CN, 18 Apr. 1915 (PRONI, MIC571/2; D3835/E/2/31).

meant Nugent had quality in depth that he did not find amongst the officers of the 36th (Ulster) Division five months later.[3] The state of training in the division was good in terms of marching and general discipline but of course neither officers nor men had experience of trench warfare. That was about to change. On 11 May, just five days after Nugent's arrival, the division received orders to move to France and he and his brigade landed at Boulogne on the 19th.

The summer of 1915 saw the start of the service on the western front of Kitchener's New Armies. Up to now the burden of the fighting had been borne by the remnants of the old regular army, reservists and Territorials, but the 14th was one of three New Army divisions rushed to France in May 1915, the 9th (Scottish) Division arriving a week earlier and the 12th (Eastern) Division following immediately after. The BEF was under significant pressure following losses of 60,000 in the defensive battle of Second Ypres (April–May) and a further 40,000 in unsuccessful attacks at Neuve Chapelle, Aubers Ridge and Festubert (March–May), and reinforcements were urgently needed. As a result the summer and autumn of 1915 saw the blooding of New Army formations in major operations in France and Flanders, notably at Loos in September. By the end of the year 19 of the 38 British infantry divisions on the western front were New Army formations.[4]

The 14th Division's uneventful crossing was followed by an administratively smooth concentration a few miles inland near St Omer and then a move to the Bailleul area near the Belgian border. It went initially to II Corps, responsible for the area immediately south of Ypres, where an intelligently-organised induction programme awaited it, involving the newcomers being attached to more experienced units to learn the basics of trench-warfare. The corps had prepared a comprehensive checklist of issues to be covered, from the construction and lay-out of trenches and the siting of machine-guns to the organisation of billets and the location of latrines.[5] While waiting to go into the line the division had several visitors. On 23 May Lieutenant-General Henry Wilson, whom Nugent knew from Ireland before the war and now the chief liaison officer at French headquarters, called in – 'full of beans', Nugent noted, 'but not very optimistic. He was most outspoken about the Dardanelles & thinks it is a rotten business, that it is going to cost us thousands of men' – followed a few days later by the Second Army commander, Herbert Plumer, who

[3] R. M. Maxwell (ed.), *Villiers-Stuart Goes To War* (1990), p. 12.

[4] Three New Army divisions, the 10th (Irish), 11th (Northern) and 13th (Western), had had their first experience of battle in Gallipoli in July and August.

[5] 2nd Corps instruction G785, 27 May 1915 (TNA, WO95/1864).

stressed the need, understandably given the experience of Second Ypres, to take precautions against gas attack. The corps commander, Sir Charles Fergusson, visited on 28 May and the next day Nugent's 41 Brigade became the first 14th Division brigade to go into the line.[6]

Nugent's headquarters and three of his battalions were attached to the 46th (North Midland) Division and the remaining battalion to the neighbouring 5th Division. Each unit was sent to a brigade of the host division, the companies being allocated to one of its battalions; each individual was then 'attached to the corresponding individual of the unit holding the trenches – company commander to company commander, platoon commander to platoon commander and so on down to private soldiers'.[7] The 46th Division's trenches were opposite Messines Ridge, scene two years later of one of the Ulster Division's greatest successes. For now, however, visiting them was merely 'a very interesting experience' for the new brigade commander, though he 'got very bored with it after a long hot afternoon walking between sandbags & crawling through tunnels':

> It is a weird existence, living in holes in the ground and uncertain at which instant one may be blown to pieces by a big shell or got by a sniper through a moment's carelessness and still stranger to think that somewhere about 5,000,000 men on both sides are facing each other in a continuous line from the North Sea to Switzerland ... I never saw a German all day though from concealed corners I examined Messines through my glasses for a long time to see if I could by chance see one.[8]

On 30 May the brigade suffered its first casualties when an officer and three men of the 8th KRRC were wounded by a mortar bomb, an event soon to become a matter of routine. Nugent visited Kemmel Hill, the one point in the sector that provided good observation of the German positions, and noted how the 'German trenches are an absolute maze, line after line of them one behind the other, joined up by communication trenches as far back as the eye can see. So different from our one line of trenches with nothing behind them'.[9] He also visited classes in bomb-throwing and the use of trench mortars (where a mortar exploded prematurely during his visit, fortunately without causing casualties), and watched aircraft from both sides flying overhead and being fired on, another new experience.

[6] ON to CN, 23, 26 and 29 May 1915 (PRONI, MIC571/2, D3835/E/2/43, 47, 49).
[7] 2nd Corps instruction G785, 27 May 1915 (TNA, WO95/1864).
[8] ON to CN, 30 May 1915 (PRONI, MIC571/2, D3835/E/2/50).
[9] ON to CN, 31 May 1915 (PRONI, MIC571/2, D3835/E/2/51).

41 Brigade finished its tour of instruction on the night of 5/6 June. The battalions had learned a good deal about trench routine – 'You would be surprised what a lot there is in it all', Maurice Crum wrote home from the 8th KRRC, 'and what a difference it makes if there is a good system and good men in charge'[10] – and so had their brigadier. But Nugent was also left with a sense of frustration. The eight-day tour had cost the brigade 40 men and, he told Kitty, 'as we do nothing to the Germans in turn so far as we know, it is very annoying to lose men to no purpose'.[11] Sitting still and taking it without retaliating was not to be Nugent's style at any period of the war.

First operations

The brigade almost immediately returned to the trenches, this time to a sector of its own. The 3rd Division, holding the front south of St Eloi, was withdrawn to prepare for an attack and Couper's headquarters took over responsibility for the line on 31 May. Since none of his brigades had completed their induction a regular brigade was loaned to him, and as soon as Nugent's brigade was ready it was sent up to take over. The relief took place on the night of 7/8 June under heavy shell fire but with few losses, and the following morning Nugent visited the right section of his new positions:

> There were long lengths of the communicating [sic] trenches that one had to go along bent double and other places where one had to run across an exposed bit and as there was no air and a blazing sun by the time we got into the front line of trenches I was absolutely wet through. Verdant Green [CO 8th KRRC] whose battalion I was visiting was even worse because he is fatter than I am. These are very unpleasant trenches. They lie where some heavy fighting took place some time ago and there are dead Frenchmen & Germans in the parapets and in front of them and behind us and underfoot and the stench is awful in places and the chlorate of lime scattered everywhere is nearly as bad.[12]

The next day he visited his left battalion, near St Eloi, and found conditions no better: 'There were many casualties here last year when the French were holding this part of the line', he wrote, 'and they were very superficially buried and in the new work my Brigade is doing, we are constantly digging

[10] Maj. F. M. Crum, *Memoirs of a Rifleman Scout* (2014), p. 197.
[11] ON to CN, 6 June 1915 (PRONI, MIC571/2, D3835/E/2/63).
[12] ON to CN, 8 June 1915 (PRONI, MIC571/2, D3835/E/2/65).

them up … I was very nearly sick on several occasions'.[13] The trenches were not only poorly constructed, they were also badly overlooked and sniping was a constant problem, particularly from a position called Piccadilly Farm just behind the German lines. On 11 June Nugent decided to retaliate: 'This evening', he wrote, 'I turned a howitzer battery on the farm and gave it 20 rounds of high explosive shells which flattened it out completely. I cannot say if we got any Germans but anyhow we got the farm'.[14] The Germans responded by shelling the British lines heavily.

This episode is revealing about Nugent as a commander and the brutal cost-benefit calculations of trench warfare. Both as a brigade and a divisional commander he was aggressive; he believed in taking the war to the enemy and had no time for a 'live and let live' approach. He hated incurring casualties while sitting passively, regarding it as both a waste of men and destructive of morale. German superiority in artillery (and also in other weapons, including mortars, machine guns and hand-grenades) was such, however, that any British aggression could expect to be repaid with interest. Indeed General Fergusson, the II Corps commander, had told Nugent as much before 41 Brigade went into the trenches, warning that any British-initiated action was met with strong retaliation and that 'unless we mean to attack on a particular front, we remain quiet in our trenches and they remain quiet in theirs, except of course the snipers who are at it day and night'.[15] If this was intended as a hint not to stir up the enemy it fell on deaf ears. Nugent, despite being a tough-minded commander, always had a genuine and deep-seated concern for his soldiers' welfare, but he saw no contradiction between that and a proactive approach to trench-fighting that could result in higher casualties. He regarded the military harm caused by ceding the initiative to the enemy as outweighing the risk of increased losses. The following month, commenting on a lull in the fighting after his battalions had come out of the line, he contrasted his approach with that of his fellow brigadiers:

> I think one reason is that the Germans leave us alone if we leave them alone. The other 2 Brigades of this Division do leave them alone. I don't think we came out here to leave them alone and we annoyed them all we could and sniped at them continually and they certainly did answer back most rudely, but we killed some of them which is the only thing to do with a German.[16]

[13] ON to CN, 9 June 1915 (PRONI, MIC571/2, D3835/E/2/68).
[14] ON to CN, 11 June 1915 (PRONI, MIC571/2, D3835/E/2/72).
[15] ON to CN, 29 May 1915 (PRONI, MIC571/2, D3835/E/2/49). See Tony Ashworth, *Trench Warfare 1914–1918: The Live and Let Live System* (1980).
[16] ON to CN, 17 July 1915 (PRONI, MIC571/2, D3835/E/2/116).

His superiors noted and admired his aggressive spirit. His soldiers may have felt differently. The German retaliatory bombardment following the shelling of Piccadilly Farm in the event killed only two men of the front-line battalion opposite, the 7th Rifle Brigade, and wounded two others, an exchange rate Nugent would have regarded as entirely acceptable.[17]

Bellewaarde Ridge

In mid-June the 14th Division became involved, though not heavily, in its first set-piece attack. The operation, though relatively small-scale, illustrates some of the tensions in the British command in the Salient in the summer of 1915 and the sometimes negative attitudes of regular officers towards the New Army.

The 3rd Division had been ordered to assault Bellewaarde Ridge, a rise about three miles east of Ypres, on 16 June. The operation, directed by V Corps, had the twin purposes of securing the higher ground and 'straightening out' the British line, and also of acting as a diversion in support of First Army's larger attack the same day at Givenchy, 15 miles to the south. Couper, told to provide two brigades to support the assault, selected 41 and 42 Brigades and on 15 June they moved to holding positions near Ypres. Nugent's reconnaissance of the route forward took him into the city for the first time and he was shocked by what he found:

> Ypres is a world's tragedy. It is awful to see a beautiful town utterly levelled to the ground, as completely destroyed as Pompeii. The walls of the houses stood in many streets, but inside they are gutted by fire or blown to pieces. In other streets every house is levelled. The great square where the Cloth Hall & Cathedral stood is a mass of ruins. The utter uselessness of it all is what one feels most in looking at destruction on so vast a scale as this.[18]

V Corps was commanded by Lieutenant-General Sir Edmund Allenby who had been a year ahead of Nugent at Staff College, and Nugent was pleased to come under his command – 'I like him and I think he is a good soldier'.[19] That positive opinion, like many of the attacking troops, would not survive the assault. Nugent expected his brigade to be heavily involved in the fighting and told Kitty, 'I hope whatever I have to do, I shall do it with wisdom and judgement'.[20]

[17] 7th Rifle Brigade war diary (TNA, WO95/1895).
[18] ON to CN, 16 June 1915 (PRONI, MIC571/2, D3835/E/2/78).
[19] ON to CN, 14 June 1915 (PRONI, MIC571/2, D3835/E/2/75).
[20] ON to CN, 14 June 1915 (PRONI, MIC571/2, D3835/E/2/76).

The commander of the 3rd Division, Major-General Aylmer Haldane, had no confidence that the man ordering the attack, Allenby, had either wisdom or judgement. Haldane's loathing of Allenby, caused by his experiences at Ypres, shines through his post-war memoirs, and his contemporary diaries and letters reflect the same views even more stridently: that Allenby as a cavalryman did not understand the way infantry operated; that the location of this attack was simply wrong, launched as it was at the tip of a salient overlooked by the enemy, with constrained gun positions and communication routes to the rear and with success promising only to drive a deeper wedge into an already unsustainable position; and that Allenby's 'offensive spirit was not balanced by adequate knowledge of the conditions to which his orders applied'. Haldane, who was not told that part of the attack's purpose was diversionary, pointed out some of the difficulties 'but my voice was as that of one crying in the wilderness and I was given a hint that it would be wiser to keep silent'.[21] Nor was he reassured by having units of the 14th Division to assist him. Its pioneer battalion had been attached to him to dig assembly trenches and he regarded it as untrained and unsteady under fire, a judgement he extended without much evidence to its parent formation, telling V Corps that having Couper's brigades in support should not be regarded as 'an unqualified benefit'.[22]

The British bombardment – which, with around 100 guns and 19,000 shells available, was relatively substantial by the impoverished standards of 1915 but pitiful compared to what would be commonplace a year later – began at 2.30am on 16 June and lasted until 4.15am, when the 3rd Division's infantry attack went in. The German front line was overrun without difficulty but succeeding waves of attackers pushed forward too enthusiastically, the troops became disorganised and ran into their own artillery fire, and the captured German front trench became overcrowded. (In fairness to Allenby, not all of this chaos could be laid at his door.) Heavy German artillery fire crashed down, and while some of Haldane's men did reach the German second line they could not remain there in the face of counterattacks and intensive shelling. By 9.30am most of the attackers were back in the German first trench.

Allenby now ordered 42 Brigade forward, to be prepared to attack at 3.30pm through the 3rd Division's lodgement, and Nugent's battalions in turn moved up behind. The Germans had put down a heavy barrage to

---

[21] Haldane, *Soldier's Saga*, pp 307–10. The quote about Allenby's offensive spirit is Liddell Hart's, cited by Haldane.
[22] Haldane diary, 12 June 1915 (National Library of Scotland (NLS), MSS.20247–52).

catch the follow-up troops and when 41 Brigade arrived at 2pm at their designated location, trenches beside a railway embankment outside Ypres, Nugent

> found the 42nd Bde still in them and we had to lie down in the open or wherever the men could get a little cover. The 42nd Brigade eventually moved out, but there seems to have been a good deal of confusion amongst them and a lack of orders. Markham their Brigadier had gone on ahead and his COs did not know where he was and the battalions of the brigade were wandering about rather like lost sheep.[23]

Markham's brigade did not reach the front line until 4pm, by when the further attack, by two of the 3rd Division's remaining battalions, had already gone in to avoid losing the barrage and been repulsed with loss. At 6pm the decision was taken to consolidate what small gains had been made. Nugent's brigade had not come into action and returned to its billets the following day.

This operation cost the 3rd Division over 3,500 men – almost as many as the combined loss of the three divisions involved in the failed attack at Givenchy.[24] 42 Brigade lost around 180 men from German shelling. The 14th Division's experience might, however, have been much worse as, according to Haldane, Allenby had insisted during the afternoon that 42 Brigade be committed even though the opportunity for further gains had passed. Haldane protested that it would result in very heavy loss with no satisfactory result. Allenby allegedly retorted, 'What the Hell does that matter. There are plenty more men in England!' 'Not like these, Sir,' Haldane answered.[25] Couper was pleased with his men's performance under their first experience of shell fire.[26] Haldane, never slow to find fault, was anything but, believing that his division had been poorly supported: 'The 42nd Bde, as I had predicted, got well shelled going up and the Shropshire LI belonging to it melted away'.[27] The 14th Division, as the first New Army division to be deployed to a very active sector, was under close scrutiny from more experienced and often unsympathetic observers. It was easy in those circumstances to get a reputation for being unlucky, or inept.

---

[23] ON to CN, 16 June 1915 (PRONI, MIC571/2, D3835/E/2/78).

[24] Sir James Edmonds, *History of the Great War. Military Operations France and Belgium* [hereafter *OH*], 1915, ii (1928), pp 98–102.

[25] Lawrence James, *Imperial Warrior: The Life and Times of Field-Marshal Viscount Allenby 1861–1936* (1993), p. 75; Haldane diary (NLS), 16 June 1915.

[26] 14 Div. Summary of Operations, 19 June 1915 (TNA, WO95/1864).

[27] Haldane diary (NLS), 16 June 1915.

Trench warfare in the Salient

Further setbacks followed. Less than a week later, on the evening of 22 June, 42 Brigade mounted a small-scale attack to capture a German redoubt. It did not go well: the supporting artillery was unable to register on the objective properly and the bombardment was ineffective; telephone lines were cut at a critical moment; the alerted Germans put down a withering fire as soon as the attackers left their trenches, to which the survivors rapidly returned; and the attack was called off almost as soon as it had started. The 5th Oxfordshire and Buckinghamshire Light Infantry suffered 60 casualties, including an officer and 14 men who reached the German trenches and were not heard of again. Allenby demanded an explanation which Couper provided, but it was an unfortunate start.[28]

The next mishap involved Nugent's own command. At the end of June 41 Brigade went back into the line just north of the Menin Road, near Railway Wood, and into the trenches the 3rd Division had captured a fortnight earlier. Nugent's men now experienced the full fury of the Salient, being subjected to heavy shelling from the start. On 30 June he spent nearly eight hours inspecting his new positions:

> They are at the very point of the Ypres Salient and I never want to be in more villainous trenches. Being at the point of the Salient we get shelled from both sides and from in front … At one place in the most forward trenches of all, we were absolutely pinned to the ground by shell fire on the particular trenches I was in. They burst with horrible regularity just over the trench. One shell burst so close to me that I was almost dazed for the moment. 2 men beside me, or rather about 5 yards from me were killed.

Grisly reminders of the 16 June attack were still evident:

> One awful trench in the first German line was still full of German dead, killed more than a fortnight ago. I could not face it as it would have meant walking over them! I gave orders that it was to be filled in on top of them tonight and fresh trenches dug. I can't think why they had not been buried by the last brigade.[29]

The Germans also fired gas shells, another new experience, but by this time Nugent was back at his HQ in the outskirts of Ypres where the density was too weak to force him to put on his respirator. It did, though, leave 'an arid

---

[28] Couper memo to V Corps, 27 June 1915 (TNA, WO95/1864).
[29] ON to CN, 30 June 1915 (PRONI, MIC571/2, D3835/E/2/98).

taste in the mouth and made my eyes smart and water for a while', and one of his staff officers, who caught a heavier dose, had to be evacuated.

The German shelling continued relentlessly and by 3 July Nugent was getting anxious 'because my Brigade has lost so many men since they came up here and there is nothing to show for it … Sitting still & doing nothing and still being shelled day and night is a very trying method of making war'.[30] The following day the Germans raided the trenches of the 8th Rifle Brigade, Nugent's left-hand battalion. They chose an exposed point where the trench-line was split by the Ypres-Roulers railway and the gap filled by a sandbag barrier, close to the boundary with the neighbouring 6th Division. After an intense two-hour bombardment, which demolished the barrier and temporarily buried the platoon commander in a collapsed trench, at 9.30am about 20 Germans rushed the position. A few defenders fled but most did not and two parties of reinforcements, one from the battalion itself and another from the 1st North Staffordshire Regiment, the adjoining battalion from the 6th Division, quickly drove the attackers out. Two German bodies were recovered; the Rifle Brigade's casualties were three men killed and 15 wounded. The North Staffordshires lost a promising officer, Lieutenant Smith, and his battalion greatly resented his death in helping recover a position lost by their inexperienced neighbours.

Again explanations were demanded by higher authorities. After discussing the action with the battalion CO, Colonel Maclachlan, Nugent mounted a strong defence. He acknowledged that some men in the absence of their officer 'did run into the lines of the adjoining Battalion', but had been quickly rallied there; there had been 'nothing in the nature of a general panic'; counter-attacks were mounted within five minutes of the initial alarm and 'there was not at any time the least appearance of a serious situation'. He expressed appreciation for the assistance of the North Staffordshires and regretted Smith's death, but noted icily that the report of their CO, Lieutenant-Colonel De Falbe, that 'his men had expelled the Germans, and were in occupation of the trenches vacated by the 8th R.B. is not in accordance with the facts and must have been sent under a misapprehension'.[31] There the matter was left, but what had in the end been a not unsuccessful small-scale action for the 14th Division had created ill-feeling with its regular neighbours. Revenge was not long in coming: on the night of 7 July the 7th KRRC raided a German listening post and bayonetted the four occupants, at a cost of one man missing and an officer wounded.[32] In the end this trench tour cost 41 Brigade over 200 casualties.

[30] ON to CN, 3 July 1915 (PRONI, MIC571/2, D3835/E/2/101).
[31] Nugent memo to HQ 14 Div, 6 July 1915 (TNA, WO95/1864).
[32] 7th KRRC war diary (TNA, WO1895/1896).

On 7 July Nugent had an unexpected diversion when he was summoned at short notice to escort two 'distinguished visitors', who proved to be Asquith and Kitchener (in France for an Anglo-French conference at Calais), round his sector of Ypres. Nugent spent some time guiding them through the ruins but was anxious throughout about their safety and eventually persuaded General Plumer, who accompanied them, to take them away.[33] His antipathy towards Asquith had not abated – 'the Prime Minister looked an absolute scallywag yesterday', he reported, 'in a very dirty old flannel suit, a soft felt hat looking like a basin and long dishevelled hair'.[34]

His once positive opinion of Allenby, however, had changed markedly. The cause was the 16 June attack and Allenby's general treatment of his subordinates. Nugent told Kitty:

> Strictly confidentially – Allenby who commands the 5th Corps to which we belong is intensely unpopular. He has the rudest manners and publishes silly orders which can't be carried out & then abuses his Divisional Generals because they are not carried out. They all hate him. No one has much confidence in him as he has been a cavalry soldier all his life and knows nothing about infantry.[35]

Couper was able to cope with Allenby better than most, refusing, according to Haldane, to take him seriously, 'in which he probably showed his wisdom'.[36] Allenby remains a contradictory figure: intelligent and well-read, he was capable of attracting intense loyalty from those who knew him well and went on to make his reputation in the Middle East. But on the western front he could be a domineering bully and Nugent's opinion of him was changed permanently by his experiences that summer.[37] On 13 July he heard with relief that the 14th Division was transferring to VI Corps. 'Nobody minds leaving the 5th which is the most unpopular Corps in the whole Army', he wrote, 'The 6th is said to be better run'.[38] The accuracy of that final comment remained to be tested.

There was now a brief lull before Nugent's brigade went back into the trenches, and he took the opportunity to visit Kitty's nephew Aubrey Parke

---

[33] ON to CN, 7 July 1915 (PRONI, MIC571/2, D3835/E/2/106).

[34] ON to CN, 8 July 1915 (PRONI, MIC571/2, D3835/E/2/111).

[35] ON to CN, currently dated 24 June 1915 (PRONI, MIC571/2, D3835/E/2/90), but almost certainly written on 10 July, this page having become detached from the original letter (E/2/108).

[36] Haldane, *Soldier's Saga*, p. 338.

[37] James, *Allenby*, pp 76–91, pp 233–4.

[38] ON to CN, 13 July 1915 (PRONI, MIC571/2, D3835/E/2/110).

(known as Pip), the popular 23-year-old son of her sister Evie, whose brother Bob had been killed the previous year and who was serving in the 10th Durham Light Infantry in 43 Brigade. His battalion was resting near Poperinghe where Nugent found him 'living under a waterproof sheet [but] very cheerful'. His unit had recently been in trenches near Hooge under heavy shell fire where all but four members of his platoon had at various times been buried by the trench being blown in on them.[39] A subaltern's life expectancy was not high in 1915 and it was the last time Nugent saw Pip alive. He was killed near Ypres on 25 September 1915, almost a month to the day after his cousin and another of Kitty's nephews, 29-year-old Sir Thomas Lees, son of her brother Elliott, died of wounds received at Gallipoli.

Nugent was always anxious to receive news from home, both as an escape from the grim realities of the war – 'How is the garden looking?', he wrote in July, 'How I wish I could see it and how I do long to see you and the children again' – and to ensure that Farren Connell remained economically viable in wartime.[40] Soon after the 16 June attack, for example, as he returned to Ypres under shell fire, part of Nugent's mind was back in Cavan as he wondered whether, if livestock prices remained as they were, he should take back more land currently rented out and employ a full time farm manager. His detailed instructions to Kitty covered, amongst much else, the purchase of cattle, cutting timber, harvesting oats, erecting fences and building a tennis court. He also had clear, and in some respects very much pre-1914 Cavan Protestant, views on the employment of staff. The replacement gardener, he told Kitty, should not be

> too young a man and don't get a R[oman] C[atholic] if you can help it. They never seem to have any authority over other men. A young RC man unless he was exceptional would simply be ignored by the old hands at FC and he would not dare open his mouth to them. Still you may find an exception to the rule.

He was against the proposed employment of a female chauffeur, who would 'almost certainly do nothing else but drive the car and quite possibly pretty badly'; her ability to maintain the vehicle had to be checked (she was not in the event taken on). A cook with a temper would, he warned Kitty, 'upset your peaceful household'. Underlying everything else, he expected the

[39] ON to CN, 8 July 1915 (PRONI, MIC571/2, D3835/E/2/112).
[40] Ibid.

country's economy to take years to recover from the war, and 'in all probability we shall have to make up our minds to live at FC or elsewhere in a very small way'.[41]

Hooge

Domestic concerns soon had to take a back seat once more, however. On the evening of 19 July 1915 the 3rd Division blew a mine under the German trenches at Hooge and immediately occupied the large crater, 120 feet wide and 20 feet deep. The captured position provided some observation over the surrounding area but proved desperately difficult to hold. The Germans reacted furiously, shelling the area intensively, while the sheer size of the crater made it hard to integrate into improvised British defences that were being blown in almost as quickly as they were dug. Haldane asked that his division's redeployment from the area be postponed to allow the position to be consolidated, but this was refused. 'I remarked', wrote Haldane waspishly later, 'that we should lose the place in a week, for I knew the value of the division newly arrived at the front that was to replace the 3rd'.[42] That division was the 14th, and others, including Haldane's ADC, Major Billy Congreve, shared his concern about inexperienced troops 'being put into such a vile place as Hooge, especially in its present state'.[43]

Nugent's brigade took over the crater sector on the night of 22/23 July and from the outset received the same hammering from the German artillery as their predecessors. He found on visiting the front line next morning that 'we have got an immense hole in the ground and a little bit of the German trenches on each side, which we have barricaded and we are on one side of the barricade and the Germans are on the other, but both of us in the same trench'.[44] On the 23rd several large German trench-mortar bombs landed inside the crater, killing or wounding 29 of 40 men working there. Nugent witnessed the aftermath:

> The bodies of our unfortunate men who had been killed were lying about in the Crater, some including the officer who had been in command, without heads, or arms and legs and legs and arms all over the place. The bodies or rather fragments could not be got at

[41] ON to CN, 19, 24 June; 9, 12 July; 24 Aug. 1915 (PRONI, MIC571/2, D3835/E/2/80, 90, 107, 109, 145).
[42] Haldane, *Soldier's Saga*, pp 316–17.
[43] Terry Norman (ed.), *Armageddon Road. A VC's Diary 1914–1916: Billy Congreve* (2014), p. 162.
[44] ON to CN, 24 July 1915 (PRONI, MIC571/2, D3835/E/2/120).

because men could not get into the Crater and we must have them out because of the awful effect of leaving them, so I have sent for ropes and tonight men will have to go down and we must get them up with ropes.[45]

It proved impossible to recover the bodies, two men being killed in the attempt which was then abandoned. The two sides were in places only 30 yards apart and on the 25th Nugent saw his first live Germans through a gap in a barricade; he at once ordered up British snipers who killed two of them. He was also covered in earth by a shell bursting nearby and noted that there had been several cases 'of men who have gone completely off their heads in the last 2 days simply from shock'.[46]

That evening he watched a spectacular aerial engagement when a British fighter attacked a German two-seater aircraft over Hooge:

Suddenly a little brown aeroplane looking like a cockchafer appeared out of the blue sky, flying at a terrific pace. It just seemed to swoop on the German: whether it dropped a bomb or fired a machine gun I could not say, but as it closed with the German, the latter suddenly swerved violently, one of the men in it fell out, and that was horrible, one could see him falling turning over and over, all legs & arms until he fell into a wood. I only hope he was dead when he fell out. The German machine then burst into flames, fell sideways then turned upside down, then seemed to right itself and finally came down nose first close to Colonel Green's headquarters. From every direction & from every nook & dugout our men seemed to emerge & cheered wildly excited.[47]

He had just witnessed Major Lanoe Hawker, one of the Royal Flying Corps's first aces, winning the Victoria Cross in his Bristol Scout for shooting down two German planes and forcing down a third on the same sortie. Nugent heard a rumour that the German aircrew had somehow survived, but that was incorrect: a couple of days later he saw the burnt-out wreckage of the German Albatros and was told that the charred remains of the pilot were in it when it crashed, while the observer who fell into Sanctuary Wood became the only German to be buried in the Commonwealth war graves cemetery later established there.[48]

[45] ON to CN, 24 July 1915 (PRONI, MIC571/2, D3835/E/2/120).
[46] ON to CN, 25 July 1915 (PRONI, MIC571/2, D3835/E/2/122).
[47] Ibid.
[48] Ralph Barker, *A Brief History of the Royal Flying Corps in World War 1* (2002), pp 100–01. The cemetery has a memorial to Hauptmann Hans Roser.

Senior officers did at least make some effort to see conditions for themselves. The following day, while Nugent was taking the VI Corps commander, Lieutenant-General Sir John Keir, and Couper round his reserve trenches they were caught by a burst of German shelling; Nugent 'bolted like a rabbit into the nearest dugout expecting them to follow', which they failed to do, and a few minutes later his brigade major, Captain Bayley, 'found them crouching behind a parapet looking very unhappy' but fortunately unhurt.[49] Keir, an artillery officer, may have appreciated the accuracy of the German fire; within days, however, Nugent would have reason to doubt Keir's grasp of infantry tactics.

On the night of 29/30 July the 7th Rifle Brigade and 8th KRRC, tired and distinctly shaken after a week under constant fire, were replaced by the 8th Rifle Brigade moving into the trenches around the crater and the 7th KRRC into the positions to their right.[50] The hand-over took place in deceptive calm, the shelling having stopped for the first time in days. It seems certain the Germans knew that new units were moving in and timed their forthcoming attack to coincide with the relief. Long stretches of the support trenches had been destroyed, which meant that the front line, itself badly damaged, was over-crowded. The two battalions settled into their new surroundings amidst a slightly eerie stillness.

At 3.15am on 30 July the quiet was shattered by a large explosion at the site of the ruined stables of Hooge chateau, near the right-hand trenches of the 8th Rifle Brigade. At the same time an intense fire began, of trench-mortars and machine-guns on the forward trenches and of artillery on the reserve lines in Zouave and Sanctuary Woods. This time, however, there was a stunning new dimension. The Rifle Brigade's forward companies heard a sudden hissing sound, a red glare illuminated the area around the crater and jets of fire arced over from the trenches of the German *53rd Reserve Division* into the British lines. This was the first use of flamethrowers against the British, the Germans using portable projectors carried on the backs of the operators.[51] An 8th Rifle Brigade subaltern near the crater saw 'three or four distinct jets of flame – like a line of powerful fire-hoses spraying fire instead of water – shoot across my fire-trench … How long this lasted it is impossible to say – probably not more than a minute; but the effect was so stupefying that, for my own part, I was utterly unable for some minutes to think collectedly'.[52] An officer of the 9th Rifle

[49] ON to CN, 28 July 1915 (PRONI, D3835/E/2/124).
[50] ON to Lt.-Gen. Sir Edward Hutton, 12 Aug. 1915, in *Nugent*, pp 12–16.
[51] *OH* 1915, ii, p. 104.
[52] Reginald Berkeley, *The History of the Rifle Brigade in the War of 1914–1918* (1927), i, p. 124.

Brigade, on Nugent's left, saw the Germans advancing 'just behind the flame projector carriers, at that queer shambling trot that the German Infantry always used'.[53]

The forward trenches in the centre of the 8th Rifle Brigade's sector, held by two companies, were quickly overrun. The Germans broke in close to the crater and fanned out left and right, occupying the ruins of Hooge village and pushing into what remained of the second-line trenches south of the Menin Road on a 500-yard front. Subsequent efforts to discover how many front-line occupants had been killed by the flames rather than trench mortars or in the infantry assault were inconclusive: Nugent afterwards attempted 'to trace witnesses who could speak as to the effect of the flame, but have been unable to trace any officer or man who got away from this trench'.[54] The battalions on the flanks held on, though the 7th KRRC on the right lost some ground. Most of the survivors of the 8th Rifle Brigade fell back to the trenches at the northern edge of Zouave Wood, though some fugitives ended up in the 9th Rifle Brigade's position to the left. The 8th Battalion's reserve company attempted to counter-attack shortly before 4am but was stopped by heavy fire.[55]

Nugent was at his headquarters in the ramparts of Ypres about three miles away when the attack began. At 3.35am the CO of the 8th, Maclachlan, phoned to alert him. Nugent at once called for artillery support, informed divisional HQ of what was happening and sent urgent orders to the recently-relieved 7th Rifle Brigade and 8th KRRC, just reaching their billets, to retrace their steps. By 5am it was clear that the Hooge position had been lost. Just after 6.15am Nugent received a fateful order from Keir, via divisional HQ, directing his brigade to mount a counter-attack that afternoon to regain the lost trenches, supported by whatever artillery could be assembled. He objected immediately, on the basis that without thorough preparation a daylight frontal attack across open ground could not succeed: 'I knew before I started that what I was asked to do was impossible and I said so to the Division that in my opinion I was asked to do what was not possible, but the Corps persisted'.[56] An hour later the order was repeated, and with the die cast Couper came forward to Nugent's HQ where they agreed the details of 41 Brigade's attack. This would be launched from the forward edge of Zouave and Sanctuary Woods at 2.45pm that afternoon following a 45-minute bombardment. Nugent would be reinforced by the

[53] Maxwell, *Villiers-Stuart*, p. 102.

[54] 41st Bde report to HQ 14 Div., 6 Aug. 1915 (TNA, WO95/1864).

[55] Berkeley, *Rifle Brigade*, pp 121–8; Maj.-Gen. Sir Steuart Hare, *The Annals of the King's Royal Rifle Corps: Volume V. The Great War* (1932), pp 96–101.

[56] ON to CN, 31 July 1915 (PRONI, MIC571/2, D3835/E/2/126).

6th Duke of Cornwall's Light Infantry (DCLI) from 43 Brigade, while Couper arranged for 42 Brigade on Nugent's left to attack simultaneously along the Menin Road with one battalion, the 9th KRRC.

Nugent now moved forward to an advanced command post at the rear edge of Zouave Wood, and on seeing the situation first-hand he again 'judged it would take a Division to get the Germans out and at least 12 hours bombardment with heavy guns'. He reported this back but once again was told the counter-attack must proceed.[57] At 11am he issued his orders to his COs at his forward HQ. The attack would be led by the 8th Rifle Brigade on the left and the 7th KRRC on the right, despite the fact that both, particularly the 8th, had suffered losses in the German assault, for the practical reason that they were already in position. The 7th Rifle Brigade and 8th KRRC would be in support, the two Rifle Brigade units advancing from Zouave Wood and the KRRC battalions from Sanctuary Wood. The DCLI remained in reserve.

Meanwhile the German artillery continued to pound away at the British positions, inflicting further casualties. At 2pm the British bombardment, by the 14th Division's own guns and a heavy artillery group, began. It was neither heavy nor accurate enough to cause any serious harm to the German defenders, who could be seen during it standing in their trenches with their rifles at the ready. The Germans had brought up, according to Maurice Crum who took part in the attack, as many as ten machine-guns to bolster the defence, some of which opened fire even before the British bombardment lifted.[58] At 2.45pm the attack went in, the lead battalions advancing in a succession of lines on a two-platoon frontage. Even before they were clear of the tree-line, however, the machine-guns began mowing them down, and seconds later heavy concentrations of German artillery fire fell on the edge of the woods. Few men got more than a few yards across the open before being hit.[59] Crum saw 'men being shot down, and could see no progress of the attack ... The fire of the Maxims was terrific; nothing could live in the open near the edge of the wood'. 'The men behaved very well', wrote Nugent afterwards, 'and the officers with a gallantry no words can adequately describe. As they came out of the woods the German machine-guns and shell fire met them and literally swept them away'. Donald Hankey, serving in the 7th Rifle Brigade, described how after the advance 'the better part of [the battalion] lay out in the wood, or in the

[57] Nugent to Hutton, 12 Aug. 1915, in *Nugent*, p. 13.
[58] Crum, *Rifleman Scout*, p. 205.
[59] Berkeley, *Rifle Brigade*, p. 129.

open before the wood, dead or dying'.[60] At 3.15pm, having got reports from the leading units, Nugent called off the attack and informed Couper. No ground had been gained on 41 Brigade's front, and indeed the German shelling was so severe the British had to pull back from the edge of Zouave Wood. The 9th KRRC on Nugent's left were able to re-occupy some trenches, but at the cost of losing their CO. Shortly after came another message from corps HQ, ordering a further attack; Nugent replied that this was impossible, and this time the issue was not pressed.[61]

Nugent remained in command at Zouave Wood for another 24 hours, his shattered battalions being withdrawn overnight and replaced by three battalions of 43 Brigade. There was an alarm in the early hours of 31 July when intense fire opened from the German positions. The British responded in kind and what may have been a German attack was repulsed, though if so it was not pushed very hard. Nugent himself left Zouave Wood that afternoon, exhausted and sick in spirit at what had happened. The fighting at Hooge over these few days cost the 14th Division 100 officers and 2,387 men, and of these 55 officers and 1,181 soldiers came from Nugent's brigade. The 8th Rifle Brigade lost over 480 officers and men, the 7th KRRC over 300, the 7th Rifle Brigade 250 and the 8th KRRC 200. The neighbouring 9th KRRC had lost 350.[62] Amongst the casualties was Nugent's soldier-servant, Pte Ackroyd, badly wounded by a shell. Nugent was devastated, not just by the scale of the losses but by their pointlessness, and his bitterness focused on Keir, telling Kitty:

> I feel one can have no confidence in leaders who send men callously or ignorantly to certain death against the opinion of the man who might know being on the spot. If they had accepted my opinion before instead of after, more than 1500 good men would have been alive today.[63]

On 5 August he was still 'very low-spirited & sad. I can't get over that terrible day & hour after hour I think of all those gallant officers & men sent to their deaths by a man who had never seen the ground & who would not listen to me who had'.[64] The point about accepting the judgement of the commander on the ground was not just a common-sense observation,

---

[60] Crum, *Rifleman Scout*, p. 206; Nugent to Hutton 12 Aug. 1915, in *Nugent*, p. 14; Donald Hankey, *A Student in Arms* (1917), p. 256.

[61] Nugent to Hutton, 12 Aug. 1915, in *Nugent*, p. 15.

[62] *OH* 1915, ii, p. 106.

[63] ON to CN, 1 Aug. 1915 (PRONI, MIC571/2, D3835/E/2/127).

[64] ON to CN, 5 Aug. 1915 (PRONI, MIC571/2, D3835/E/2/129).

it was also a doctrinal one. The 1909 Field Service Regulations Part 1 (FSR1) represented the closest thing the army had to a formal doctrine at the outbreak of war, setting out general principles for the guidance of officers during operations. One of FSR1's important tenets was the concept of 'the man on the spot' in interpreting orders in the light of changed circumstances.[65] The purpose, of course, was to grant subordinates the initiative to modify orders to achieve their commander's intent rather than give them permission to disobey. But in paying no regard at all to Nugent's objections, particularly after he had seen the situation in Zouave Wood personally, Keir breached that principle. Whatever Allenby's failings as a corps commander in 1915, Haldane was able on 16 June to dissuade him from committing 42 Brigade to a hopeless attack. On 31 July Nugent and Couper were unable similarly to convince Keir, with disastrous consequences for 41 Brigade.

In 1915 British tactics were still hovering uncomfortably between, on the one hand, recognition that trench warfare required technological solutions and, on the other, pre-war concepts of the ability of high morale and determination in the attack to compensate for material deficiencies. Hooge, as it proved, formed part of a pattern of Second Army operations between mid-1915 and the summer of 1916, in which the Germans would capture a position, the British would respond with hasty counterattacks – too slow to take the enemy off-balance but too rushed to be effective – and then press them for too long, after which, following a pause, properly-prepared and often successful attacks were mounted. This happened not only at Hooge in July 1915 but at the Bluff in February 1916, St Eloi in April 1916 and Mount Sorrel in June 1916. In these four almost unremembered actions the British and Canadians lost nearly 20,000 men, which helps explain why in early 1916 Haig, the newly-appointed commander-in-chief, considered removing Plumer. The remark famously attributed to Marshal Foch, that it took 15,000 casualties to train a major-general, seems apposite here.[66]

The high social status of the regiments involved meant that 41 Brigade's officers had been drawn disproportionately from Britain's elite. Nugent told Lieutenant-General Sir Edward Hutton, Colonel of the KRRC:

> It nearly broke my heart to see my brigade come back. Officers of a class we shall never be able to replace, the pick of English or British public school and Varsity life. Heroes in battle, they led their men

---

[65] Andy Simpson, *Directing Operations: British Corps Command on the Western Front 1914–18* (2006), pp 6–7.

[66] Robert Heinl Jr, *The Dictionary of Military and Naval Quotations* (1966).

with the most sublime courage, knowing as I am certain they did that they were going to certain death. The splendour of it, and the utter waste! 8th R.B. have 3 officers left, other battns 6 or 7 and the best all gone.[67]

The dead included 2nd Lieutenant Billy Grenfell of the 8th Rifle Brigade, brother of the poet Julian Grenfell and son of Lord Desborough, and also 2nd Lieutenant Sidney Woodroffe of the same battalion, who won a posthumous Victoria Cross, the first awarded to the New Army. The losses were felt at the top of government. The Desboroughs, understandably desolate over the deaths of two sons (Julian had been fatally wounded in May), dined at 10 Downing Street on 3 August with Asquith, Kitchener, Bonar Law, Churchill and others; Kitchener was close to the Desboroughs and on 16 August Nugent reported that 'Lord K telegraphed out that every endeavour was to be made to recover the Grenfell boy's body'. Colonel Maclachlan and another officer located it outside Zouave Wood but because of the shelling could not bring it in, instead arranging for it to be buried where it lay when circumstances allowed. 'It would be impossible to touch the body now anyhow', noted Nugent grimly.[68]

In the early hours of 9 August the 6th Division recaptured some of the lost trenches at Hooge in a set-piece attack with massive artillery support, including French heavy guns. Initially the operation went well, the trenches at the crater and the chateau stables being reoccupied as well as some positions beyond them, 130 prisoners taken and an estimated 500 enemy killed. The Germans then subjected the British to a murderous bombardment, requiring some of the gains (though not the crater) to be abandoned. The two attacking brigades lost over 2,100 men, mostly from shelling.[69] A week later Nugent had lunch with Congreve, commander of the 6th Division, whom he knew from before the war:

> Congreve told me that … Zouave Wood which used to be a delightful shady wood where we could walk about quite safely has now not a tree left standing and is simply ploughed up with shells and has been abandoned. He says the desolation of it is terrible. When they captured the Crater they found over 200 dead Germans in the bottom of it, mostly in pieces. There are dead Germans lying all over the front of the line we now hold as well as hundreds of our

[67] ON to Hutton, 12 Aug. 1915, in *Nugent*, p. 16.
[68] ON to CN, 16 Aug. 1915 (PRONI, MIC571/2, D3835/E/2/138).
[69] *OH* 1915, ii, pp 106–08; Mark Connelly, *Steady the Buffs! A Regiment, a Region and the Great War* (2006), pp 60–64.

own dead, but as no one can go out to bury them and the stench is so appalling that even the men who seem to enjoy stinks are retching.[70]

The positive spin put on the recapture of the crater in official communiques and the press annoyed Nugent – on 17 August he complained that '[t]he account in the papers today of the recapture of those trenches is absolutely misleading' – because of the implicit contrast with the 14th Division's performance.[71]

Aftermath

In fact the recriminations over the loss of the crater on 30 July began almost at once. Troops from the 6th Division jeered soldiers of the 14th as they passed 'as rotten fellows who couldn't hold a trench' (when Congreve's men a few days later were blasted out of those same trenches Nugent simply commented, 'I fancy they wouldn't jeer them now').[72] Haldane was scathing in the immediate aftermath, writing that it had taken just one day longer than he had predicted for the captured position to be lost and blaming 41 Brigade for not making it secure – 'it is the officers and men who must have been at fault', he wrote, adding that this demonstrated 'the folly of putting divisions composed of new troops into the field and not mixing them up with experienced troops'.[73] A sapper officer involved in the original detonation of the mine at the crater heard that the 14th Division defenders had been 'caught half asleep, fell into a panic and ran. A *real* bad show', adding that 'I had my own opinion of that Division'.[74] While Nugent would not have agreed he did accept, after talking to survivors, that the 8th Rifle Brigade 'which met the brunt of the attack and the liquid fire lost their heads and didn't make as strong a resistance as they could have done'.[75]

In addition to his grief over the losses Nugent was understandably worried about his own position. The Hooge attack had already resulted in the sacking of one 14th Division brigadier. On the morning of 31 July George Cockburn of 43 Brigade had been told to take over from Nugent in Zouave Wood. At 7pm, however, he was still in Ypres and Couper peremptorily ordered him forward, but it took him almost five hours to

[70] ON to CN, 16 Aug. 1915 (PRONI, MIC571/2, D3835/E/2/138).
[71] ON to CN, 17 Aug. 1915 (PRONI, MIC571/2, D3835/E/2/140).
[72] ON to Hutton, 12 Aug. 1915, in *Nugent*, p. 16.
[73] Haldane diary (NLS), 3 Aug. 1915.
[74] Lyn MacDonald, *1915: The Death of Innocence* (1997), p. 424.
[75] ON to CN, 5 Aug. 1915, in *Nugent*, p. 11.

make the three-mile journey from Ypres to his advanced HQ through admittedly heavy shelling. Couper was forced in his absence to appoint a temporary replacement and afterwards reported pointedly that the 'situation at this time was somewhat hampered by my being unable to communicate with B.G.C 43rd Infantry Bde'. Cockburn was relieved of his command on 2 August and sent home.[76]

Nugent was under no illusion about his own vulnerability, or that muttering against him had started. His nephew 'Pip' Parke even felt it necessary to write home a few days after the attack defending him against the charge of uselessly squandering his men.[77] Couper in his after-action report went out of his way to praise Nugent, who took some comfort from being invited to dinner by Keir on 3 August, which he thought was meant to show he was not being blamed for the attack's failure. He may have been too sanguine. A divisional commander in the Salient in 1915 later recalled that in this period 'the higher commands were determined to whitewash themselves for the unsatisfactory state of affairs by making scapegoats of subordinates, and many brigadiers were relieved of their commands'.[78] Receipt of Nugent's and Couper's after-action reports prompted a series of questions from VI Corps whose tone was less about learning lessons than assigning culpability: why had there been a delay in Nugent notifying divisional HQ of the German attack, why had communication with the artillery not been better, what were the details of the 8th Rifle Brigade's deployments, how quickly did reserve platoons move into position, what action had been taken against a platoon that apparently abandoned a section of trench without orders, and so on. Most of the queries reflected VI Corps's ignorance of what had actually happened and Couper answered them calmly, including pointing out that the platoon that had 'abandoned' a trench had been enfiladed by machine-guns, and that its commander had been killed trying to recapture it.[79]

Nugent, meanwhile, turned to two of his patrons, General Hutton and Archie Murray, still Deputy CIGS, sending both detailed accounts setting out his version of events. Hutton forwarded Nugent's narrative to the King and in his covering letter said protectively:

[76] Couper memo to 6 Corps, 7 Aug. 1915 (TNA, WO97/1864); Maj. A. F. Becke, *Order of Battle, Divisions: Part 3A. New Army Divisions* (1938), p. 46.

[77] ON to CN, 23 Aug. 1915 (MIC571/2, D3835/E/2/144).

[78] Lt.-Gen. Sir Thomas Snow, 'Memoir: 27th Division Nov. 1914 to June 1915', quoted in Simon Robbins, *British Generalship on the Western Front 1914–18* (2005), p. 60.

[79] The following memos in the 14 Div. war diary record the exchanges: Nugent to HQ 14 Div., 6 Aug.; Couper to 6 Corps, 7 Aug.; Loch (BGGS 6 Corps) to 14 Div., 9 Aug.; Couper to 6 Corps, 10 Aug. 1915 (TNA, WO97/1864).

There are sure to be unkind things said of the Brigadier General and his command upon the occasion of a reverse such as this sad business, but in such cases I always think there are two sides to a question. In this I am convinced that Nugent and his Riflemen are not to blame.[80]

Murray's hand-written reply on 17 August was more directly reassuring:

I was so glad to get your letter of the 21st [sic – 12th?] and to hear the full truth of the 14th Division's hard fight. I want to show it to Lord Kitchener for I do not think that your troops have got the credit that they should for gallant and brave work. I am sure the 41st is safe in your hands and I look forward to your getting a division very soon.[81]

Nugent remained cautious despite this 'nice letter', telling Kitty:

As to what he says about my getting a Division soon, I do not lay great stress on it. There are so many out here who have been longer out than I have and who have borne the burden and heat of the day longer that their claims would rightly weigh with Sir J French's staff and himself before me. Besides I failed even if it was not my fault, still I did fail and that counts against one.[82]

The remorseless grind of trench warfare continued. 41 Brigade went back into the line in mid-August to a quieter sector north of Ypres. Nugent's hatred of the Salient and the losses associated with it was now deeply ingrained, and he wrote on 11 August:

I only hope that Army HQ will at last recognise hard facts and that we shall at last withdraw from a line which has cost us 80,000 men since we first went into it and which has never had a shadow of reason to justify its retention except sentiment and the wish to hold the last town in Belgium, but as this has long been a heap of ruins what possible good can there be in holding a line which will cost thousands still. Sir H Smith-Dorrien said the line of the Salient east of Ypres ought to be abandoned and he was sent home. I wonder if Sir H Plumer will have the moral courage to say what everyone out here knows. There is to be a conference this evening to discuss the

80 Hutton to Lord Stamfordham 18 Sep. 1915, in *Nugent*, p. 10.
81 Murray to ON, 17 Aug. 1915, in *Nugent*, p. 251n.
82 ON to CN, 30 Aug. 1915 (PRONI, MIC571/2, D3835/E/2/150).

situation. I shall be anxious to hear the result. I have implored
Couper to speak up in the interests of his Division and of the whole
army.[83]

His wish went unfulfilled, and the Ypres sector continued to play a major
part, for good and ill, in his career on the western front. The mention of
Plumer highlights how different Nugent's dispiriting period in Second
Army in 1915 was from the positive experience he would have in 1916–17.
The explanation lies, in addition to the operational disadvantages facing the
BEF in 1915, in Plumer's newness in the role and the fact that Tim
Harington, his outstanding chief of staff who transformed the army's
administration and relationship with subordinate commanders, would not
arrive until the following summer. But it also reflects the personal
command style of some of Plumer's subordinates, particularly Allenby and
Keir. Even allowing for the painful learning process that commanders at all
levels were undergoing, the strategic constraints under which they laboured
and the doctrinal and technological transition that was underway, their
leadership that summer was strikingly insensitive and wasteful.[84]

Preoccupied with operational concerns, Nugent had little time to think
about Irish politics in the summer of 1915; in any event Ireland seemed
relatively stable after the dramas of the previous year, and there were other
issues on the home front, like the munitions shortage, industrial unrest and
the prospects for compulsory service (which like most senior officers he
strongly supported) that caught his attention. But Irish politics periodically
cropped up. 'I wonder if it is conceivable that the country will go back to
the Home Rule state of feeling after the war. I know one person who will
have nothing to do with any civil war rot if he lives', he wrote on 18
August.[85] He also followed the progress of the Ulster Division and was glad
to hear in June that it was moving to England, as it would 'be so much
better to take them out of Ireland and let them see something outside their
own little corners'.[86] In August he wrote: 'I think it is a good thing that the
Ulster Division has left Ulster now and I hope it will soon be out here and
have some hard fighting. They won't want to talk so much of civil war when

[83] ON to CN, 11 Aug. 1915 (PRONI, MIC571/2, D3835/E/2/135).

[84] For the BEF, in 1915 see Spencer Jones, '"To make war as we must, and not as we
   should like": the British Army and the problem of the Western Front, 1915', in
   Spencer Jones (ed.), *Courage Without Glory: The British Army on the Western
   Front 1915* (2015), pp 31–55. Keir was himself sacked by Allenby in August
   1916 when serving in the latter's Third Army

[85] ON to CN, 18 Aug. 1915 (PRONI, MIC571/2, D3835/E/2/141).

[86] ON to CN, 5 June 1915 (PRONI, MIC571/2, D3835/E/2/62).

they have seen what war is really like'.[87] The Ulster Division would indeed soon be out in France and in due course would see some very hard fighting. What Nugent had not expected was that he would be leading it. Murray was as good as his word. On 6 September Nugent told Kitty:

> Dearest, I have news which will thrill you but which you must not breathe till it is official. I have been told I have been given command of a Division & so will be promoted to Major General. The Division is the Ulster Division of all others. It is now I believe at Aldershot & is coming out almost at once but at any rate I shall be home for a while & I may be on my way home before you get this even.[88]

On 10 September he left the Salient to take up the command that would define his professional career. He had some regrets about leaving the 14th Division, but none at all about leaving Ypres. He had had a searing introduction to trench warfare and had important principles reinforced, such as relying on the opinion of the officer on the spot when it came to operational decisions. He had also witnessed some poor generalship and developed outspoken opinions on the undesirability of cavalry and gunner officers commanding infantry formations or directing operations in which infantry played the dominant role. It was a theme that would recur more than once over the next two-and-a-half years.

[87] ON to CN, 18 Aug. 1915 (PRONI, MIC571/2, D3835/E/2/141).
[88] ON to CN, 6 Sep. 1915 (PRONI, MIC571/2, D3835/E/2/152).

4

Divisional Commander

Politics and professionalism in the Ulster Division, September 1915–June 1916

Introduction

Nugent's new command was one of the most distinctive New Army formations. Formed in significant part from the UVF, the Ulster Division embodied Ulster unionism's commitment to the war effort and its activities were followed with intense interest by people at home. Nugent would lead it for 31 of the 37 months it spent on operations on the western front and, as Cyril Falls put it, '[a]s long as the 36th Division is remembered, General Nugent's name will be associated with it. His whole existence was centred upon it; he was intensely proud of its achievements and jealous for its good name'.[1]

From the outset, however, his relationship with the division's political supporters was complex. Commanding it had some of the characteristics of leading a Dominion formation, in that with operational responsibility came political expectation. Nugent was now the commander of the military component of a distinct political community whose leaders felt they had a right to a say in the running of 'their' division. While the military aspects of his role gave him few qualms, he was less comfortable handling its political dimension. Despite his Cavan background and UVF connections he did not, as we have seen, share all the political aspirations of the Ulster unionist leadership, nor their view of what the war meant for Ireland. For him, as for others – including, for different reasons, both southern unionists and moderate nationalists – it was a potentially unifying experience, a chance to submerge domestic political differences and create a basis for future cooperation. For many Ulster unionists it was an opportunity to differentiate loyal Ulster from nationalist Ireland; common cause with their political opponents was not what they sought.

There were from the outset, therefore, underlying tensions between Nugent and important figures in Ulster, including James Craig, over both

---

[1] Cyril Falls, *The History of the 36th (Ulster) Division* (1922), p. 244.

influence within the division – Nugent was determined to resist any political 'interference' in his command – and Ireland's political future. Over the next 18 months these would be exacerbated by intensive fighting at the front and rebellion at home, spilling over into directly military issues such as keeping the division up to strength and making senior appointments within it. Nugent's two priorities for his new command – to professionalise and as far as possible to depoliticise it – would soon bring him into conflict with both politicians and military superiors.

The Ulster Division

After snatching a few days with Kitty in London, Nugent joined the division at Bordon, near Aldershot, on 14 September. It had moved there a fortnight earlier from Seaford on the Sussex coast, where it had been training since arriving from Ireland in July, to complete its musketry courses before deploying overseas.

Nugent found himself for the second time in four months in the awkward position of replacing an officer who had expected to take his formation to war. His predecessor, Major-General Herbert Powell, a retired Indian army officer who had also served in the UVF, and who had been recalled to the colours in 1914, was still in France on a pre-deployment visit and was naturally bitterly disappointed to find on his return that he had been superseded. There was considerable personal sympathy for him in the division but also a recognition that he was too old and out-of-date for operational service.[2]

Nugent took over a formation whose strength stood at about 18,000 men, two-thirds of whom were serving in the infantry. Including the pioneers, five of its 13 battalions were recruited in Belfast, two each in counties Antrim and Down and four in the rest of the province (see Annex A). Most had strong local associations as effectively the Irish equivalent of pals battalions. The 9th Royal Irish Rifles, for example, were known as the West Belfast Volunteers, the 10th Royal Inniskilling Fusiliers were called the Derrys, and many of those Cavan Volunteers who had enlisted now formed part of the 9th Royal Irish Fusiliers (the Armagh, Cavan and Monaghan Volunteers). The bulk of the supporting arms had also been raised in Ulster, the major exception being the artillery: no Irish division in the Great War had artillery units recruited in Ireland.

Research in recent years has modified earlier views of the 36th Division as composed almost entirely of pre-war UVF volunteers. An estimated 31,000 UVF members enlisted during the war. Of these, around 16,500 had joined up by December 1914, of whom perhaps a quarter were army

[2] Falls, *Ulster Division*, p. 20.

reservists recalled to their original units. Other UVF personnel enlisted in other formations, particularly the 10th (Irish) Division, before the creation of the Ulster Division was finally agreed and relatively high proportions of some UVF units, especially in rural areas like Cavan, did not volunteer for overseas service. Even allowing for these caveats, however, UVF members undoubtedly joined in large enough numbers to make up the great majority in the division's Belfast battalions and a substantial proportion in the others, representing a critical mass more than sufficient to shape its ethos.[3]

That was certainly true of the division's leadership, which in September 1915 was dominated by UVF figures. They included, in addition to Nugent himself, all three infantry brigadiers: George Couchman (107 Brigade) had commanded the Belfast UVF, William Hacket Pain (108) had been the UVF's chief of staff and Thomas Hickman (109), an English MP, had been its inspector general. Seven of the 12 infantry battalions were commanded by ex-UVF officers (though all 12 had had pre-war regular experience, including two in the Indian army). At lower levels, of a sample of 231 infantry officers with the division in January 1915, at least 102 (44%) had served in the UVF.[4] James Craig had been invalided from the divisional staff some months previously but Captain Wilfrid Spender, an English ex-regular who had resigned his commission to play a leading role in organising the UVF, remained as GSO2.[5] Unionist MPs serving with the division in the autumn of 1915 along with Hickman were Craig's brother Charles (11th Royal Irish Rifles), Hugh McCalmont (12th Royal Irish Rifles), Peter Ker-Smiley (14th Royal Irish Rifles) and Hugh O'Neill (divisional staff), while other members of the UUC included Lord Leitrim (11th Royal Inniskilling Fusiliers) and Lord Farnham (Nugent's ADC), leaders respectively of Donegal and Cavan unionism.

The division was not alone amongst United Kingdom formations in having a distinctive political identity. The 16th (Irish) Division performed a similar role for moderate nationalism, though the core of National Volunteers around which it was formed was somewhat smaller than the

---

[3] Timothy Bowman, *Carson's Army: The Ulster Volunteer Force, 1910–22* (2007), pp 171–8; idem, 'The Ulster Volunteer Force and the Formation of the 36th (Ulster) Division', *Irish Historical Studies*, 32 (2001), pp 498–518; Richard Grayson, *Belfast Boys: How Unionists and Nationalists Fought and Died Together in the First World War* (2009), pp 9–13; David Fitzpatrick, 'The logic of collective sacrifice: Ireland and the British Army, 1914–18', *Historical Journal*, 38:4 (1995), pp 1,028–9; Stephen Sandford, *Neither Unionist Nor Nationalist: The 10th (Irish) Division in the Great War* (2015), pp 13–25.

[4] Bowman, 'Formation of the 36th (Ulster) Division', p. 509.

[5] General Staff Officer, grade 2.

UVF component of the Ulster Division. In a different context the 38th (Welsh) Division owed its existence to Lloyd George's wish to create a Welsh army corps and to the Liberal party's machinery in Wales, and Welsh politicians monitored its fortunes as closely as their Irish counterparts did the 16th and 36th Divisions. More broadly, the army's territorial regimental structure and the network of regional relationships it embodied, and the fact that many New Army units had been raised through local rather than central initiatives, provided opportunities for a range of groups – MPs, municipal bodies, the Territorial associations, local grandees – to exert pressure on behalf of their 'clients', whether units or individuals, within the army. The political issues confronting Nugent were therefore an extreme example of a phenomenon facing other divisional commanders, particularly William Hickie, commanding the 16th Division.[6] Nugent's initial contacts with the unionist leadership were cordial enough and gave no hint of the storms to come. Both Carson and Craig sent messages of congratulation and Nugent called to see Carson (still Attorney-General in the coalition government, though soon to resign) in London. Carson was one politician Nugent continued to admire, probably because Carson's original all-Ireland unionist outlook, even though circumstances had made him an advocate of Ulster separatism, mirrored his own.

Early days

Nugent, it transpired, had less than three weeks to finalise preparations before the division's departure for France. There were pressing operational matters to address, including the state of the division's artillery. The allocated artillery (the 153rd, 154th, 172nd and 173rd Brigades, Royal Field Artillery (RFA)), raised in May 1915 in north London and Croydon, had arrived at the end of August, when it quickly became apparent that their level of training was inadequate. They were sent off for urgent additional instruction and temporary replacements, in the form of the 1st/1st London Territorial Artillery, were attached in their place.[7] This was

---

[6] See Terence Denman, *Ireland's Unknown Soldiers: The 16th (Irish) Division in the Great War* (1992); Colin Hughes, *Mametz: Lloyd George's Welsh Army at the Battle of the Somme* (1982); Peter Simkins, *Kitchener's Army* (1998); Ian Beckett, 'The Territorial Force', in Ian Beckett and Keith Simpson (eds), *A Nation in Arms: A Social Study of the British Army in the First World War* (1985), pp 127–63; Ewen A. Cameron and Iain J. M. Robertson, 'Fighting and Bleeding for the Land: the Scottish Highlands and the Great War', in Catriona M. M. MacDonald and E. W. McFarland, *Scotland and the Great War* (2014), pp 81–100.

[7] Falls, *Ulster Division*, p. 19. The London artillery comprised the 1/1st, 1/2nd, 1/3rd & 1/4th London Brigades RFA.

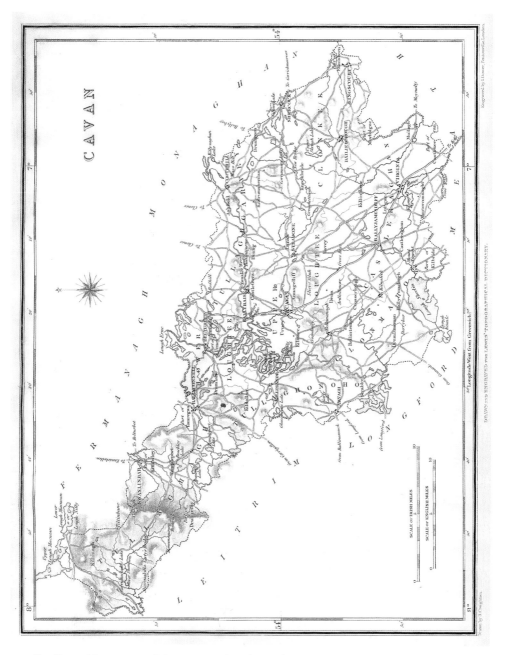

Co. Cavan: Mountnugent (Mount Nugent) in the south (Lewis, *Topographical Dictionary*, 1837)

Major-General Sir Oliver Nugent (William Conor)
This portrait is reproduced by the kind permission of Belfast City Council.
The original can be viewed at City Hall, Belfast

GOC Ulster Division (PRONI)

Ulster's
Solemn League and Covenant.

Being convinced in our consciences that Home Rule would be disastrous to the material well-being of Ulster as well as of the whole of Ireland, subversive of our civil and religious freedom, destructive of our citizenship and perilous to the unity of the Empire, we, whose names are under-written, men of Ulster, loyal subjects of His Gracious Majesty King George V., humbly relying on the God whom our fathers in days of stress and trial confidently trusted, do hereby pledge ourselves in solemn Covenant throughout this our time of threatened calamity to stand by one another in defending for ourselves and our children our cherished position of equal citizen-ship in the United Kingdom and in using all means which may be found necessary to defeat the present conspiracy to set up a Home Rule Parliament in Ireland. ¶ And in the event of such a Parliament being forced upon us we further solemnly and mutually pledge ourselves to refuse to recognise its authority. ¶ In sure confidence that God will defend the right we hereto subscribe our names. ¶ And further, we individually declare that we have not already signed this Covenant.

The above was signed by me at _Dublin_ "Ulster Day." Saturday, 28th September, 1912.

God Save the King.

Nugent's signed copy of the Ulster Covenant, 1912 (Nugent family)

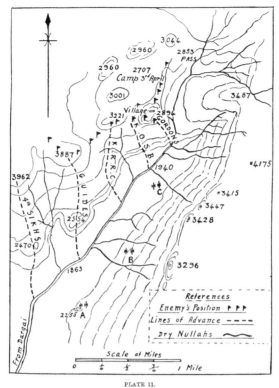

PLATE 11.

MAP TO ILLUSTRATE ACTION AT THE MALAKHAND PASS, APRIL 3, 1895.

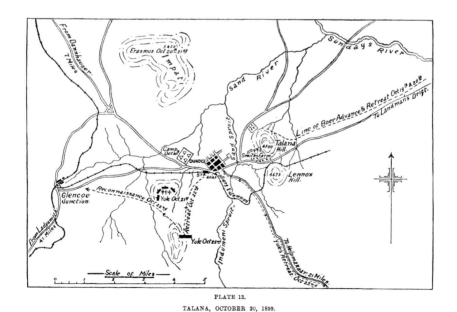

PLATE 13.

TALANA, OCTOBER 20, 1899.

Malakand 1895 and Talana 1899 (see Chapter 1) (KRRC regimental history)

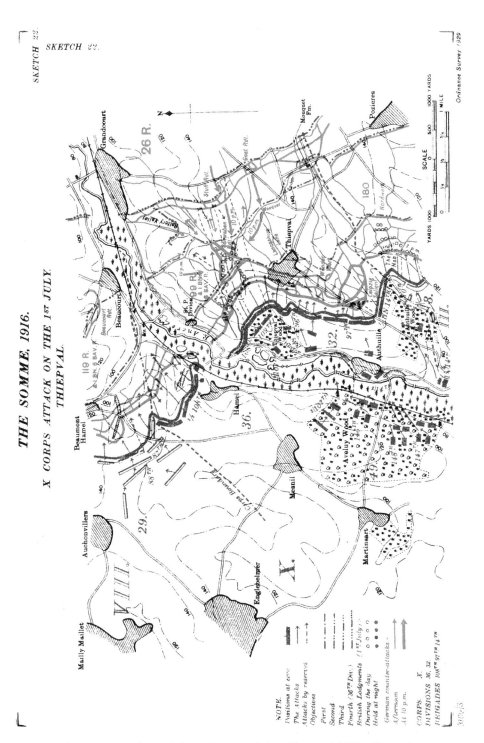

The Somme, 1 July 1916: the X Corps attack (see Chapter 5) (Official history)

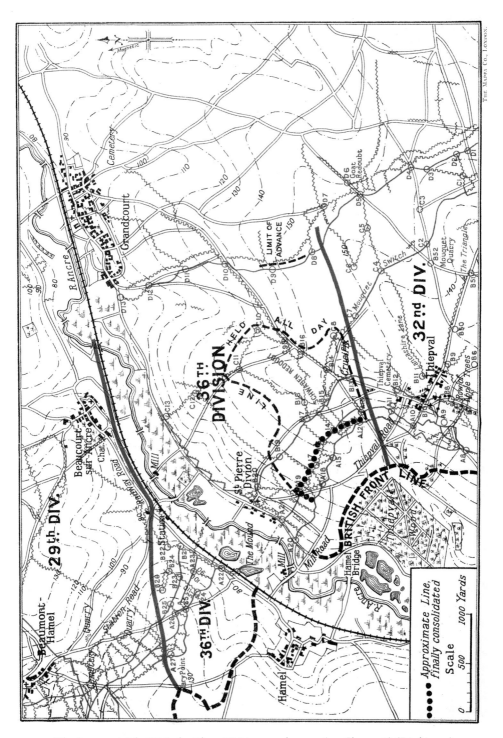

The Somme, 1 July 1916: the Ulster Division attack sector (see Chapter 5) (Div history)

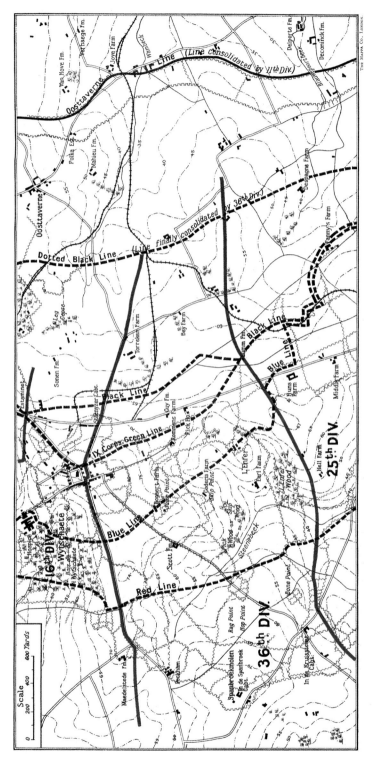

The Mappa. Co. London.

Messines, June 1917 (see Chapter 7) (Div history)

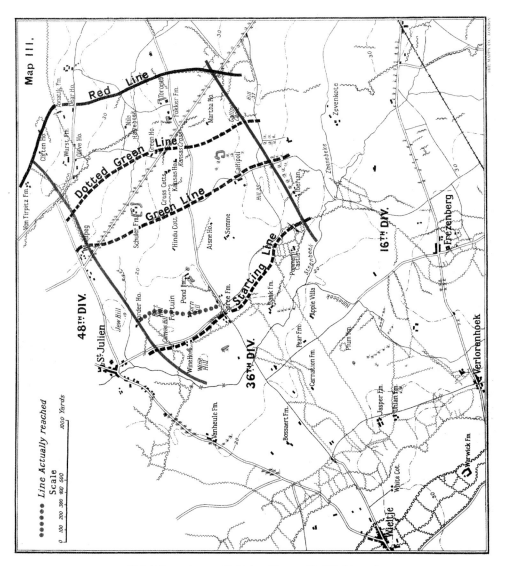

Map III.

Red Line

Dotted Green Line

Green Line

Starting Line

48TH DIV.

36TH DIV.

16TH DIV.

Line Actually reached

Scale

0 100 200 300 400 500   1000 Yards

St. Julien

Verlorenhoek

Frezenberg

Wietje

Von Tirpitz Fm.

Clifton Ho.

Wurst. Fm.

Olive Ho.

Avatık Fm.

Bear Ho.

Toronto

Nile

Hanebeke

Green Ho.

Fokker Fm.

Martha Ho.

Hill 35

Hill 37

Zevenkote

Zonnebeke

Winnipeg

Cross Cotts.

Schuler Fm.

Kansas Ho.

Hindu Cott.

Kansas Cross

Gallipoli

Iberian

Aisne Ho.

Somme

Hill 35

Pommern Castle

Steenbeek

Hanebeek

Border Ho.

Pond Fm.

Corn Hill

Fort Luin

Spree Fm.

Bank Fm.

Apple Villa

Pear Fm.

Plum Fm.

Jew Hill

Gallows Hill

Winehouse

White Hill

Vanheule Fm.

Carnation Fm.

Jasper Fm.

Uhlan Fm.

Bossaert Fm.

White Cot.

Warwick Cot.

THE MAPPA CO. LONDON

Third Ypres, August 1917 (see Chapter 7) (Div history)

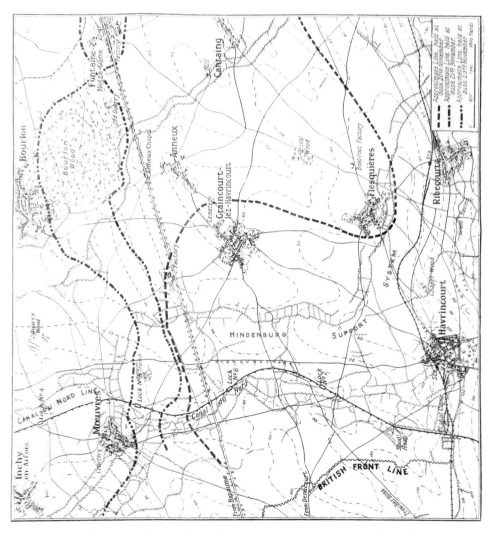

Cambrai, November 1917: the Ulster Division attack sector (see Chapter 8) (Div history)

CAMBRAI, 1917.

Cambrai 1917: Welsh Ridge, held by the Ulster Division in the December fighting,
shown in the centre (see Chapter 8) (Official history)

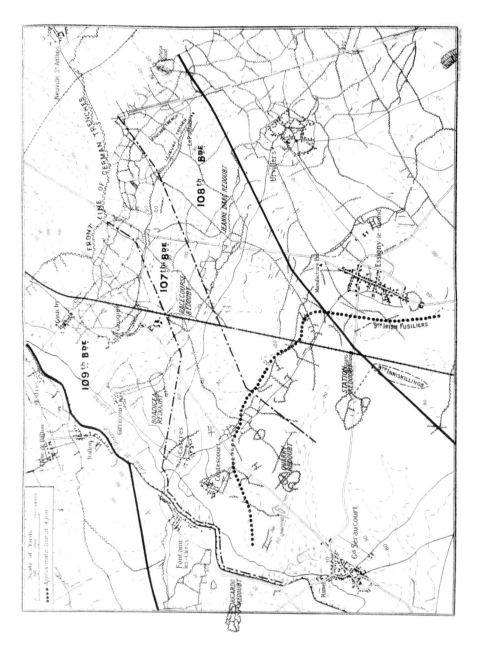

St Quentin, March 1918 (see Chapter 9) (Div history)

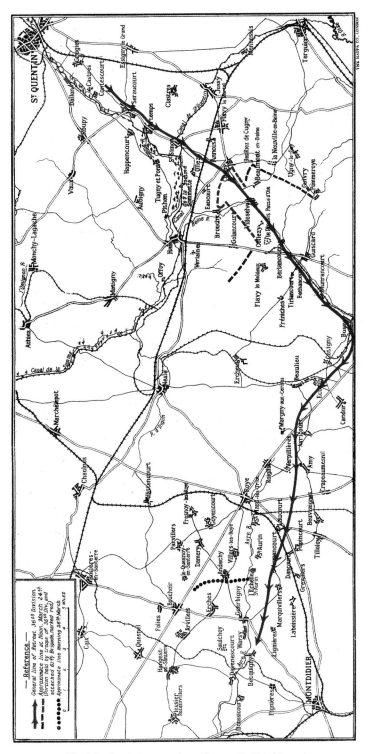

The March 1918 retreat (see Chapter 9) (Div history)

Attack of the Ulster Division, 1 July 1916 (J. P. Beadle)
This painting is reproduced by the kind permission of Belfast City Council.
The original can be viewed at City Hall, Belfast

Medals of Major-General Sir Oliver Nugent (Author's collection)

not unusual: in several New Army divisions the artillery units, which required higher levels of technical expertise than their infantry colleagues, had to be exchanged between formations as embarkation dates approached. Unlike others, however, the Ulster Division's artillery would re-join relatively quickly.

There was also an important ceremonial occasion to fit in. Wherever possible the King visited in person formations preparing to go overseas, and on 30 September he reviewed the division on Hankley Common, near Aldershot, a large-scale set-piece event. The parade, as surviving film footage shows, was a great success. The King was impressed and so were other onlookers, including Kitchener, and the divisional historian later wrote: 'None of those who saw them is likely to forget the physique or the bearing of that splendid body of men. It is hard to think without emotion of what the Division was that day and the fate that awaited it'.[8]

Even as the review took place, however, the 36th Division's advance parties were leaving for France. The next day Nugent delivered a lecture to a large audience of officers and NCOs. In it he stressed the importance of traditional military virtues – care for their men, discipline, loyalty – and the key features of war on the western front, including the use of artillery, machine-guns, grenades and new weapons like gas and flamethrowers. He was characteristically direct, warning them, for example, of the impact of trench mortars ('I have seen men crying like children after a series of these shells … reduced to gibbering idiots'). He was clear on the responsibilities of leaders: 'you must work on the principle that there is nothing too small to worry over if it tends to the comfort, health or fighting efficiency of your men'. He stressed the importance of discipline:

> In all my experience of life as a soldier, I have never seen a regiment which made or maintained a reputation which had not discipline … It is the spirit of discipline which enables you and the men you have to lead to face losses, to go steadily to your front and to confront difficulties and dangers which would probably have frightened you into a lunatic asylum 8 months ago.

He also delivered an uncompromising message about maintaining control in action: 'The bad example of one man is contagious and may affect a number in his vicinity. Every officer and NCO has a great responsibility at such times. A rot must always be stopped before it spreads'. He ended with

---

[8] Falls, *Ulster Division*, p. 21. The film of the review is in the Imperial War Museum's collection (IWM 580, 'Britain Prepared: a review of the activities of his Majesty's naval and military forces').

his initial impressions of the division: in terms of physique it was the finest he had seen; discipline, given the relative absence of serious crime, was good; and he paid tribute to General Powell, the officers and NCOs for the fact that he was able 'to take command of a division fit and ready to take the field'. He would revise the last part of his judgement when the division reached France, but the lecture made a positive impression. Major Bob Perceval-Maxwell of the 13th Royal Irish Rifles noted that night, 'Our new General made all the officers and NCOs a very good address today. Very straight and sensible and gave us some very useful hints about things in general. I feel that he will be a very good man for his job and I think we are lucky to have got him'.[9]

Deployment to France

In early October the main body of the division crossed the channel, Nugent himself doing so on the 3rd, and by 9 October it was concentrated around Flesselles, near Amiens. It shifted further west to Bernaville a few days later. The build-up of New Army divisions in France had accelerated since the 14th had been rushed over in May. Six more Kitchener formations had deployed in July, two in August and four in September, two of which went on to Salonika. The Ulster Division arrived in October and five more would disembark by the end of the year, including most of the 16th Division (its third brigade and artillery did not arrive until early 1916).[10] Arrangements for receiving them were now well-established and the Ulster Division's induction programme began almost at once. It was similar to the 14th Division's six months earlier, each brigade in turn going into the line under the tutelage of an experienced division. Unlike the 14th, however, the 36th had the luxury of finding its feet in a genuinely quiet sector, which was – ironically, given what would happen the following summer – in the Somme area just north of the River Ancre. On 9 October 107 Brigade moved up for their attachment to the 4th Division; eight days later it was 108 Brigade's turn, two battalions going to the 4th Division and two to the 48th, further north; and after that it was 109 Brigade's turn with the same two divisions.[11]

Nugent now had his first opportunity to examine closely the state of training of his units and the quality of his senior subordinates. Neither, in his view, met the standards required. He quickly decided that Brigadier-General George Couchman of 107 Brigade was not up to the job, telling

---

[9] Lecture, 1 Oct. 1915 (PRONI, D/3835/E/10/3A); Perceval-Maxwell to his mother, 1 Oct. 1915 (PRONI, D/2480/6/4); Bowman, *Irish Regiments*, p. 110.

[10] Becke, *Order of Battle, Divisions, Part 3A* (1938) and *Part 3B* (1945).

[11] Falls, *Ulster Division*, p. 23.

Kitty that he had had 'to write to one of my Brigadiers and tell him he won't do, so beastly but quite unavoidable. I might have delayed it, but what good and a good man is badly wanted at once'.[12] Couchman, at 55 less than a year older than Nugent, had followed a similar career path. A Somerset Light Infantry officer, he won a DSO in Burma in the 1880s and subsequently commanded both a regular battalion and, from 1911 to 1914, the neighbouring Territorial brigade to Nugent's in southern England: while they had met, Nugent's opinion of him at that time is unclear. Following Couchman's retirement in early 1914 he had joined the UVF. Nugent's unceremonious removal of him stemmed directly from the serious disciplinary problems already apparent in 107 Brigade.[13] Comprising four of the division's five Belfast battalions – the 8th, 9th, 10th and 15th Royal Irish Rifles – it was a challenging command, recruited from working-class loyalist districts in a tough industrial-port city, and its brigadier in Nugent's view had lost control. On 26 October 1915 he wrote:

> The Belfast Brigade is awful. They have absolutely no discipline and their officers are awful. I am very much disturbed about them. I don't think they are fit for service and I should be very sorry to have to trust them. Don't breathe one word of this to a living soul please. It is all due to putting a weak man in command of the Brigade to start with and giving commissions to men of the wrong class.[14]

His comment on the brigade's officers obviously reflected a bias at this stage of the war in favour of officers from traditional backgrounds, but others shared his overall assessment of 107 Brigade. Even Wilfrid Spender – no fan, it was emerging, of Nugent's – agreed that a change was necessary, saying of Couchman, 'I'm afraid he has not been a success. He is too fussy one moment and too kindly to his officers at the next'.[15] Couchman left on 20 October. His successor, William Withycombe, almost 10 years younger, had extensive recent operational experience, having commanded the 2nd King's Own Yorkshire Light Infantry in France since November 1914 and survived the German gas attack at Ypres in May 1915.[16] He had energy and grip and would become one of Nugent's most trusted subordinates, but his arrival did not immediately resolve 107 Brigade's problems.

[12] ON to CN, 10 Oct. 1915, in *Nugent*, p. 32.
[13] Bowman, *Irish Regiments*, pp 111–16.
[14] ON to CN, 26 Oct. 1915, in *Nugent*, p. 34.
[15] Spender to his wife, 10 Oct. 1915, in *Nugent*, p. 253n.
[16] Lt.-Col. R. C. Bond, *The King's Own Yorkshire Light Infantry in the Great War* (1929), p. 746.

Before appointing him, Nugent had had to see off efforts by Theresa, Lady Londonderry, to secure a brigade in the division for her son Charlie (the seventh Marquess of Londonderry, who in the 1930s would become Secretary of State for Air and interlocutor with the Nazis).[17] Londonderry was a major in the Household Cavalry and ADC to Lieutenant-General Sir William Pulteney, commander of III Corps. Both his mother and his wife Edith were formidable political operators and even before the division left England Theresa was lobbying hard for his promotion, asking Pulteney and General Sir John Cowans, Quartermaster General at the War Office, to make representations on Charlie's behalf. Nugent turned these approaches down flat, the status of those asking the favour notwithstanding. As Cowans acknowledged to Theresa in early October:

> Of course there is a certain amount in what the General [Nugent] urged when approached, that C[harlie] had no infantry experience, and that it meant the lives of about 4000 men being put under a man without sufficient experience. Against that I urged that he had a year's experience out here, and that they might give him good staff officers, as no doubt the Ulstermen would follow him far better than any other man; and after all, local influence and experience of war combined, seem to make a pretty good case for him. We will have to see what the General replies from France, as they have now gone over there.[18]

By 12 October word had come back that Nugent was sticking to his guns. Pulteney wrote apologetically to Edith that he was 'sorry about Charley and the Ulster Division but [I] understand that Nugent was opposed to it'. Perhaps to reassure her that Charlie was well out of it he added, 'The Ulster Division went down to 3rd Army where they ought to be able to train them all right, am afraid that the discipline is none too good from all accounts but they will pull themselves together out here just like the Canadians did'.[19]

---

[17] See Ian Kershaw, *Making Friends with Hitler: Lord Londonderry and Britain's Road to War* (2004).

[18] Anthony Leask, *Putty. From Tel-el-Kebir to Cambrai: The Life and Letters of Lieutenant General Sir William Pulteney* (2015), p. 331; N. C. Fleming, *The Marquess of Londonderry: Aristocracy, Power and Politics in Britain and Ireland* (2005), pp 19–44.

[19] Leask, *Putty*, p. 332.

The reference to the Canadians was to disciplinary issues the 1st Canadian Division had encountered on arriving at the front.[20] Pulteney's comments underscored the close scrutiny the Ulster Division could expect. Partly this was the normal supervision of military superiors: in its first few months in France the division passed quickly through a number of different corps in Third Army – VII, XIII and XIV, commanded respectively by Lieutenant-Generals Sir Thomas Snow, Sir Walter Congreve and Lord Cavan – with the commanders of which Nugent got on well and of whom Cavan in particular made a positive impression. Trickier was the fact that, shortly after its arrival, Allenby replaced General Monro as Third Army's commander, to Nugent's chagrin. 'Allenby is here and no one is particularly rejoiced I can assure you', he complained in late October, and in November he asked Kitty: 'Did you call on Lady Allenby? Don't tell her that her husband is the most cordially hated man in the British Army'.[21] Fortunately his dealings with Allenby were limited. Some of the attention from external military observers had a more political aspect, however, as the aftermath of the Curragh crisis lingered on. When the division left XIII Corps in December 1915 Spender thought the change timely because 'two of the Corps staff were formerly very anti-Ulster. General Greenly, who is an old staff college friend of mine, took a very strong line against us then … it is better for many reasons that we should be moved'.[22]

Commanders and staff

Meanwhile command changes in 107 Brigade continued. Before the division left England the CO of the 8th Royal Irish Rifles, Lieutenant-Colonel Lyle, had been removed and his successor, Lieutenant-Colonel Chute, followed shortly after arriving in France. In the 15th Royal Irish Rifles Lieutenant-Colonel Ford-Hutchinson went equally quickly. In the 9th Royal Irish Rifles Lieutenant-Colonel Ormerod, who suffered from ill-health, was evacuated after a few weeks and though a medical board passed him fit to return Nugent had him taken off the boat at Southampton as unsuited to operational service.[23] By early 1916 only Colonel Bernard of the 10th Royal Irish Rifles, an Indian army officer, remained of 107 Brigade's original COs. It is easy to be dismissive of these 'dug-outs', but some had had impressive careers. Hugh Lyle was a Welsh Fusiliers officer with a DSO from Burma, described by Frank Richards, author of *Old*

---

[20] Paul Dickson, 'The end of the beginning', in Geoffrey Hayes et al., *Vimy Ridge: A Canadian Reassessment* (2007), pp 36–40.

[21] ON to CN, 31 Oct. and 24 Nov. 1915, in *Nugent*, pp 35, 254n.

[22] Spender to his wife, 3 Dec. 1915, in *Nugent*, p. 40.

[23] Bowman, *Irish Regiments*, pp 111–12; Crozier, *Brass Hat*, p. 102.

Soldier Sahib, as one of the best COs he ever had.[24] George Ford-Hutchinson, formerly of the Connaught Rangers, won a DSO in the Sudan with the Egyptian army and was replaced, according to Lieutenant Stewart-Moore, his cousin, also in the division, 'because he was not sufficiently robust … It must have been a sad blow to him when he was adjudged too old at fifty'.[25] Often these older officers simply were not up to the strains of modern war.

Changes were less extensive in the other two brigades, only one CO in each leaving before June 1916. In 108 Brigade Lieutenant-Colonel McCalmont of the 12th Royal Irish Rifles, an Irish Guards officer and MP, went to command a battalion of his own regiment before Christmas and was promoted to brigadier shortly after. In 109 Brigade, on the other hand, the situation with the 14th Royal Irish Rifles (Young Citizen Volunteers), Nugent's fifth Belfast battalion, was more complicated. The only unit in the division to pre-date the war, having been raised with the support of Belfast Corporation in 1912 as part of an initiative to encourage volunteering, its CO, Lieutenant-Colonel Chichester, was absent for long periods because of ill-health.[26] He was finally invalided in March 1916 but the instability while temporary replacements came and went had a lasting impact on the unit's efficiency. Spender believed that 'General Nugent does not think Irishmen are good in command of their own countrymen, but prefers a mixture, I think'.[27] That was not, in fact, the case but he did believe the division's leadership needed an injection of fresh blood. Of five new COs in place by the end of May 1916, two were regulars posted in – Bowen (14th Royal Irish Rifles) and Bull (12th Royal Irish Rifles); one was a British ex-regular officer seconded from a Canadian regiment – Pelly (8th Royal Irish Rifles); and two were 'internal' promotions – Crozier (9th Royal Irish Rifles) and Gordon (15th Royal Irish Rifles), both with pre-war regular service.[28]

Pressure from supporters at home was applied in respect of vacancies at battalion level also. The departure of Chichester from the 14th Rifles left

[24] Frank Richards, *Old Soldier Sahib* (1936), p. 298.
[25] *Nugent*, p. 254n.
[26] Steven Moore, *The Chocolate Soldiers: The Story of the Young Citizen Volunteers and 14th Royal Irish Rifles during the Great War* (2016), pp 15–22.
[27] Spender to Carson, 25 Nov. 1915, in *Nugent*, p. 38.
[28] The other six, in addition to Bernard (10th R. Irish Rifles), were Pakenham (11th R. Irish Rifles), Savage (13th R. Irish Rifles, another Indian army officer), Blacker (9th R. Irish Fusiliers), Ricardo (9th R. Inniskilling Fusiliers), Ross Smyth (10th R. Inniskilling Fusiliers), and Hessey (11th R. Inniskilling Fusiliers), all of whom save Blacker, a gunner, had seen service as regular infantry officers before the war.

an opening that the wife of Peter Ker-Smiley MP, the battalion 2ic, felt was rightfully her husband's and Lady Farnham was asked to recommend him. The response from France was sharp. After confirming there was no prospect of Nugent appointing Ker-Smiley, Farnham explained:

> He has been passed over as it was mutually agreed by everybody that he was unfit for command. I fear I can do nothing in the matter. I don't think that anything Mrs Smiley can do will have the least effect out here. Out here the higher command are very strict about making you get rid of anybody you cannot rely on.[29]

Nugent's scrutiny fell too on his immediate staff. Where possible the headquarters of New Army formations going overseas were bolstered by staff-trained officers, despite the shortage of such men across the BEF. All 19 New Army divisions on the western front at the end of 1915 deployed with Camberley-trained GSO1s (chief operations officer); the position with Assistant Adjutant & Quartermaster Generals (AA&QMG, the principal personnel and logistics officer) was more mixed, with about half being staff-qualified, though a number of others were supply specialists from the Army Service Corps.[30] Arriving in the Ulster Division with Nugent in September 1915, therefore, were a new AA&QMG and GSO1, respectively Lieutenant-Colonels Godfrey Meynell and Alick Russell, both Staff College graduates. Camberley-trained or not, however, they still had to meet Nugent's exacting standards, Farnham noting in early October that 'Oliver fairly keeps his staff up to the mark'.[31] Nugent soon concluded that change was necessary:

> Meynell is, I am afraid a useless staff officer, always making heavy weather of everything and no more initiative than a clerk. I have to think of everything in his branch and he gets on my nerves. I am afraid I shall have to get him removed. It is horrible work and it is so wrong to send staff officers to staff appointments who are no use. Not fair on them or on their General.[32]

Meynell left at the end of October to command a battalion of the King's Shropshire Light Infantry (and later, briefly, a brigade). His replacement

---

[29] Farnham to his wife, 3 Mar. 1916 (PRONI, D3975/E/8/6/1).

[30] For an overview of the BEF and operational staff-work, see P. M. Harris, 'The men who planned the war: A study of the staff of the British Army on the Western Front 1914–1918' (PhD thesis, King's College London, 2013).

[31] Farnham to his wife, 11 Oct. 1915 (PRONI, D3975/E/8/1/3).

[32] ON to CN, 12 Oct. 1915, in *Nugent*, p. 32.

was Lewis Comyn, a 43-year-old lieutenant-colonel in the Connaught Rangers, who had already demonstrated his competence as a staff officer in France despite not having attended Staff College. He was also a Catholic, one of the first appointed to a senior position in the division. This caused a stir because Spender told his wife, who in turn told Lady Carson. Spender was anxious that this, as he put it, might cause mischief and 'create a wrong impression', and he wrote hurriedly to tell Carson that 'Comyn and Mayne [a more junior Catholic officer posted in at the same time], are both good chaps and Unionist, and though it is not a tactful thing to have done on the part of the authorities, I feel sure they are not themselves intriguers'.[33] Nugent, who hated any manifestation of sectarian feeling, was fortunately unaware of this episode. Comyn proved an efficient and resourceful head of the division's administrative planning until November 1917, when he was promoted into the War Office.

On paper the credentials of Alick Russell, the division's GSO1, were impeccable. The son of Lord Odo Russell, a British diplomat, he had been commissioned into the Grenadier Guards, served in South Africa and was from 1910 to 1914 military attaché in Berlin. He was well-connected, charming and possessed a detailed knowledge of the German army.[34] What he lacked was an aptitude for operational planning of the sort required by an infantry division on active service and by February 1916 he had begun to grate on Nugent:

> To tell the truth I am rather sick of Russell. He is no use as a Staff Officer and he is so overcoated with the manners of courts that he remains permanently artificial. I get so bored at being spoken to as if I were the Kaiser, with a sort of catch and gasp at the end of every sentence … If he were a good staff officer I shouldn't mind but he is absolutely useless and some day I shall have to tell him so.[35]

For the time being that issue remained unresolved. At lower levels, however, Nugent had other capable officers. Spender, whatever his and Nugent's political differences, was exceptionally able and though only a captain had been at Camberley with many men now holding senior appointments (a constant source of frustration to him), while Major Somerville, deputy on the logistics side, and Captain Richardson, the GSO3 responsible for intelligence matters, were both very competent. All three were promoted

---

[33] Spender to his wife, 3 Dec. 1915, in *Nugent*, p. 40.
[34] Matthew S. Seligmann (ed.), *Military Intelligence from Germany, 1906–14* (2014), pp 12–14.
[35] ON to CN, 13 Feb. 1916, in *Nugent*, pp 46–7.

out of the division within 18 months. Bright young officers also joined as 'staff learners', one of them, Cyril Falls, being a future official historian and Chichele Professor of the History of War at Oxford.

Two further senior command changes came before the end of 1915. Brigadier-General George Hacket Pain of 108 Brigade, formerly of the Queen's Regiment and the UVF's chief of staff in 1914, had served in the Sudan and South Africa and commanded a regular battalion of the Worcestershire Regiment before retiring in 1912. At nearly 60, however, and seriously overweight he was too old and unfit for trench warfare, and Nugent in any event had doubts about his competence. In December he left to take command of a reserve brigade at home. Again Nugent got a battle-experienced replacement, Galway-born Charles Griffith (48), who had won a DSO in South Africa and commanded the 1st Bedfordshire Regiment at Mons and in the First and Second Battles of Ypres.[36] Like Withycombe he proved a reliable, efficient commander. Also in December the Ulster Division's own artillery arrived to replace the London Territorial gunners, and with them came a new Commander Royal Artillery (CRA), 45-year-old Henry Brock, younger brother of Rear-Admiral (later Admiral of the Fleet Sir) Osmond Brock. Brock, who had been wounded in the Boer War leading a unit of colonial light horse and until October 1915 had commanded an artillery brigade in the 4th Division, remained with the division for the rest of the war.

Nugent's first three months in command therefore saw a high degree of churn at senior level, with further changes to come: by mid-May 1916 all three infantry brigadiers and both senior staff officers had left as he put together an efficient leadership team. Changes of this sort were the norm in New Army divisions. In the 19 Kitchener divisions that deployed to the western front between May and December 1915, for example, 29 of 57 infantry brigadiers, just over 50%, were replaced shortly before embarkation or within 12 weeks of arriving; so were four divisional commanders, four GSO1s and six AA&QMGs, as older officers like General Powell who had borne the brunt of raising the New Armies were replaced by those better suited to front-line service.[37] The picture in the Ulster Division thereafter was, however, one of remarkable stability. Nugent commanded on the western front for just over two-and-a-half years. Comyn stayed with him as AA&QMG for 24 months, Brock as CRA for

---

36 Steven Fuller, *1st Bedfordshires. Part One: Mons to the Somme* (2011), pp 24–5, 136–7.

37 Becke, *Order of Battle: Parts 3A and B* (1938, 1945). A small number of the changes arose from promotions or casualties.

29 months, and two infantry brigadiers, Withycombe and Griffith, for 27 and 29 months respectively. This represented continuity unusual in the Great War. Once Nugent had officers in whom he had confidence he was loyal to them.

Training and discipline

While sorting out the division's leadership, Nugent had also been assessing its tactical training. His initial impact had been positive – 'Oliver is in great form', recorded Farnham on 14 October, 'and has I think instilled gr[ea]t confidence in all the COs. Ricardo said he wished to goodness they had had him from the beginning' – but the mood soon became more challenging.[38] On 16 October he held his first large-scale field exercise after which, he said, 'I delivered a long criticism. There were too many mistakes and shortcomings I am sorry to say for a Division supposed to be ready for war'.[39] Only 108 and 109 Brigades were involved, 107 being in the trenches, but Nugent's incisive de-brief went down in Ulster Division folklore. Spender thought the performance 'not very good I'm afraid, but the General's summing up was first rate'. Major Macrory of the 10th Royal Inniskilling Fusiliers, noting that 'few of the officers who were privileged to listen to his pow-wow after the performance will forget it', recalled:

> Very gravely, he opened his remarks by saying how glad he was to have at last seen the famous Ulster Division going through an attack practice, but (still more gravely) how much more glad he was to know that it was only a practice attack, for had it been a pukker attack on the German lines he very much feared that he would not have had the pleasure of speaking to any of the participating officers again in this world! The general went on to congratulate the officers on the excellence of their North of Ireland eyesight – he had observed that although they all were equipped with field glasses, none of them had ever found it necessary to use them.

Macrory added that as a lecture 'it was superb, and did a lot of good, even though the officers did feel a little bit small, and more than a little bit aggrieved, at the nature of their commander's witticisms'. An officer of the 12th Royal Irish Rifles recollected that the 'remarks of our General on the day's performance were, to say the least of them, hardly as complimentary as we should have wished. They left an impression on the minds of those who heard them that will never fade'. A platoon commander in the 11th

---

[38] Farnham to his wife, 14 Oct. 1915 (PRONI, D3975/E/8/1/5).
[39] ON to CN, 16 Oct. 1915, in *Nugent*, p. 33.

Royal Inniskilling Fusiliers wrote that Nugent 'told us quietly and firmly what he thought of us … we had a good name as a division but he did not know how we got it. Every rudimentary mistake that could be made had been made by officers that day … He did not know what sort of training we had had in Ireland, but it was very poor'. The pace of tactical training accelerated.[40]

So too did a general tightening of discipline, as Nugent's personality began to be felt throughout the division. As a commander he had always been demanding and suffered fools not at all. He believed in high standards of planning and discipline as the keys to success and keeping his men alive. He was far more inclined to find fault than to praise, particularly in the early days, and had no interest in being popular. He cared deeply about his officers and men but his style was what one historian has described as 'the stern, patriarchal approach'.[41] In that regard he belonged to a particular type of Great War divisional general – others included Heneker (8th Division), Robertson (17th Division), Shute (32nd Division) and Russell (New Zealand Division) – in being professional, tough-minded and, on occasion, severe.

His reputation had preceded him: word in the 10th Royal Inniskilling Fusiliers before his arrival was that their new general was 'very soldierly but the devil of a straffer'. Cyril Falls, who served on the division's staff from 1916 to 1918, wrote later, 'I have nothing to say against any of the divisional commanders whom I served, except that the first [Nugent] had a shocking temper'. This was due in part, as has been seen, to his South African injuries: prolonged spells in the saddle or long walks over difficult ground caused him pain. Farnham noted in November 1915 that Nugent was suffering from headaches and 'is pretty severe at times'. Spender observed of him in April 1916 that '[b]ut for his temper he would have done better as there are elements of greatness in him'. Frank Crozier later wrote that Nugent 'did his own shooting so well (in the front line with weapons, on paper with such an acid pen, and in the conference room with such a cutting tongue and subtle wit) that he was sent to India at a critical period when he should have been promoted to an army corps'. Sir Edward

---

[40] Spender to his wife, 16 Oct. 1915 (PRONI, D1633/1/1/18); Lt.-Col. Frank Macrory, 'Account of the service of the 10th Royal Inniskilling Fusiliers' (TNA, WO95/2510); API & DG [Samuels], *With the Ulster Division in France* (n.d. [1917]), pp 15–16; diary of 2nd Lt. Young, 11th R. Inniskilling Fusiliers (PRONI, D3045/6/11).

[41] J. M. Bourne, 'British generals in the First World War', in G. D. Sheffield (ed.), *Leadership and Command: The Anglo-American Military Experience Since 1861* (1997), p. 100.

Hutton commented after Nugent's death that he had 'an unbending will, was self-confident in his judgments and had not the happy knack, which a few strong characters have, of subordinating his own judgment when it clashed with that of authority'.[42]

There were two particular aspects to his focus on discipline. The first was his determination to impose, as matters of military efficiency, pre-war regular standards of cleanliness and obedience. His insistence on spotless accommodation led his men to joke that the division was 'sweeping onward through village after village in the North of France'. A stream of orders issued about standards of dress, saluting and behaviour. No aspect of life in the division escaped his notice, including disagreements between his chaplains. 'I have had to settle such a silly dispute between the Presbyterian and Church of Ireland chaplains of the Division', he wrote crossly on 9 November (the row being due to the Presbyterian chaplains' reluctance to accept orders from the division's senior chaplain, an Anglican), 'so to avoid friction I said that orders to them should come from my office direct. Silly idiots'.[43]

This experience of occasionally uncomfortable adjustment to operational conditions was common to all New Army divisions. The second aspect, however, was specific to the Ulster Division, and that was Nugent's concern to manage its sense of identity in a way that accorded with the army's expectations. He had no difficulty with his men expressing their Ulster Protestant heritage, for example by celebrating the Twelfth of July – indeed, the division contained many members of the Orange Order and several battalions had their own Orange lodges.[44] Nor did he object to his soldiers' sometimes vehement expressions of loyalty to the Crown. What he was determined to do was to contain those expressions within boundaries the army found acceptable. The entire regimental system was based on the controlled recognition of regional and national distinctiveness. It was not, though, designed to accommodate the kind of geographically-focused political radicalism that had led to the formation of the UVF, and Nugent knew there was nervousness in the military hierarchy that so political a

[42] Macrory, '10th Inniskillings'; Cyril Falls, 'Contact with troops: commanders and staff in the First World War', *Army Quarterly*, 88:2 (1964), p. 178; Farnham to his wife, 9 Nov. 1915 (PRONI, D3975/E/3/2/1); Spender to his wife, 3 Apr. 1916, in Margaret Baguley (ed.), *World War I and the Question of Ulster: The correspondence of Lilian and Wilfrid Spender* (2009), p. 65; F. P. Crozier, *The Men I Killed* (1937), p. 67; Hutton obituary of Nugent, *The King's Royal Rifle Corps Chronicle* (1927).

[43] Falls, *Ulster Division*, p. 25; ON to CN, 9 Nov. 1915, in *Nugent*, p. 36.

[44] Bowman, *Irish Regiments*, pp 28–9; Fitzpatrick, *Descendancy*, pp 34–40.

formation might prove disruptive. For him the threshold of acceptability was crossed if political views were expressed in ways that could be regarded as divisive, sectarian or overtly party-political. In February 1916 he told General Hutton 'that by unanimous consent there are no references in this Division to politics now'.[45] This was simply wishful thinking, but he did succeed, building on the work of his predecessor, in sublimating to a considerable extent the UVF sense of identity into wider regimental traditions such as the wearing of shamrocks on St Patrick's Day, and into identification with the division.

There were some behaviours he would not tolerate. On 1 December he noted in divisional orders that there were reports of members of the division 'wounding (no doubt unintentionally) the religious feelings of the country' by entering churches without removing their head-dress and, more seriously, by pilfering items from a church in the village of Vignacourt. 'The Divisional Commander considers that this is almost incredible ... such an act not only constitutes theft, but also sacrilege', he announced, and added that he relied 'on the good feeling of all under his command' to prevent a repetition. His concern was about both discipline and civil-military relations (something he always took seriously, though personally he felt considerably more affinity for the French than the Belgians). His Catholic chaplain, Father Strickland, reported the episode to the Vatican, and to Nugent's amusement he received a papal medal – 'The Pope seems to have been much touched', he wrote, 'and sent me a silver medal with his blessing!' Some people at home were less impressed when they heard, which provoked a characteristic response: 'I don't mind. I have no sympathy with the narrow-minded outlook of the extremists in the north, any more than I have with the Sinn Feiners'.[46]

107 Brigade

Meanwhile problems with 107 Brigade and the 14th Royal Irish Rifles had persisted, and other observers shared Nugent's concerns about these units. An officer of the 4th Division told Spender that while the 12th Royal Irish Rifles was a first-class battalion, the 14th 'had no officers worth anything and very few NCOs'. Spender himself regarded the 14th as 'our weakest unit' and saw 107 Brigade's soldiers as 'a hot lot [who] require careful handling whilst their present officers would many of them be better for a change'. Crozier believed that, while the 9th and 10th Royal Irish Rifles

[45] ON to CN, 5 Feb. 1916, in *Nugent*, p. 47.
[46] 36 Div. Routine Orders, 1 Dec. 1915 (PRONI, D3835/E/10/4); ON to CN, 19 Jan. and 3 Feb. 1916, in *Nugent*, pp 43–5.

were competent units, the 8th and 15th were not. Farnham thought that of the three brigades 107 Brigade was 'much the worst, and one battalion is hopeless'.[47] The number of courts-martial in 107 Brigade in October and November 1915 had been higher than in the other two brigades combined (26 in 107 Brigade, 24 in 108 and 109).[48] More generally, the unruliness and indiscipline in the brigade spilled over into operational performance, Spender noting in early November that '107 Bde appears to have got rather a bad name for slackness in the trenches, not fear but lack of care in rebuilding and a general tendency to idleness'.[49] Nugent blamed weak leadership and summoned the officers to tell them so. Crozier recalled:

> General Nugent … assembles all the officers of our brigade in a village schoolroom and delivers a strafe, not wholly deserved but very good for us, which I shall always treasure in my mind as the complete example of what can be said by the powerful to the powerless in the shortest space of time possible, consistent with the regulation of words for breathing, in the most offensive, sarcastic and uncompromising manner possible.[50]

An experiment in the autumn of 1915, following the difficult experience of raw New Army divisions at Loos, under which a New Army brigade was exchanged for a regular one in a number of Kitchener divisions, led to 107 Brigade being sent to the 4th Division in early November, 12 Brigade exchanging places with it. Nugent opposed the change but when it was clear that it would happen nevertheless, he arranged for 107 Brigade to be transferred rather than the originally selected 108 Brigade.[51]

When 12 Brigade arrived two of its battalions were sent to 108 and 109 Brigades (2nd Lancashire Fusiliers to the former, 2nd Essex Regiment to the latter), being replaced by the 11th and 14th Royal Irish Rifles. Regular units or not, however, the newcomers were treated just the same as the rest of the division. On 19 November Nugent watched one of 12 Brigade's exercises and was unimpressed.[52] Movement, he told them, had been 'altogether too slow and wanting in vigour'; discipline in the firing line

---

[47] Spender to his wife 1 Nov. and 13 Dec. 1915, 7 Apr. 1916, in *Nugent*, pp 57, 252n; Crozier, *Brass Hat*, p. 77; Farnham to his wife, 26 Oct. 1915 (PRONI, D3975/E/8/1/11).

[48] Bowman, *Irish Regiments*, p. 113.

[49] Spender to his wife, 12 Nov. 1915, in *Nugent*, p. 254n.

[50] Crozier, *Brass Hat*, p. 77.

[51] Farnham to his wife, 30 Oct. 1915 (PRONI, D3975/E/3/2/1).

[52] 36 Div. Routine Orders, memorandum dated 19 Nov. 1915 (PRONI, D3835/E/10/4).

required 'immediate attention', the 1st King's Own (Royal Lancaster Regiment) and 11th Royal Irish Rifles being particularly at fault; the Lancasters' transport was 'very dirty and showed no apparent sign of proper care'. The 14th Rifles were for once praised, for the turn-out of their wagons, but any glow of satisfaction was dispelled when Nugent a few days later visited an exercise being run by Major Ker-Smiley; after five minutes he ordered the battalion back to camp, commenting witheringly that 'he was not out to watch children's play'.[53] Overall 12 Brigade's attachment was not a success. Nugent pressed for the decision to be reversed and in February 107 Brigade returned to the Ulster Division and 12 Brigade went back to the 4th.[54]

Shot at dawn

By common consent 107 Brigade had improved while away but problems, particularly with desertion, remained and with the 36th Division now in the line Nugent decided drastic action was needed. Only four men of the Ulster Division were executed during the war but it is no coincidence that three, all from 107 Brigade, were shot in early 1916, all for desertion. Nugent had previously recommended clemency for soldiers facing the death penalty and would do so again, but in these cases he supported Withycombe's recommendation that the sentences be carried out. On 26 February he told Kitty 'I have to shoot a man of this Division tomorrow morning I'm sorry to say. He deserted from the trenches'.[55] Private James Crozier (18) of the 9th Royal Irish Rifles was executed on 27 February; Privates McCracken (19) and Templeton (20) of the 15th Royal Irish Rifles were shot on 19 March.[56]

The number of executions in the two Irish divisions in France – in addition to the four in the 36th, there were three in the 16th – was lower than in many others. The death penalty was more often carried out in regular than New Army or Territorial formations, but of the other 18 New Army divisions which deployed to France in 1915, nine executed more men than the Ulster Division and two the same number.[57] Military justice being exemplary justice, however, Nugent recommended that these particular sentences be carried out – final confirmation rested with Haig as

[53] Spender to his wife, 28 Nov. 1915, in *Nugent*, p. 38.
[54] Falls, *Ulster Division*, p. 28.
[55] ON to CN, 26 Feb. 1916, in *Nugent*, p. 52.
[56] Julian Putkowski and Julian Sykes, *Shot At Dawn: Executions in World War One by authority of the British Army Act* (2003), pp 67–70, 213–14. The fourth soldier, Pte. Hanna of the 9th R. Irish Fusiliers, was shot for desertion in Nov. 1917.
[57] Putowski and Sykes, *Shot at Dawn*, pp 286–91.

commander-in-chief – to send a stark message: in Crozier's case because 'there have been previous cases of desertion in the 107th Brigade'; in Templeton's because 'there have been recently 3 cases of desertion in the 15th Battalion Royal Irish Rifles for which the extreme penalty was not awarded' and he hoped this would act 'as a deterrent to other men in this unit'; and in McCracken's, similarly, because of 'several recent cases of desertion in the 15th R.I.R'. These soldiers were unlucky, in that their convictions came at a point when the military authorities had run out of patience, but there were aggravating factors also. Crozier, who had two previous convictions for absence, had been on sentry duty in a forward position when he disappeared and when apprehended five days later, on 4 February, was 25 miles behind the lines without his rifle and equipment and admitted immediately to being a deserter. Templeton deserted from the trenches on 20 February and gave himself up 24 hours later six miles to the rear: he had previous convictions for absence and disobeying orders. McCracken had three previous convictions, two for absence.

The executions of Crozier and, to a lesser extent, McCracken have remained controversial, partly because of their age and partly because of the vivid account of Crozier's death left by his CO, Lieutenant-Colonel Frank Crozier (no relation), in his post-war memoir *A Brass Hat in No Man's Land*, using the fictitious name Crocker for the victim. Their ages were in the end not felt to offer sufficient extenuation: as it happened, in February and March 1916 the division buried, in addition to these two youths, at least fifteen more teenaged soldiers killed in the trenches – one, only 16 and who had enlisted under-age, was Samuel Williamson from Crozier's battalion – and would bury several hundred more after 1 July; to a tragic extent it was a very young man's war. Frank Crozier also alleged, however, that a 9th Royal Irish Rifles officer, called Rochdale in *Brass Hat* but in fact 2nd Lieutenant A. J. Annandale, had displayed cowardice at around the same time but was treated less harshly. Annandale seemingly cracked under mortar fire and fled from a forward trench, to be found later asleep in a dug-out in the support lines. He was dismissed from the army in August 1916 as suffering from shell-shock and other underlying medical conditions exacerbated by active service. Some in the battalion thought that if a private soldier had been executed for desertion then so should he. The circumstances of the Annandale case seem, however, to have been objectively different. One should also, perhaps, treat Frank Crozier's post-war account with caution. He actively sought James Crozier's execution, his evidence at the court-martial that the prisoner was a shirker and 'of no fighting value' probably being decisive in securing both conviction and sentence. In retrospect he may have been uncomfortable about his role and seeking to deflect attention from it.[58]

Politics

By early 1916 political tensions in Nugent's relationships within the division and outside it were emerging. He had, as the Home Rule crisis had demonstrated, little in common with the largely Belfast-based unionist leadership, as he explained to Kitty in February 1916:

> You see, people in the north of Ireland don't really know anything about me, nor of the Nugent family. We are not really a N of Ireland family and as a matter of fact, the Nugents were for James and against William in the days when the North was founding itself. All our family associations lie in the midlands of Ireland and it is merely a geographical accident that we live inside Ulster.

He was coming increasingly to the view that a compromise settlement should be accepted by Ulster unionism in exchange for full nationalist support for the war effort, including conscription.[59] Unionists like Spender of course felt differently. Their contrasting reactions to a speech by John Redmond in November 1915 calling for nationalists and unionists to fight side by side illustrate the point. Nugent thought the speech a good one and that Carson should respond in kind; Spender was alarmed and indignant and saw it as a trap to lure Ulster into a Home Rule settlement. He reacted similarly to a rumour in late 1915 that the 16th and 36th Divisions were to be brigaded together.[60] Spender was increasingly suspicious of Nugent's politics, which he reported back to Carson and Craig through his wife. In late November, for example, he warned that 'Gen N[ugent] is not at all keen about a separate Ulster and would willingly compromise with the Nationalist party if it meant support by the Govt. There is no fervour about his faith in this respect and he will want watching later after the war. I think

[58] Crozier, *Brass Hat*, pp 96–100. For careful analyses of the context of these executions see Bowman, *Irish Regiments*, pp 116–18; Grayson, *Belfast Boys*, pp 68–71; and, for Crozier, Cathryn Corns and John Hughes-Wilson, *Blindfold and Alone: British Military Executions in the Great War* (2002), pp 304–07; Charles Messenger, *Broken Sword: The Tumultuous Life of General Frank Crozier 1879–1937* (2013), pp 62–3. Deaths of teenaged soldiers calculated from Commonwealth War Graves Commission online registers.

[59] ON to CN, 18 Feb. 1916, in *Nugent*, p. 48.

[60] Spender to his wife, 25 Nov. and 14 Dec. 1915, ON to CN, 3 Dec. 1915, in *Nugent*, pp 37–41.

Sir E[dward] ought to know this'.[61] Nugent was aware of this – in December Spender noted that he 'has once or twice cut short his conversation when I am there showing that our views in relation to Ulster ideals do not coincide and that he knows that I write freely to Sir Edward about them' – and was even more guarded and prickly with Spender as a result.[62] But Nugent's differences were not only with him. In late 1915 he had had a heated political disagreement with Ricardo, Pakenham and (especially) Leitrim which strained relations for several weeks, despite the efforts of Kitty and Lady Leitrim to mend fences from a distance.[63]

A particular episode in February and March 1916 illustrates Nugent's political views. This involved a dispute between two Ulster unionist ladies' committees – the Ulster Women's Unionist Council Gift Fund in Belfast, run by the formidable Lady Richardson, and its offshoot in London, headed by the Duchess of Abercorn, of which both Kitty and Lily Spender were members – and the Irish Women's Association (IWA), avowedly non-political but led by the Catholic Lady MacDonnell and with John Redmond's wife as an active member, over which should support Ulster Division prisoners of war. The Belfast committee were strongly opposed to any IWA involvement and wrote to Nugent to protest. This provoked a blunt response: 'I wrote back quite straight and said I did not regard Lady MacD's act as "interference" but as a kindly act and that I would welcome any such acts from whatever source they came and I deprecated any suggestion of unworthy motives for any act of kindness done to prisoners of war. I hope they liked it'.[64] Nugent and Spender, anxious to prevent a row between the division and the committee members (and their politician husbands), issued a stream of advice to their wives and a compromise was eventually reached, but Nugent was left deeply irritated. 'What does it matter so long as they are doing good whether a Committee is composed of Nationalists or Unionists', he wrote, 'Why should we out here be asked to take sides in such a dispute. D—n politics while the war lasts and at all times in the Army'.[65]

There were lighter moments, however. In December 1915 Nugent arranged for the purchase of a film projector and screen for the division, the £200 cost to be recouped by admission charges as it toured the different

[61] Spender to his wife, 28 Nov. 1915, in *Nugent*, p. 38.

[62] Spender to his wife, 25 Nov. 1915, in *Nugent*, p. 252n.

[63] See, for example, ON to CN, 1 Nov. 1916, in *Nugent*, p. 261n. Ricardo commanded the 9th R. Inniskilling Fusiliers and Pakenham the 11th R. Irish Rifles; Leitrim was 2ic of the 11th R. Inniskilling Fusiliers.

[64] ON to CN, 25 Mar. 1915, in *Nugent*, pp 55–6.

[65] ON to CN, 25 Feb. 1916, in *Nugent*, p. 51.

units. It proved extremely popular and Nugent had a private viewing at the beginning of February, telling Kitty, 'I saw the Ulster Review, one of the principal episodes depicted is my kissing the King's hand at the end. I come out very well and quite overshadow the King as I am nearest the camera'. The divisional concert party, the Merry Mauves (or Follies), was also in great demand.[66]

Recruitment

Meanwhile the whole question of Irish recruitment cast a deepening shadow. From the time he was appointed Nugent was aware of the difficulties the Irish divisions would face once they began sustaining heavy casualties, given falling recruitment rates in Ireland, and his initial conversation with Carson in September 1915 had focused on the issue.[67] It was the unevenness of Irish recruiting as well as the total numbers that posed such acute problems. An estimated 210,000 Irishmen, excluding enlistments in Britain or the Dominions, served in the British armed forces during the war: 21,000 regular soldiers in August 1914, along with 5,000 sailors and 2,000 officers, were joined on mobilisation by 30,000 reservists, and during the war a further 134,000 men enlisted in the army (along with 10,000 recruits to the navy and RAF and about 4,000 direct commissions). Significant though the total was, however, it represented enlistment levels proportionally much lower than in the rest of the United Kingdom; in 1914–15 Irish enlistment rates were less than a third of those in Britain, even before the introduction there of compulsory service, and from 1916 would fall away further. In the 17 months from August 1914 to December 1915, for example, around 90,000 men enlisted in the army in Ireland; in the remaining 34 months of the war, without conscription, only 44,000 more joined up.[68] The slump predated the Easter rising, often blamed for the collapse of recruitment across much of the country.

The recruiting pattern reflected various factors. Political allegiance was one, and it was to this that unionist politicians attributed the fact that Irish

[66] ON to CN, 5 Feb. 1916, in *Nugent*, p. 46; Falls, *Ulster Division*, p. 137.
[67] Carson to Nugent, 23 Sep. 1915, in *Nugent*, p. 30.
[68] Between August 1914 and December 1915 about 8% of Ireland's male population aged 15–49 enlisted (the equivalent rates for England and Wales and Scotland respectively were 24% and 27%); from Jan. 1916 to the end of the war the percentage in Ireland fell to less than 4% (in England and Wales and Scotland, underpinned by conscription, the rates were respectively 22% and 15%). See Keith Jeffery, *Ireland and the Great War* (2000), pp 5–9; Fitzpatrick, 'Logic of collective sacrifice', pp 1,017–30; Nicholas Perry, 'Nationality in the Irish infantry regiments in the First World War', *War and Society*, 12:1 (1994), p. 69.

Protestants – the majority of whom lived in Ulster and most of whom were unionist – were disproportionately represented, providing, according to one estimate, around 45% of recruits despite comprising only 25% of the island's population. There was, however, no simple correlation between political or religious affiliation and willingness to serve. After the initial surge recruiting fell away in unionist areas almost as markedly as nationalist ones: indeed, more Catholics than Protestants enlisted in Ulster in 1915. Social and economic factors were of central importance, with men of all religious denominations being more likely to enlist in the industrialised north than elsewhere in the country; throughout Ireland urban workers were more likely to enlist than agricultural ones; and membership of collective organisations like the Ulster or National Volunteers or the Orange Order seems to have been a positive factor in individuals' willingness to enlist.[69]

Whatever the underlying drivers, the shortage of recruits was already apparent by late 1915. Soon after arriving in France Nugent convened a conference of COs to consider what more could be done to stimulate recruiting, following which various measures were taken, including a post-card writing campaign to potential recruits by men in the division. In December the *Belfast Newsletter* published an appeal from Nugent to those at home 'to keep us up to our numbers in trained men' and to join the division's reserve units.[70] These steps had little effect, and like most senior officers Nugent favoured the introduction of conscription in Ireland. In April 1916 he told Carson that 'this Division cannot exist unless we do [have conscription] … it would be so bad for the future if there were 2 parties in the north of Ireland, those who gave their sons or husbands and the cowards who lurked at home, that if we must suffer, do let us all suffer together and so have a common bond of union'.[71] On 27 May the CIGS, Sir William Robertson, called in on his way to Paris to meet Joffre. Their discussion alarmed Nugent sufficiently to write to Carson about the 'inconceivable' possibility of the Ulster Division being broken up:

> In discipline and physique it is superior to any Division I have seen out here, Regular or New. It is Ulster to the backbone, and full of esprit de corps, an all Ulster unit … I hate asking you to interest

[69] Patrick Callan, 'Recruiting for the British Army in Ireland during the First World War', *Irish Sword*, 66 (Summer 1987), pp 42–56; Fitzpatrick, 'Logic of collective sacrifice', pp 1,017–30.

[70] *Belfast Newsletter*, 18 Nov. and 31 Dec. 1915.

[71] ON to CN, 13 Apr. 1916, in *Nugent*, pp 63, 256n.

yourself in this question, but for the sake of the Division and the Province which raised them, I hope you may be able to ascertain whether the project is really being considered and quash it if it is.[72]

Carson raised the issue with Robertson, who assured him on 7 June that there was no such intention but noted that 'there was some difficulty about the provision of drafts', which the Adjutant-General, Sir Nevil Macready, hoped to meet Carson to discuss. His and Macready's attempts to engineer a joint meeting with Carson and Redmond in June failed, however, there being more pressing political matters preoccupying them.[73]

The Easter Rising

The most dramatic development in Ireland in 1916 was the Easter Rising. Nugent was in England on leave during the fighting in Dublin from 24–29 April and his immediate reactions are not reflected in his correspondence. Like many unionists, however, he saw it as the work of a lunatic fringe 'confined to the worst elements of Sinn Feiners and Dublin roughs' and rejected by most moderate nationalists. He put much of the blame on Chief Secretary Birrell's irresolute (in Nugent's view) administration and regarded the insurrection as an argument for firmness rather than conciliation, describing Redmond's protests in parliament over the executions of rebel leaders as 'the coolest piece of cynical impertinence I have heard for a long time'. He noted with satisfaction the involvement of troops from his reserve brigade in suppressing the Rising (1,000 men of the Belfast-based 15 Reserve Brigade arrived in Dublin on Easter Monday), and felt as far as the rebels were concerned 'a little more shooting wouldn't do them any harm'.[74] The far-reaching political consequences were no more immediately apparent to him than they were to most others.

By this stage Kitty and the girls had moved to rented accommodation in London (St George was away at Eton) so as to be close at hand when Nugent came home on leave. His higher pay as a major-general made this affordable and they spent the next two years moving between addresses in London and Hampshire. In addition to her work on the Ulster Women's Committee Kitty was also involved in helping with wounded soldiers. The family returned regularly to Ireland, however, and in May Nugent sought to reassure her about going home that summer. Cavan, he told her, had been largely unaffected by the rebellion and the anxieties of Neills, the

[72] Ian Colvin, *The Life of Lord Carson* (1934), iii, pp 181–2.
[73] Robertson to Carson, 7 June 1916 (PRONI, D1507/A/17/10).
[74] ON to CN, 10, 14 and 26 May, 8 June 1916, in *Nugent*, pp 62, 64, 66–7, 73.

steward at Farren Connell, were to be expected from an elderly northerner who feared that southern Catholics were all 'hankering to go out and kill a protestant'. But he acknowledged Kitty's concerns by offering to write to the local resident magistrate for advice – 'I would not for the world that you should go home and feel a strain all the time'.[75]

Trench warfare

Meanwhile trench warfare intensified. New equipment was arriving – Lewis guns were distributed to battalions in early 1916, as were steel helmets – while organisational changes were almost continuous. Brigade machine-gun companies were formed in January, and brigade trench mortar batteries in April; the divisional cyclist company disappeared in May and the artillery was restructured (from three brigades of 18-pdrs and one of 4.5in. howitzers, to three 'mixed' brigades each of three 18-pdr and one howitzer batteries, and one of three 18-pdr batteries only); and the attached cavalry squadron was removed in June. In early March, as divisions 'squeezed up' to make room for new formations in preparation for the forthcoming offensive, the Ulster Division came under command of General Rawlinson's Fourth Army and shifted its boundary southward to take in Thiepval Wood, south of the Ancre.

It was from the wood that on the night of 7/8 May the 9th Royal Inniskilling Fusiliers carried out the division's first full-scale raid. The 90-strong raiding party, led by Major John Peacocke, had undergone extensive rehearsals beforehand and Nugent took a close interest, visiting the Inniskillings on the day to wish them luck: 'It has all been very carefully rehearsed and all the plans were settled before I came home the other day but I would not allow it to be carried out in my absence in case of unforeseen contingencies happening'.[76]

In the event unforeseen contingencies did happen. After dark the party moved into No Man's Land but by chance the Germans simultaneously mounted a raid of their own against the left of the 32nd Division, a few hundred yards to the south. Ricardo and Peacocke decided to go ahead nevertheless and at midnight the raiders stormed the German front-line trench. There was a brisk fight but the Inniskillings' casualties were light and they believed they inflicted heavy losses, bombing several dug-outs. No prisoners were taken, however, and on the way back the party was trapped in a sunken road by heavy shelling and suffered around 30 casualties, including nine dead. Meanwhile, on the right, the 10th Royal Inniskilling

---

[75] ON to CN, 26 May 1916, in *Nugent*, pp 66–7.
[76] ON to CN, 8 May 1916, in *Nugent*, p. 60.

Fusiliers helped repel the German raid on the 2nd Dorset Regiment. The shelling here too was intense, and while eventually the Germans were driven off with loss, the Dorsets suffered 60 casualties and the 10th Inniskillings almost 80, including 19 killed. The following morning Nugent visited Thiepval Wood:

> The wood is tremendously battered and big trees are lying about everywhere, trenches flattened out and wire cut to pieces. A good few German dead lying about outside. It was the biggest small affair we have had hitherto and the Division did very well indeed. What a contrast between such a life and the conditions of only 4 days ago when I was with you.[77]

There followed on 5 June a raid by the 12th Royal Irish Rifles on a German outpost, Railway Sap, in the Ancre valley. The raiding party broke into the German trenches and, while again no prisoners were taken, a possible mine-shaft heading for the British lines was blown in, as were a number of dug-outs; one was reported to be an officer's and when Nugent asked how it had been identified 'the answer was it was hung with highly improper photographs'. A German retaliatory raid a few nights later on William Redan, a post opposite Railway Sap, was successfully driven off, though the 15th Royal Irish Rifles suffered 65 casualties.[78] Proactive trench warfare was becoming costlier and some were already wondering whether the gains were commensurate. Spender described the 12th Rifles' raid as 'a very fine performance', but added 'the enemy bolted into a tunnel and I'm afraid we suffered much more than he did … I am very doubtful if these minor exploits do us much good, but there is a mad fashion for them'.[79] The value or otherwise of raiding would become an increasing issue later in the year.

The blood-letting was still not confined to France. On the morning of 8 May, as Ricardo's men made their final preparations, Eamonn Ceannt, Con Colbert, Sean Heuston and Michael Mallin were shot by firing squad in Kilmainham Jail; the following morning, as Nugent toured his battered trenches and the dead of the 9th and 10th Royal Inniskilling Fusiliers were being brought to the rear, Thomas Kent was executed in Cork. Eight other rebel leaders, including Patrick Pearse, were already dead and two more would follow. The political divide in Ireland was deepening.

[77] ON to CN, 9 May 1916, in *Nugent*, p. 62.
[78] 12th Rifles war diary (TNA, WO95/2506); ON to CN, 6 June 1916, in *Nugent*, p. 71.
[79] Spender to his wife, 6 June 1916 (PRONI, D1633/1/1/297).

The Lloyd George negotiations

It was for that reason that, between May and July 1916, Lloyd George led negotiations with Redmond on one hand and Carson and Craig on the other to try to secure a political settlement, negotiations that would impact on Nugent and others in the division in a directly personal way. Lloyd George's proposal was based on the near-immediate introduction of Home Rule for 26 counties and the exclusion of the six north-eastern counties, an idea first mooted in 1914. He deliberately left vague the period of Ulster's exclusion, allowing nationalists to believe it to be only for the duration of the war and unionists that it would be permanent, or at the very least a matter for fresh negotiations when peace came. Either way, Cavan, Monaghan and Donegal would not be part of the excluded area. The MPs and peers in the Ulster Division, including Farnham, were summoned home in early June for consultations, at which point it became clear that Carson and Craig would support the deal. Farnham at once reported to Nugent and Spender 'the damnable position' in which the unionists of the three counties had been placed, asking bitterly 'what becomes of the Covenant?'[80] On 8 June Nugent summed up the position: 'it is Craig and the politicians of Belfast who want now to cut out those 3 counties because they realise as Devlin [Joe Devlin, nationalist MP in Belfast] does that if they are included in Ulster, there is a very good chance of a Nationalist majority in Ulster which would certainly not help the solution of the Irish Question'.[81]

Spender, despite his close relationship with Carson, reacted furiously to the news of 'this betrayal' – 'I could not have believed it would have been possible that many whom we know would have been ready to sacrifice their pledged word'. Others in the division were equally outraged. Ricardo, who was in England on leave, confronted Craig and told him that he had gone mad. Lord Leitrim, in hospital and unable to support Farnham in person at the UUC meeting, was said to be 'fretting his heart out' and demanding that Carson explain to the division 'why this course had to be followed'. Colonel Blacker, from County Armagh, while believing personally that the proposed deal was the least worst option, noted on 17 June that in the 9th Royal Irish Fusiliers opinion 'is, from what I hear, strongly against, as we

---

[80] Farnham to Spender, n.d. but before 12 June 1916 (PRONI, D1295/7/1). For serving officer MPs and parliament see Matthew Johnson, 'Leading from the front: the 'Service Members' in Parliament, the armed forces, and British politics during the Great War', *English Historical Review*, 130:544 (June 2013), pp 613–45.

[81] ON to CN, 8 June 1916, in *Nugent*, p. 73.

have Cavan and Monaghan men'.[82] Nugent himself was dismayed but unsurprised, telling Spender that he had never trusted 'the Belfast people who were now looking forward to their own little dung-heap'. He neither knew nor cared about the political pressure the Ulster unionists were under to agree or risk losing parliamentary and public support in Britain, Lloyd George having stressed heavily to them the demands for an Irish settlement coming from MPs, the Dominions and America.[83] Nugent told Kitty on 9 June that

> the Belfast people won't hesitate to chuck us over. I see Arthur spoke against excluding Cavan but what is the use of talking about it. It won't stop it if the Belfast people want us to be handed over to save themselves. The only thing that is certain is that it will not satisfy the nationalists.[84]

His anger, exacerbated by the recruiting issue, focused particularly on Craig as he fumed 'I hear James Craig told Colonel Ricardo that he had no time to talk about recruiting, that the H[ome] R[ule] question must be settled first. He ought to be shot if that is true'. On 10 June he joked to Kitty that, with immediate Home Rule on the table, 'you and I may as well join the Sinn Feiners at once'.[85]

For Nugent and his fellow unionists in the three 'abandoned' counties the writing was now unequivocally on the wall as to the political future. The episode reinforced his essentially southern unionist opinions and his alienation from the Ulster unionist leadership, other than Carson, was much increased. On 12 June the UUC voted in principle to accept the Lloyd George offer, with apparent unanimity but after bitter debate. The issue of Ireland's future and Ulster's place in it was, however, still unresolved when the Ulster Division launched its most famous attack.

[82] Spender to his wife, 3 June 1916, in *Nugent*, p. 69; Ricardo to Hugh de Fellenberg Montgomery, 11 Apr. 1920 (PRONI, D627/435/28); Blacker letters, Blacker to his wife, 17 June 1916 (website: https://blackersletters.com).

[83] Spender to his wife, 3 June 1916 (PRONI, D1633/1/1/293); Thomas Hennessey, *Dividing Ireland: World War 1 and Partition* (1998), pp 152–5.

[84] ON to CN, 9 June 1916, in *Nugent*, pp 73–4.

[85] ON to CN, 6 and 10 June 1916, in *Nugent*, pp 72, 74.

5

Sacrifice on the Somme
Operational failure, reputational triumph, July 1916

Introduction

The Ulster Division's capture of the Schwaben Redoubt on 1 July 1916, its most celebrated battle, was a genuinely impressive feat of arms, and one that became a defining experience of the Ulster Protestant unionist tradition in the twentieth century. Although the assault ended in a heavy defeat the division's reputation had been made.

The tendency, unsurprisingly given the action's iconic status, is to see its achievement in isolation, but its attack was part of an integrated corps-level operation to capture an important objective, the central section of the Pozieres-Serre ridge. This involved three divisions and 36 infantry battalions, supported by 256 guns; in all around 58,000 men, of whom over 9,000 would become casualties.[1] The generals directly concerned – the commander of X Corps, Lieutenant-General Sir Thomas Morland, and his three divisional commanders, Nugent, Rycroft of the 32nd Division and Perceval of the 49th – and their staffs worked hard to develop a plan they hoped and expected to succeed. Ultimately the outcome of 1 July was determined by the failure of the over-stretched artillery to suppress the German defences, exacerbated by the employment of excessively rigid infantry tactics along parts of the front and the absence of effective battlefield communications. Even so, the result in X Corps's sector was not inevitable. There were important decisions, particularly around the commitment of reserves, that these four men had to take under extreme pressure which (with the benefit of hindsight), had they been different, might have influenced the outcome. The story of the attack has been told in several detailed accounts.[2] The focus of this chapter is instead on the key

---

[1] *OH*, 1916, i, pp 398, 421.
[2] See, especially, Falls, *Ulster Division*, pp 41–63; also Philip Orr, *The Road to the Somme* (1987), pp 140–202; David Truesdale and David Orr, *'Ulster Will Fight …', Vol 2: The 36th (Ulster) Division from Formation to the Armistice* (2016), pp 226–46.

decisions Nugent and other senior officers had to make, during both the planning of the assault and its execution.

Fourth Army plan

The decision for an Anglo-French offensive on the Somme was taken at a meeting between Joffre and Haig on 14 February 1916. The opening of the German attack on Verdun a week later meant that the BEF's share would be proportionately greater than originally intended and by the end of March Henry Rawlinson, the Fourth Army commander, and his chief of staff Archie Montgomery (whose County Tyrone family Nugent knew well) had devised a two-stage 'bite and hold' operation. This involved an initial attack by ten divisions on a front of 20,000 yards to capture the German First Position - the German defences on the Somme in July 1916 consisting of a First and a Second Position, with a third in construction behind them - and then, after a pause of 72 hours or so, a further advance to capture the Second Position between Serre and Pozieres.[3]

X Corps's commander, Thomas Morland, was a capable officer whom Nugent knew of old: in fact he, Morland and Rawlinson had all joined the KRRC within 12 months of each other in 1883–4, a unique regimental line-up on 1 July. The corps faced a challenging task. The Germans regarded the ridge between Pozieres and the Ancre valley as defensively critical and the fortifications around Thiepval were among the strongest on the entire front. The topography meant that the First and Second Positions here ran close together, only some 600 yards apart in places. Morland's intention was to use the 32nd and 36th Divisions to capture the First Position on the high ground south of the Ancre before halting to prepare the assault on the Second Position, and Nugent and his staff began planning accordingly; as early as 23 March he 'spent the morning crawling about as near as I could get to the Germans, reconnoitring ground over which we may eventually have to attack'.[4] When Haig saw Rawlinson's plan, however, he objected to what he perceived as its lack of ambition: he wanted the opening assault to aim for a complete breakthrough of the German lines, or at least to have that option if the initial stages went well. In mid-April Rawlinson reluctantly produced a revised version, which now envisaged capturing the Second Position along much of the front in the opening assault, coupled with a widening of the attack frontage. This significantly extended the depth of the attack without increasing the

---

[3] Robin Prior and Trevor Wilson, *Command on the Western Front: The Military Career of Sir Henry Rawlinson 1914–18* (1992), pp 141–6.
[4] ON to CN, 23 Mar. 1916, in *Nugent*, p. 55.

artillery available to support it, and this dilution of the artillery's impact would have disastrous operational consequences.[5] The new plan, as one scholar has put it, was 'not to be bite and hold, but rush and hope'.[6]

The Corps plan

On 17 April Morland held an important conference with Nugent, Rycroft and Perceval to consider the revised Fourth Army plan, outlined to him and the other corps commanders by Rawlinson the previous day.[7] Nugent was accompanied by his new GSO1, Lieutenant-Colonel Otley Place: once operational planning had begun in earnest he could no longer put off making a change and on 4 April the unfortunate Alick Russell had left for a staff appointment at home. Nugent told Kitty 'I was really sorry for him. He felt it so much and said when he left that he was sorry he had failed me … I would not say 'I'm so sorry you have become ungummed' when you meet him'.[8] Place, a 40-year-old Royal Engineer officer, Staff College graduate and holder of the DSO from South Africa, joined on promotion from the staff of the 19th Division. 'I hope he will be a success', Nugent wrote. In fact he turned out to be a considerable success, remaining as, effectively, Nugent's chief of staff until his capture in March 1918 (only one GOC/GSO1partnership in a New Army division lasted longer than their 23 months together, the 26 months of Hickie and Jackson in the 16th Division). Cyril Falls summarised Place's attributes:

> As a staff officer he was far more than merely able and efficient. His sympathy and imagination enabled him to grasp all points of view, and to understand those which were different to his own. He never seemed to require, as do so many men engaged on difficult tasks, an hour free from interruption, but could switch his mind on to each new problem presented to him, and return to his own where he had left it.[9]

[5] Prior and Wilson, *Command on the Western Front*, pp 146–51; J. P. Harris, *Douglas Haig and the First World War* (2008), pp 220–23; Rodney Atwood, *General Lord Rawlinson: From Tragedy to Triumph* (2018), pp 133–42.
[6] William Philpott, *Bloody Victory: The Sacrifice on the Somme and the Making of the Twentieth Century* (2009), p. 119.
[7] 'Notes on Conference held at [X] Corps Headquarters on 17th April 1916' (TNA, WO95/850).
[8] ON to CN, 4 Apr. 1916, in *Nugent*, p. 56. 'Ungummed' was a term, borrowed from the French, for being dismissed.
[9] Falls, *Ulster Division*, p. 223.

His skills were needed immediately as Morland and his subordinates pondered a difficult operation. The Germans had embedded a series of mutually-supporting strongpoints in their defences opposite X Corps: these included the Leipzig Redoubt, Wunderwerk and Thiepval village facing the 32nd Division, the Schwaben Redoubt and St Pierre Divion opposite the Ulster Division, and, north of the Ancre, the Beaucourt Redoubt, able to enfilade from the high ground there any assault south of the river.

On the Ulster Division's front, the German First Position comprised three lines of trenches stretching up onto Thiepval ridge – a front-line trench, with a support trench immediately behind, known together to the British as the A line, and 500 yards behind them a reserve trench, called the B line. About 700 yards beyond the B line, and between it and the Second Position, was an intermediate trench-line, referred to as the C line (that part of it running down to the Ancre valley being also known as the Hansa line). Connecting the B and C lines on top of the ridge were two communication trenches, forming a rough triangle 400 yards wide and 800 yards deep: this had been wired-in and fortified with multiple machine-gun posts and deep dugouts to create the formidable Schwaben Redoubt. And 600 yards beyond the C line, at the rear edge of the ridge, was the front trench of the Second Position, called the D line, which at its closest point was about 2,500 yards from Thiepval Wood.

Morland's staff had prepared for the conference an updated version of the corps plan. The 32nd and 36th would still be the right and left assault divisions with the 49th in reserve.[10] The Ulster Division's final objective, however, was now considerably more distant, a 1,500-yard section of the D line south of the Ancre; it also had a subsidiary task, a limited attack north of the river towards Beaucourt station, to protect both its own flank and that of the 29th Division to the north. Similarly, the 32nd's objective had become the D line around Mouquet Farm, several hundred yards beyond Thiepval village. Neither Morland nor his divisional commanders were happy with objectives this deep but they had no alternative, given Rawlinson's directive, but to plan to reach them in a single attack. They initially considered leap-frogging one wave through another but eventually concluded that it would be less disruptive if the first-wave battalions pressed on all the way to the C line, the second-wave units occupying the captured trenches behind them; the reserve brigades of the 32nd and 36th Divisions would then attack the final objective, the D line. Within days Morland was

[10] The 49th was earmarked, in the event of a major success, to form part of an exploitation force under General Gough.

able to send Rawlinson an amended plan.[11] When doing so he made a final plea for a halt on the C line to check progress and allow patrols to probe forward, but Rawlinson again insisted that the attack on the D line be mounted as part of one continuous forward movement.

At corps and divisional level the techniques of operational planning and staff-work were still developing in 1916.[12] Morland had also forwarded to Rawlinson the plans of the 32nd and 36th Divisions which he acknowledged varied 'both in the depth to which it is proposed to penetrate the hostile positions in one effort and in the time it is calculated will be required to reach the enemy's different lines of defence'; coordinating them, he added, needed Fourth Army's confirmation of the overall approach. This method of requiring subordinate headquarters to develop detailed plans and then trying to align them was, as a X Corps staff officer later accepted, a recipe for nugatory effort:

> [A] very great deal of extra work was thrown on div and bde staffs by the practice which was at its worst then of asking for plans and then trying to coordinate them at Corps HQ and Army HQ, with the result that they were often sent back to be done again. I think that the 36th Division plan was made three times.[13]

The result was that in mid-May, only weeks before the opening of the offensive, the separately-developed plans of the 36th and 32nd Divisions were incompatible. Rycroft intended a conventional frontal assault on Thiepval and wanted the Ulster Division to attack immediately alongside to provide support. Nugent, by contrast, wished to make a relatively narrow thrust on either side of the Ancre valley, enveloping the Schwaben Redoubt from the north. This would leave a gap between the two divisions and Rycroft was not happy. On 13 May Nugent wrote bluntly to X Corps: 'As Corps Headquarters will eventually have to coordinate the plans of attack of the 32nd and 36th Divisions, it may be useful to the Corps Commander if the reasons for the plan of attack prepared for the 36th Division are stated in detail'.[14] He outlined the reasons for his preferred approach, including the protection it would provide from the enfilading machine-guns in Thiepval. How Nugent's plan would have fared in reality is a moot point, given the damage caused on the day by the defenders of St Pierre Divion and Beaucourt Redoubt, both commanding the Ancre valley, but in the end

[11] Morland memorandum to Fourth Army (GS 187/2/4), Apr. 1916 (no day given, but sent in the last week of April) (TNA, WO95/850).
[12] Simpson, *Directing Operations*, pp 25–36.
[13] Col. S. J. P. Scobell to Edmonds 23 June 1930 (TNA, CAB45/191).
[14] Nugent to X Corps G, 13 May 1916 (TNA, WO95/2491).

Morland supported Rycroft and the Ulster Division plan had to be re-done. The prediction about the Thiepval machine-guns would prove all too accurate.

There were plenty of teething problems, therefore, in the planning process. The Army Group commander, Haig, imposed on the Army commander, Rawlinson, a plan he did not believe in. Rawlinson in his turn refused to modify that plan to take account of the particular problems facing Morland, attacking a key objective. Morland failed to provide his divisional commanders with sufficiently detailed guidance to enable them to produce mutually supporting plans of their own. And within the Ulster Division, as will be seen, Nugent would make controversial decisions about his own command arrangements impacting on his brigadiers and battalion COs. The Somme was a steep learning experience for commanders at every level.

Ulster Division plan

The final divisional plan, issued on 16 June, was devised by Nugent, Place, Comyn and Brock in the small chateau of Hedauville, five miles behind the line. One particular aspect of the preparations demonstrated the profound changes in military technology in the course of Nugent's career. On 22 May he told Kitty:

> I have thought for a long time that I would like to know much more of the German lines than I do, so today I went over them in an aeroplane ... The actual flying was nothing. I confess to being in a blue funk when I got into the machine and for the first minute while we were rising, afterwards I got so interested I never thought about being in the air. We went up to 7000 feet and we cruised up and down the line. I am sure every Divisional General ought to go up and see his own lines and the German lines in front of him ... The most interesting thing is to note how we show ourselves and the Germans seem to conceal everything. The roads behind our lines were full of motors, and men and constant movement whereas in the German area one could see no sign of anyone moving.[15]

Almost certainly he was flying in a BE2c aircraft belonging to 4 Squadron RFC, attached to X Corps. There was one near mishap. Nugent at one point waved the pilot towards Thiepval Wood, which he wanted to see from the air, but failed to tell him to turn back until 'I suddenly realised we were well behind the German lines and still going on, I frantically waved to him

[15] ON to CN, 22 May 1916, in *Nugent*, p. 65.

to turn and retreated back over our lines'. On Nugent's recommendation Morland went up a few days later himself, as did members of Nugent's staff. They could do so because the allies at this point enjoyed air superiority over the Somme: these flights would have been much riskier a few weeks later as the Germans deployed new fighters (including the famous Albatros DI) piloted by men like Boelke and von Richthofen to contest control of the sky.[16]

The Ulster Division's eventual plan of attack differed considerably from Nugent's original conception. On 1 July the division would open its attack south of the Ancre with two brigades, their objective the C line on top of the ridge, including the Schwaben Redoubt. 109 Brigade on the right, next to the 32nd Division, would have two battalions in its leading wave (9th Royal Inniskilling Fusiliers on the right, 10th Royal Inniskilling Fusiliers on the left) and two in support (11th Royal Inniskilling Fusiliers right, 14th Royal Irish Rifles left). 108 Brigade on its left would advance south of the Ancre with two battalions in the first wave (11th Royal Irish Rifles right, 13th Royal Irish Rifles left) and one in the second (15th Royal Irish Rifles, attached from 107 Brigade). There was then a gap of about half a mile across the Ancre valley where no attack would be mounted, due to insufficient troops and the difficulties of the ground. North of the Ancre the other two battalions of 108 Brigade, the 9th Royal Irish Fusiliers and 12th Royal Irish Rifles, would attack side by side in a more or less self-contained operation to clear the northern slopes of the Ancre valley as far as Beaucourt station. Once the C line was taken 107 Brigade, with the 8th, 9th and 10th Royal Irish Rifles, would advance to capture the D line.

Nugent was well aware of the threat from the powerful German defences and did what he could to reduce it. He decided to push his leading waves into No Man's Land before zero to enable them to rush the German trenches as soon as the barrage lifted. He was not alone: a brigade of the 32nd Division did the same and there were other examples elsewhere, but the tactic proved particularly successful here. He arranged for smoke-screens to mask the German positions in the Ancre valley, where the machine-guns in St Pierre Divion and Beaucourt Redoubt posed a particular threat. He remained very concerned about Thiepval and the lack of damage being done to its defences by the opening bombardment and asked for additional concentrations of artillery on the village in the days before the attack, to little effect.

---

[16] James Corum, 'Air war over the Somme', in Matthias Strohn (ed.), *The Battle of the Somme* (2016), pp 84–9; Peter Hart, *Somme Success: The Royal Flying Corps and the Battle of the Somme 1916* (2001), pp 157–83.

In support the division had its four artillery brigades, comprising 48 18-pdr field guns and twelve 4.5-in. howitzers, supplemented by an artillery brigade from the 49th Division and a French 'groupe' of twelve 75mm guns from the 20th Artillery Regiment. In addition, it had its share of the 80 heavy guns X Corps had available, as well as its three Stokes mortar batteries and an attached battery of medium and heavy mortars.[17] The true creeping barrage had yet to be introduced by the British and on 1 July the screen of shells in front of the infantry would move forward in a series of lifts. The final intense bombardment would shift at 7.30am from the German front-line trench onto the support line immediately behind; three minutes later it would advance onto the B line. The infantry had 15 minutes to get there before the barrage lifted again, onto the C line. There the shelling would remain for an hour before moving to the D line, where it would rest for a further 80 minutes before, at 10.08, lifting again to form a defensive screen 300 yards beyond the D line. The artillery programme would drive, and at a crucial stage delay, the speed of the division's advance, the attacking infantry having almost no control over it.

Training

Meanwhile training for the Big Push had begun in earnest. This was centred on Clairfaye Farm, in the corps rear area about seven miles behind the front, where a replica of the trenches the division would attack had been laid out. Each brigade in turn came out of the line for rehearsals: 107 Brigade in late April and early May, with a brief 'refresher' in late June; 109 Brigade for much of May; and 108 Brigade in the first half of June. Most battalions practised their attacks at least a dozen times, as well as taking part in brigade and divisional exercises and watching demonstrations of the use of Stokes mortars, air-ground cooperation and the consolidation of captured trenches. Other divisions were doing the same, but as ever Nugent injected intensity:

> A month before the attack I had dug an exact plan of the German trenches, on the full size scale, taken from aeroplane photos, on ground behind our lines and the battalions and Brigades were practised day after day in going over them. Every company and every man always went to the exact same part every day until they were so drilled into the exact piece of the programme each man was expected to carry out that they went instinctively when in the attack to where they had been trained to go.[18]

[17] *OH*, 1916, i, p. 398; Falls, *Ulster Division*, pp 46–7.
[18] ON to CN, 11 July 1916, in *Nugent*, p. 89.

No matter how thorough the training, however, it could not replicate the reality the assaulting battalions would encounter. 'It all seems so simple above ground', wrote an officer of the 14th Royal Irish Rifles presciently in May, 'I don't think we quite realise what is before us'.[19]

Tactical guidance came, controversially as it proved, in the form of GHQ's 8 May memorandum on 'Training of Divisions for Offensive Action' and Fourth Army's 'Tactical Notes' of 17 May, both of which recommended attacking in a series of waves. The 'Notes', for example, suggested – without making it an absolute requirement – that 'as a general guide, the leading lines should not be more than 100 yards apart', advancing at a steady pace with 'the men in each line extended at two or three paces interval'.[20] The extent to which these tactics caused the catastrophic losses on 1 July has been a matter of debate. In places they were certainly a contributory factor, but there was considerable variation in the approaches used by different divisions, the 36th being an example.[21] On the day Nugent's six leading battalions attacked in lines, but he expected more flexible tactics to become necessary as the advance continued and on 1 June he issued orders to ensure that training did not become too much a matter of drill:

> [I]t is probable that the 'A' and 'B' lines will be carried without much difficulty, before the Germans have time to recover from the bombardment and offer any organised resistance. The 'C' line, however, is in places 700 yards from the 'B' line and it must be anticipated that the Germans will put up a fight on this line and certainly on the 'D' line behind. If the 'C' line is held, the advance from the 'B' line will be in the nature of an attack across the open and would be carried out in accordance with the principles laid down in 'Infantry Training' and 'Field Service Regulations'.[22]

His assumption was clearly that fire and movement would be used beyond the B line. His directive also included the tactical use of Lewis guns, still a new weapon: 'At present in practice attacks it is not unusual to see the Lewis gun teams just walking along, without seeking any opportunity of assisting the advance by fire, and apparently pledged to inaction until the Infantry have captured some particular line of trench'. Commanders were ordered to

[19] 14th R. Irish Rifles war diary, 13 May 1916 (TNA, WO95/2511).
[20] *OH*, 1916, i, pp 290–92.
[21] Harris, *Douglas Haig*, pp 223–4; Gary Sheffield, *Forgotten Victory. The First World War: Myths and Realities* (2001), pp 138–40; Falls, *Ulster Division*, p. 46; Connelly, *Steady the Buffs*, pp 94–8.
[22] 36 Div. war diary (TNA, WO95/2491).

plan to use them to provide covering fire during the attack, including taking on previously concealed machine-guns. Nugent supervised the training closely and was joined on 8 June by Rawlinson and Morland to watch 108 and 109 Brigades practising their attacks.

Final preparations

With the battle fast approaching, 109 Brigade underwent two important leadership changes. In early May Brigadier-General Hickman asked to return full-time to the House of Commons. Although the most competent of the brigadiers he had inherited Nugent was delighted – he told Haig, who happened to be visiting, that 'it would be such a relief to get rid of him without having to push him out. He will be the last of the politicians. I like him personally but I shall be glad to be quit of him'.[23] (Spender wrote hopefully that on his return home Hickman would 'probably succeed in cooking N[ugent]'s chances', but in fact Hickman did not bear Nugent the same resentment that Hacket Pain and Spender did.)[24] In his stead Nugent got Reginald Shuter, a 39-year-old Royal Irish Fusiliers officer with a DSO from South Africa, who had gone to France with his battalion in 1914 and been commanding it since January 1916.[25]

Nugent regretted the second change more. At the beginning of June William Hessey of the 11th Royal Inniskilling Fusiliers was promoted to command a brigade in the 37th Division. A regular Inniskilling Fusiliers officer who had served in South Africa before retiring in 1913 as a captain, he had assumed command of the battalion just before it left for France. He was widely regarded as one of the division's best COs and Nugent had pressed for his promotion in the hope of being able to keep him. He could not, having to tell Hessey on 9 June, 'I wish you were staying here as Brigadier, but it is not the policy to give a man a Brigade in his own Division as a rule'.[26] Nugent's support at least enabled Hessey to circumvent one prior requirement for promotion, Nugent noting that 'the experience of actual fighting which Kiggell or Rawlinson, I forget which, said you ought to have first does not seem to have been a sine qua non after all'. Hessey was replaced by George Brush, an ex-Liverpool Regiment officer who had been serving as 2ic of the 10th Royal Inniskillings Fusiliers.

The British bombardment that began on 24 June had two functions: to destroy the German defences, including the wire, and, on the day itself, to

[23] ON to CN, 11 May 1916, in *Nugent*, p. 63.
[24] Spender to his wife, 12 May 1916, in *Nugent*, p. 252.
[25] Brig.-Gen. A. R. Burrowes, *The 1st Battalion The Faugh-a-Ballaghs in the Great War* (n.d.), pp 61, 69.
[26] Nugent to Hessey, 9 June 1916 (Hessey papers).

screen the attacking infantry and suppress enemy artillery and strongpoints. The density of guns proved wholly insufficient to perform either task effectively along much of the front. Fortunately for the Ulster Division observation in its sector was relatively good and south of the Ancre – though not to the north – the German wire was largely destroyed and their front-line trenches badly battered, the attached French 75s doing especially good work. In addition, on the night of 26/27 June an experimental gas attack was mounted against the German front line from Thiepval Wood; in Falls's words, it was 'the first time the Division had had to do with the abominable stuff which brought no good fortune'.[27] German shells burst a number of cylinders, resulting in some of the operators, from a specialist Royal Engineers unit, and their Ulster Division helpers being gassed themselves, but the vapour was released as planned. When two hours later the 13th Royal Irish Rifles raided the trenches opposite they found the defenders unaffected by the gas but cowed by the shelling, and took 13 prisoners including an officer, the first ones taken by the division, at a cost of 15 casualties.

Torrential rain on the 27th and 28th caused the British attack to be postponed for 48 hours and Nugent relieved the assault battalions, already in the forward trenches, to give them some respite; during this change-over a shell landed in the midst of a column of the 13th Royal Irish Rifles setting out from Martinsart, just behind the line, causing almost 50 casualties. Nugent visited the 9th Royal Inniskilling Fusiliers, 11th Royal Irish Rifles and 9th Royal Irish Fusiliers the following day and in the early hours of 1 July the first-wave battalions moved back into position. There were mishaps on the way – Lieutenant-Colonel Ross Smyth of the 10th Royal Inniskilling Fusiliers was thrown from his horse and injured following a shell-burst, Major Macrory taking over just a couple of hours before H-hour; while in the assembly trenches of the 14th Royal Irish Rifles a box of bombs was dropped, the safety pins of two came out and Private M'Fadzean saved his comrades by throwing himself on top of the bombs (he was awarded a posthumous Victoria Cross).[28] Nugent and his operations staff moved to their forward headquarters near Martinsart at 9pm on 30 June; by 5am on 1 July both assault brigades had reported they were in position; and the final intensive phase of the bombardment began at 6.25am, supplemented at 7am by a hurricane mortar bombardment on the German front line. Nugent went to an observation post (OP) in a tree on the Mesnil Ridge to

27 Falls, *Ulster Division*, p. 49.
28 ON to CN, 29 June 1916, in *Nugent*, p. 78; Gardiner Mitchell, *'Three Cheers for the Derrys!' A History of the 10th Royal Inniskilling Fusiliers in the 1914–18 War* (1991), p. 81; Falls, *Ulster Division*, p. 315.

watch the attack but found the haze obscuring his view and returned to his forward HQ. At 7.15am the division's leading waves south of the Ancre moved into No Man's Land and lay down 150 yards from the German line, waiting for the barrage to lift.

1 July: The assault

At 7.30am the barrage moved off the German front-line trench and the division's first six battalions went in. The contrast over the next 60 minutes between the experience of the units on the right of the attack and those on the left could not have been greater. The three on the right created the Ulster Division legend, overrunning four sets of trenches in one of the furthest advances of the day, taking the Schwaben Redoubt and opening up the German Second Position to direct assault. The three on the left attacking either side of the Ancre were effectively destroyed by machine-guns and artillery before reaching the German front line.

On the right the 9th and 10th Royal Inniskilling Fusiliers of 109 Brigade and, beside them, the 11th Royal Irish Rifles of 108 Brigade achieved their spectacular success for three reasons. First, as already noted, on this part of the front the German wire had been well cut and the front-line trenches badly damaged. Second, the German machine-guns in Thiepval were fully engaged at first in repulsing the 32nd Division's attack on the village; in the end, rather than the Ulster Division helping Rycroft's men onto their objective it was the other way round. And, thirdly, Nugent's decision to push his leading troops into No Man's Land before zero did make a decisive difference. Even with the wire cut the race for the parapet was close, several German machine-gun teams being overrun while in the process of setting up their weapons. Had they succeeded the story on the Ulster Division's right might have been the same as on the left. Within three minutes the leading waves were across the German front-line trench and entering the support trench immediately beyond. As they pushed on towards the B line the second-wave battalions – from right to left the 11th Royal Inniskilling Fusiliers and 14th Royal Irish Rifles of 109 Brigade and the 15th Royal Irish Rifles of 108 Brigade – were already crossing No Man's Land. A heavy German barrage had begun, in line with their standard practice of sealing off the attackers from support, while the machine-guns in Thiepval, having dealt with the immediate threat from the 32nd Division, began switching their fire north to catch the Ulster troops in enfilade. Nevertheless, by 8am Nugent had encouraging news that on the right the first wave had reached and were clearing the B line, including the western face of the Schwaben Redoubt.[29]

[29] *OH*, 1916, i, p. 405.

His optimism that the attack north of the Ancre would go well was, however, misplaced. The curve of the valley of the Ancre, with St Pierre Divion tucked under the slope of its southern bank, and the steep gradient north of the river, intersected by a north-south ravine half-way across No Man's Land, meant that significant stretches of the German trenches and wire were in dead ground. Both battalions – two of Nugent's best, the 12th Royal Irish Rifles and 9th Royal Irish Fusiliers – took casualties while filing out through their own wire before zero and suffered further losses while forming up. When the barrage did move forward it became clear that the German defences were intact; men fell in droves, a previously concealed machine-gun in a railway embankment causing especially heavy casualties, and the advance in lines had quickly to be abandoned. The attackers then attempted to get forward in a series of rushes but were virtually annihilated, the two battalions losing three-quarters of their men. The 13th Royal Irish Rifles, the left-hand battalion of the attack south of the river, fared no better. Its line of advance took it from the northern part of Thiepval Wood up the slope towards the top of the ridge, and as it did so the German machine-guns in St Pierre Divion and on the Beaucourt ridge caught it – the smoke screens were ineffective – inflicting shattering losses, only a few small parties making it to the German trenches.

The commitment of 107 Brigade

Just after 8am 107 Brigade left Thiepval Wood in line with the timetable and began moving across No Man's Land, the 10th Royal Irish Rifles on the right, the 9th on the left and the 8th in support. The shelling of the wood had stripped the foliage from many of the trees and the 10th Rifles suffered casualties from machine-guns while moving through it. Nugent had forbidden his infantry COs to accompany their units into the attack: instead they were to remain at their battle headquarters and re-join their units on the objective once captured. Two of the three COs in 107 Brigade disobeyed the order. Colonel Bernard of the 10th Rifles went forward with his men to ensure they crossed the start-line safely and was killed in the wood; Crozier of the 9th Rifles accompanied his soldiers as far as No Man's Land, returning unscathed and later claiming that Nugent had blocked the DSO for which he was recommended because of his disobedience.[30] The brigade's advance across No Man's Land fortunately coincided with a lull in the German shelling and losses were relatively light.

On top of the ridge the 9th and 10th Royal Inniskilling Fusiliers and the 11th Royal Irish Rifles, aided by the arrival of most of the 15th Royal Irish

[30] Crozier to Edmonds, 23 Mar. 1930 (TNA, CAB45/188).

Rifles, were continuing to fight their way into the C line and through the Schwaben Redoubt. Casualties were now mounting fast, particularly in the 9th Inniskillings, exposed to close-range flanking fire from Thiepval. At the same time the 14th Rifles and the remnants of the 11th Inniskillings, which had suffered serious losses crossing No Man's Land, were consolidating the German A and B lines. By 8.30am, however, it was clear to Nugent that despite these successes the X Corps attack was not going to plan; the failure of the 32nd Division's attack on Thiepval was already evident and news was coming in of the 29th Division's repulse further north. At 8.32am Place, on his orders, asked X Corps whether 107 Brigade should halt on the C line until the situation became clearer. The reply was that the advance should continue pending confirmation from the corps commander, away at his forward OP. Forty minutes later, at 9.10am, Morland's order came through to hold 107 Brigade back. It was too late: the brigade was now advancing towards the C line and strenuous efforts to get a message through were unsuccessful.[31] As Nugent told Kitty:

> [A]s soon as I saw how things were going on either flank of us I wired at once that in my opinion any advance beyond a certain line would leave us dangerously exposed. The answer was, 'carry out the programme'. I could have stopped it then. An hour [sic] later a message came approving my proposal and telling me to stop further advance but it was too late then, even if I could have got a message through. People at home may imagine COs and Generals can alter or change a plan once put in operation. It is impossible. Once troops begin to move under such conditions as the Division encountered on 1st July nothing can be stopped or changed.[32]

Assault on the D line

By 9.15am 107 Brigade had reached the C line. After pausing to reorganise, its three battalions resumed their advance, accompanied by enthusiastic parties from the other two brigades. The generally accepted account of what happened next, based on the official history, is that the brave but over-keen Ulstermen, not properly controlled by their officers, were only a hundred yards or so from the D line at around 10am when they 'ran into the British

---

[31] Cyril Falls believed Morland's delayed reply was due to technical problems: 'The Corps Commander was in an O.P. in a tree. The telephone line to him got out of order for perhaps quarter of an hour and Nugent felt he could not stop the brigade on his own responsibility. Permission came just too late and a great sacrifice resulted in only more loss.' Falls to Liddell Hart, 28 June 1964 (Liddell Hart Centre for Military Archives, LH1/276/60).

[32] ON to CN, 11 July 1916, in *Nugent*, p. 88.

barrage, which was not to lift from that line until 10.10am. Heavy casualties were suffered in consequence, and the extended lines had to lie down on an open stretch of rank grassland, which offered no cover'.[33] This is not, in fact, what happened.

Just after 10am 107 Brigade approached the D line. About 150 yards from it, slightly ahead of schedule, the advancing troops halted and lay down, waiting for the barrage to move on. They did not run into it, because they could see it in front of them. The tactic of getting close to the barrage and waiting for it to lift before rushing the objective had been built into the division's planning: not only had it been used in the opening assault on the A line, it was also reflected in the orders for the advance to the B and C lines.[34] What seems to have happened is that the artillery, perhaps putting in a final burst of intensive fire before shifting beyond the D line at 1008, fired short or, as sometimes occurred, the barrage 'crept back' towards the helplessly waiting troops. Casualties were heavy, but just as devastating were the German machine-guns. The enforced pause in 107 Brigade's advance had given the Germans time to confirm that these troops were British rather than their own men retiring, and as soon as the barrage lifted the massed machine-guns in Beaucourt, Grandcourt and elsewhere opened up, inflicting severe losses. A number of men dashed forward and entered the Second Position: one party reached Stuff Redoubt and found it empty; another group broke in about 600 yards to the north and hastily barricaded themselves in. A third party, about 200-strong, took up position on the left in some abandoned German artillery emplacements at the head of Battery Valley, a re-entrant between the C and D lines. But most of the survivors fell back and joined the jumbled mix of soldiers, from at least six different battalions and three brigades, holding the C line and the Schwaben Redoubt.

The Corps reserve

With all three of his brigades committed Nugent now had no means of influencing the battle, other than to a limited degree with artillery. Morland still had the 49th Division available, however, and the central, and urgent, question became the deployment of the X Corps reserve. At around 9am Major-General Perceval (himself from a County Down family), who had heard of the Ulster Division's early gains and expected his troops to be used to reinforce them, had gone to Nugent's HQ. 'I saw Nugent and his staff', he wrote later, 'The impression that I got after talking to them was that

---

[33] *OH*, 1916, i, p. 407.

[34] See, for example, 108 Bde's orders (TNA, WO95/2504). For 107 Bde lying down waiting for the barrage to lift off the D line, see the war diaries of 107 Bde and 8th and 9th Royal Irish Rifles (TNA, WO95/2502 & 2503), and the letter of Maj. McCallum (8th Rifles) to Edmonds, 30 Mar. 1930 (TNA, CAB45/198).

there was not a moment to be lost and that it might be too late to do more than secure what had been gained'.[35] Perceval hurried to Morland to urge him to use all or part of his division to assist the 36th. Morland refused, instead deciding to use the 49th Division to support renewed efforts to take Thiepval village. He told Perceval to send his 146 Brigade up to Thiepval Wood, but to be prepared to attack the village rather than reinforce the Ulstermen. Later in the morning Morland ordered 147 Brigade to move up to Authuille Wood, behind the 32nd Division. His one concession was to send a battalion of Perceval's third brigade (1st/5th York & Lancaster Regiment, 148 Brigade) to occupy the northern part of Thiepval Wood, left exposed by the losses suffered by 108 Brigade.[36]

It is easy to be wise after the event. Morland's decision was based on various factors. It would take almost two hours for 146 Brigade to get through Thiepval Wood and reach the German lines, and with Thiepval unsubdued its casualties crossing No Man's Land would have been heavy. It would also be advancing into an exposed salient under fire from three sides. Incorrect reports suggested that some 32nd Division attackers were in Thiepval and he was understandably anxious to reinforce them and reluctant to bombard the village indiscriminately for fear of killing his own men. Even so, the commitment of even one of the 49th Division's brigades to reinforce the Ulster Division's gains, with the possibility of securing a foothold in the Second Position and outflanking Thiepval from the north, might have had a major operational impact. Nor is this a matter of retrospective wisdom: not only Nugent and Perceval but also Rycroft, when Perceval spoke to him later in the morning, urged the use of at least part of the 49th Division to reinforce the 36th. Otley Place believed that the opportunity to reinforce lasted for two or three hours after the initial attack, and was surprised, given the known strength of Thiepval, that X Corps had no pre-prepared plan to reinforce any success on either side of it, while an officer of the 32nd Division felt that if troops of the 49th Division had followed up the 36th immediately, Thiepval would have been captured by 11am.[37] This confusion reflected the fact that the BEF's operational techniques were still developing: by 1918 reinforcing success rather than

[35] Perceval to Edmonds, 29 May 1930 (TNA, CAB45/198). In a previous letter to Edmonds (2 Mar. 1925, also in CAB45/198), Perceval says his meeting with Nugent took place at around 11am, but the second letter suggests it was earlier. The internal evidence in both letters reinforces that view, and the official history puts the meeting shortly after 107 Brigade left Thiepval Wood (*OH*, 1916, i, p. 408).

[36] *OH*, 1916, i, pp 412–13.

[37] *OH*, 1916, i, p. 413; Place to Edmonds, 31 May 1930 (TNA, CAB45/198); Brig.-Gen. J. B. Jardine, 97 Bde, to Edmonds, 13 June 1930 (TNA, CAB45/137).

attempting to retrieve failure would have been the instinctive response of a commander in Morland's position.[38] Whatever the merits or otherwise of his decision, however, the implementation of his preferred approach, the reinforcement of the 32nd Division to capture Thiepval, rapidly descended through a combination of indecision and the friction of battle into chaos.

Consolidation

With no reinforcements from X Corps, Nugent concentrated on trying to organise additional fire support and supplies for his troops on the ridge. He was hampered by not having a clear understanding of what was happening there since so many messages failed to make it back. The extent to which this was his own fault would become a matter of contention. Nugent's refusal to allow his COs to accompany their battalions meant that some 48 rifle companies had been committed to the attack without a single officer above the rank of major to coordinate their activities or pass back high-level assessments of the situation. Nugent, then and later, was entirely unapologetic, writing after the battle:

> The COs were not allowed to go forward with their men. They could do nothing if they had and in trying to do something would all have been killed or wounded. I absolutely forbid them to go beyond Thiepval Wood. Now at any rate I have the COs to start rebuilding their battalions. They all protested when I told them they were not to go forward, but they all realise now, they could have done nothing and they are far more valuable as live men than dead heroes.[39]

That may be what they said, but it is not what many of them thought at the time. Nor have historians subsequently shared his view. Sir James Edmonds, writing in the official history of the failure to exploit information brought in by patrols in late morning that the Mouquet Switch Line behind Thiepval was unoccupied, thought a great opportunity had been missed and that the 'instructions that no officer of the battalion or brigade staffs was to go forward with the assaulting troops now had dire consequences'; Martin Middlebrook forty years later followed him in believing that 'with no central command in the Schwaben, no one took advantage of this opportunity'; while Anthony Farrar-Hockley in the 1960s similarly regretted that the assault battalions 'had been sent forward

---

[38] See Martin Samuels, *Command or Control: Command, Training and Tactics in the British and German Armies 1888–1918* (1995), pp 143–57.
[39] ON to CN, 11 July 1916, in *Nugent*, p. 89.

without a coordinator of any sort between themselves, the mortars, machine-gunners and two sections of Royal Engineers accompanying the force', and attributed 107 Brigade's running into its own barrage to having no senior officer to control them.[40]

Nugent's decision may have been influenced by his experience at Hooge and the heavy losses amongst officers there. It seems he was confident that the attack up to the capture of the D line, intensively practised as it had been, would succeed and he wished to preserve his key commanders for the fighting after that. His fear that losses amongst them would be high was certainly realistic: along the front, 52 COs in the 14 assault divisions (including Third Army) became casualties, 30 of them killed or died of wounds; five divisions lost more than half their COs on 1 July.[41] Some of the criticism was unjustified. 107 Brigade's misfortune with its own barrage has already been discussed. The failure to exploit the empty Mouquet Switch Line was due not to the absence of senior officers but to shortage of men; as would soon become clear, without reinforcements the defenders were too few to hold what they already had. In fact the possibility of using the Mouquet Switch to outflank Thiepval was already being considered, Rycroft suggesting to Perceval around midday that 146 Brigade be given to Nugent for precisely that purpose, but Morland decided to await the outcome of the next attack on the village.[42] Nugent's decision did, however, undoubtedly hamper both coordinated defensive operations once German counterattacks began and the relaying to the rear of an authoritative picture of what was happening; in retrospect it seems to have been a mistake and was not one he repeated. While the presence of the COs would not have changed the outcome, their absence imposed a huge strain on company officers, though several rose to the challenge outstandingly. A number of officers from battalion staffs did nevertheless cross No Man's Land to try to discover what was going on. They included Major Peacocke, 2ic of the 9th Royal Inniskilling Fusiliers, who reached the Crucifix area south-west of the Schwaben Redoubt at 11am and stayed there to take command.

Nugent hoped that the 32nd Division's renewed attack on Thiepval at 1.30pm would bring relief, but this never properly got off the ground because of the difficulty of getting the troops and a fire-plan in place in time, and Morland ordered a further attack for 4pm. In No Man's Land, meanwhile, lashed by artillery and machine-gun fire, carrying parties with supplies, groups of reinforcements, runners carrying messages, walking

---

[40] *OH*, 1916, i, p. 417; Martin Middlebrook, *The First Day on the Somme* (1971), p. 178; Anthony Farrar-Hockley, *The Somme* (1964), pp 133–5.

[41] Middlebrook, *First Day*, pp 326–8.

[42] *OH*, 1916, i, p. 413.

wounded and prisoners, attempted the journey in one or both directions: while some made it unscathed, many did not. An attempt by the 16th Royal Irish Rifles, the divisional pioneers, to dig a communication trench from Thiepval Wood to the A line had to be abandoned under intense fire.

The German response

The German defenders facing the Ulster Division were from Generalmajor von Soden's impressive *26th (Wuertemberg) Reserve Division*, holding the front from Serre to Ovillers. On 1 July they were attacked by five British divisions with two more in immediate support, a ratio similar to that the Ulster Division would face on 21 March 1918 (though the strength of the defences and effectiveness of the attacking artillery then would be very different).[43] These odds were offset by the strength of their fortifications and the fact that the *26th Division* had four infantry regiments instead of the usual three, had been reinforced by a fifth (*8th Bavarian Reserve Regiment*), and had powerful artillery support (154 guns). The framework of the defence was built around eight machine-gun companies, with 90 heavy and 30 light machine-guns.[44]

Bearing the brunt of the opening Ulster Division attack south of the Ancre was the *3rd Battalion 99th Reserve Regiment*, reinforced by elements of the *1st and 3rd Battalions 8th Bavarian Regiment*, holding the First Position and the Schwaben Redoubt. The defenders of the first three lines were mostly killed or captured during the assault, making up the bulk of the 543 prisoners taken by the Ulster Division: others were killed by their own artillery and machine-guns in No Man's Land while being escorted to the rear. North of the Ancre, their comrades in the *119th Regiment* had a much easier time in repulsing 108 Brigade's assault there. In immediate support south of the river von Soden had in Grandcourt the *180th Recruit Battalion*, one of the *26th Division's* holding units for replacements, together with four companies of the *8th Bavarians*. Four miles to the rear, at Irles, was the *2nd Battalion 8th Bavarians*, the divisional reserve. Elements of all these units delivered, at around 2pm, the first heavy coordinated counterattacks against Nugent's men (though there had been local attacks, particularly from the valley of the Ancre, in the course of the morning). These comprised two main thrusts, an advance by the *180th*

---

[43] The British 8th, 29th, 36th, 32nd and 8th Divisions in the initial attack, with the 49th and 19th in close support.

[44] *OH*, 1916, i, pp 422–3; Matthias Strohn, 'The German army at war', in Strohn (ed.) *Battle of the Somme* (2016), pp 181–97; Samuels, *Command or Control*, pp 137–8; Christopher Duffy, *Through German Eyes: The British and the Somme 1916* (2006), pp 148–53.

Battalion and two machine-gun companies up the slope from Grandcourt, and an attack by five companies of Bavarians from the Second Position. The Grandcourt attack forced back the Ulster soldiers at the top of Battery Valley, many of whom were killed retreating across the open: the Germans were eventually halted at 3pm in the Hansa line about 600 yards from the Schwaben Redoubt. The Bavarians cleared the remaining isolated parties of Ulstermen from the D line, including Stuff Redoubt, and then attacked towards the C line where they were stopped by machine-gun and rifle fire.

This marked the start of repeated attacks on the C line from north, east and south; the fighting was intense (during it Captain Bell, an Inniskilling Fusiliers officer attached to a trench mortar battery, earned a posthumous Victoria Cross for courageous leadership) and the defenders' casualties began mounting as rapidly as their ammunition supplies dwindled. A message from Major Gaffikin of the 9th Royal Irish Rifles in the Schwaben Redoubt, to take one example, written about 4pm but not received until after 6pm by which time he had been mortally wounded, was stark:

> We are in considerable difficulty … I do not think we shall be able to hold out tonight if attacked, as we can be taken from front to rear unless Thiepval falls, and the men are very exhausted, and both Lewis guns and M. guns are short of ammo. We are short of bombs. Could you send us water tonight. Roughly position is that we are hanging on by our eyebrows to the SW sides of the Parallelogram [Schwaben Redoubt] and C9 in the E front of it. The men are not fit to attack again.[45]

Between 3.30pm and 4pm the defence on the ridge started showing signs of weakening. Observers saw men falling back from the C line, some halting in the A or B lines but others continuing across No Man's Land towards Thiepval Wood. A number were walking wounded or prisoners but others were soldiers who had reached the end of their tether and were coming back without orders. On this occasion, as on a number of others during the day, officers drew, and sometimes used, their revolvers on panic-stricken soldiers.[46]

Although Nugent had known his men were hard-pressed these reports brought home for the first time the urgency of the situation; indeed, his immediate response reveals how out-dated his picture of the position on the ridge had become. Shortly after 4pm he ordered 107 Brigade to suspend efforts to reach the D line, and instead to reinforce the Schwaben Redoubt

[45] 107 Bde war diary (TNA, WO95/2502).
[46] See Middlebrook, *First Day*, p. 209; Crozier, *Brass Hat*, p. 126.

and C line and shore up the left flank overlooking the Ancre valley. As there had been no prospect of a further advance on the D line for some time the brigade merely 'answered that 107th Bde is already merged into the 108th and 109th Bdes in the holding of C Line and Fort Schwaben'.[47] Nugent's hopes that the 4pm attack on Thiepval by 146 Brigade and a battalion of the 32nd Division would improve the situation were dashed. That assault, like its predecessors, misfired; fewer than half the attackers could get into position in time, and when the initial waves were mown down it was with difficulty halted. Morland did, however, at last respond to Nugent's appeals for reinforcements, but his intervention merely added to the confusion. He agreed just before 4pm that, in view of the deteriorating position on the ridge, two battalions of 146 Brigade, in the wood to support the attack on Thiepval, should be diverted instead to help the Ulster Division.

As on so many occasions on 1 July it proved easier to issue an instruction than make it happen. Nugent told Withycombe of 107 Brigade, the senior brigadier in Thiepval Wood, to take command of the two 146 Brigade battalions and use them to reinforce the C line. (At no stage during the day did Nugent enter the wood himself: there was nothing he could have done there, and he would have been separated from his communications with Morland, the flanking divisions and the guns.) When Withycombe's staff officer arrived at 146 Brigade's HQ, however, its commander refused to cooperate. While Morland's order had been phoned through to the 49th Division it had not been passed on to Brigadier-General Goring-Jones, on the grounds that it was too late to change 146 Brigade's plans for the Thiepval attack. He understandably replied, therefore, that with two battalions already attacking Thiepval and the other two standing by to assist he was unable to help. On being shown the written order he reluctantly agreed to release two companies of 1/7th West Yorkshire Regiment but declined to do more without confirmation from Perceval.

There followed a prolonged period of order and counter-order as different levels of command tried to influence a situation they only partially understood and which was rapidly slipping away from them. At 5.30pm Nugent sent a further order to Withycombe, telling him 'to counter attack with all available troops of 49th Div placed under his orders. Rally the men falling back and see they go forward again. Schwaben must be held at all costs'.[48] Such orders, however forcefully expressed, were increasingly detached from the realities on the ground. The confusion in Thiepval Wood, under constant artillery fire and crowded with wounded and

---

[47] 107 Bde war diary (TNA, WO95/2502).
[48] 107 Bde war diary (TNA, WO95/2502).

stragglers, was enormous. It was matched by the confusion between Morland and Perceval over what the 49th Division was to do. At 6.46pm the 49th's war diary noted that the orders received from X Corps 'were not quite clear' and it took a phone conversation between the two headquarters at 7pm to confirm (again) that two battalions of 146 Brigade were to support the Ulster Division and that 148 Brigade was to send two battalions to reinforce the 32nd Division and another to support Nugent.[49] It was almost 8pm before Goring-Jones's units at last started moving and not until 9pm that the equivalent of two battalions – 1/5th West Yorkshire Regiment and two companies each from the 1/7th and 1/8th West Yorkshires – began crossing No Man's Land heading for the Schwaben Redoubt.[50]

The withdrawal

The moment for reinforcement had, however, passed as the defenders on the ridge had reached breaking-point. Since Morland's decision at 4pm to release part of 146 Brigade Nugent's men had fought for over six hours without assistance. There were further concerted German pushes at 5pm and 6.15pm from the D line, along the Mouquet Switch and from the Ancre valley, which were stopped but which, along with continuous smaller ones, had eroded the division's lodgement. At around 10pm came another determined attack, this time spearheaded by two fresh battalions of the *185th Regiment*, sent forward by the German *XIV Reserve Corps, 26th Division's* parent formation.[51] Although they failed to break into the south-western end of the Schwaben Redoubt, the only part still in British hands, they did succeed in surrounding it on three sides and at 10.30pm, in danger of being cut off, Peacocke withdrew the exhausted survivors. As they pulled back they met the men of 146 Brigade moving up but it was too late. All of them headed back down the slope towards Thiepval Wood, carrying with them as many wounded as they could.

Morland and Nugent were still trying to retrieve something from the wreckage. An attempt to mount yet another attack on Thiepval just after 6pm had failed, but Morland promised Nugent units from the 49th Division's 148 Brigade to launch a night attack, to coincide with a further assault on the village. Once again there was a breakdown in communication between X Corps and the 49th Division. When Perceval received the order at 9.30pm to provide two more battalions to Nugent he was unclear

---

[49] 49th Div. war diary (TNA, WO95/2765).
[50] *OH*, 1916, i, pp 414–15.
[51] Samuels, *Command or Control*, p. 155.

whether this was as well as or instead of reinforcing the 32nd Division, and he went in person to see Morland get clarity. Over an hour was lost as a result.

Just after 11.30pm Nugent told Withycombe that three battalions of 148 Brigade were being made available to launch a further assault. The 1st/4th York & Lancaster Regiment duly arrived and Withycombe sent them to the forward edge of the wood to prepare for the attack. But by 1am on 2 July there was still no sign of the other two battalions, the 1st/4th and 1st/5th KOYLI, and Withycombe, judging that the attack could not now be made before daylight, recommended it be cancelled (as the proposed renewed attack on Thiepval village already had been). Nugent agreed, but since the corps reserve was involved he referred the recommendation with his endorsement to Morland. Morland's response – in contrast to Keir's the previous summer – was that the man on the spot should decide and the attack was called off. Withycombe had nevertheless made a morally brave call, and he took care to record his reasons in detail in the brigade war diary. He also took energetic steps to ease the chaos in the wood, using the 4th York & Lancasters to hold the trenches along its forward edge, deploying the two battalions of 146 Brigade, now returned from the German lines, to occupy the northern part and ordering Colonel Ricardo to reorganise what was left of 107 and 109 Brigades to hold the southern sector.

With a degree of stability now restored Nugent and Withycombe waited for daylight, believing no British troops were still fighting in the German trenches. Meanwhile, in testimony to the confusion that had reigned at corps level throughout, Perceval's 147 Brigade, waiting since morning near Authuille Wood behind the 32nd Division, received no orders and remained inactive there all day. As the official history put it, '[t]he piecemeal employment of the 49th Division by X Corps headquarters had accomplished nothing'.[52]

2 and 3 July

When dawn came on 2 July Nugent and Withycombe found that the information of the previous evening was incorrect. An OP on Mesnil Ridge reported British troops in the German front line, a sighting soon confirmed by other observers, and just after 10am Nugent ordered Withycombe to reinforce them. Withycombe gave the task to Crozier who by late morning had assembled a force of about 400, drawn mostly from 107 Brigade. At 2pm the 9th Royal Irish Rifles' 2ic, Major Woods, led them over under a protective barrage; while the party lost about a third of its strength in doing so it was subsequently reinforced by further small groups. In the German

---

[52] *OH*, 1916, i, p. 416.

trenches they found some 120 Ulster soldiers holding out, and with them 40 men of the 7th West Yorkshire Regiment under Corporal Sanders, who had been fighting hard there since the previous evening and who was awarded the Victoria Cross for his leadership. This toe-hold in the German line was consolidated and the wounded evacuated. The intention was that Woods's force would be relieved that evening, but in the event the process was not completed until mid-morning on 3 July. The Germans retook these trenches a few days later.

Meanwhile the relief of the rest of the division had taken place. By 5pm on 2 July Nugent's units in Thiepval Wood had been replaced by the 49th Division, and at 7pm he finally handed over responsibility to Perceval. The division's participation in the battle of the Somme had not yet ended, however, the gunners, pioneers and sappers having to remain in action for several more days to support the fresh divisions moving into the line. There was still urgent work for the infantry also, which brought displays of heroism matching those of the assault itself. Of 9,000 men in the attack over 5,000 had become casualties, including 190 of 300 officers; nearly 2,000 had been killed but hundreds of the wounded were still lying out between the British and German lines. On the night of 1/2 July and for several nights afterwards, and during daylight also, parties risked their lives in No Man's Land to bring in their wounded comrades, and two of the four Victoria Crosses won by the division on the Somme were awarded for rescuing wounded men, Lieutenant Cather of the 9th Royal Irish Fusiliers (posthumously) and Private Quigg of the 12th Royal Irish Rifles.[53]

Nugent's experience in the 36 hours between 7am on 1 July and 7pm on the 2nd underscored the limitations on a Great War divisional commander's ability to influence events once battle was joined - as has rightly been observed, armies in the First World War could kill better than they could communicate.[54] His tactical plans for the assault, particularly moving his leading waves into No Man's Land before zero, had been successful on the right of his attack, though not on the left. Once his reserve brigade had been committed he was effectively a spectator for much of the rest of the day, and one whose picture of what was going on was less complete than it might have been as a result of his decision to hold back his COs. He did what he could, nevertheless, to assist his men on the ridge and, having delegated tactical authority to Withycombe in Thiepval Wood, supported him in the actions he took. The critical decisions about the deployment of the X Corps reserve were not his to make, though he tried to influence them: and the failure to reinforce the division's success on the

---

[53] Falls, *Ulster Division*, pp 59–60.
[54] Alexander Turner, *Messines 1917* (2000), p. 15.

morning of 1 July, and the lengthy delay in deploying reinforcements in the evening, ended any hopes there were of holding onto the Schwaben Redoubt and other Ulster Division gains.

However glorious, the battle had been a costly defeat and Nugent now faced the task of rebuilding his command. Its sacrifice also took on, inevitably, a major political significance. The division's military performance on 1 July would remain a matter of intense pride to him for the rest of his life; the political use to which that performance was now to be put was a different matter.

6

Manpower and Politics

Recruitment and trench warfare, August 1916–March 1917

Introduction

The 1 July battle left the Ulster Division shattered as a fighting formation and incapable of further large-scale operations until brought up to strength. How to do so became a highly politicised issue that over the next few months brought the division to the brink of disbandment, destroyed what remained of Nugent's relationship with the Ulster unionist leadership and undermined his relations with Douglas Haig.

The scale of the casualties and their impact on close-knit communities left an enduring imprint of grief and pride on the consciousness of Protestant Ulster. The division's heroism also created a strong sense amongst its supporters that the sacrifice had earned special treatment for the province in any future political settlement. The accounts of the battle appearing immediately afterwards played directly into the debate about Ireland's future, sometimes in ways of which Nugent did not approve. The aftermath also demonstrated how the pattern of the Ulster Division's service on the western front, like the 16th (Irish) Division's, would differ from that of most British formations. Because of their recruiting problems every major battle involving significant casualties now posed an existential crisis for the Irish divisions. Their losses on the Somme left both in limbo for months, unable like other divisions to return to the fighting for a second, third or even fourth time. The Irish infantry was a wasting asset and Nugent had to manage the issues this raised in terms of morale, identity and military performance for the rest of his time in command.

Central to the division's ability to continue functioning effectively were its battalion COs, to the selection and development of whom Nugent devoted considerable personal attention. His relationship with this constantly changing group reveals a good deal about his evolving command style as he and his division entered their second year on active service.

After the battle

Nugent's immediate preoccupation on getting the division out of the line was to establish the full extent of its casualties. On 2 July he estimated them at 150 officers and 6,000 soldiers (at a time when the division was still in action); two days later the figures had been adjusted downwards to 210 officers and 5,200 men. Subsequently Cyril Falls in the divisional history in 1922 gave the total as 5,500, the figure still most generally cited, though the official history ten years later recorded an amended 5,104 casualties.[1] Whatever the precise number the losses were by any measure severe (though four other divisions lost more heavily on 1 July) and included over 2,000 dead or missing. They had fallen overwhelmingly on the infantry: three battalions had lost over 500 men and five more over 400. Small wonder, as Falls described, that the survivors were very silent in the days after the battle; a grief-stricken Colonel Blacker of the 9th Royal Irish Fusiliers spoke for the rest when he wrote on 2 July, 'My beloved Battalion and the companions of the last two years swept away in a few short hours … I am heartbroken'.[2]

On 3 July Nugent issued an order of the day expressing his admiration and appreciation for what had been achieved – nothing finer, he declared, had been done in the war – praising the discipline and courage shown by all ranks, regretting the heavy losses and adding that he was

> proud beyond description, as every Officer and Man in the Division may well be, of the magnificent example of sublime courage and discipline which the Ulster Division has given to the Army. Ulster has every reason to be proud of the men she has given to the service of our country. Though many of our best men have gone the spirit which animated them remains in the Division and will never die.[3]

The following day he visited the survivors of 108 and 109 Brigades – 'I assembled the remnants of 2 of my Brigades today', he told Kitty sadly, 'and thanked them for the work they had done' – and saw 107 Brigade on the morning of the 5th. These were emotional occasions. Spender told his wife, 'The Genl wrote an excellent order of the day, and made a very nice speech to all the Bdes nearly breaking down'; the 10th Royal Irish Rifles reported the glowing tribute the general paid to 107 Brigade; Blacker noted Nugent's complimentary address to 108 Brigade and his 'very fine Order of the Day

[1] ON to CN, 2 July 1916, and to the King, 5 July 1916, in *Nugent*, pp 80, 84; Falls, *Ulster Division*, p. 59; *OH*, i, p. 421.
[2] Falls, *Ulster Division*, p. 63; Blacker letters, 2 July 1916.
[3] 36 Div. war diary (TNA, WO95/2493)

on the operations and the behaviour of the Division'. Not everyone was impressed; a disgruntled soldier of the 14th Royal Irish Rifles complained that Nugent had told them they had done well but could have done better and thought him 'anything but a gentleman'.[4] On 5 July the division moved back 20 or so miles to Rubempre, seven miles north of Amiens.

Reaction to the attack

As soon as the attack was over the process of shaping the narrative around it, both consciously and unconsciously, had begun. Nugent wrote to several key figures in the days after the battle. On 4 July, for example, he sent the King a detailed description:

> I cannot attempt to describe in adequate terms the extraordinary gallantry and discipline displayed by every battalion in the Division … I am sure, Sir, that you would have been satisfied with these incomparably gallant men, could you have seen their attack and their absolute disregard of personal danger. We shall no doubt be made up again but I fear we shall never have men of such splendid qualities again.[5]

On 5 July he wrote similarly to Carson:

> The attack carried out by the Ulster Division was the finest thing the new armies have done in this war. Observers from outside the Division who saw it say it was a superb example of discipline and courage … It was magnificent beyond description. Officers led their men with a gallantry to which I cannot do justice and the men followed them with equal gallantry and when the officers went down they went on alone.[6]

Within days the first official account, an initial summary by Falls, had been prepared and on 6 July Spender sent a copy to Lily: 'If you are with Sir Edward when this letter arrives', he told her, 'he will be interested in the enclosed by Falls, which tho' based largely on what I told him, is very much better than anything I could write myself'. At the same time other accounts from survivors and observers were flooding home, many of which were published in newspapers and helped shape the public understanding of the

[4] ON to CN, 4 July 1916, in *Nugent*, p. 82; Spender to his wife, 5 July 1916 (PRONI, D1633/1/1/335); 10th R. Irish Rif. war diary (TNA, WO95/2503); Blacker letters, 4 July 1916; Middlebrook, *First Day*, pp 255–6.

[5] Nugent to the King, 4 July 1916, in *Nugent*, pp 82–4.

[6] Colvin, *Carson*, pp 184–5.

battle. Sometimes the writers were taken aback to find letters they had thought personal in print: it had 'never occurred' to Spender that a letter of condolence he had sent would be published – 'it seems lacking in delicacy and I should certainly have written very differently had I known'.[7]

But other letters were definitely written for publication, and a particularly influential one was by Spender himself. Composed on 2 July while the division was still in the line, he sent it to his wife the following day. Presented as an anonymous account by a 'Staff Officer', it began memorably 'I am not an Ulsterman, but yesterday as I followed their amazing attack I felt I would rather be an Ulsterman than anything else in the world'. It was a powerful piece of writing and was the more effective for coming from an apparently detached observer.[8] When Lily received it she forwarded it to Carson and to Howell Gwynne, editor of the Conservative-supporting *Morning Post*, and on 6 July it appeared in both *The Times* and the *Morning Post*, as well as being circulated by the Press Association. It was picked up by other papers, national and regional, including the Ulster press, in the coming days, Craig telling Spender on 9 July that he and his colleagues had managed to get it 'into the whole British press'.[9] There were two versions, however. The one in *The Times* contained the account of the attack but omitted most of Spender's explicitly political concluding paragraph, which the *Morning Post* retained:

> The Ulster Division has lost more than half the men who attacked, and in doing so has sacrificed itself for the Empire which has treated them none too well. The much derided Ulster Volunteer Force has won a name which equals any in History. Their devotion, which no doubt has helped the advance elsewhere, deserves the gratitude of the British Empire. It is due to the memory of these brave heroes that their beloved Province shall be fairly treated.[10]

The paragraph summed up the view, not only of unionist politicians, but of most of the Ulster unionist population also, that the division's sacrifice had earned Ulster special consideration when it came to determining Ireland's future. The unionist leadership shared at a personal level both the pride and the sense of loss: James Craig's brother Charles had been wounded and taken prisoner, while Carson told Nugent that he had lost a

[7] Spender to his wife, 6 and 12 July 1916 (PRONI, D1633/1/1/337; Baguley, *Question of Ulster*, p. 111).
[8] Baguley, *Question of Ulster*, pp 104–05.
[9] Craig to Spender, 9 July 1916 (PRONI, D1295/4/15).
[10] Baguley, *Question of Ulster*, p. 105.

great number of personal friends.[11] Their immediate political objective, however, was to use the 1 July attack to maintain pressure on the government for the exclusion from Home Rule of the six north-eastern counties. On 5 July Carson had written to Nugent saying how moved he and his Ulster parliamentary colleagues had been by the bravery and losses of the division and asking that their appreciation be made known.[12] Nugent sent, via Kitty, his thanks and confirmed that the letter's contents would be published, but added for Kitty's benefit, 'I am not going to hurry about it. I have my doubts about Sir EC now. Anyhow I think he sold us over Cavan'.[13] Increasingly anxious over the political use to which the division's attack was being put, he went on:

> I hope to goodness the politicians won't try and make political capital out of us. I should hate that and so should we all I think. We are quite satisfied with the knowledge that the Army and the people at home know what we have done, without politicians using us as stalking horses.[14]

There was, of course, never any prospect of avoiding that. Carson, defending his support for the six-county option at a political meeting in London on 7 July, made reference to the division's attack: 'The day the war broke out ... we changed our volunteers into soldiers, and then last week they have made the supreme sacrifice'. Craig wrote similarly in his letter to Spender on 9 July of the 'glorious page in war's history written by those who at a critical time shamed England by the stand they made for liberty and home'.[15]

Nugent initially had been pleased by the many congratulatory messages that poured in, from family members, Morland, Gough, Sir George Richardson (head of the UVF), General Powell and others, and by the recognition the division was receiving in the press. As the days passed, however, with the letters to the newspapers showing no sign of abating and the political purpose behind some of them becoming clearer, he grew more concerned. 'I am getting rather worried over the continual mention of us', he wrote on 9 July, 'and I am so afraid it is being done for political purposes. I wish they would leave us alone now'. Two days later he complained, 'I am

[11] Carson to ON, 5 July 1916 in *Nugent*, p. 86.
[12] Ibid.
[13] ON to CN, 8 July 1916, in *Nugent*, pp 87–8.
[14] Ibid.
[15] Deirdre McMahon (ed.), 'The Irish settlement meeting of the Unionist party, 7 July 1916', *Analecta Hibernica*, 41 (2009), p. 233; Craig to Spender, 9 July 1916 (PRONI, D1295/4/15).

greatly annoyed at my letter to Sir G Richardson being published. One cannot even write a private letter without having it stuffed into the papers. It is all politics of course'.[16] He was not alone: Stewart Blacker also felt that there had been 'a lot of extravagant stuff published in the press, which is a great pity. The Division behaved magnificently and the point does not want labouring'.[17]

Nugent's frustration was exacerbated by his knowledge of the casualties sustained by soldiers from Cavan, Monaghan and Donegal. Of the 820 fatalities suffered on 1 July by the division's three Inniskilling Fusilier battalions and the 9th Royal Irish Fusiliers, which recruited in south and west Ulster, around a hundred, or 12%, came from these three counties and at least as many again had been wounded.[18] At home his fellow Cavan unionist, Somerset Saunderson, attempted to turn the argument about the division's sacrifice against the UUC when he denounced the proposed deal as a 'gross breach of the pledge under which the men of the Ulster Division had gone to the Front'.[19] In fact the political negotiations were already breaking down over whether the exclusion of the north-eastern counties would be permanent (and also the extent to which the cabinet had been aware of Lloyd George's proposals) and the process was formally abandoned on 27 July. The damage had been done, however, as far as Nugent's faith in the unionist leadership was concerned.[20]

By the time the talks ended so too had Wilfrid Spender's service with the division. His departure was both hastened and over-shadowed by a serious row with Nugent over yet another letter in the press. This one he had written to Sir George Richardson, claiming later it had not been intended for publication, but whether it was or not it contained the fateful sentence, when describing the division's performance, that their general 'now knows he has commanded the best troops in the world and confesses it'. Nugent was incandescent at the implication he had not previously appreciated the quality of his men and even Spender acknowledged that he had reason to be angry.[21] Spender's contrition soon turned to resentment, however, even though he was leaving on a double promotion (on Nugent's recommendation he was jumping from captain to lieutenant-colonel to

---

[16] ON to CN, 2 and 11 July 1916 (PRONI, D3835/E/2/297; *Nugent*, p. 88).

[17] Orr, *Road to the Somme*, p. 240.

[18] Calculated from *Soldiers Died in the Great War*.

[19] Saunderson to the Unionist delegates of County Monaghan, 11 July 1916 (PRONI, D1507/A/18/12).

[20] Hennessey, *Dividing Ireland*, pp 144–53; John Stubbs, 'The Unionists and Ireland, 1914–18', *Historical Journal*, 33:4 (1990), p. 883.

[21] Baguley, *Question of Ulster*, p. 115.

take up a GSO1 appointment). He departed on 23 July and Nugent was glad to see him go – 'I think he will be better away', he told Kitty, 'He is too much mixed up with the politicals in Belfast and talks and writes too much to them'.[22] Spender's hostility lasted for the rest of the war, despite the fact that Nugent intervened after his departure to get his promotion confirmed.[23] By contrast, Nugent was sorry to say farewell to Farnham, recalled in August to his regiment, the North Irish Horse. His replacement as ADC was Somerset Saunderson; as another leading Cavan unionist disenchanted with Carson and Craig, his arrival made no difference to the political outlook at the top of the division.

Talk of promotion

As the scale of the disaster on 1 July sank in, rumours spread of impending changes at senior level. On 13 July Nugent told Kitty:

> We hear that both the Corps commanders, our late Corps commander and the one on our left, are very shaky and may possibly be on their way home soon. It is also rumoured but must not be repeated that Allenby is not unlikely to be going home too, but none of these matters may even be whispered.[24]

Allenby remained in charge of Third Army until the following spring, while the two corps commanders, Morland and Hunter-Weston (VIII Corps), stayed in post until 1918. Hunter-Weston's headquarters, which had presided over the heaviest casualties of the opening day, was however shifted north away from the fighting and despite his protestations that he had not been 'stellenbosched', a Boer War expression for sacked, he had effectively been sidelined.[25] Morland too felt the pressure, telling his daughter on 10 July: 'Eddie Wortly has been sent home – his Divn was engaged to the N of me. "Brief life is here our portion." My turn may come next'.[26] He survived but other heads did roll, the first of them indeed being the commander of the 46th Division, Major-General Eddie Montagu-Stuart-Wortley, another former KRRC officer to whose division Nugent's brigade had been attached back in May 1915. On 20 July Nugent informed Kitty

[22] ON to CN, 20 July 1916 in *Nugent*, p. 93.
[23] Spender to Lily, 15 Oct. 1916 in Baguley, *Question of Ulster*, p. 148.
[24] ON to CN, 13 July 1916 in *Nugent*, p. 90.
[25] Simpson, *Directing Operations*, p. 27; Elaine McFarland, *'A Slashing Man of Action': The Life of Lieutenant-General Sir Aylmer Hunter-Weston MP* (2014), pp 246–7.
[26] Bill Thompson (ed.), *Morland – Great War Corps Commander* (2015), p. 152.

that '[a] good many Divisional Generals have gone home already, including the man who was on my left'.[27] By that stage, three weeks into the battle, four divisional generals had been replaced – in addition to Stuart-Wortley, they were Pilcher of the 17th Division, Philipps of the 38th and Dawson of the 39th; none had served directly alongside the 36th, however, so the reference was probably to Stuart-Wortley. Others would follow as the battle continued, including the unfortunate William Rycroft of the 32rd Division, sacked by Gough in November.[28]

One man's misfortune was another's opportunity and by mid-July the talk in London and France was that Nugent was to be promoted. He discounted the suggestion, on the basis that there were no vacancies and that even if there were, there were many generals senior to him; he also claimed, not wholly convincingly, that he would not care to leave the Ulster Division.[29] He need not have worried. The rumours proved unfounded, though his hopes rose momentarily in August when he briefly assumed command of V Corps. It quickly became clear that the appointment was temporary, and when on moving to IX Corps later that month Nugent had another short stint in charge he warned Kitty, 'Dolly [his sister-in-law] need not write a 2nd letter of congratulation. It is only for a while'.[30] While not excessively ambitious he was a capable professional soldier, and a source of frustration for him over the coming months would be the lack of opportunity to gain further laurels for his division and himself while others were carving out reputations in the continuing fighting on the Somme.

Rebuilding the division

Nugent's temper became distinctly frayed in mid-July. Partly this was a reaction to the strain of the Thiepval assault and the heavy losses, which he felt deeply, but it was also due to the news that the division was bound for Flanders: 'I simply loathe the thought of Belgium', he complained, 'its dirt, trenches, flies and inhabitants'.[31] The division entrained on 11–12 July and spent a couple of weeks in the Second Army rear area before going into the line; on the Twelfth he watched 107 Brigade marching to their new billets playing Orange songs and wearing marigolds in their caps, a sign, Falls thought, that confidence was returning.[32] It did not improve Nugent's mood, however, and the same day he wrote, 'The man I loathe is Harry

[27] ON to CN, 20 July 1916 (PRONI, D3835/E/2/305).
[28] Peter Simkins, *From the Somme to Victory: The British Army's Experience on the Western Front 1916–1918* (2014), pp 71–80.
[29] ON to CN, 20 July 1916 (PRONI, D3835/E/2/305).
[30] ON to CN, 25 Aug. 1916, in *Nugent*, p. 261n.
[31] ON to CN, 11 July 1916, in *Nugent*, p. 88.
[32] Falls, *Ulster Division*, p. 63.

Rawlinson, the Army Commander whose senseless optimism is responsible for the practical wiping out of the Division. He is the only man too who has never sent the Division one word of acknowledgement, thanks or praise for what they did for him'.[33] Given that Rawlinson was busy fighting a major battle this was perhaps unfair, but he was not Nugent's only target. A few days later his irritation was directed at the division: 'If you are not Ulster and if you don't subscribe to every Ulster prejudice and if you are not as intolerant as they are, they will have nothing to do with you. … I have found that for 10 months and I feel today no nearer them and no more in touch with them than when I came'.[34] These private comments, written to let off steam, give a misleading impression, and his essential admiration for his men was clear in the same letter:

> They are magnificent soldiers but very hard to know. They think nothing of and know nothing of the months of unceasing preparation and organisation for their attack. Well, all the preparation and organisation in the world would have been useless if there had not been their splendid courage and determination to carry them through.

A further outburst was provoked by criticism, picked up by Kitty, about the conduct of the 1 July attack and the commitment of 107 Brigade, as those at home struggled to come to terms with the scale of the losses. Nugent wrote angrily on 18 July:

> People no doubt talk a lot of ignorant rubbish. I suppose they think I ought to have refused to obey orders for fear someone should get hurt. Don't they understand that I have to carry out orders just as the men under me have to carry out theirs. I get my orders how far I am to go and then my job [is] to work out how we are to do it. Do they think I started the Division off on its own into the German trenches. I am afraid Ulster women are a narrow-minded clique and I dislike them all intensely though I don't know any of them and don't want to.[35]

The main issue now worrying Nugent was again the problem of keeping the division up to strength. In the course of July just over 2,300 replacements joined, less than half the requirement, and Nugent noted with

[33] ON to CN, 12 July 1916, in *Nugent*, pp 89–90.
[34] ON to CN, 15 July 1916, in *Nugent*, pp 90–91.
[35] ON to CN, 18 July 1916, in *Nugent*, p. 92.

concern how slowly drafts were coming in.[36] Fresh divisions were badly needed on the Somme, however, and on 23 July, under-strength or not, the Ulster Division relieved the 20th Division in the trenches opposite Messines. 108 Brigade, the first to go in, was so short-handed – it had less than 3,000 men, a thousand fewer than on 1 July – that its four battalions replaced two of the 20th's, and the other brigades were in the same position. In August the flow of replacements virtually ceased, while that month the division suffered 220 casualties holding the line.[37] One source of replacements Nugent had hoped for, the return of his lightly wounded, had not materialised. As early as 5 July he had sought Carson's help: 'Unless a special point is made of it they will … be sent wherever drafts happen to be most wanted … They must come back to the Division; they would not be happy elsewhere, nor could the Division do without them'. Even Carson, however, could do nothing and later in July Farnham reported that the division was 'gradually getting made up again, but with all sorts, from everywhere which is a great pity, and worst of all a lot of our slightly wounded have been sent to other battalions instead of coming back to us, which is most annoying. Oliver is bucking up a row about it, but fears they will not take much notice'.[38]

The reinforcements reaching the 9th Royal Irish Fusiliers demonstrate the piecemeal nature of the process. Their losses on 1 July, 17 officers and 518 men, were amongst the heaviest anywhere that day, Blacker writing afterwards, 'I feel ashamed almost to be alive'. By 16 July 80 replacements, mostly Irish, had arrived. By then ten of the battalion's slightly wounded men had also returned – though they proved, understandably, 'nervy' when back in the trenches – but 40 others had been posted to the 2nd Royal Irish Rifles, a regular battalion, and despite strenuous efforts it proved impossible to retrieve them. On the night of 23/24 July the Fusiliers and the 12th Royal Irish Rifles jointly took over a stretch of the line previously held by one full-strength battalion. A draft of 40 men arrived on the 24th, and by the 27th the battalion was 513 strong, but with a trench strength of only 200. On 8 August a group of 88 men from the Sherwood Foresters arrived, the first substantial draft of non-Irish soldiers to join, but it was the last significant reinforcement the Fusiliers would receive from any source for the next four months.[39]

---

[36] Ibid.

[37] 108 Bde & 36 Div. AA&QMG war diaries (TNA, WO95/2504 and 2493).

[38] Colvin, *Carson*, iii, p. 185; Farnham to his wife, 25 July 1916 (PRONI, D3975/E/8/10/7).

[39] Blacker letters, 10, 13, 16, 27, 28 July and 8 Aug. 1916.

Once again the division did what it could to stimulate recruiting. A recruiting party was sent home in early August to capitalise on the publicity around 1 July but achieved little, and Nugent was furious: 'The people we wrote to had done nothing', he complained, 'Such a shame and I am so angry about it. I loathe the people of Belfast'.[40] An unfortunately-timed letter from the head of the Orange Order in Belfast, congratulating the division and saying that the Order's hearts went out to it, caused him to let fly: 'I thought this was about the limit, considering that none of them are enlisting, so I replied that if their bodies accompanied their hearts, it would be much more to the point. I think it is sheer impertinence to write flapdoodle of that kind at the present time'.[41]

Second Army

As the division settled back into trench routine, Nugent found the command atmosphere in Second Army very different from 1915. Plumer was more experienced and confident, Allenby and Keir had gone and Tim Harington had arrived as Plumer's chief-of-staff to form one of the western front's most effective command partnerships. Over the next few months Nugent's relationship with them would become very close. The division was now in IX Corps, commanded by Lieutenant-General Sir Alexander Hamilton Gordon, a competent if rather lugubrious officer, and in September they were joined there by the 16th Division. The relationship between the two Irish divisions is considered in the next chapter.

The routine of operations was briefly broken on 14 August when the King visited Second Army and Nugent arranged for him to meet 30 officers and men from the division who had distinguished themselves on 1 July. The conversation over lunch provided an insight into George V's political views:

> [The King] would talk and so did Lord Stamfordham [his private secretary] of the Ulster Divn as the Irish Divn and I had finally to explain that we were the Ulster Divn and that there was an Irish Divn so he said he thought it was a pity we were not called the Irish Divn too as he thought 'Ulster' savoured of politics. I firmly and gently put him right and said there were no politics in the Ulster Division.[42]

Political or not, the division soon found itself playing an active role in Second Army's attempts to harry the opposing German forces, both to

[40] ON to CN, 22 Aug. 1916, in *Nugent*, p. 107.
[41] ON to CN, 10 Aug. 1916, in *Nugent*, p. 104.
[42] ON to CN, 14 Aug. 1916, in *Nugent*, pp 105–06.

prevent their transfer to the Somme and to deny rest to formations sent to Flanders to recover. The methods included all the techniques of aggressive trench warfare, patrolling, sniping, intensive artillery bombardments and, particularly, trench raids, Second Army conducting no fewer than 104 raids between July and mid-November.[43] The policy of raids became increasingly controversial as the war progressed. Falls, while noting the high success rate of Ulster Division raids throughout the war, concluded that they were 'frequently useful, and sometimes imperatively necessary; but the British raided too often'. He cited one brigadier who believed that while raids might have had a good general effect on a unit's morale, that was not necessarily true of the raiders themselves, given the intense strain involved, and that battalions deplored the high casualties amongst 'the very cream of their officers, NCOs and men'.[44] Nugent would not, at this stage of the war, have agreed. He was, as we have seen, an aggressive commander and no front where he was in charge remained quiet for long. On 17 September he told Kitty with macabre enthusiasm:

> Yesterday I gave a part of the German trenches from which they have been giving me great annoyance a real doing, 2 hours in the morning and 2 hours in the afternoon. I had every big gun I could borrow 9", 6" and 4.7". I looked on and it was most pleasing to see the German trenches and dugouts going up into the air, trenches and beams and corrugated iron and one German who went up like a Catherine wheel and came down more or less in pieces on to their wire where he was hanging all yesterday.[45]

A few weeks later he reported:

> This Division has received much commendation for its activity. We were told we were the best Division at strafing the Boche in the 2nd Army, which is satisfactory and encouraging. We certainly do give them a bad time. I have a weekly bombardment and blow his trenches to pieces … and we constantly raid his trenches and blow up his dugouts. He really has a rather bad time with us.[46]

While he went into detail about what his men were doing to the Germans he tended to resort to euphemism when describing the effect of the inevitable response (the Germans had replied 'most rudely', for example, or

---

[43] *OH*, 1916, ii, p. 544.
[44] Falls, *Ulster Division*, p. 71.
[45] ON to CN, 17 Sep. 1916, in *Nugent*, p. 108.
[46] ON to CN, 2 Nov. 1916, in *Nugent*, p. 117.

'the dirty worm has turned'). He was well aware that retaliation was virtually guaranteed – after the September bombardment of the German lines he commented, 'The Boche made no response which is most unusual and I can't think what they are up to. I fully expect something awful in a day or two' – but he continued to believe the military gains were worth it.[47] The most intensive phase of raiding carried out by the division during the war came between mid-September and mid-November 1916: in those eight weeks it made ten raids, involving eight of its twelve infantry battalions.[48] Six were regarded as clear successes, the German trenches being entered and a total of eight prisoners taken, 32 confirmed fatalities inflicted and a further 70 or so 'probables' claimed, in addition to any defenders who may have been in the many dug-outs bombed but not searched. But the raiding parties, which varied in size from 40 to 200, suffered about 120 casualties including seven officers. Two raids by the 11th Royal Inniskilling Fusiliers, at either end of the ten-raid sequence, illustrate the techniques and the challenges.

The first raid was one of six carried out on the night of 15/16 September by IX Corps, four by the 19th Division and two by the Ulster Division. The Inniskillings launched their foray from the Bull Ring, in the British lines, at a section of the German line a short distance away. The raiding party, comprising an officer and 44 men, successfully entered the enemy trenches but the defenders, cut off by a box barrage, fought back hard, the grimness of the fighting illustrated by the fact that one of the Inniskillings had his trouser leg torn off by a German he was bludgeoning to death.[49] The raiders eventually retired with a prisoner and claiming to have inflicted at least 33 other casualties, but their own losses, in addition to nine wounded, included four men missing, three of whom were later reported killed. (The other Ulster raid, by the 9th Royal Irish Rifles, was regarded as a neat success, with the capture of a prisoner and at least six Germans killed for a British loss of an officer and two men wounded.) IX Corps judged the series of raids that night as 'on the whole successful' with seven prisoners taken and an estimated 79 Germans killed, a figure almost certainly inflated. British losses were six officers and 52 men.[50]

[47] ON to CN, 17 Sep. 1916, in *Nugent*, p. 108.

[48] 15 Sep., 9th R. Irish Rifles and 11th R. Inniskilling Fusiliers; 30 Sep., 10th R. Irish Rifles and 10th R. Inniskilling Fusiliers (11th R. Irish Rifles' raid was aborted because of an accidental explosion); 12 Oct., 9th R. Irish Rifles, 9th R. Irish Fusiliers and 9th R. Inniskilling Fusiliers; 31 Oct., 11th R. Irish Rifles and 14th R. Irish Rifles; 16 Nov., 11th R. Inniskilling Fusiliers.

[49] 11th R. Inniskilling Fusiliers war diary (TNA, WO95/2510).

[50] IX Corps war diary (TNA, WO95/835).

The final raid of the series, against the Spanbroek salient on the night of 16 November, was a more clear-cut success. It was bigger, involving four officers and 104 men of the 11th Royal Inniskilling Fusiliers, and the raiders took the defenders, from a newly-arrived Saxon division, completely by surprise. In Falls's words they 'dealt with them in terrible fashion', killing 23 and inflicting perhaps twice as many 'unconfirmed' casualties, and taking three prisoners.[51] The Inniskillings had one man killed, one missing and 14 wounded. When they pulled out they left various booby-traps behind, including grenades under some of the German bodies. Nugent visited the battalion the next day and found its CO, Audley Pratt, 'so excited he was foaming. His battalion is tremendously pleased with itself and cheered itself half the night after it got back. The Army are very pleased as they very much wanted prisoners to establish identifications of troops opposite us'.[52] There was a less satisfactory aspect, however: 'I was rather annoyed that the parties did not take more prisoners but our men wouldn't trust them. They had been had before by Boches holding up their hands and shouting 'Kamerad' while another man took a pot shot from behind him, so they killed everyone almost that they met'.[53] It was not the last time he would complain of Ulster Division raiding parties' reluctance to take prisoners.

Nugent was out constantly visiting – and sometimes 'strafing' – his units. As Falls later recalled:

> One day, when I was commanding a platoon, I saw my then divisional commander on his way to the trenches and had to ask who he was. Yet when a little later I went to divisional headquarters as a staff 'learner' I found that he went out five or six days a week, though often not beyond brigade headquarters. So far as I recall, he visited the trenches at least once a week, but … the average platoon commander might not encounter him for months on end.[54]

He had his share of narrow escapes in the front line. On 1 January 1917, for example, he 'got into the middle of a rather severe shelling and 2 poor men were blown to pieces almost beside me', while a few weeks later, in

[51] Falls, *Ulster Division*, p. 75. For a discussion of the differential performance of regional contingents, including the Saxons, within the German army, see Tony Cowan, 'A picture of German unity? Federal contingents in the German army, 1916–17', in Jonathan Krause (ed.), *The Greater War: Other Combatants and Other Fronts, 1914–1918* (2014), pp 141–60.

[52] ON to CN, 17 Nov. 1916, in *Nugent*, pp 119–20.

[53] ON to St George, 27 Nov. 1916, in *Nugent*, pp 120–21.

[54] Falls, 'Contacts with troops', pp 173–4.

separate incidents within a few days, a German aircraft machine-gunned the trench he was in, a sniper's bullet narrowly missed his head, and enemy artillery pursued him across a field and along a road as he sprinted for safety – presumably, he remarked, because they had 'seen my red band through their telescope and thought a general was worth trying to bag'.[55]

Manpower crisis

While trench warfare continued the crisis over Irish recruitment was coming to a head. It did so in the autumn of 1916 because of the coincidence of the losses of the 16th and 36th Divisions on the Somme (and in the regular Irish battalions also) with the decimation of the 10th (Irish) Division by malaria in Macedonia; the immediate catalyst was the 4,000 casualties suffered by the 16th Division at Guillemont and Ginchy in early September.[56] There were not enough Irish replacements to bring the Irish formations back up to strength and on 29 September the Army Council, chaired by Lloyd George, now at the War Office, met to discuss a paper on Irish recruitment prepared by the Adjutant General, General Macready.

The position it described was serious. Irish infantry units across the army were more than 17,000 below strength: the 10th Division had a deficit of 4,613 men, the 16th Division 4,370, the 36th Division 4,460, and the remaining regular battalions 3,751. Assuming a wastage rate of 10% per month the paper projected that the shortfall would rise to nearly 48,000 within six months. Macready offered five options: introduction of conscription in Ireland; amalgamation of the 16th and 36th; reinforcing the Irish divisions with Englishmen; allowing the divisions gradually to waste away; or transferring Irish units from non-Irish formations to the Irish divisions.[57] The Army Council opted for rationalisation, concluding that as recruiting in Ireland had almost ceased the maintenance of three Irish divisions was no longer possible. Recognising that, for now, conscription was politically unacceptable, they decided that the 16th and 36th Divisions should be amalgamated; but aware of the political implications of this course also, they agreed that John Redmond and Sir Edward Carson should be informed. The proposal was duly relayed to them

[55] ON to CN, 1 Jan., 5 and 19 Mar. 1917, in *Nugent*, pp 129, 134–6.

[56] Denman, *Ireland's Unknown Soldiers: The 16th (Irish) Division in the Great War* (1992), pp 78–103.

[57] Minutes of the Proceedings of, and Precis prepared for, the Army Council for the years 1915 and 1916, p. 55, (TNA, WO163/21); Bowman, *Irish Regiments*, pp 140–42. The Irish divisions were not the only ones under threat: the 38th (Welsh) Division was also identified in Macready's paper as critically under-strength – by over 2,800 men – and at risk of disbandment.

by Lloyd George and their reaction was predictably hostile.[58] Redmond warned that this would have a disastrous effect on Irish recruiting.[59] Carson objected also, writing to Nugent on 10 October that he had been told

> that the amalgamated Division will be called the Irish Division and the name of Ulster will disappear ... I feel perfectly certain that there would be great disappointment in Ulster, and indeed resentment, particularly as the 16th (Irish) Division was never really a Division at all and is now only little more than a brigade.[60]

If the Ulster Division had to be amalgamated, he believed, it should be with the 51st (Highland) Division. Nugent, in London on leave, had already been told of Carson's views by Macready. He was horrified and had written at once to Carson saying that in his opinion this would be a disastrous mistake, arguing that if the two divisions had to disappear as separate formations they should be merged with each other.[61] On receiving Carson's letter he wrote again, expressing disappointment at Carson's prediction there was no hope of Irish conscription. The two options, in his view, were therefore amalgamation or acceptance of drafts from Britain. He continued:

> In the case of the Irish Divisions, I think we must face the fact that amalgamation, whether of Divisions or of Battalions of the same Regiment, can only be a temporary arrest of decay, because the flow of recruits from Ireland has practically ceased. ... Your point that amalgamation would mean the disappearance of the designation 'Ulster' would be equally applicable to amalgamation with a Highland or English Division. As regards the second alternative, I am told that the Secretary of State [Lloyd George] objects to drafts from Great Britain being sent to Irish Divisions. It must be conceded that if we are to be kept going by English or Scotch recruits we cannot claim to be Irish.[62]

Nugent's view was driven as much by political considerations as by military ones and he made no secret of the fact, telling Macready:

> It [amalgamation with non-Irish formations] would mean the complete disappearance of two Irish Divisions and it would be read as an admission that the two Irish Divisions could not combine, that

[58] General Sir Nevil Macready, *Annals of an Active Life* (1924), ii, p. 255.
[59] Denis Gwynn, *Life of John Redmond* (1932), p. 530.
[60] ON to CN, 10 Oct. 1916, in *Nugent*, pp 111–12.
[61] ON to Carson, n.d. but around 8 Oct. 1916, in *Nugent*, pp 111–12.
[62] ON to Carson, 16 Oct. 1916, in *Nugent*, pp 114–15.

Irish creeds and politics were carried into the fighting line. It would be a libel on both Divisions. There are no politics whatever, and I am sure there could be no better cure for Irish home troubles than that Protestants and Catholics should fight together in the same unit.[63]

Ireland was not the only country struggling in the autumn of 1916 to maintain all-volunteer forces, and nor was Nugent the only divisional commander being drawn into political controversy. The Dominions too were feeling the strain, and conscription, introduced in Britain in January 1916 and New Zealand in May, was as fiercely divisive an issue in Australia and Canada as it was in Ireland. In October, as the future of the 16th and 36th Divisions hung in the balance, campaigning in Australia in the first conscription referendum was in full swing, generating 'a public debate that has never been rivalled in Australian political history for its bitterness, divisiveness and violence', and in the run-up to the 28 October vote – which the opponents of conscription narrowly won, as they did a second a year later – the sustainability of Australian formations, like Irish ones, formed part of the debate.[64]

There, as in Ireland, the prospect of formations being disbanded was for the military authorities not just a practical response to manpower shortages but also a source of political pressure. In August 1916 the Army Council had warned the Australian government that the 3rd Australian Division might have to be broken up to provide replacements unless 70,000 men were found by the end of the year. Its commander, John Monash, a supporter of conscription, found himself like Nugent protesting against the possibility of a high-quality division being disbanded: to do so, he argued, would be 'a cruel shame' as his soldiers would be 'torn asunder who enlisted together, represented the same districts and home interests, and hoped to work and fight side by side'.[65] Despite his objections, in September almost 3,000 of his men were transferred to other formations before General Birdwood, the ANZAC commander, persuaded Haig to halt the process. (In the summer of 1917 Arthur Currie, commander of the Canadian Corps, would become embroiled in his turn as a supporter of compulsory service in the equally bitter Canadian debate, though his enthusiasm for conscription had waned by the time the measure was introduced at the end

[63] ON to Macready, 6 Oct. 1916, in *Nugent*, pp 108–09.
[64] Joan Beaumont, *Broken Nation: Australians in the Great War* (2013), p. 223; for Australia's manpower difficulties, see Jean Bou and Peter Dennis, *The Australian Imperial Force* (2016), pp 60–70.
[65] Geoffrey Serle, *John Monash* (1982), p. 268.

of 1917.)[66] Nugent's problems were not, therefore, unique. Hickie too faced them, though in the absence of his correspondence it is harder to see in detail how he handled the challenging task of dealing with nationalist politicians on the issue: he was, however, more tactful than Nugent and seems to have maintained good working relations with them.

In a parliamentary debate on 18 October John Redmond spoke of his sadness that, despite all he could do, Irish regiments at the front might not be kept up to strength, but when he asked whether Irish recruits drafted to Scottish regiments would be returned to Irish units the Secretary of State's response was pointed: 'That involves another question. It involves restoring to English regiments the Englishmen put into Irish regiments. I am sorry to say that there are a great many battalions that have really ceased to be Irish'.[67] At the time he made it Lloyd George's statement was incorrect but that was about to change. The Army Council met again the following day and, recognising that political considerations would have to take precedence, referred the issue to the War Cabinet, which duly decided to drop the amalgamation proposal and allow drafts of English troops to be sent to Irish units instead. On 26 October GHQ in France received approval from the War Office for 'reinforcing Irish units with Englishmen, keeping the Regular Irish bns supplied with Irishmen', and shortly afterwards Macready explained to Redmond that the army regarded it as particularly important to retain the Irish character of the regular battalions.[68] On 5 November Nugent wrote to Hacket Pain, commanding the reserve brigade in Ireland:

> This, I understand, is the policy which has been adopted. The 'Ulster' designation, or 'Irish', as the case may be, will be taken away as soon as the Irish Divisions have more than 50% of men from Great Britain in their ranks. This is reasonable. Anything which gives us men is better than the state of suspended animation in which we have lived for the last four months.[69]

The first conscripts began to arrive soon after – the 9th Royal Irish Fusiliers, for example, at last got a fresh draft of 103 men, mostly from the London

---

[66] A. M. J. Hyatt, *General Sir Arthur Currie: A Military Biography* (1987), pp 91–5.

[67] House of Commons: Parliamentary Debates 1916, 86: Cols 647–50.

[68] Minutes of the Proceedings of, and Precis prepared for, the Army Council for the years 1915 and 1916, p. 26, (TNA, WO163/21); AG GHQ France War Diary, 26 Oct. 1916 (TNA WO95/26); Macready to Redmond, 31 Oct. 1916 (Perry, 'Nationality', pp 82–3).

[69] ON to Hacket Pain, 5 Nov. 1916, in *Nugent*, p. 118.

Regiment, in November and a further 89 men of the West Yorkshire Regiment in December – and on 24 November Nugent inspected 300 new arrivals:

> I found artisans of all sorts, cooks of all kinds, entree cooks, pastry cooks, plain cooks, and one great find, a music hall comedian. I asked him what line he did and he said 'I'm versatile, sing, dance or juggle', so I have said he is to be marked down for our Follies. I gave them an address and good advice and said I hoped they would be very happy and well looked after and at the end they called out 'Thank you Sir'! I nearly fainted. Such want of discipline, on parade too. Besides the idea of the British soldier thanking one for anything was too much.[70]

Battalion commanders

For Nugent, as for every divisional commander, his infantry COs were of vital importance and he devoted considerable attention to their assessment, development and replacement: this was not a task he left to his brigadiers. He made a particular effort to get to know them as individuals at a level beyond simply meeting them on inspection visits or at conferences. Soon after arriving in France he had instituted weekly lunches at his headquarters with three or four COs and after the Somme he resumed the practice but extended it to an overnight stay. Stewart Blacker was one of the first invitees, in mid-August, and enjoyed the experience. He was collected by car in time for lunch, at which Nugent and his principal staff officers were 'very affable', and was then left to relax. Having just come out of the line he found the peace and quiet restful – divisional HQ at that point was in the attractive chateau of Mont Noir – and the following day he

> lay out in the hay in the shade, and listened to the wood pigeons. After a 9.00 a.m. breakfast I read the 'Times' and then went and inspected the two offices – 'G' branch with Place and Bruce, and then 'Q' with Singleton, and put forward various suggestions and views, which were received in a most friendly spirit. The Gen. went off to the trench line about 9.30 a.m. and is only just back. I must say he's more than kind and thoughtful, and insists on my doing exactly what I like, always ready to chat and discuss men and affairs.

Two other COs had been invited but made their excuses, which Blacker thought was because they were frightened of Nugent.[71] Once word got out,

---

[70] ON to CN, 24 Nov. 1916, in *Nugent*, p. 120.
[71] Blacker letters, 16, 17 and 18 Aug. 1916.

however, the invitations were eagerly taken up and Nugent told Kitty a short time later that the officers liked the surroundings and seemed to enjoy themselves, adding, 'I get a chance of knowing them better than if I only see them in the trenches'.[72] In February 1917 he told Plumer:

> I have made a point of … getting to know COs and giving them a chance to meet the Divisional staff. Until the weather got too cold, I always had a weekend party of a couple of COs. They seemed to like it, and anyhow I think they appreciated being asked. It is a good thing to ask COs from different Brigades as they scarcely ever meet each other. I have found it most beneficial in mitigating the repugnance with which the Divisional Commander is usually regarded by the Battalion CO.[73]

Turnover amongst COs was high. Although the division was not involved in a major engagement between the Somme and Messines, only two of the eleven COs to survive the 1 July attack (Bernard of the 10th Royal Irish Rifles was killed in Thiepval wood) were still in post in June 1917, Macrory (10th Royal Inniskilling Fusiliers) and Gordon (15th Royal Irish Rifles). Three had left on promotion by the end of 1916 – Bull (12th Royal Irish Rifles), Crozier (9th Royal Irish Rifles) and Ricardo (9th Royal Inniskilling Fusiliers) – while a fourth, Pelly (8th Royal Irish Rifles), returned briefly to his parent unit, the Princess Patricia's Canadian Light Infantry, before being promoted early in 1917. Whether or not Nugent's refusal to allow his colonels to go over the top on 1 July had been wise, their preservation was now of real benefit to the army. The unfortunate George Bull lasted only four days in command of 8 Brigade before being fatally wounded on 7 December 1916, but the others survived the war.

Of the other five COs, Brush (11th Royal Inniskilling Fusiliers) went in August 1916; Bowen (14th Royal Irish Rifles) was evacuated sick in October (his successor, Lloyd, followed suit in January 1917); and Pakenham (11th Royal Irish Rifles), Savage (13th Royal Irish Rifles) and Blacker (9th Royal Irish Fusiliers), all in their fifties with a year or more of honourable front-line service behind them, left during the winter through ill-health or transfer to non-operational roles, Blacker being the last to go in March 1917. All but one of the resulting vacancies were filled by internal promotion of officers already serving in the division as battalion 2ic's or senior majors (two of whom, Burnand and Somerville, were regulars who

---

[72] ON to CN, 21 Aug 1916, in *Nugent*, p. 106.
[73] ON to Plumer, 2 Feb. 1917, in *Nugent*, p. 132.

had been posted in as 2ic's, effectively as COs in waiting).[74] The final vacancy was filled by a regular officer transferred in directly from outside, Cheape of the 14th Royal Irish Rifles, of whom more below. The pattern here reflected a broader development in the BEF, the emergence by the second half of 1916 of a cadre of battalion commanders whose expertise was based on wartime rather than pre-war service.[75] When Nugent took over in September 1915 ten of his COs were retired officers recalled to service ('dug-outs') and two were Indian army officers diverted to the New Armies. By 1 July 1916 the balance had shifted, to two regulars, seven dug-outs, two Indian army and a wartime officer, i.e. without pre-war regular commissioned service (Frank Macrory, 10th Royal Inniskilling Fusiliers). By June 1917 the make-up had changed again, to three regulars, three dug-outs and six wartime officers.[76] This trend was seen in New Army divisions across the BEF and by the end of the war one third of all service battalions were commanded by wartime officers.

Nugent had, however, constantly to wrestle with a lack of depth in the quality of his officer cadre. He had found this when he assumed command, and others identified the same problem – Place, for example, on joining regarded the division's soldiers as being as good as any in the army, but was less impressed by the officers.[77] When Ricardo wrote to Nugent in December 1916 from his new division, the 37th, he offered a comparison of the two formations: his assessment was that the 37th's soldiers were not nearly as good as the Ulster Division's, but that its officers and NCOs were generally better and it had 'more material for 2nd in Comd and future COs than we had in 36th'.[78] After the wave of CO departures in the second half of 1916 Nugent's resources were getting thin with the consequence that he shouldered even more of the load himself. 'I find my work increasing daily', he noted in September:

---

[74] Blair Oliphant (11th R. Irish Rifles), Burnand (10th R. Irish Rifles), Cole-Hamilton (8th R. Irish Rifles), Goodwin (12th R. Irish Rifles), Peacocke (9th R. Inniskilling Fusiliers), Perceval-Maxwell (13th R. Irish Rifles), Pratt (11th R. Inniskilling Fusiliers), Somerville (9th R. Irish Fusiliers) and Woods (9th R. Irish Rifles).

[75] Peter E. Hodgkinson, *British Infantry Battalion Commanders in the First World War* (2015), pp 47–68.

[76] Regulars – Burnand, Cheape & Somerville; dug-outs – Blair Oliphant, Gordon & Pratt; wartime – Cole-Hamilton, Goodwin, Macrory, Peacocke, Perceval-Maxwell and Woods (Cole-Hamilton had served in South Africa as a militia officer).

[77] Spender to his wife, 7 May 1916, in *Nugent*, p. 256n.

[78] Ricardo to Nugent, 12 Dec. 1916, in *Nugent*, p. 123.

Our Army has got too big for the number of trained officers available to fill such positions as Commanding Officers and even Brigadiers. Result I have to supervise and investigate and poke my nose into questions of detail which ought not to be necessary … This adds very materially to one's daily work, I can assure you, also to one's anxieties and responsibilities.[79]

By the end of the year the situation was no better – '[m]ost of my best COs have gone home on sick leave or got brigades' he told Kitty, 'and so I am having to run things more myself than I had to do'.[80]

He asked GHQ for help in respect of one unit in particular, the 14th Royal Irish Rifles still being a cause of concern. The battalion had been unlucky in the high turnover of its COs, always a source of disruption – its war diary noted in January 1917, '[u]sual luck of this Bn, cannot keep a CO, this is number seven since we came on service' – but Nugent regarded it as unreliable and asked the Adjutant General's branch for 'a CO and a large draft of Englishmen to try to create a fighting spirit in them'.[81] Every unit in the division was receiving such drafts by the winter of 1916/17 but a capable new CO, Lieutenant-Colonel Cheape, a cavalry officer who had proved himself with the 7th Black Watch, was posted in in February 1917 to provide the Rifles with some badly-needed stability.

Nugent's relationship with his senior COs evolved over time. Formidable though he was, his high regard for officers like Hessey, Ricardo, Peacocke and Blacker was increasingly reciprocated with a degree of affection. Blacker detected a softening in him after the Thiepval attack, writing on 1 August, 'The Gen. was round this morning and was most pleasant. He has quite changed, and it's now quite a pleasure to meet him', and some months later George Bruce, then on Nugent's staff, told Spender that Nugent 'was a changed man and was doing all he could – with success – to be popular with the Division'.[82] In his letter of December 1916 Ricardo was effusive:

> I rejoiced when I heard you were going to command the Division
> and I never for one moment changed that feeling. I have always
> admired and respected you as a chief and you won my affection as
> an unfailing friend – you'd be surprised perhaps to know how widely
> that feeling for you is throughout the Division – we are an

[79] ON to CN, 13 Sep. 1916, in *Nugent*, p. 262n.
[80] ON to CN, 10 Dec. 1916 (PRONI, D3835/E/2/379).
[81] 14th Rifles war diary, 17 Jan. 1917 (TNA, WO95/2511); ON to AG, GHQ, 11 Dec. 1917, in *Nugent*, p. 196.
[82] Blacker letters, 1 Aug. 1916; Spender to his wife, 27 Mar. 1917, in Baguley, *Question of Ulster*, p. 210.

inarticulate nation. You should have had a Corps long ago and I
hope for the Army's sake that you soon get one but it will be a black
day when you leave the Ulster Division.[83]

Even allowing for his gratitude for his promotion and the fact that he was
lobbying for a return to the division (which he obtained the following
month, when Shuter left to instruct at the Senior Officers' School at
Aldershot), there was genuine warmth in Ricardo's remarks. Frank Crozier,
another beneficiary of promotion, was equally admiring, describing Nugent
as a great friend and recalling his advice, when Crozier left in November
1916 to command 119 Brigade in the 40th Division, to treat his four
battalions as 'four big companies'.[84] Nugent's view of him, though, was
more equivocal, Crozier having been one of his strangest subordinates.[85]
Originally commissioned into the Manchester Regiment before being
forced to resign for bouncing cheques, he subsequently joined the UVF and
became CO of the 9th Royal Irish Rifles early in 1916. Admired by some
as a fine fighting soldier, disliked by others as a ruthless bully, he showed in
his various post-war autobiographical works something of an obsession
with shooting his own men to maintain discipline. According to Spender,
Nugent thought long and hard before recommending Crozier for
promotion because he was so rough with his soldiers, but in the end
Crozier's undoubted aptitude for fighting overcame Nugent's doubts.[86]

The Christmas message

As 1916 drew to a close one positive development from Nugent's
perspective was Asquith's replacement by Lloyd George, who, whatever his
role in the Irish negotiations, he rightly believed would prosecute the war
with resolution.[87] Less encouraging was the manpower situation. Despite
the War Cabinet's October decision, the division at the turn of the year was
still badly under strength and Nugent described the wearing effect of this
in a frustrated memo to GHQ in early 1917. The division had been
operating for the past six months, he pointed out, with a manpower deficit
of between 4,500 and 3,679; the men, overworked and tired, were going

---

[83] Ricardo to Nugent, 12 Dec. 1916, in *Nugent*, p. 124.

[84] Crozier to Edmonds, 23 Mar. 1930 (TNA, CAB45/188); F. P. Crozier, *Impressions
and Recollections* (1930), p. 178.

[85] See Messenger, *Broken Sword, passim*; see also Michael Taylor, 'The history of 119
Infantry Brigade in the Great War with special reference to the command of
Brigadier-General Frank Percy Crozier' (PhD thesis, University of Birmingham,
2016).

[86] Spender to Edmonds, 3 May 1930 (TNA, CAB45/191).

[87] ON to CN, 7 Dec. 1916, in *Nugent*, p. 122.

sick in increasing numbers and morale was suffering. It was neither fair nor sensible, he warned, to keep the division languishing in this condition.[88] It was against this backdrop that in December 1916, when the *Belfast Newsletter* asked him for a Christmas message to the people of Ulster, Nugent leapt at the chance. 'I am giving them beans and no mistake', he remarked happily, 'laying it on with scorpions'.[89] His message duly appeared on 26 December:

> A message to the people of Ulster from the Ulster Division must contain, besides greetings and good wishes, some hard truths ... the Ulster Division is growing stronger day by day, but its ranks are being filled up by Englishmen and Scotchmen: men who have not shirked duty, and who have done for Ulster what she has, as yet, failed to do for herself.[90]

He also referred to 'the contempt which Ireland is heaping up for herself' on the recruitment issue and to 'the road upon which Ireland is drifting leaderless today'. He sent the press cutting to Kitty a few days later: 'I enclose the Belfast News Letter with my message to the Ulster loafers ... Don't you think it a rather good message, just some plain speaking. I have had 2 letters of protest already which shows that it left a sting'.[91] In fact it caused deep offence, made worse when nationalist demonstrators in Dublin reproduced it on placards as evidence that unionist criticisms of the nationalist contribution to the war effort were hypocritical. Ulster unionism generally was outraged (its leaders were reported to be still furious the following May), there were calls in the Belfast press for his removal and it was rumoured that Craig had refused to have anything to do with the division while Nugent remained in command.[92] In January 1917 Lily Spender described how Lady Carson 'was sniffing very much ... over General Nugent's message to Ulster in the papers, as so were we all', while Spender heard that 'Belfast's main topic of conversation is ON's unpopularity and that this is mainly responsible for no more men coming forward now'.[93] However well-received the message was in France – 'people

[88] ON to AG GHQ, n.d. but around 1 Feb. 1917, in *Nugent*, pp 130–31.

[89] ON to CN, 19 Dec. 1916, in *Nugent*, p. 263n.

[90] *Belfast Newsletter*, 26 Dec. 1916.

[91] ON to CN, 30 Dec. 1916, in *Nugent*, p. 129.

[92] ON to CN, 3 Mar. and 26 May 1917, in *Nugent*, pp 148, 260n.

[93] Lily Spender to Spender, 2 Feb. 1917, in Baguley, *Question of Ulster*, p. 176; Spender to his wife, 9 Jan. 1917 (PRONI, D1633/1/1/554).

out here', claimed Nugent, 'were delighted with it' – its impact in terms of political relationships was counter-productive.[94]

Indeed, there seems to have been, at some point in 1917, a politically-motivated attempt to remove him from command. After the war Crozier claimed that, while on leave from the 40th Division, he had been asked by Craig to meet Andrew Bonar Law, the Conservative leader; while Crozier does not say when this was, he mentions that Craig was holding a minor government appointment (Craig was a government whip until January 1918) and one possibility is March 1917, when Crozier may have been at home. According to Crozier, Bonar Law told him that 'it could be arranged at GHQ, that I should get the Ulster Division', but once Crozier realised that this would involve Nugent's removal rather than promotion he rejected the offer – 'although naturally any soldier wants promotion, yet not at the expense of his Chief, to whom he owed everything in France' – and told Nugent. Crozier is not always a reliable witness and there is no mention of this episode in Nugent's correspondence, but if accurate it helps explain his vehement dislike of Craig by mid-1917.[95]

While this controversy continued, in February and March further large-scale drafts arrived with the 36th Division, at last bringing it up to strength. The price, however, was the continuing dilution of its Ulster identity. The 14th Royal Irish Rifles provides an example: when the battalion arrived in France in October 1915, just under a thousand strong, 98% of its soldiers were Protestant and at least 97% had next of kin living in Ulster, mostly Belfast. Between December 1915 and May 1916, a further 87 reinforcements arrived, of whom 93% were Protestant and 95% Ulstermen. On 1 July the battalion suffered over 300 casualties, and during the rest of July it received 171 replacements. In the first departure from its Ulster identity these included 87 men from Britain (mostly from the KRRC) and 30 southern Irish Catholics. There followed a lengthy period when it received very few replacements: only 80 men, all but seven Ulster Protestants, joined between August 1916 and the end of January 1917. In February 1917 the battalion at last received the long-awaited drafts to bring it up to strength, but of the 382 men who joined three-quarters were English.[96] A majority of the Ulster Division was still Irish in the spring of 1917 – almost two-thirds in the infantry – but the proportion was falling, prompting hostile questions in parliament about the number of Irish battalions receiving non-Irish drafts.[97]

[94] ON to CN, 26 May 1917, in *Nugent*, p. 148.
[95] F. P. Crozier, *Impressions and Recollections* (1930), pp 207–08.
[96] Perry, 'Nationality', pp 83–4.
[97] House of Commons Parliamentary Debates 1917, 91, Col. 376.

The title

At the end of April 1917 Nugent received an unwelcome message from a visiting GHQ staff officer:

> The gist of it is that the C in C out here won't use us for any purpose but holding the line so long as we call ourselves the Ulster Division, because he considers that it is unfair to Englishmen who have compulsory service that they should be sent to fill up a Division supposed to be composed of volunteers from Ulster, but who won't volunteer, that if we want to be called Ulster we must fill up our own ranks, but that if we are prepared to drop the title of Ulster we shall be treated as any other Division, get men and be used in something more glorious than trench drudges. Now the whole difficulty is this, that GHQ won't put this in writing, but they want me to start the correspondence by offering on behalf of the Division to drop the title of Ulster.[98]

Nugent was dismayed, less by the thought of losing the title than by the fear he was being used. The understanding of the previous autumn had been that the titles of the Irish divisions would be reconsidered once their proportion of Irish soldiers fell below 50%. For the Ulster Division that point had now been reached; while its infantry was still 64% Irish, when all arms were included the overall proportion was around 50%.[99] (The 16th Division was in the same position, but if there was a similar approach by Haig to Hickie evidence of it has not survived.) It was one thing to acquiesce in a change if imposed, another to take the opprobrium of volunteering it:

> What would happen? The politicians at home would at once kick up a row, call it an insult to Ulster and so on. The War Office would then say 'we never suggested it. The GOC the Ulster Divn suggested it of his own initiative'. Can't you imagine the outcry amongst the cats round Lady Carson's com[mi]tee table and the stayathomes of Belfast. They would never rest till they got me hounded out and we have to live in Ireland after the war. I would do it all the same tomorrow if it is the only way, but it is so unfair to try and throw the onus of taking the first step upon me that I am trying to get GHQ to say it in writing. Why should I be made the scapegoat for the wrath of the dirty politicians of the Craig type.[100]

[98] ON to CN, 29 Apr. 1917, in *Nugent*, p. 139.
[99] Plumer to AG GHQ, 3 May 1917, in *Nugent*, p. 142.
[100] ON to CN, 29 Apr. 1917, in *Nugent*, pp 139–40.

Nugent also vented his anger at his division's inability to play its full part in the fighting: 'Not that I have a word to say against the men out here. They are always good, but I wish I had never seen a political Division and the people who thought they were going to run it can never forgive me because I would not allow any politics in it'. His situation was made more difficult because of his strained relationship with Haig, dating back to their time at Staff College. Their recent meetings had been friendly enough, not least one in December 1916 to which Nugent had not looked forward but which in fact went well:

> Nothing could have been more charming. He said 'I must thank you for all the splendid work done by your Division since it came out. You did magnificently on the Somme and I always think with regret that we failed to give you all the support we ought to have done'. I thanked him and said I thought that perhaps we had all been rather optimistic as to what it was possible to do. He replied 'Well, we were all learning'.[101]

Behind this encouraging exchange, however, the old tensions remained: 'Alas for my prospects', Nugent told Kitty, 'I never got on with him and we have always been anti sympatica or antipathetic or mutually antagonistic or whatever one may call it'.[102] He therefore sought Plumer's advice on how to respond, and to his relief Plumer offered to raise the issue himself. He did so on 3 May, suggesting to GHQ that, given a possible reluctance amongst non-Ulstermen to be drafted into a formation with such a distinctive title, it was 'for consideration whether it would not now be generally advantageous to omit the title 'Ulster' and let the Division be styled the 36th simply'.[103] Nugent in turn consulted his COs, and at a conference on 16 May their unanimous view was that that the title should be retained, though at his insistence they emphasised that their attachment to it was 'from association and sentiment and in no way political' and that whatever the decision was it would be loyally supported. Nugent also warned them 'that they must remember they were soldiers and must not start work behind the backs of higher authority by writing to their political friends'. He then reported to Hamilton Gordon that in the opinion of his officers and himself the title was highly valued, not just by Ulstermen but by a majority of the Englishmen serving with the division, that its loss would be deeply felt and that they wished to keep it, but that the decision

[101] ON to CN, 20 Dec. 1916, in *Nugent*, p. 126.
[102] ON to CN, 20 May 1917, in *Nugent*, p. 145.
[103] Plumer to AG GHQ, 3 May 1917, in *Nugent*, p. 142.

rested with the higher command.[104] Faced with this, GHQ dropped the proposal but the Ulster Division, like the 16th Division, received no further large-scale drafts of English troops from this point on. The Irish infantry had to depend increasingly on the cannibalisation of its own units to provide replacements. Nor had Nugent done himself any favours with Haig.

For the rest of the summer he was too busy concentrating on fighting two major battles to worry overmuch about titles. The fact that both were fought alongside the 16th Division, with all the symbolic issues that raised, was further evidence that for officers commanding Irish formations in the Great War, politics and operations could never be entirely separated.

[104] Nugent to IX Corps, 16 May 1917, and ON to CN, 17 May 1917, in *Nugent*, pp 143–5.

7

Wearing Out

The Irish Divisions, attrition and the limits of partnership, April–August 1917

Introduction

The summer of 1917 was one of stark contrasts for Nugent, with the spectacular and widely-celebrated success of Messines in early June, directed by a commander whom he admired deeply, being followed just ten weeks later by a costly and demoralising defeat at Ypres under a general he held in contempt ever after.

With the Ulster Division's manpower difficulties temporarily resolved the first half of 1917 was for it, like the rest of the army, a period of significant operational development. The introduction of new tactics and technology and the associated organisational changes not only altered the way Nugent's soldiers fought on the battlefield, it also had implications for the role he and his headquarters, like their counterparts in other divisions, played within the BEF's evolving command framework. The new methods worked well at Messines and the successful cooperation there of the 16th and 36th Divisions, which Nugent and Hickie worked hard to bring about, was regarded by many as symbolising the possibility of reconciling political differences in Ireland. Its timing, as the Irish Convention prepared to meet in Dublin in another attempt to reach a settlement, invested the sight of Irishmen from both traditions fighting alongside each other with particular force. Yet that partnership collapsed amidst mud, machine-gun fire and a degree of mutual recrimination at Ypres in August, a failure that affected Nugent personally more than any of his other battles, while the disappointed hopes in Flanders would be mirrored in the coming months by ebbing optimism for the Convention's prospects.

The 36th and 16th Divisions

When, in September 1916, the 16th Division joined the Ulster Division in IX Corps it seemed to some a step towards the outcome long sought by John Redmond and his Irish Party colleagues, the creation of an 'Irish Corps' comparable to the Australian and Canadian Corps, with its implication of Dominion status. Redmond, like Nugent, believed that shared service could help bridge domestic divides and in late 1915, as the 16th Division prepared to follow the 36th to France, he had declared, 'I pray that whenever a battalion of the Irish Brigade goes into action there may be a battalion of the Ulster Division alongside them … Let Irishmen come together in the trenches and spill their blood together and I say there is no power on earth when they come home can induce them to turn as enemies one upon the other'.[1] Ulster unionists like Spender were equally strongly opposed to the idea of brigading the divisions. 'It would be a doubtful experiment in peace but in war it is criminal', he warned in December 1915:

> Imagine what will happen if one of our units is late in coming up in support through no fault of their own, or vice versa, or if one of their patrols gets fired on by our guns. The mutual suspicion will become certain distrust, and then military cooperation the secret of success would go overboard and the Germans would get in.

His fundamental concern, though, was political rather than operational:

> To mix the N and S Irish in this way is presumably to make them willing to agree to set up an independent household together apart from the British, to remove their mutual antagonisms so that they may be content to have Home Rule. In a few days the papers will be rhapsodizing over the reconciliation of the Irish etc etc, and people will begin to think that Home Rule will not be so bad after all and the trickiness of Redmond will begin to work.[2]

His alarm may have been overdone but he was describing accurately enough Redmond's political objective, while his prediction of the press reaction to a joint success is precisely what occurred after Messines. Nor was nervousness about how well the two formations would get on confined to unionists: officers in the 2nd Royal Dublin Fusiliers, a regular battalion that joined the 16th Division in late 1916, were worried that their men's morale might be undermined by bringing the divisions together.[3] In fact the British command had no intention of creating a permanent Irish corps in the autumn of 1916. The 16th Division was transferred to the Ypres sector for the same reason as the Ulster Division, to recover from its losses and release fresh divisions for the Somme. If there was a deeper motive for posting them to the same corps at this point it may have been that their

[1] Denman, *Ireland's Unknown Soldiers*, pp 28–9.
[2] Spender to his wife, 14 Dec. 1915, in *Nugent*, pp 40–41.
[3] W. T. Colyer memoir (IWM), quoted in Bowman, *Irish Regiments*, p. 155.

amalgamation was being considered, which collocation would have facilitated.

When the move eventually happened Spender's reaction (he was no longer with the division) was relatively restrained: 'I hear that the 16th has been plumped down next to the 36th', he told Lily in October 1916, 'and tho' I think it will not matter, I wish these political experiments could be avoided by well-meaning soldiers, and some time-serving wire pullers'. They both assumed Nugent was behind the move, partly because Lady Carson had told people, based on the exchanges with her husband, that Nugent favoured amalgamation of the two divisions.[4] There is no evidence at all that Nugent had any influence on the decision but from the outset he saw it as an opportunity to promote reconciliation and demonstrate Irish solidarity in support of the war effort. It followed that he and his opposite number, Hickie – a capable and charming Catholic officer from a Tipperary land-owning family, known to be sympathetic to Home Rule – were determined to make the partnership a success.

Over the coming months relations between the divisions proved to be very good at officer level and generally so amongst the soldiers. A potentially tricky moment came in late September when units from the two formations first encountered each other in the line, and it was with relief that Lewis Comyn on the divisional staff was able to tell Farnham that '[t]he 16th have come in on our flank and so far everything goes all right and the men are hobnobbing quite amicably in the trenches. It is fortunate that both Divs have done so well and that neither can reproach the other'.[5] Historians have, however, pointed out that the goodwill had its limits, and also the relatively sparse and rather mixed testimony from the lower ranks.[6] An officer of the 14th Royal Irish Rifles described handing over the line to a Dublin Fusiliers battalion before Messines – 'As the Dublins came in one of them remarked "Glory be to God will you look at the Carson Boys". "Get the hell out of that you bloody Fenians"'; Stephen Gwynn, a nationalist MP serving with the 6th Connaught Rangers, which included many Belfast Catholics, noted that while 'fraternisation worked gradually' there were initial suspicions; an Englishman serving in the 9th Royal Irish Rifles recalled an air of restraint between the two formations.[7] The impression nevertheless remains that the soldiers of both divisions mostly

---

[4] Spender to his wife, 17 Oct. 1916 and her reply of 20 Oct., in Baguley, *Question of Ulster*, pp 149–51.

[5] Comyn to Farnham, 24 Sep. 1916 (PRONI, D3975/E/8/11).

[6] Bowman, *Irish Regiments*, pp 154–5; Grayson, *Belfast Boys*, p. 103.

[7] Sir Percy McElwaine memoir (IWM), quoted in *Nugent*, p. 260n; Denman, *Ireland's Forgotten Soldiers*, p. 150; Grayson, *Belfast Boys*, p. 103.

got on well. Gwynn was soon writing that 'we are alongside of the Ulster Division and making great friends with them', after the war referring to the good relations between the divisions that were 'undone later in Ireland', while an Ulster soldier later recalled the friendly visits he and his comrades exchanged with their 16th Division neighbours.[8] Perceval-Maxwell of the 13th Royal Irish Rifles observed in May 1917 that '[t]he men get on very well though of course now there is a very big English element in both' and in July, after Messines, he described how when his battalion took over billets from a 16th Division unit 'when they left our band played them out of camp and the men cheered them. They were Munsters. As Holt [Waring] and I watched it we couldn't help laughing as three years ago it would not have been safe to let the two Batts into the same Parish much less the same field'.[9] Nugent and Hickie saw sport as a means of building relationships, and in December 1916 Nugent told Kitty:

> The 16th Irish Division next door to us is very friendly. They have presented 4 cups for boxing competition to be competed for by the Ulster Division. Quite embarrassing as of course we shall have to do likewise. Still it's all for good and as I have no doubt L[loyd] G[eorge] means to give Ireland Home Rule all round as the price of men, anything which tends to promote good feeling will tell afterwards.[10]

The boxing match in January 1917 was very successful, and an Ulster Division officer described the speeches made afterwards by Hickie and Nugent:

> They said the greatest compliment one could have was to fight beside, behind, or in front of each other, and neither wished for anything better and had perfect confidence in each other. It was grand to hear it and would have done all extreme "Sinn Feiners" and Orangemen quite a lot of good if they heard it. But I expect when they all get home into the "Unfortunate Country" it will be forgotten and they will be at each others' throats again.[11]

A football match between the 9th Royal Irish Fusiliers and 6th Connaught Rangers in April 1917 attracted a crowd of up to 3,000 and was played,

---

[8] Bowman, *Irish Regiments*, p. 154; Grayson, *Belfast Boys*, p. 103; Colin Reid, 'Stephen Gwynn and the failure of constitutional nationalism in Ireland, 1919–21', *Historical Journal*, 53:3 (2010), p. 725.

[9] Perceval-Maxwell to his parents, 12 May and 25 July 1917, in *Nugent*, p. 260n.

[10] ON to CN, 17 Dec. 1916, in *Nugent*, p. 125.

[11] Herdman to his mother, 1 Feb. 1917 (PRONI, T2510/1).

according to Rowland Feilding, the Rangers' English CO, 'in a spirit of friendliness which ... seems unattainable on Ireland's home soil'; an Ulsterman wondered in jest if they would get into trouble for fraternising with the enemy.[12] These cordial relations would soon be tested against a real enemy.

Before then Nugent had met, and like many of his military colleagues was impressed by, Willie Redmond, John Redmond's brother, whose engaging personality and example in serving at the front despite being in his fifties made him the Home Ruler British officers most admired. After entertaining Redmond to dinner in December 1916 Nugent told Kitty: 'All I can say is that if all Nationalists were like him, I am not surprised that Chief Secretaries and Viceroys after a short time in Ireland become H[ome] R[uler]s. He is the most charming and delightful person I ever met'.[13] Others found Redmond equally disarming. He, Stephen Gwynn, Nugent and Somerset Saunderson not long afterwards were entertained by Lieutenant-General Sir Alexander Godley, commanding II ANZAC Corps and a friend of Nugent's from Ireland, who used almost identical language to describe Redmond and his 'moderate and reasonable views' – 'we are all quite of the opinion that the Irish question will be settled in the trenches in Flanders, where the Ulster Division and the South Irish Division ... are lying side by side'.[14] Redmond himself repeatedly stressed the potentially transformative effect of shared service. In December 1916 he recounted in a parliamentary speech how, when visiting the forward trenches, he had passed without realising it from a sector held by an Inniskilling battalion of the 16th Division to that of a neighbouring Inniskilling unit in the 36th. If it was possible, he argued, for men with such divergent views in politics and religion to stand shoulder to shoulder in face of the common enemy it had to be possible for them to agree on the future government of Ireland.[15] In late May 1917, in what would be their last meeting, Nugent described how

> after lunch we had a long talk in my hut on the prospects of a settlement in Ireland. He is very hopeful though he recognises that the people of NE Ulster and Belfast will be the obstacle. He said all the respectable Nationalist classes in Ireland sincerely desire a

[12] Rowland Feilding, *War Letters to a Wife: France & Flanders 1915–1919* (1929), p. 170.

[13] ON to CN, 5 Dec. 1916, in *Nugent*, p. 121.

[14] Ann Godley (ed.), *Letters of Arthur, Lord Kilbracken and General Sir Alexander Godley, GCB, KCMG, 1898–1932* (n.d. but *c.* 1940), p. 82.

[15] Terence Denman, *A Lonely Grave: The life and death of William Redmond* (1995), p. 102.

settlement and would make any concession almost to the extreme party in Ulster in order to gain a settlement by consent but short of partition to which no Nationalist will agree.[16]

Both of them, moderate nationalist and all-island unionist, were pinning their hopes on shared war experience and the deliberations of the Convention. Both were equally unrealistic. It was too much to expect, as one scholar has observed, that centuries of mistrust could be overcome by a few years' joint service in France and Belgium, and the more sons of Ulster who died fighting for the Union and the more nationalists who gave their lives for an Ireland free and undivided, the harder a settlement became: the reality was that, however comradely the feelings at the front, at home the war 'was driving Ireland apart, not bringing Ireland together'.[17]

Beyond Ireland the spring of 1917 saw two seismic international developments which Nugent thought boded well for the allies' prospects. 'What a stupendous affair the Russian Revolution is', he noted in March, 'I hope it is all for good so far as the progress of the war is concerned'. His hopes that the overthrow of the Tsar would re-energise the Russian war-effort would prove illusory but his assessment of the impact of America's declaration of war was more accurate: 'The entry of America is a great moral affair even if she is not able to add much at present to the effective fighting strength of the Allies … At the end of this year if the war is still going on a big American Army of 500,000 men would be a very decisive factor'. He foresaw, too, the implications for the government's Irish policy of Irish-American pressure: 'Personally I think the North of Ireland should be compelled to submit to a settlement in the interests of the Empire', he wrote, 'I believe an Irish Home Rule govt would probably be the worst in the world but in the interests of the Empire and of civilisation against the Huns we should put up with it if it is necessary'.[18]

Tactical reforms and strategic decisions

With the division now back up to strength, the period from late March to May was taken up with intensive training. The British had used the winter of 1916–17 to take stock of their experiences on the Somme and those of the French at Verdun to develop new tactics and organisations. Although an important contribution was a Canadian study, led by Arthur Currie, of French and British/Canadian operational techniques, similar thinking was going on elsewhere in the BEF and ideas were being exchanged well before

[16] ON to CN, 27 May 1917, in *Nugent*, pp 148–9.
[17] Denman, *Redmond*, p. 103.
[18] ON to CN, 17 Mar., 6 and 8 Apr. 1917, in *Nugent*, pp 134, 137–8.

the learning was codified into official guidance.[19] An example is Ricardo's letter to Nugent of 16 December 1916 from the 37th Division, in which he reported that he had been 'reading a heap of literature on the later experiences on the Ancre. So many points you contended for, getting out in front during the intense bombardment, getting close up to and following up close and quick etc are now laid down as indispensable to success'. He wrote again later in the month enclosing 'some literature which may interest you. Gough's army were very keen on this French training – which is nothing new. It is making the platoon the little fighting self-dependent unit – with its own quota of specialists'.[20] The publication of two important pamphlets, 'Instructions for the Training of Infantry Divisions for Offensive Action' (SS135) in December 1916 and 'Instructions for the training of platoons in offensive action' (SS143) in February 1917, was therefore a consolidation of as well as a major step forward in the development of British doctrine and practice.[21] There were two parallel processes at work, the decentralisation of infantry tactics and the increasing centralisation of artillery and other specialist support. Both had implications for the way Nugent exercised command.

The new platoon organisation, with its four sections comprising Lewis gun, bombers, rifle grenadiers and riflemen, was becoming standardised across the BEF in early 1917. It was designed to reintroduce the capacity for independent fire and manoeuvre at that level, so enabling the infantry to fight their way forward after their supporting artillery had lifted onto other targets. The introduction of these tactics into the Ulster Division in a five-week period in March and April 1917 illustrates the mechanics of operational learning in an infantry division at this stage of the war. Each brigade in turn came out of the line for an intensive course, starting with a lecture and demonstration for officers at the Second Army School at Wisques, followed by a 12-day training cycle in which three days were spent successively on platoon, company, battalion and brigade practices. Participants were in no doubt the changes were important – the adjutant of the 14th Royal Irish Rifles commented on the 'attention being given to the

---

[19] Bill Rawling, *Surviving Trench Warfare: Technology and the Canadian Corps 1914–1918* (1992), pp 87–113; Chris Pugsley, *The ANZAC Experience: New Zealand, Australia and Empire in the First World War* (2004), pp 165–203; Hyatt, *Currie*, pp 63–7; Connelly, *Steady the Buffs*, pp 131–3.

[20] Ricardo to ON, 12 and 29 Dec. 1916, in *Nugent*, pp 123, 128.

[21] Jim Beach, 'Issued by the General Staff: doctrine writing at British GHQ, 1917–1918', *War in History*, 19:4 (2012), pp 464–91; Paddy Griffith, *Battle Tactics of the Western Front: The British Army's Art of Attack, 1916–18* (1994), pp 76–9.

platoon and company in attack. Significant!' – and Nugent supervised matters closely.[22] In the case of 107 Brigade, for example, he attended the initial conference for COs organised by Brigadier-General Rowley (filling in temporarily for Withycombe), and then spent three days watching the brigade going through the different training phases; Plumer himself came to see the final brigade exercise on 28 April. Learning new tactical drills was one thing, however, changing mind-sets another. At the training's conclusion 107 Brigade's war diary commented thoughtfully:

> In these 12 days an entirely new system of warfare had to be learnt and adopted viz the platoon as the unit armed with its own particular weapons. The period available was not really long enough to allow of sufficient being taught, but nevertheless very considerable progress was made. The men were very keen and took considerable interest throughout. The greatest difficulty was the junior officer. It was difficult to make the platoon commander understand that he was in command of his platoon and his difficulty was considerably increased by his lack of imagination or initiative. At the end of the 12 days junior officers were just beginning to understand the importance of their position.[23]

In early May 107 Brigade ran a week-long course for over 30 of its young officers and platoon sergeants 'with the object of improving the imagination and initiative of the officers and senior NCOs'. The results were judged to be very satisfactory. Nugent supported these efforts, the encouragement of initiative at lower levels being a theme throughout his time in command: as early as January 1916 he had lectured junior officers on the need to show more initiative, warning them 'that they would probably be d—-d if they did but it would certainly be d—-d if they did nothing and there was just the off chance that if they did something they might do the right thing'.[24] It was no coincidence, therefore, that in the spring of 1917, as the responsibilities of platoon commanders increased, there was a sharp disagreement between him and Hacket Pain, commanding 15 Reserve Brigade in Ireland, about the poor training of new officers joining the division. Amongst the deficiencies, about which Nugent made a formal complaint, was the failure of 15 Brigade to utilise properly the operational experience of wounded officers attached to it while recuperating.[25]

---

[22] 14th R. Irish Rifles war diary (TNA, WO95/2511).
[23] 107 Bde war diary (TNA, WO95/2502).
[24] ON to CN, 16 Jan. 1916, in *Nugent*, p. 44.
[25] ON to Hacket Pain, n.d. but late Mar./early Apr. 1917 (PRONI, D3835/E/7/11).

The need for a change in attitude applied to him also, however, as implicit in the new tactics was the delegation of greater authority from division to brigades and battalions. This was in contrast to the Thiepval attack, where his refusal to allow COs to accompany their units had epitomised centralised control. All the brigades – including their trench mortar and machine-gun companies, crucial adjuncts to the development of tactical self-reliance at brigade level and below – continued training during May between spells in the line to embed the new methods. Nugent also sent a brigadier, probably Ricardo, and two staff officers down to Arras to visit one of the Canadian divisions that had captured Vimy Ridge and 'get the latest tips and information from their experience'.[26]

At the same time the expanding role of corps headquarters was also impacting on the conduct of command at divisional level. The Somme had demonstrated that in large-scale operations artillery, engineer and logistics assets were best coordinated at corps level and by 1917 the trend had accelerated significantly.[27] At Messines, for example, though his own artillery formed part of the supporting bombardment and though he helped shape the fire-plan, Nugent himself had direct control during the attack over only four batteries, while his heavy machine-guns were integrated into IX Corps's machine-gun barrage, his trench mortars were firing on targets largely designated by corps, and in the build-up to the battle many of the engineering tasks carried out by his sapper field companies and pioneers were in support of others. The same was true of the fighting later in the summer at Ypres. The divisional artillery, though it supported the division's attacks on both 7 June and 16 August, effectively ceased to be under his direct operational command from late May until the end of August: when the division was pulled out of the line after Messines the gunners stayed on supporting other formations, went straight from there into action at Ypres ahead of the rest of the division, and then once again remained in the line after the Ulster infantry had been withdrawn. The same was true of the equally hard-worked engineers and pioneers who were detached from the division between Messines and Ypres, the 16th Royal Irish Rifles not re-joining until mid-September. The BEF was

---

[26] ON to CN, 21 May 1917, in *Nugent*, p. 146.

[27] For the evolution of the relationship between the corps and divisional levels of command see Simpson, *Directing Operations*, pp 61–114; Robert Stevenson, *To Win The Battle: The 1st Australian Division in the Great War, 1914–1918* (2013), pp 48–57; for the development of divisional command in the twentieth century, including the Great War, see Anthony King, *Command: The Twenty-First-Century General* (2019), pp 73–213.

becoming a more sophisticated military machine that required increased flexibility from both its structures and its commanders.[28]

The evolving organisation of the divisional artillery in 1916–17, reflecting better techniques and improved command and control, is another case in point. At the Somme Nugent's four artillery brigades had deployed 60 guns (48 18-pdrs and twelve 4.5in. howitzers). In September 1916 one artillery brigade (the 154th) was broken up in line with army-wide changes to strengthen control and save manpower, its guns being re-distributed to two of the other brigades to enhance their hitting power. In February 1917 a second brigade, the 172nd, left to become the 113th Army Brigade RFA, part of a general reorganisation to concentrate additional artillery assets at army and corps level. For the rest of the war the Ulster Division had just two artillery brigades (153rd and 173rd), deploying between them 36 field guns and twelve howitzers, the 20% reduction in the number of artillery pieces reflecting the shifting balance between division and corps in the management of firepower.[29]

British plans, summer 1917

Meanwhile the war for the allies was not going well. In May the fighting at Arras finally ground to a halt and the French army experienced a wave of mutinies following the Nivelle offensive. Although Nugent was unaware of the scale of the crisis in French morale he had heard rumours in late April that 'the French military authorities are so disgusted with General Nivelle's failure that he was on the point of being ungummed' (Nivelle was succeeded by Petain on 15 May), and by mid-May in his view the 'poor old French are about finished'.[30] The British for the rest of the year would bear the brunt of the fighting in the west and at a conference with his Army commanders at Doullens on 7 May Haig outlined his plans. His ambitious strategic objective was to break through the German lines around Ypres, advance to the Belgian coast to link up with coastal operations there (including an amphibious landing), clear out the enemy's submarine bases and, with luck, unhinge the entire German position in Flanders. The main offensive would be preceded by a preliminary operation to take Messines

---

[28] Falls, *Ulster Division*, pp 106–08, 125, 130–31; Stuart White, *The Terrors: A History of the 16th (Pioneer) Battalion Royal Irish Rifles 1914–1919* (1996), pp 145–73.

[29] Gen. Sir Martin Farndale, *History of the Royal Regiment of Artillery: Western Front 1914–18* (1986), pp 348–9; Falls, *Ulster Division*, pp 306–07.

[30] ON to CN, 30 Apr. and 16 May 1917 (PRONI, D3835/E/2/12/437 & 441).

Ridge, to protect its southern flank. Haig and Plumer agreed that this initial attack should begin in just one month's time, on 7 June.[31]

Messines: the preparations

That short timescale was possible only because Second Army had been planning the attack for over a year, preparations for which included driving a series of mines under the ridge and whose detonation would be the battle's defining feature. Messines was a limited 'bite and hold' operation mounted with all the care and attention to detail that Plumer and Harington could bring to bear, and for which Plumer had available three corps – from north to south X, IX and II ANZAC – comprising 12 divisions. His plan involved each corps attacking with three divisions in line and one in support, on a total frontage of 17,000 yards: the objective of the nine divisions in the first wave was the Black line, running along the top of the ridge, following which the three reserve divisions would pass through to take the final objective, the Oostaverne line, 2,000 yards further east. The attack would be preceded by the detonation of the mines under the German positions (19 in the end exploded), but almost as impressive was the concentration of 2,266 British guns and howitzers to support the attack, 756 of them heavy and medium pieces, supplemented by hundreds of trench mortars and a machine-gun barrage by 700 Vickers guns.[32]

Hamilton Gordon's IX Corps was earmarked to attack the centre of the ridge. He decided to do so using the Ulster Division on the right, the 16th in the centre and the 19th on the left, with the 11th Division in reserve; on Nugent's right would be II ANZAC Corps's 25th Division. The 36th and 16th would attack either side of the village of Wytschaete, their final objective being about 2,500 yards from the start-line. The planning process was far more streamlined than it had been on the Somme. Divisional plans were already well-developed and in early April, over a month before the final decision to mount the Messines operation, Nugent had been able to circulate a detailed outline to his brigadiers. As usual the corps and divisional plans were confirmed through a series of conferences, and following Hamilton Gordon's meeting with his divisional commanders on 29 May Nugent issued his final orders.[33] The Ulster Division on 7 June would attack on a two-brigade front, each with two battalions in its first wave and two in the second: both brigades would also have an attached battalion from the reserve brigade to assist in mopping up.

---

[31] Ian Passingham, *Pillars of Fire: The Battle of Messines Ridge, June 1917* (2012), pp 16–20; *OH*, 1917, ii, pp 24–5.

[32] *OH*, 1917, ii, p. 41.

[33] IX Corps war diary (TNA, WO95/835).

The thoroughness of Second Army's preparations impressed participants. Nugent after the war described the attack as 'a perfect example of trained effort in which nothing essential to success had been overlooked, in which cooperation and mutual help between units and between the man in the field and the Army Staff reached its fullest expression'.[34] A detailed scale model had been constructed in the IX Corps rear area where whole companies at a time could be briefed and, as on the Somme, full-size mock-ups of the German positions had been laid out over which units rehearsed their attacks.[35] Nugent's relationship with Plumer and Harington by now was very strong. He and Plumer got on well (to the extent of occasionally exchanging light-hearted banter, not something Plumer, who did not welcome over-familiarity, always encouraged), and Nugent regarded him as 'a delightful, loyal person to soldier with … always accessible and friendly'.[36] They also respected each other professionally: Plumer told Nugent in March that the 36th was the best division in Second Army, while for Nugent Second Army had become 'the Army I shall always swear by. They know how to get things done, and what is far more important they know and understand the British Infantryman. At least Sir H Plumer does'.[37]

On 23 May, however, as preparations intensified, Nugent had a visitor, Douglas Haig, whose opinion of him was less positive. Nugent found the experience unsettling: 'For him he was quite genial but he always makes me feel like a small boy saying his lessons. Prickles rise along my backbone'.[38] The point about reciting lessons was more accurate than he may have realised. Haig had come to hear his generals' plans, visiting Second Army and its subordinate headquarters over a three-day period, and it was an oral exam that could be failed. Also on 23 May Haig saw the recently-appointed Major-General Dick Stuart-Wortley of the 19th Division, who had been with Nugent at Talana. Their discussion went badly and Stuart-Wortley was removed the following day because Haig 'did not like his arrangements. He had broken up a brigade to provide 2 battalions as "moppers up" to another brigade … I felt he had hardly got beyond the fringe of the problem which confronted him. He was also very nervous and fussy'.[39] In fact Stuart-

34 ON address at unveiling of Lisburn war memorial, 28 Apr. 1923, in *Nugent*, p. 260n.
35 Falls, *Ulster Division*, pp 82–4.
36 ON to CN, 4 July and 20 Sep. 1917, in *Nugent*, pp 159–60, 178.
37 Blacker letters, 10 Mar. 1917; ON to CN, 17 June 1917, in *Nugent*, pp 158–9.
38 ON to CN, 23 May 1917, in *Nugent*, p. 147.
39 Gary Sheffield and John Bourne, *Douglas Haig: War Diaries and Letters 1914–1918* (2005), p. 295.

Wortley's plan was similar to those of both Nugent and Hickie, but Haig had lost confidence in him and he exchanged places with Cameron ('Tiger') Shute, commanding the 32nd Division in a quiet sector, where he lasted only a few more months. Haig had acted decisively, though whether a commander-in-chief reaching down three command levels to remove a divisional general shortly before a major offensive reflected the ideal delineation of responsibilities is debatable.[40] Neither Hamilton Gordon nor Plumer challenged his decision, however, and Nugent for his part was just relieved his session with Haig had gone well – 'He even got so far as to call me by my Christian name and take my arm ... I think perhaps he meant to convey that he had heard well of me and that he didn't think me as impossible or incompetent, or whatever he may have thought me, as he used to do'.[41] At this stage the issue of the title seems not to have damaged their relationship, though news of the division's request to retain it may not yet have reached Haig.

Minor operations continued in the run-up to the offensive, with raids made or attempted by both sides. The opposing artillery was also very active and on 27 May the Ulster Division's main HQ, recently established in the purpose-built 'Ulster Camp' near the village of Dranoutre, was heavily shelled and had to be evacuated: Nugent and his staff 'spent the night dodging from one place to another ... One shell covered me with earth but that was the nearest I was to one, but that was unpleasantly close'. Others were not so fortunate and amongst the casualties, to Nugent's regret, was the division's popular Commander Royal Engineers, Lieutenant-Colonel King, while 70 horses were also killed.[42] The following day Nugent and his operational staff moved to their forward HQ, tucked into the slopes of Kemmel Hill, and on 31 May the preliminary bombardment of the battle of Messines began.

Between late May and 6 June the British fired three-and-a-half million shells onto the ridge, destroying much of the German wire, obliterating long stretches of their trenches, knocking out many artillery batteries and forcing the remainder to keep moving to avoid destruction. Even so the exchanges were not all one way: on 6 June Nugent's main OP was destroyed by a heavy German shell, fortunately with no one in it. While it was intact, however, he had been able to observe two daylight Ulster Division raids, on 3 and 4 June, mounted under cover of the British bombardment. The first, by the 13th Royal Irish Rifles, took 19 prisoners and the second, by the 9th

[40] Harris, *Douglas Haig*, pp 343–4.
[41] ON to CN, 25 May 1917, in *Nugent*, pp 147–8.
[42] Falls, *Ulster Division*, pp 80–81; ON to CN, 28 May 1917, in *Nugent*, pp 149–50.

Royal Irish Fusiliers, took 31, including an officer, at a cost of two killed and six wounded.[43] 'I really could hardly bear to watch them', Nugent wrote:

> It looked such a little lonely party going out from our trenches into the awful country beyond the German lines ... I must say it was horribly thrilling to watch through the telescope, our men bombing the dugouts and dragging out Germans, some of whom had to be bayonetted because they wouldn't come along. In each case we had very few casualties. The men are delighted and it has given them great confidence both in themselves and in the Artillery.[44]

Plumer too was pleased and ordered the rest of Second Army to conduct similar raids. Nugent met the captured officer (of the *40th (Saxon) Division*) and 'did the heavy General out of the book', expressing his 'sympathy on the fortunes of war'; the officer told him 'they had been told that we kept black troops behind the line to kill the prisoners ... He honestly believed it himself which shows the kind of barbarians the Germans are'.[45]

Messines: the attack

By the evening of 6 June, the division's assault troops were in position. On the left 109 Brigade deployed the 11th Royal Inniskilling Fusiliers (left) and 14th Royal Irish Rifles (right) in its first wave and 9th and 10th Royal Inniskilling Fusiliers in the second, with the attached 11th Royal Irish Rifles mopping up behind the first wave; on the right, 107 Brigade had the 9th Royal Irish Rifles (left) and 8th Royal Irish Rifles (right) in the first wave, the 10th and 15th Royal Irish Rifles in the second and 12th Royal Irish Rifles acting as moppers-up. Each battalion would attack with two companies up and two in support, each company advancing in two lines. The division also had attached a section of four Mark IV tanks, its first experience of working with armour. The first wave was to take the Blue line, half-way up the ridge (passing through an intermediate objective, the Red line, en route); the second wave battalions would then advance to the Black line, the division's final objective. Once established there both brigades would push forward strong patrols to an outpost line a thousand yards further on – the Mauve line – to cover the advance of the 11th Division to Second Army's furthest objective, the Oosttaverne line. Supporting them

[43] Falls, *Ulster Division*, pp 89–90.
[44] ON to CN, 4 June 1917, in *Nugent*, pp 151–2.
[45] ON to CN, 5 June 1917, in *Nugent*, p. 152.

were almost 190 field guns and howitzers: twelve 18-pdr batteries would put down a creeping barrage moving forward at a rate of 100 yards every three minutes, while nine 18-pdr and five 4.5in. howitzer batteries put down a standing barrage on successive trench lines and strongpoints, lifting onto the next series of targets as the creeping barrage reached them. In addition nine heavy batteries would fire on depth targets on the division's front.[46]

In the early hours of 7 June Nugent went to Kemmel Hill to watch the start of the attack. There were five mines on the Ulster Division's front, called (from north to south) Peckham, Spanbroekmoelen and Kruisstraat, the last a triple-mine. The sappers had suggested that the Kruisstraat mines be blown sequentially rather than simultaneously, to catch the defenders as they fled towards the rear, but following a demonstration behind the lines Nugent vetoed the idea; nor was it clear that Spanbroekmoelen, the largest, would detonate at all following recent German counter-mining efforts, though shortly before the attack divisional HQ at last received word that it was 'almost certain' to work.[47]

At 3.10am on 7 June 19 mines, containing almost a million pounds of ammonal, 'went up', in Nugent's words, 'in a lurid gigantic sheet of flame', and then

> something like 3000 guns opened fire along the 2nd Army front and the whole country beyond the German front line became a sheet of flame and smoke. It might have been literally the end of a world. There was no wind and the dense pall of smoke and dust from the mines and shells hung like a black pall over the ground, lit up continually by the flash of bursting shells and as for the noise no words could describe that. It absolutely cowed one, because the roar prevented one from hearing anyone speak and the continual concussion became painful.[48]

He returned to his command post announcing that he had seen 'a vision of hell'.[49] As the first wave left their trenches some men were thrown off their

[46] Falls, *Ulster Division*, p. 86; *OH*, 1917, ii, pp 46–9.
[47] Interview by Alexander Barrie with Henry Hudspeth, OC 171st Tunnelling Company, in 1961 about the Kruisstraat mines (Royal Engineers Museum, Library & Archive, Barrie papers) – I am indebted to Dr Simon Jones for this reference; Falls, *Ulster Division*, p. 88.
[48] ON to CN, 7 June 1917, in *Nugent*, pp 153–4.
[49] Falls, *Ulster Division*, p. 92. For the Messines attack, see Falls, *Ulster Division*, pp 91–102; Orr and Truesdale, *"Ulster Will Fight"*, ii, pp 254–82; Denman, *Ireland's Unknown Soldiers*, pp 110–15; Tom Burke, *The 16th (Irish) and 36th (Ulster) Divisions at The Battle of Wijtschate-Messines Ridge, 7 June 1917* (2007), *passim*.

feet by the delayed detonation of the Spanbroekmolen mine, which went off 20 seconds late, but casualties were light and the main problem was maintaining direction in the smoke and dust. Moving forward rapidly behind the barrage the first-wave battalions encountered little resistance in the German front-line or support trenches, the few dazed survivors (from the *3rd Bavarian Division*) surrendering, while the German counter-barrage was extremely weak. By 3.45am the Red line had been reached and, after a short pause, the assault moved on to the Blue line. Patchy resistance was encountered from fortified farmhouses and other strongpoints, but the new platoon tactics quickly proved their worth. A British staff officer wrote afterwards that 'there was no quarter given to the machine gunners, they now have the satisfaction of knowing we have got our own back on the brutes who got us on July 1st'.[50] Skip Point was taken by men of the 9th and 14th Royal Irish Rifles along with 150 prisoners and by 4.50am the leading battalions were consolidating on the Blue line.

After a two-hour halt the second wave units resumed the advance behind the barrage. Once again pockets of resistance, particularly near the top of the ridge, were efficiently eliminated. A strongpoint called Pick House in the centre, for example, attacked by the 10th Royal Irish Rifles, was suppressed by Lewis guns, rifle grenades and a captured machine-gun and then surrounded: before the final assault could go in the garrison, including a battalion commander, surrendered. The 10th Royal Inniskilling Fusiliers were held up by a machine-gun post until an accompanying tank, its attention attracted by a sergeant beating on its side with a Mills bomb, destroyed the German position; on the left the 9th Royal Inniskilling Fusiliers and 1st Royal Munster Fusiliers of the 16th Division jointly cleared the ruins of Wytschaete; on the right Lumm Farm was taken by the 15th Royal Irish Rifles in hand-to-hand fighting. By 8.40am the second-wave battalions had gone firm on the Black line and patrols were moving forward to the Mauve line. Supporting arms hurried forward to help secure the captured positions, including 12 Vickers machine-guns, but the expected early German counter-attacks did not materialise. Their reserves had been held too far back, a mistake that cost the German commander, General von Laffert, his job, and when the attacks eventually came they fell on II ANZAC Corps on Nugent's right and were easily repulsed.[51] Shortly after midday Nugent updated his letter to Kitty:

---

[50] Herdman to his mother, 9 June 1917 (PRONI, T2510/1).

[51] Passingham, *Pillars of Fire*, pp 94–153. For weaknesses in German defensive methods in 1917, see Tony Cowan, 'Genius for war? German operational command on the Western Front in early 1917' (PhD, King's College London, 2016).

> Up to now, thank God, all seems to have gone well. We have captured Wytschaete side by side with the 16th Irish Division. The Anzacs on our right have got Messines and the 36th Divn have got all the ridge between the two places. For over 2½ years the Germans have looked down from Wytschaete and the ridge and Messines on us at the bottom of the hill. I hope they will never get it back now.[52]

Even in a battle as well-managed as this, tactical adjustments had to be made: Hamilton Gordon called in to congratulate Nugent on progress but also to order him to occupy the Mauve line in greater strength than originally intended. The 11th and 12th Royal Irish Rifles were rushed into position by 3pm, just ten minutes before the leading brigade of the 11th Division passed through.

Over 1,200 prisoners had been taken by the Ulster Division and hundreds of the enemy had been killed. Nugent was delighted by how the battle had gone, describing the operation as 'the most successful the British Army has had in this war' and adding that 'I am very happy over the share in it of this Division and the splendid way they fought today. I feel I have done some share of good work'.[53] His men were also pleased with themselves:

> Our men are in great heart. They say they have got their own back at last. They did most extraordinarily well. I have learned that this Division took all its objectives with less loss than any other Division in the Army and we took more prisoners. This may be accounted for by the fact that our men are kinder hearted.[54]

Nugent walked over the battlefield the next day:

> It is a terrible scene. Most of the dead and all the wounded have been removed, but there are a goodish number of German dead and some of our own still scattered about and other gruesome sights. The contorted attitudes of most are horrible. The most pathetic sight of all I think, is to see where a man's little belongings have been scattered on the ground, private letters, photos of wives and children, all sorts of little things which the poor miserable Boche had evidently treasured. I even pitied the Boche. He had such an appalling ordeal to go through.[55]

---

[52] ON to CN 7 June 1917, in *Nugent*, p. 154.
[53] Ibid., p. 155.
[54] ON to CN 8 June 1917, in *Nugent*, p. 156.
[55] ON to CN, 8 June 1917, in *Nugent*, p. 155.

Plumer called in to congratulate him on 8 June, as did Haig the following day, praising 'the splendid performance of the Division'.[56] The one error the British had made in an otherwise skilfully mounted operation was overcrowding the ridge, where the attackers were vulnerable to German shelling; Nugent had, however, thinned out his troops on the crest on the night of 7 June by replacing the two assault brigades with 108 Brigade, so his losses over the next 48 hours were less heavy than they might have been. By the time the division was relieved on the night of 9 June its total casualties stood at 61 officers and 1,058 men, lighter than expected, of whom about 700 had been incurred in the initial assault. (When, by contrast, the division went back into the captured positions at the end of June for a week they encountered heavy shelling and lost almost 300 men just holding the line: as Falls noted, holding a newly-won position after a major attack was always an unpleasant task.)[57]

The after-action reports of Nugent's brigadiers were uniformly enthusiastic. 107 Brigade thought the 'complete success of the operations was undoubtedly due to the thoroughness of the barrage and to the way in which the Infantry kept close up to it … The new platoon organization was a complete success'. 109 Brigade attributed success

> chiefly to the platoon system of training, to thorough organisation and to the dissemination to all ranks of information they should know. Every man went over knowing what to do and how to do it; the lesson learnt from the Canadians at Vimy as regards dealing with enemy machine guns was acted upon with excellent results, and it was confirmed in our operations that the platoon as now organised has at its disposal all the arms necessary to deal with any enemy machine gun which may come into action at close range.

There were still lessons to be learned, though – 108 Brigade commented that the 'whole subject of consolidation needs practice: the efforts of some parties merely resulted in a safe and inconspicuous shell hole being converted into an insecure and very obvious target, with a few sandbags to give it a home-like appearance'.[58]

Reaction to the battle

Nugent was delighted too by the political message the Irish divisions' success sent:

[56] ON to CN, 10 June 1917, in *Nugent*, p. 157.
[57] 36 Div. AA&QMG war diary (TNA, WO95/2463); Falls, *Ulster Division*, pp 101–04.
[58] 36 Div. narrative of operations against Messines-Wytschaete Ridge (TNA, WO95/2491).

Farren Connell, Co Cavan, in winter, *c.* 1900 (Nugent family)

Nugent as a young man in the 1880s (PRONI)

Shooting party, Ireland, 1890s, Nugent standing 5th from left (PRONI)

1st King's Royal Rifle Corps, Chitral relief force 1895, officers in front,
Nugent (probably) the second dismounted officer from the right (Nugent family)

The Malakand Pass 1895, where Nugent won his DSO (Nugent family)

Three generations of a Boer family in the field against the British, 1900 (PRONI)

Nugent (left) after his release from Boer captivity, with his brothers-in-law
Elliott Lees (right) and Percy Browne (standing), Pretoria, 1900 (PRONI)

Kitty with St George and Theffania, 1905 (Nugent family)

Nugent as Commanding Officer of 4th KRRC, 1908 (PRONI)

Nugent (seated front) and another officer on a shooting expedition, River Ganges, 1910
(Nugent family)

Nugent at Farren Connell, *c.* 1913 (Nugent family)

O.C.
1st
2nd **BATTN. CAVAN REGIMENT (U.V.F.)**
3rd

Please circulate following Order verbatim to your Battalion :—

DAY PARADES—

Owing to the lateness of the Season and the consequent necessity of utilizing every fine day for work on the farms, the Officer Commanding the Cavan Regiment, U.V.F., directs that Day Parades shall be suspended until further orders.

The Officer Commanding wishes to take this opportunity of expressing his satisfaction at the generally high average of attendances during the Winter, often under adverse conditions of weather.

He desires to impress upon all ranks that this Order merely suspends Day Parades for a time, in the interests of farmers, but that it is essential that these Parades should be resumed as soon as possible.

In any case the usual Evening Drills are not to be suspended.

O. S. NUGENT. COLONEL.
Commanding Cavan Regiment, U.V.F.

April 9th, 1914.

Orders to the Cavan Volunteer Force issued by Nugent, April 1914 (PRONI)

Brigadier-General Nugent, 41 Brigade, in France, summer 1915 (PRONI)

Nugent and one of his staff officers, Capt Harry Altham (later President of MCC),
at Snipers Willow, Ypres Salient, summer 1915 (courtesy of R. Brodhurst)

The King's inspection of the Ulster Division, Aldershot, September 1915, Nugent the left of the three riders behind him, next to Kitchener (Nugent family)

Ulster Division, royal review, Aldershot, September 1915, the divisional artillery (Nugent family)

Ulster Division, royal review, Aldershot, September 1915, the divisional cyclists
(Nugent family)

Ulster Division training, 1915 (PRONI)

VICTORIA CROSSES OF THE 36th (Ulster) DIVISION – 1916.

The late Lt. G. St. G. S. CATHER
9th Royal Irish Fusiliers.

The late Pte. W. F. Mc FADZEAN
14th Royal Irish Rifles.

The late Capt. E.N.F. BELL
9th Royal Inniskilling Fusiliers.

· Pte. R. QUIGG ·
12th Royal Irish Rifles.

The Late 2/Lt. J. S. EMERSON
9th Royal Inniskilling Fusiliers.

The Ulster Division's four VC winners at the Somme, along with Emerson, who won his at Cambrai
(Div history)

Nugent and Kitty on horseback, India, 1920 (Nugent family)

The Ulster Tower: Nugent took part in the opening ceremony in 1921
(Div history)

THE HISTORY
OF THE
36TH (ULSTER) DIVISION

By
CYRIL FALLS
*Late Lieutenant, Royal Inniskilling Fusiliers
and Captain, G.S., 36th Division*

WITH AN INTRODUCTION BY
FIELD MARSHAL THE LORD PLUMER
G.C.B., G.C.M.G., G.C.V.O.

M'CAW, STEVENSON & ORR, LIMITED
THE LINENHALL PRESS, BELFAST
AND 329 HIGH HOLBORN, LONDON, W.C.
1922

The Divisional History, on which Nugent worked closely with Cyril Falls (Div history)

Nugent, 6th from left, presiding at an Ulster Division officers' club dinner, early 1920s (PRONI)

Nugent unveiling the Lisburn war memorial, 1923, Sir James Craig
next but one to his left looking up (PRONI)

Memorial plaque, Mountnugent parish church (PRONI)

> What pleases me more than anything is that the 16th Division did equally well and there was nothing to choose between them so neither side can make any capital out of the performance of its own Division in Ireland. As a matter of fact we were first on top of the ridge, because the 16th were hung up by wire in a wood, but there was nothing to choose between the Divisions, nor in fact any Division so far as I can hear. It was a great success.[59]

Others felt the same. Feilding of the 6th Connaught Rangers wrote to his wife, 'I hope you and all the world will have learnt also that the South Irish Division and the Ulster Division went forward side by side'.[60] Press reporting was enthusiastic – the *Belfast Newsletter* quoted front-line correspondents describing units from north and south fighting alongside each other 'in the finest and friendliest rivalry ... there was no chance for either to do better than the other, for both did the best possible'; the *Ballymena Observer* noted that 'a very pleasing feature of the battle is that Ulster regiments are fighting in most friendly rivalry side by side with Southern Irish battalions'.[61] Not everyone was pleased by the coverage. Spender, who predicted once again that Nugent would be promoted, told Lily, 'I am glad the 36th seems to have had some luck at last, but dislike this slobber of the N and S Irish – especially as by now more than half the latter at any rate must be English!' In fact, based on the casualties at Messines, the infantry of both divisions were at this point still over 60% Irish.[62]

Amongst those casualties, to Nugent's sorrow, was Willie Redmond, fatally wounded during the 16th Division's attack and brought in by Ulster Division stretcher-bearers. Warm tributes were paid to him across the political spectrum, including by Edward Carson in parliament where, though acknowledging their political differences, he spoke of his respect for his 'much lamented lifelong opponent'. (Carson also articulated unionism's variant on Redmond's shared service ideal: 'if in the trenches they could fight side by side for the common cause of liberty', he looked forward to an Irish settlement that met 'the ideas of liberty of all parties in Ireland'.) James Craig and other unionist politicians attended a requiem mass for Redmond in Westminster Cathedral. Some unionist commentators, however, while praising Redmond's personal example, contrasted this with wider

---

[59] ON to CN, 10 June 1917, in *Nugent*, p. 157.

[60] Feilding, *War Letters*, p. 189.

[61] *Belfast Newsletter*, 9 June 1917; *Ballymena Observer*, 15 June 1917.

[62] Spender to his wife, 10 June 1917, in Baguley, *Question of Ulster*, p. 242; Perry, 'Nationality', p. 79; Richard Grayson, 'Ireland's new memory of the First World War: forgotten aspects of the Battle of Messines, June 1917', *British Journal for Military History*, 1:1 (Oct. 2014), pp 58–61.

nationalist lack of support for the war effort and bemoaned the 'disproportionate' attention being paid to his death, and a few were openly hostile.[63] They had a point about Redmond's lack of representativeness by 1917: in a symbol of shifting political opinion the by-election on 10 July for Redmond's East Clare seat was won by Eamon de Valera of Sinn Fein with 71% of the vote.[64] The Ulster Division marked Redmond's passing by providing a joint guard of honour with the 16th Division at his funeral.[65] Nugent also sent £100 from divisional funds to his memorial fund (to which Carson also contributed), though the gesture was not universally appreciated: 'Most of the Division favoured the idea', he noted in September 1917, 'but some of the Belfast lot objected. However they were in a minority so I overruled them. Another black mark against me though'.[66]

In early July the division left Second Army for Gough's Fifth Army in high spirits, Nugent telling Kitty that his men were 'quite the bright, particular boys or stars of this Army' and that Hamilton Gordon and his staff were 'almost in tears at losing us'.[67] The 16th Division moved too, and both now came under the command of Lieutenant-General Herbert Watts's XIX Corps. Their transfer together suggests that the idea of maintaining their partnership was becoming established, and another success like Messines might have resulted in the creation of a permanent Irish corps after all. Tragically, however, their next joint action was nothing at all like Messines.

Third Ypres: planning

The Third Battle of Ypres was a low point for the Ulster Division during the war. It was also an unusual experience operationally for the division, in that it was the only occasion during Nugent's time in command that it was inserted into an offensive battle already underway (on the Somme, at Messines and at Cambrai it formed part of the opening assault, preceded in each case by weeks of planning). What was not new was that for the second successive summer it was taking part in a battle over the conduct of which there was disagreement between Haig and his Army commander. The debate over Haig's intentions was still raging when the official history was being written thirty years later but it seems that by the opening of the offensive in late July, and in contrast to the Somme, he favoured making

[63] *Belfast Newsletter*, 9, 12, 13, 19 and 22 June 1917.
[64] Denman, *Redmond*, p. 134.
[65] Denman, *Redmond*, p. 121.
[66] ON to CN, 5 Sep. 1917, in *Nugent*, p. 176.
[67] ON to CN, 17 June 1917, in *Nugent*, p. 158.

progress through a succession of 'bite-and-hold' operations.[68] Gough, on the basis of previous discussions with Haig and also because of his own appointment to command as a 'thruster', rather than the more cautious Plumer, believed he was to seek a breakthrough, and that even if this required a series of pushes these should be mounted in rapid succession and with stretching tactical objectives. The misfortune for Fifth Army's subordinate formations was that Gough's interpretation played into his weaknesses as well as his strengths, and in particular his failure to recognise, despite his experiences on the Somme and at Bullecourt, that success on the western front required precision and thorough preparation as well as energy and drive. This was especially so as the German defences had recently been reorganised by their defensive expert, Colonel (soon to be Major-General) von Lossberg, into a series of zones each 2–3,000 yards deep. These were designed to absorb an attacker's momentum in a forward zone, halt him in a main battle zone (the area being dotted with scores of pill-boxes constructed of reinforced concrete), and then defeat him by counterattacks, either by local reserves or, if necessary, by dedicated counterattack divisions.[69]

The Fifth Army's opening attack, on 31 July, made by nine divisions supported by almost 2,200 guns, nevertheless gained valuable ground, especially on the left. British losses were heavy but German casualties were nearly as severe and compared to the first day of the Somme progress was encouraging.[70] It was, however, well short of the ambitious objectives Gough had set, particularly on the right or southern part of the front, which included XIX Corps's sector. This was overlooked by the Gheluvelt plateau – though not high, any elevation in the Salient offered a significant tactical advantage – giving the Germans both observation and protection for their artillery behind it. (Haig had urged Gough to give the capture of the plateau priority, but Gough had opted instead to spread his divisions across a broad front.) On 31 July XIX Corps had used the 55th (West Lancashire) and 15th (Scottish) Divisions to attack between St Julien and Frezenberg, keeping the Ulster Division and the 16th in reserve. They had

---

[68] Tim Travers, *The Killing Ground: The British Army, the Western Front and the Emergence of Modern Warfare* (1987), pp 203–19; Andrew Green, *Writing the Great War: Sir James Edmonds and the Official Histories 1915–1948* (2003), pp 167–94; Robin Prior and Trevor Wilson, *Passchendaele: The Untold Story* (1996), pp 73–7.

[69] *OH*, 1917, ii, p. 144.

[70] British losses between 31 July & 3 Aug. were almost 32,000, German casualties from 21–31 July about 30,000: Nick Lloyd, *Passchendaele: A New History* (2017), pp 119–21.

initially done well, overrunning the first two defensive zones and reaching the German Third Position, before being hit by powerful counterattacks and forced back to the Second Position, known to the British as the Black line, which from the evening of 31 July formed the new front-line.[71] They had suffered almost 3,500 casualties apiece and were exhausted. To add to their difficulties, on the night of 31 July torrential rain began teeming down and by the following day the battlefield had turned into a swamp.[72]

Third Ypres: Holding the line

Gough had intended keeping his leading divisions in action until their objectives had been secured, but in the southern sector the losses, the weather and the weight of German shelling forced a change of plan. Already on 2 August Watts had directed Nugent to provide a brigade to support the 55th Division. Nugent duly sent up 107 Brigade, with no expectation of its immediate use, but Jeudwine, GOC of the 55th, ordered it to relieve at once his two brigades in the front-line trenches. On the night of 2/3 August Withycombe's men did so, in continuous rain and under heavy shell fire, the 10th Royal Irish Rifles taking over the right of the position in the Black line and the 15th Royal Irish Rifles the left, with the 9th and 8th Royal Irish Rifles respectively in support trenches close behind. Casualties during the relief were so heavy that, to quote Falls, 'after that night's work … there could be no question of employing those battalions in the coming attack'.[73]

The following day Nugent was ordered to relieve the remainder of the 55th Division and on the night of 3/4 August the rest of the division moved up in lashing rain – 'The weather conditions are indescribable', he wrote – with divisional HQ moving into Mersey Camp near Ypres. At the same time the 16th Division replaced the 15th Division on Nugent's right. Later that day he went up as close to the front as he could, the foremost trenches not being approachable in daylight, and already, he noted, 'it was really pitiful to see the conditions in which these unlucky men were living … there is nothing but water and mud everywhere'.[74] Casualties mounted rapidly and as soon as possible he reduced the forward troops to the minimum necessary to hold the line. Even so, for his soldiers the conditions were grim. The war diary of the 8th Royal Irish Rifles for the period from 3–7 August stands for the others: for the first three days, in support, the entries read simply 'Very bad time. Heavy hostile shelling'; the next two, in the front line itself, read 'Bad time. Enemy very active'; and the entry on 7

---

[71] *OH*, 1917, ii, pp 147–80.
[72] ON to CN, 1 Aug. 1917, in *Nugent*, p. 162.
[73] Falls, *Ulster Division*, p. 112.
[74] ON to CN, 4 Aug. 1917, in *Nugent*, pp 162–3.

August noted 'Bad relief. During this tour the Battalion had the following casualties; – 7 officers and 167 ORs'.[75] They included the CO, Cole-Hamilton, who was wounded and evacuated. Nugent observed, as he had at Hooge in 1915, that casualties in such conditions were always the most unsatisfactory 'because it goes on day after day gradually frittering the men away and shaking their morale with no tangible results'.[76]

Gough wanted to renew the attack quickly, but the weather and the water-logged ground forced repeated postponements. Nugent had earmarked 108 and 109 Brigades for the assault and hoped to keep them out of the line, but so punishing were the conditions that he had no option but to relieve 107 Brigade on the night of 7/8 August with a composite brigade of two battalions each from 108 and 109 Brigades (the 11th and 12th Royal Irish Rifles, and 9th and 10th Royal Inniskilling Fusiliers). They stayed in for six days, with the two brigade HQs spending three days each in command, and during this period a second CO, Macrory of the 10th Inniskillings, was wounded. The remaining four battalions were held back from the foremost trenches but even units not in the line got no rest, constantly providing carrying-parties and work details. Nugent, unusually for him, was unable to get right forward: 'I can't go up to the front line', he wrote on 6 August, 'partly because I can't get there and partly because there is constant heavy shelling and it isn't my business to get knocked over if I can help it, also I can't go far away lest the Germans take it into their heads to start an attack'.[77] Gough called to see him on 8 August 'and stayed quite a long time. I liked him as far as one can judge from a first impression'.[78] It was to Gough's credit that he visited his subordinate commanders, though Nugent's positive impression would not last long.

At this point Gough still hoped to mount a further assault soon and the day after his visit Nugent issued his own orders for the renewed offensive, but again the weather and terrain imposed delays. Reluctantly Gough had accepted Haig's advice to try to take the Gheluvelt plateau before launching a further general push and the attempt, by II Corps, took place on 10 August. It made some progress, albeit with loss, but most of the plateau remained in German hands. Gough despite this decided to resume the attack across the entire Fifth Army front on 15 August, but the saturated ground forced a 24-hour postponement and zero hour was finally set for dawn on the 16th.

[75] 8th Rifles war diary (TNA, WO95/2503).
[76] ON to CN, 6 Aug. 1917, in *Nugent*, p. 163.
[77] ON to CN, 6 Aug. 1917, in *Nugent*, p. 164.
[78] ON to CN, 8 Aug. 1917, in *Nugent*, p. 164.

What Gough did not do was arrange for fresh divisions, other than in II Corps, to carry out the attack, even though the Irish divisions, which had been in the line longer than any other Fifth Army formations and in one of the worst parts of the front, were now in a parlous state. By 15 August the Ulster Division had lost over 1,500 officers and men, mostly from its infantry battalions, and was exhausted; the 16th Division was in a similar condition. Nugent's detailed exchanges with Watts at this time have not survived. He certainly made XIX Corps aware of the extent of his losses and the strain on his men but there is no indication that he lodged any kind of formal objection, as he had at Hooge, probably because other formations were suffering similarly and he believed that military necessity required them all to stick it out. There was, however, a pervading sense in the division that the conditions for success had not been established. The war diary of one battalion afterwards noted: 'We went into this battle knowing that things were not right and that spirit is fatal, but all round us the signs were very clear', while Falls contrasted unfavourably the Fifth Army's preparations with Second Army's 'precision, care and forethought' and quoted an experienced officer of the division 'that the Battle of Messines was won at Zero, and that the Battle of Ypres was lost long before it'.[79]

Superficially Nugent's attack plan was like the one used at Messines. The division would attack on a two-brigade front – on the left 109 Brigade with the 11th Royal Inniskilling Fusiliers (left) and 14th Royal Irish Rifles (right) in its first wave supported by the 10th Royal Inniskilling Fusiliers; on the right 108 Brigade with the 13th Royal Irish Rifles (left) and 9th Royal Irish Fusiliers (right) leading and the 12th Royal Irish Rifles in support. The leading battalions each had half a company from their supporting battalions attached as moppers-up. The final objective was the Red line in the German Third Position, about 2,000 yards from the start-line, with an intermediate objective, the Green line, about half that distance. Yet the actual fighting power the division could deploy was very different. Nugent was attacking with six battalions rather than ten, none at more than two-thirds strength; his infantry numbers were therefore scarcely 40% of those at Messines and the men were worn out. There were no huge mines this time to obliterate the German defences, and at St Julien these were formidable, the ground between the Black and Green lines being covered by a network of powerful pill-boxes, often protected by uncut wire. The creeping barrage was provided by fourteen 18-pdr batteries, and as at Messines there was a standing barrage on known strongpoints.[80] Unlike Messines, however, observation was poor, the artillery's gun platforms were often unstable

---

[79] 14th Rifles war diary (TNA, WO95/2511); Falls, *Ulster Division*, pp 121–2.
[80] Falls, *Ulster Division*, p. 115.

because of the ground conditions, and the Germans, who had at least parity in artillery and in the air, were hammering the British gun-lines hard. The terrain, in contrast to the good going at Messines, was a quagmire.

On the night of 12/13 August 107 Brigade had taken over the line once more and two nights later the other two brigades, having reorganised, returned to the trenches. Neil Malcolm, Gough's chief of staff, called to see Nugent on 15 August to check on arrangements (Malcolm was not popular with the Ulster Division, Ricardo for one commenting after the war that he 'was answerable for a good many failures').[81] On the night of 15/16 August the assault brigades deployed into their final positions but since the approaches to the Black line across the flooded Steenbeck valley were being heavily shelled losses were considerable, the battalions losing an average of 50 men apiece moving up. Amongst the dead was Lieutenant-Colonel Pratt of the 11th Royal Inniskilling Fusiliers, one of Nugent's subordinates in the CVF, killed leaving 109 Brigade HQ at Wieltje: his 2ic, Major Knott, took over.

Third Ypres: The attack

At 4.45am on 16 August the leading waves left their trenches behind the creeping barrage. They were raked by machine-gun fire immediately, the pill-boxes so little affected by the barrage that they were able to fire through it. The weather was dry even if the ground was not and visibility for the German defenders, from the *5th Bavarian Division*, was good. Despite enduring awful conditions themselves they would put up a fierce resistance.

Each attacking battalion, as at Messines, advanced in two waves, each of two companies, the companies in their turn being deployed in two lines. So depleted were they, however, that a sergeant described the attack as looking 'more like a big raid than anything else', and Falls estimated that the first line out of the trenches across both brigades totalled no more than 300 men, of whom a third were hit in the first thirty seconds.[82] The creeping barrage's rate of advance of 100 yards every five minutes, thought to be extraordinarily slow, proved impossibly fast for the conditions and soon out-distanced the struggling infantry. Despite this, all four attacking battalions managed to get forward a few hundred yards and some parties, travelling close behind the barrage over ground relatively less water-logged

---

[81] Malcolm diary (privately held: I am grateful to Professor Ian Beckett for this reference); Ricardo to ON, 2 Jan. 1922, in *Nugent*, p. 239.

[82] Falls, *Ulster Division*, p. 116. For the St Julien (or Langemarck) attack, see Falls, *Ulster Division*, pp 107–24; Orr and Truesdale, *"Ulster Will Fight"*, ii, pp 285–317; Denman, *Ireland's Unknown Soldiers*, pp 116–24; Lloyd, *Passchendaele*, pp 128–33.

than elsewhere, reached the Green line. The majority, however, were held up in the interlocking fire of the pill-boxes, as were the two supporting battalions following them.

On the right the 9th Royal Irish Fusiliers captured a low rise, Hill 35, near the Green line, but in the twenty minutes it took to clear the position the creeping barrage had moved ahead and the flank of the 16th Division's left-hand battalion, the 7th Royal Inniskilling Fusiliers, was left exposed. The depleted Irish Fusiliers then advanced on their main objective, the Gallipoli Farm pill-box complex, but were held up by uncut wire and after suffering heavy casualties fell back to Hill 35. On their left the 13th Royal Irish Rifles attacked another large pill-box, Somme; the leading wave by-passed it but the platoon designated to take it was too weak to do so and the battalion's advance stalled under fire from at least five German positions, with officer casualties especially heavy. The 14th Royal Irish Rifles, the right-hand unit of 109 Brigade, encountered ground even worse than elsewhere, the troops struggling through water almost waist deep in places. They too came under withering machine-gun fire, but some parties nevertheless managed to advance up to 700 yards and a group almost surrounded Pond Farm, the key defensive position in this sector; again, however, they were too few to capture it and the supporting troops from the 9th Royal Inniskilling Fusiliers could not get forward through the machine-gun fire ('Supports cannot be found', wrote the adjutant of the Rifles angrily, 'they have melted into the "Blue" somewhere, but certainly not out in front').[83] On the extreme left the 11th Royal Inniskilling Fusiliers faced the same combination of bad going and heavy fire. Limited progress was made on the right but the left-hand company managed, after a hard fight, to take an enemy position called Fort Hill, on a slight rise to its front. As at Hill 35, however, by the time this was done the barrage had gone and attempts to by-pass other German strongpoints were unsuccessful.

At around 6am the Ulster Division attack began to collapse, starting with the uncontrolled withdrawal of the survivors of the 13th Royal Irish Rifles' left-hand companies but spreading quickly to neighbouring sub-units. When the 11th Royal Irish Rifles, 108 Brigade's reserve battalion, arrived to occupy the British front-line trench just after 6am it found that 'stragglers from the two Assaulting Battalions and also from the Supporting Battalion were streaming back to and beyond the Black line'.[84] Lieutenant-Colonel Somerville of the 9th Royal Irish Fusiliers ordered two companies to form a defensive line in No Man's Land before going forward to organise the defence on Hill 35, where he was fatally wounded soon after. His fellow

[83] 14th R. Irish Rifles war diary (TNA, WO95/2511).
[84] 11th Rifles war diary (TNA, WO95/2506).

COs, also in their command posts in the Black line, reacted similarly to news that the attack was faltering. Perceval-Maxwell of the 13th Royal Irish Rifles raced forward with his headquarters staff to rally his men and was wounded leading an attack on the Somme pill-box. Major Vivian, commanding the 14th Royal Irish Rifles in the absence of Cheape, 'on hearing that the attack was failing, and knowing that the Black Line was to be held at all costs', took a group of 24 officers and men forward to consolidate some captured German trenches to provide a rallying-point.[85] These interventions stabilised the line temporarily but by 7am it was nowhere in front of the Black line by more than about 300 yards. Even these small gains would soon be lost almost everywhere. At about 9am, in the words of the official history, 'waves of German infantry streamed over the crest of the Zonnebeke-St Julien spur against the 16th and 36th Divisions', preceded by a heavy bombardment.[86] This devastating counter-attack, delivered by the *5th Bavarian Division's* reserve regiment *21st Bavarian Regiment*, reinforced by elements of *12th Reserve Division*, first struck the 16th Division, which had managed to advance further than Nugent's men, and sent it reeling back to its start-line. When the German attack reached the Ulster Division's sector the survivors here too fell back, in some cases considerably disorganised, and by 10am were back in the Black line. The only gains retained were around Fort Hill on 109 Brigade's left.

At 10.15am Watts spoke by phone to Nugent and Hickie and they agreed reluctantly to bring the British barrage back to the start-line along most of the front, despite the fact that parties of their men were still in No Man's Land; Watts also told them to prepare for another attempt to reach the Green line.[87] The reports reaching Nugent from Griffith and Ricardo about the state of their men, however, and visits to the front by staff officers soon made it clear that the scale of the losses, especially amongst officers, made this impossible. (Captain Godson, 108 Brigade's intelligence officer, who had just seen for himself the chaos in the front line, was with Griffith at brigade HQ in mid-morning when 'the Div'l Commander telephoned saying he wanted to have another attack made at 7.30pm. This I did my best to help oppose. The men were in a state to do nothing but a dud show'.)[88] Shortly after 2pm Gough ordered XIX Corps to make a further

---

[85] 14th Rifles war diary (TNA, WO95/2511).

[86] *OH*, 1917, ii, p. 196.

[87] XIX Corps war diary (TNA, WO95/959).

[88] Nick Metcalfe, *Blacker's Boys: 9th (Service) Battalion, Princess Victoria's (Royal Irish Fusiliers) (County Armagh) and 9th (North Irish Horse) Battalion, Princess Victoria's (Royal Irish Fusiliers) 1914–1919* (2012), p. 139.

effort to capture the Green line and at 4pm Watts issued orders to Nugent and Hickie to this effect, asking when they intended to carry them out. They objected strongly: Nugent made clear that nothing could be attempted until the morning, but he and Hickie both argued against any resumption, pointing out that none of their four assault brigades could now muster more than 500 men each.[89] An attack next morning was still on the cards, however, when Nugent wrote to Kitty that evening:

> It has been a truly terrible day. Worse than the 1st July I am afraid. Our losses have been very heavy indeed and we have failed all along the line, so far as this Division is concerned and the whole Division has been driven back with terrible losses. Audley Pratt is gone, Somerville another of my Colonels also gone, Bob Maxwell I grieve to say was last seen wounded and lying out in front and we have been driven in since then and he was not brought back. Blair Oliphant another of my Colonels has not been heard of for several hours. Peacocke another Commanding Officer has not been seen or heard of since early morning and his whole battalion has disappeared. We don't know where they are but we hope they may be holding out in shell holes in front and will get back after dark. [Peacocke and Blair Oliphant were in fact uninjured.] Tomorrow we have to make another attack at dawn and I have no men to do it with. It is a ghastly business ... I am heartbroken over it and I fear we shall be absolutely wiped out tomorrow. We have not enough men left to do the attack or to hold the line we are to hold, even if we get it. My poor men.[90]

Between them, fortunately, Nugent and Hickie were able to convince Watts that an attack next day was not practicable, and at 8pm he told Gough that the order could not be carried out. As Nugent told Kitty, 'My Division did not make any further attack. When we went into numbers available it was realised how serious the losses had been and I pointed out that it was out of the question. Other Divisions on my right and left all agreed as to their own men. The losses had been so heavy that there was nothing more to be done'.[91]

In addition to his grief over the casualties Nugent was despondent because the division had apparently let others down: 'Our failure has involved the failure of the Divisions on both sides of us and that is so bitter a pill' he wrote, 'In July of last year, we did our work but failed because the

[89] *OH*, 1917, ii, p. 197; XIX Corps war diary (TNA, WO95/959); Falls, *Ulster Division*, pp 118–19.
[90] ON to CN, 16 Aug. 1917, in *Nugent*, p. 166.
[91] ON to CN, 16 Aug. 1917, in *Nugent*, p. 167.

Divisions on either side failed us. This time it is the Ulster Division which has failed the Army'. Within 24 hours, however, the position had become clearer:

> I thought my Division was the only one to fail but it isn't so. On the left the Guards and French and 2 other Divisions got where they were supposed to go, but it was recognised that they had a comparatively easy job and that they are not in touch yet with the German main position. On the right we are right up against it and no one got on. It was not only the Ulster Divn which failed but nearly all. A poor satisfaction certainly but still some.

He gave full credit to the defenders ('We had Bavarians against us and they were magnificent fighters').[92] Two days later he could be more reflective, and objective, about the division's performance:

> It was the MGs that stopped the whole attack. They were everywhere, that and wire which the Germans had put up between the first and second attacks. I do not think we could have done more than we did. At any rate we could not have got through. I am not quite satisfied all the same that we couldn't have done a little more than we did do, but it is easy for us behind to criticise those in front.[93]

It was indeed easy for those behind to criticise and Gough and Watts started at once. On 17 August Haig visited Gough who, he noted in his diary, 'was not pleased with the action of the Irish Divisions of the XIX Corps (36th and 16th). They seem to have gone forward, but failed to keep what they had won. These 2 divisions were in the Messines battle and had an easy victory. The men are Irish and apparently did not like the enemy's shelling, so Gough said'. From there Haig went to see Watts and heard a similar story: 'At XIX Corps I saw General Watts who gave a bad account of the two Irish Divisions (36th and 16th). Nugent and Hickie are the respective GOCs'. It was left to Haig himself to suggest mitigating factors: 'But I gather the attacking troops had a long march up the evening before the battle through Ypres to the front line and then had to fight from zero 4.45am until nightfall. The men could have had no sleep and must have been dead tired'.[94]

[92] ON to CN, 17 Aug. 1917, in *Nugent*, p. 167.
[93] ON to CN, 19 Aug. 1917, in *Nugent*, p. 168.
[94] Sheffield and Bourne, *Haig Diaries*, pp 317–18.

The self-exculpatory comments of Gough in particular, about exhausted men committed to a virtually hopeless attack, go far to explain the Fifth Army's negative reputation. The two Irish divisions who 'did not like the enemy's shelling' had lost between them over 4,000 men on 16 August and nearly 8,000 in total since the beginning of August: for the Ulster Division the casualties were 144 officers and 3,441 other ranks from 2–18 August, of which 81 officers and 1,955 men occurred during the attack.[95] Nugent saw Gough on 21 August and afterwards told Kitty, 'He was very pleasant and is a charming person as he always is, but my dearest, no one can talk to him and come away thinking that he is mentally or intellectually fit to command a big Army. He isn't and it is wrong that the lives of thousands of good men should be sacrificed through want of forethought and higher leading'. Nugent's opinion of Gough had changed permanently because of the division's losses: 'Being a good cavalry soldier and a good fellow are not the only qualifications for the command of great armies in which cavalry takes no part'.[96]

The attack affected Nugent deeply, as Farnham, who saw him on the night of the 21st, reported to his wife: 'I dined with O. He feels it very much I fear. It is very bad luck, and is such absolute waste of good material'. The next day Farnham, who had also seen Hickie, was able to write more frankly in a letter brought home by an officer going on leave, so evading the censor:

> It was very bad luck on the Div and also on 16th Div. They had both had fearful casualties and had an awful time, holding the line for a fortnight before the attack took place. They went over very weak, and were asked to do the impossible, and suffered very severely. However they did their best, and as far as I know are not blamed for the failure.

Farnham was clearly not aware of Gough's comments about the Irish divisions. He was, though, aware of the Irish divisions' comments about Gough:

> I fear this show is not really going at all well. Everyone seems to think Goughie is quite mad, and have a poor opinion of the 5th Army, and very different from the 2nd Army and old Plumer. We have had fearful casualties up to date trying to take this Passchendaele Ridge and really are no forreder [sic] than we were when we started.[97]

[95] *OH*, 1917, ii, pp 197–8.
[96] ON to CN, 21 Aug. 1917, in *Nugent*, pp 168–9.
[97] Farnham to his wife, 21 and 22 Aug. 1917 (PRONI, D3975/E/8/23/11, 12).

The next day, and following a further failed attack in the St Julien sector, Nugent gave vent to his feelings in another bitter letter to Kitty:

> 2 fresh Divisions attacked the same ground that we and the 16th attacked over. They attacked yesterday and before I left for Boulogne I heard the attack was a complete failure. They could do no more than we could. If this is so it means that 6 Divisions have now been wasted over the same piece of ground and so far as I can see the Corps have learned nothing from our experiences nor from the experiences of the Divisions that attacked before us. Neither apparently has the 5th Army. We can't go on losing men like this. We haven't got them. As it is the whole summer is being wasted in useless loss of life and we have gained nothing of value, except the Messines Ridge, the attack on which was a very different show than anything the 5th Army have ever done.[98]

The six 'wasted' divisions (in fact five, the luckless 15th Division going twice), were the 15th and 55th Divisions on 31 July, the 16th and 36th on 16 August, and the 15th and 61st Divisions on 22 August. The attacks cost these five divisions over 14,000 casualties for, after the first morning, minimal gains. The opinion that Nugent had heard of Watts – 'He is said to be a very good Corps Comdr and a good fighting general' – is scarcely borne out by these figures; Haig's assessment that Watts was 'a plucky hard little man' but also 'a distinctly stupid man and lacks imagination' seems closer to the mark.[99]

The end of the partnership

There were other recriminations. The bitterness of the troops was reflected in the war diary of the 14th Royal Irish Rifles, which suffered over 330 casualties:

> The whole thing has been a miserable failure for reasons which are obvious to us all. Our men did all that was asked of them, but the peculiar attitude of the enemy and his methods were not properly appreciated by the powers that be. Our Divisional staff and Brigade staff did everything that was humanly possible.[100]

Spender heard that the division did not hold Nugent responsible but also that the defeat had taken its toll on him ('They do not blame ON who is

[98] ON to CN, 21 [in fact 23] Aug. 1917, in *Nugent*, p. 169.
[99] ON to CN, 14 July 1917, in *Nugent*, p. 265n; Robbins, *British Generalship*, p. 54.
[100] 14th R. Irish Rifles war diary (TNA, WO95/2511).

not well by the way', he told Lily) while his brother Rex, serving with the division, reported in September that 'ON is not at all well, evidently nervy'.[101] As with every failed attack units and formations were quick to blame those on their flanks. In the 16th Division's 49 Brigade, which had advanced beside 108 Brigade, the view in the 7th Royal Inniskilling Fusiliers was that the 9th Royal Irish Fusiliers 'gave way before a Counter-attack and left the Battalion with both flanks in the air'; the 7th/8th Royal Irish Fusiliers reported that 'the division on our left began to waver and it was reported they had been driven back by a counter-attack'; the 2nd Royal Irish Regiment attributed 49 Brigade's failure to the 9th Fusiliers, who 'were seen to retire in disorder'. The 9th Irish Fusiliers, predictably, maintained that they had been holding Hill 35 successfully until the 16th Division's precipitate retreat to the Black line forced them to follow suit, while Spender was told shortly after the attack that 'the 36th has been very badly hit again, due so they say to the 16th in a large measure but I do not know the facts'.[102] Both versions, in fact, had an element of truth: the left of the 16th Division had advanced further than the 36th and held its ground until struck by the German counterattack, but had then been forced back to the Black line ahead of the 36th. The finger-pointing was still going on when Spender visited in September: 'The 36th undoubtedly were not given a fair chance this last time – chiefly the Corps, and this and the failure of the 16th were perhaps equally responsible, and of course optimism'.[103] He was partly right – neither division had had a fair chance, for which XIX Corps bore considerable responsibility. In contrast to Messines the press reporting was sombre:

> The part played by the Irish battalions in the last attack north-east of Ypres was in some respects a tragic one … There is a limit to human endurance, and if you can appreciate the ordeal of the Ulster and South Irishmen – again fighting and dying together as they did at Messines – you will realise that no soldiers could have accomplished more, and that many would have accomplished less without failing in their duty.[104]

[101] Spender to his wife, 25 and 28 Sep. 1917, in *Nugent*, pp 260–61n.
[102] War diaries of 7th R. Inniskilling Fusiliers, 7th/8th R. Irish Fusiliers, 2nd R. Irish Regt and 9th R. Irish Fusiliers (TNA, WO95/1977, 1978, 1979, 2505); Spender to his wife, 19 Aug. 1917, in *Nugent*, p. 103; Metcalfe, *Blacker's Boys*, pp 137–8.
[103] Spender to his wife, 25 Sep. 1917, in *Nugent*, pp 260–61n.
[104] *Belfast Newsletter*, 23 Aug. 1917 (quoting *Morning Post* correspondent).

At the end of August the Ulster Division left Fifth Army, without regret, to join IV Corps in Byng's Third Army. The 16th Division went to Third Army also, but to VI Corps. Spender had predicted that the two divisions would be split up – 'I imagine the stupid experiment of the partnership will now be given up', he had written on 19 August, 'another of ON's awful mistakes by a man who said that he would have nothing to do with politics'.[105] Third Ypres brought to an end the experiment of operating the two Irish divisions side by side. The decision was unlikely to have been taken because of any perceived animosity between the two formations, but because of their fragility; manpower problems meant that both now required significant reorganisation and putting them in the same corps would have been operationally risky. Some argued retrospectively that a partnership between such opposites could only ever have been temporary, a perspective reflected in a post-war biography of Carson which claimed that 'these fine loyalties of war seemed to make but little difference to the age-old animosities of the Irish race' and citing a 1917 letter to Carson from an Irish Rifles officer that

> the Ulstermen and the 16th (Irish) Division were "friendly enough when they were going over the top together but it's when they are behind the lines that they are apt to scrap a bit … After the 'show' the Ulstermen went about playing Dolly's Brae and Derry Walls and other aggressively Orange ditties, which didn't exactly please the 16th". He was forced to think that their being thrown together would not make the slightest difference in the long run.[106]

That was not a view Nugent would have accepted.

Learning curve?

The Ulster Division's experience in the summer of 1917 raises the question of the relevance to it of the concept of a 'learning curve'.[107] It is now generally acknowledged that the British army in the Great War was an organisation that learned from its experiences, and that was certainly true of the 36th Division: because of the high turnover amongst its COs, the continuity of leadership it enjoyed at divisional and brigade level seems to

[105] Spender to his wife, 19 Aug. 1917, in *Nugent*, p. 103.
[106] Colvin, *Carson*, iii, p. 295.
[107] For the learning process on operations, see Jonathan Boff, *Winning and Losing on the Western Front: The British Third* (2012), pp 1–21, 243–51; Connelly, *Steady the Buffs*, pp 229–33; Aimee Fox, *Learning to Fight: Military Innovation and Change in the British Army, 1914–1918* (2018), *passim*.

have been particularly important in this regard. The learning trajectory was for it, however, less a curve, with its implication of uninterrupted progress, than a series of uneven steps (not least because the Germans were learning too, and each side had to react to the other's innovations). The highly-motivated, well-rehearsed formation that attacked on 1 July 1916 then experienced several months of stagnation in the winter of 1916–17; that hiatus, however, was due more to manpower shortages than to an inability to absorb operational lessons, and Nugent's correspondence with Ricardo that December demonstrates informal learning networks and information exchange at work. Re-energised by both reinforcements and the new tactics it assimilated in the spring of 1917, the division in June achieved its spectacular success at Messines. Yet just weeks later at Third Ypres it suffered an unnecessarily severe setback (even allowing for the conditions), not because the division had become de-skilled between 7 June and 16 August but because Gough, Malcolm and Watts were further down the learning curve operationally than Plumer, Harington and Hamilton Gordon. It was a reminder that for improvement to be consistent the learning had to occur simultaneously at different levels of command. Nugent's next battle, in complete contrast to Langemarck, would mark a further step change in the BEF's operational development.

8

New Ways of War

Cambrai and the birth of military modernity, September 1917–February 1918

Introduction

Cambrai was one of Nugent's most complex battles. For the Ulster Division the assault phases of the Somme, Messines and Third Ypres had lasted less than 36 hours, whereas at Cambrai it was in action continuously for seven days during the British attack and a further ten days during the German counter-stroke, and the duration alone imposed demands on him as a commander he had not previously encountered. More fundamentally, Cambrai saw the emergence of a genuinely modern operational technique, with the use by the British for the first time in combination of massed armour, predicted artillery fire and tactical airpower in a way that would have been recognisable to a Second World War commander. Nugent had no difficulty in adjusting mentally to this new operational world, his roots as a Victorian soldier notwithstanding. His biggest problem here, as in other battles, would be the failure of tactical communications to match progress in other aspects of military capability.

Even as the division made operational and technological strides, however, its human component was wearing out. Manpower shortages forced a further restructuring of its infantry in the autumn of 1917. A setback just before Cambrai raised questions about the morale of some of its soldiers, while the aftermath of the fighting demonstrated that individuals, and even entire units, were coming to the end of their tether. Rebuilding the division after the battle was a major challenge for a general who was himself beginning to feel the strain of over two years in command.

Reorganisation

The 36th Division was now in the Cambrai sector, used by both sides to rest divisions recovering from the fighting at Ypres. The division had some recovering to do. Once again both it and the 16th Division faced serious manpower problems, and with the army short of men and political opposition to posting non-Irish soldiers to Irish units still strong, the policy of transferring in regular battalions was now the only way of sustaining them. That process was already underway in the 16th Division – by August 1917 it contained three regular units, rising to four by December – and for the Ulster Division it had been clear since Messines that external reinforcement was essential. In early August the 1st Royal Irish Fusiliers arrived unenthusiastically from the 4th Division (the men were reportedly 'all mud sick' about the move).[1] No changes could be made immediately, but when the division came out of the line the 8th and 9th Royal Irish Rifles in 107 Brigade were merged to make room for the newcomers. This was followed in September by the North Irish Horse, now dismounted, being absorbed by the 9th Royal Irish Fusiliers.[2]

These changes were relatively straightforward; the next ones were less so. In October, the 7th Royal Irish Rifles arrived from the 16th Division and were attached temporarily to 108 Brigade. They were followed on 14 November by the 2nd Royal Irish Rifles (from the 25th Division), which triggered a series of pre-planned changes, the 2nd Battalion absorbing the 7th, and the 11th and 13th Royal Irish Rifles, also in 108 Brigade, being amalgamated. The reorganisation of battalions of the same regiment would elsewhere have been a piece of routine military house-keeping, but here it brought out the tensions inherent in Ireland's participation in the war. Although their identities were now much diluted the four units still bore the imprint of their origins – the 2nd Battalion a pre-war regular unit with an 'all-island' ethos, the 7th from the nationalist 16th Division, and the 11th and 13th Rifles originally UVF units in east Ulster. The officers of the 2nd Battalion had heard with dismay of their transfer to what some considered, according to John Lucy, the 'poisonously loyal' 36th. He had brought back with him from leave in Cork several small flags bearing the Irish harp which were used to decorate the room at a dinner the battalion gave before Cambrai, but in the event the gesture caused no disharmony because the Ulster Division officers present 'affected no surprise at our very Irish table … and we had a very merry evening'.[3]

An identity clash involving the 7th Irish Rifles nearly ended more badly. They were temporarily commanded by Denys Reitz, a Boer fighter turned British officer who had fought at Talana and whom Nugent met and liked ('We both agreed', he told Kitty, 'that that was a gentleman's war compared with this one and he is coming to dine with me tonight'). But shortly after

[1] Capt. A. J. Trousdell, quoted in Bowman, *Irish Regiments*, p. 153.
[2] Marcus Cunliffe, *The Royal Irish Fusiliers 1793–1950* (1952), p. 326; Metcalfe, *Blacker's Boys*, pp 154–8; Richard Doherty, *The North Irish Horse: A Hundred Years of Service* (2002), p. 25; Philip Tardif, *The North Irish Horse in the Great War* (2015), pp 139–84.
[3] John Lucy, *There's a Devil in the Drum* (1938), pp 378–9.

the battalion's arrival Reitz heard a commotion from the stores tent and found his men 'wrecking the place'. The reason was the delivery of soda-water from the Ulster Division's bottling-plant, labelled as usual 'Boyne Water' but which Reitz's men misinterpreted as deliberate provocation, and uttering 'threats and curses against the bloody Orangemen' they 'started off in a body … to avenge what they considered a mortal insult'. Reitz hurriedly rang ahead to divisional HQ which turned out a guard to intercept them. Fortunately, they were persuaded to return to camp without further incident and the next day 'they were playing football with the Ulsterites as if nothing had happened'.[4] It was a reminder, though, that there were deeper attachments than to a regimental cap-badge impacting on soldiers' attitudes. The 7th Rifles had had persistent disciplinary problems in the 16th Division which reflected poor leadership but also, perhaps, political views – Reitz had heard that one reason for their transfer and disbandment was that 'there were too many Sinn Feiners amongst us'; sending the battalion to the Ulster Division to be broken up did not represent sensitive handling by the authorities.[5]

The softening some had detected in Nugent's style after the Somme was only relative, and he remained a demanding and occasionally intimidating commander. His refusal to treat the regular units being posted in with the respect they felt they deserved caused resentment. Following an inspection of the 2nd Royal Irish Rifles and his subsequent address to them early in 1918, for example, their chaplain reported that the CO had complained to the brigadier: 'The only consolation he got was to be told by that officer that he had never heard the general so complimentary before! As we learned later, his praise was always well salted with abuse'.[6]

Nugent, at the same time as reorganising his infantry units, had to rebuild his group of infantry COs, five having become casualties at Ypres while another, Cheape (14th Royal Irish Rifles), was promoted in August to command a brigade in the 29th Division.[7] Two other command changes, both in 107 Brigade, had already come at Nugent's initiative after Messines. On 20 July he told Kitty that he had had 'to inform 2 of my COs the other day that I did not think they were up to the mark and must try some other job', the officers concerned being Lieutenant-Colonels Woods (9th Royal

---

[4] ON to CN, 23 Sep. 1917, in *Nugent*, p. 179; Denys Reitz, *Trekking On* (1933), p. 182.

[5] Bowman, *Irish Regiments*, pp 147–8, 154–5; Reitz, *Trekking On*, pp 184–5.

[6] J. W. Taylor, *The 2nd Royal Irish Rifles in the Great War* (2005), p. 111.

[7] Pratt (11th R. Inniskilling Fusiliers) and Somerville (9th R. Irish Fusiliers) had been killed in August and Cole-Hamilton (8th R. Irish Rifles), Macrory (10th R. Inniskilling Fusiliers) and Perceval-Maxwell (13th R. Irish Rifles) wounded.

Irish Rifles) and Gordon (15th Royal Irish Rifles).[8] In the case of Gordon, a pre-war regular who had done a competent job at Thiepval and Messines, it is likely that Nugent had simply concluded he was tired (he had been absent through illness in June). Woods, however, was a different case. A protégé of Frank Crozier, he had done well on the Somme where he earned the DSO, but he did not get on with his fellow officers and Crozier later acknowledged that in recommending him for promotion he had wanted this to be in a different formation.[9] Woods was, it seems, a disruptive influence and Nugent and Withycombe wanted rid of him, but he did not go without protest. His wife was the daughter of Stewart Quin, a leading member of the UUC, and on 20 July Woods saw Nugent and

> calmly informed me that unless he was given a better job there could be a row made at home as his father in law was a very influential politician in Belfast and would be sure to have a try to raise a row in Parliament I suppose. I don't think he meant that he himself would do anything to down me but that his father in law would. I am very curious to know who his father in l[aw] is. I forgot to ask him. We do have our trials out here. Needless to say I told him that his father in l[aw] might do what he pleases.[10]

Securing capable COs remained a critical issue for Nugent, as he explained when Kitty took him and Farnham to task over their apparent indifference to casualties:

> Arthur was as sorry as any of us at losing Audley Pratt, but my child all our feelings in that way are blunted out here. It is too much the occurrence of every day to stir one over much. I find that however much I really liked a man who gets knocked out, my first thought always is 'Who shall I put in to replace him'.[11]

The eight CO replacements in the autumn of 1917 came from a variety of sources. Three were regulars: Lieutenant-Colonels Goodman and Incledon-Webber were posted in with, respectively, the 2nd Royal Irish Rifles and 1st

---

[8] ON to CN, 20 July 1917, in *Nugent*, p. 160.

[9] Crozier, *Impressions and Recollections*, pp 178–9; Messenger, *Broken Sword*, p. 117.

[10] ON to CN, 20 July 1917, in *Nugent*, pp 160–61. Woods, despite this setback, went on to perform well in Russia during the Allied intervention there in 1918, after a spell commanding a reserve battalion at home: see Nick Baron, *The King of Karelia: Colonel P. J. Woods and the British Intervention in North Russia 1918–19* (2007).

[11] ON to CN, 2 Sep. 1917, in *Nugent*, p. 175.

Royal Irish Fusiliers, while Philip Kelly, a regular Irish Fusiliers officer in his twenties, took over the 9th Royal Irish Fusiliers. Another external appointment was Lieutenant-Colonel Elwes, a recalled Scots Guards officer who had assumed command of the 9th Royal Irish Rifles just before Langemarck and remained in charge of the amalgamated 8th/9th Royal Irish Rifles thereafter. Three others were internal appointments: Cole-Hamilton returned from his wounds in August to take over the 15th Royal Irish Rifles, while Vivian (14th Royal Irish Rifles) and Knott (11th Royal Inniskilling Fusiliers) had been serving as battalion 2ic's.[12] Knott in particular was an example of an emerging group of younger 'home-grown' officers – others included McCallum (8th Royal Irish Rifles), Montgomery (9th Royal Irish Rifles) and Knox (10th Royal Inniskilling Fusiliers) – who would play increasingly influential roles in 1917–18. Unlike the older officers, they served almost continuously with the division from 1915 onwards and benefited from the BEF's more structured approach to training, several, for example, attending the Senior Officers Course at Aldershot, though not all would end up as battalion commanders. The changes of late 1917 provided opportunities for a number of them, including Knox and Montgomery, to have temporary spells in command and gain experience.

The remaining replacement CO was an officer whose services Nugent had specifically sought. In August he asked Farnham to take over the 10th Royal Inniskilling Fusiliers, telling Kitty in September that 'I am hoping to get Arthur Farnham as a Commanding Officer for one of my battalions very shortly. I shall be glad to have him. The difficulty of replacing officers in command of battalions gets greater every day'.[13] In doing so he was short-circuiting the usual arrangements, which were that if a division had no suitable internal candidate for a command vacancy a qualified officer would be offered from a central list, as Elwes had been. He got his way, and Farnham eventually arrived on 24 September, though when he did Nugent had a pang of anxiety about appointing him to such a dangerous role – 'if anything happened him I should feel very bad about it'.[14] By contrast he successfully resisted attempts by Frank Macrory, the previous CO of the

---

[12] By Cambrai the composition of the division's infantry COs had changed since June 1917, albeit slightly. Four had been serving regular officers in 1914 [Lucas-Clements (vice Incledon-Webber), Burnand, Kelly and Goodman], three were dug-outs [Blair Oliphant, Elwes, Farnham] and five were wartime officers [Cole-Hamilton, Goodwin, Peacocke, Knott and Vivian, though Cole-Hamilton and Vivian had held pre-war special reserve commissions].

[13] ON to CN, 9 Sep. 1917 (PRONI, D3835/E/2/Pte 69/1993).

[14] ON to CN, 21 Sep. 1917 (PRONI, D3835/E/2/523).

10th Inniskillings and now recovered from his injuries at Ypres, to re-join the division. Nugent's reply mixed appreciation with directness, praising Macrory's leadership and service but making clear that his brigade commander, Ricardo, had problems with his attitude (the family story was that this related to his refusal once to parade his tired men for inspection after coming out of the line) and did not want him back. 'I cannot overrule the Brigadier in this matter', Nugent told him, 'and the best advice I can give you is that you should now leave the Army and go home to Ulster to the retirement which you have so well and honourably earned'. As Macrory's son later wrote, it was 'a very nice letter and he preserved it for the rest of his life, proudly showing it to all and sundry at every opportunity, although when analysed it was nothing less than the sack'.[15] There had been changes in divisional HQ too. Somerset Saunderson had transferred to the Tank Corps some months previously and Nugent's long-serving second ADC, Robin Henry, now returned to his parent artillery unit. To replace them he got, after some searching, two officers wounded earlier in the war, Major Guy Campbell and Captain Freddie Drummond, the latter having lost an arm at Hooge in 1915. Lewis Comyn also went, to Nugent's considerable regret, on promotion to the War Office, being replaced as AA&QMG by his deputy, Major S. H. Green.

In September 1917 Carson, now Minister without Portfolio in the War Cabinet, visited France and Nugent took him and another unionist politician, Ronald McNeill, on a tour of the Somme battlefield. They did not have time to walk over the ground, but Nugent showed them various locations from the car and they came across the skeleton of a German soldier in a shell-crater. Not unusually, Carson was pessimistic about the war's progress, being particularly concerned by allied shipping losses (he had until recently been First Lord of the Admiralty). They also had a revealing exchange while driving through Albert:

> The troops in it were very slack about saluting us or me as we drove through and I said 'I wonder who this rabble is. If they were the Ulster Division they would hear about it'. Carson laughed and said 'Yes, I imagine they would. I have heard many things about you, but failure to say what you think or being slack in matters of discipline have not been mentioned as failings of yours'. I said 'I suppose you have heard lots of things, but I can assure you I do not care a d—— what you hear. I know what I expect and I take no less and you may also believe that popularity hunting isn't one of my failings either'.

[15] Patrick Macrory, *Days That Are Gone* (1983), p. 71.

He said 'No, I know it isn't and no one respects you the less for it and they know now that you know your business' or words to that effect.[16]

Trench warfare

When the division went back into the line near Havrincourt at the end of August, replacing the 9th (Scottish) Division, it immediately found itself engaged in a struggle for Yorkshire Bank, a spoil heap beside the Canal du Nord. Both sides had had posts on it until the 9th Division expelled the Germans in the early hours of 30 August. The Germans retook it that night, 108 Brigade's first night in the line, but were driven out; they took it again on the night of 1 September, but were ejected early on the 2nd. Nugent was unimpressed, visiting 108 Brigade to 'inquire into why the garrison allowed it to be taken by the Germans a 2nd time and to see that better arrangements were made for tonight'. The changes worked, in that the next three German attempts were successfully driven off.[17] The next significant action came on 4 November, when the 9th Royal Irish Fusiliers raided German trenches at Wigan Copse, also near Havrincourt. Nugent gave Kitty a detailed if gruesome account:

> We had a very good raid last night into the German lines. Killed over 40 and blew in dugouts which we know contained men. It was a complete surprise carried out without any preliminary bombardment. The whole party 64 of them crawled on their bellies for over an hour until they got up to the German wire where there was a gap. Then they rushed in and first met a party of 16 men coming out of their trenches. They had a lively fight with them and eventually bayonetted the whole lot. Another party of Germans were hunted out of the trenches up against their own wire and they were either bayonetted or shot. The squealing of the Germans could be heard back in our lines.

Pointing out the strong resistance the defenders put up (the Fusiliers suffered 20 casualties, including four dead), Nugent again noted the propensity of pumped-up soldiers not to take captives:

> Our men were rather excited and saw red and they took no prisoners. They did take some at first but got bored with them and killed them … They are men of the North Irish Horse recently sent

[16] ON to CN, 16 and 20 Sep. 1917, in *Nugent*, pp 177–9.
[17] Falls, *Ulster Division*, pp 128–9; ON to CN, 2 Sep. 1917, in *Nugent*, p. 175.

to us and have never yet had a chance of killing a German and they got excited and killed everyone instead of taking some prisoners as proof of success[.][18]

Such episodes were not uncommon on both sides, and Nugent's matter-of-fact description is indicative, coming from an essentially humane man, of battlefield realities.[19] As far as the overall British offensive effort in late 1917 was concerned, however, even the aggressive Nugent was beginning to have doubts.[20] On 8 November, he commented on the fighting at Passchendaele:

> I sometimes wonder if these terrible losses for such apparently small results are really worth it. The ground in Flanders is responsible for nearly as many lives as the German shells. Men get drowned in the shell craters, falling into them wounded. I have been talking lately to some of the Divisions recently down from there and they say they don't know how the men can stick it in holding a line, much less in attacking from it.[21]

Cambrai preparations

On 13 October 1917 Haig had approved the plan of General Sir Julian Byng, commander of Third Army, for a limited offensive at Cambrai. The underlying concept was the use of massed armour to mount a surprise attack, supported by artillery 'firing off the map', exploiting the latest survey techniques to dispense with the usual preliminary registration. The intention was to seize part of the Hindenburg line near Havrincourt; depending on the strength of resistance the attack could then either be closed down or, if going well, exploited using cavalry to try to cut off the enemy forces east of Cambrai and perhaps capture the city itself.[22] Byng's plan involved seven infantry and five cavalry divisions, almost 500 tanks and around 1,000 guns, divided between III Corps (Lieutenant-General Pulteney) on the right, attacking initially towards Marcoing, and IV Corps (Lieutenant-General Woollcombe), which included the Ulster Division, on the left aiming for Bourlon.[23]

---

[18] ON to CN, 4 Nov. 1917, in *Nugent*, pp 179–80; Metcalfe, *Blacker's Boys*, pp 162–3.

[19] See, for example, Tim Cook, 'The politics of surrender: Canadian soldiers and the killing of prisoners', *Journal of Military History*, 70:3 (2006), pp 637–65.

[20] Harris, *Douglas Haig*, pp 383–5.

[21] ON to CN, 8 Nov. 1917 (PRONI, D3835/E/2/538).

[22] Ian Beckett, Timothy Bowman and Mark Connelly, *The British Army and the First World War* (2017), pp 338–9.

[23] *OH*, 1917, iii (1948), pp 4–9.

On 3 November Nugent, along with other senior officers, attended a tank demonstration and was impressed: it was, he felt, 'really rather wonderful to see how they can get over fences and flatten out wire. They are a great improvement on what they were last year'.[24] There followed a series of corps conferences, the most important of which was chaired by Woollcombe at 11am on 11 November, a year to the minute from the end of the war, to go through the IV Corps plan in detail. Present were his divisional commanders, who in addition to Nugent included Major-Generals Braithwaite (62nd Division), Harper (51st) and Dudgeon (56th), as well as Colonel Baker-Carr of the 1st Tank Brigade. Baker-Carr later claimed that at this stage there was little enthusiasm in the corps for the employment of tanks and would be very critical of the Highland Division's use of them, but there is no hint in Nugent's correspondence of any reluctance. The following morning, he met his own brigadiers to finalise the Ulster Division's plan, and they briefed their COs that afternoon.[25]

Nugent had been given two tasks, to protect the left flank of Third Army's advance and to act as the IV Corps reserve. The other two assault divisions of IV Corps, the 62nd and 51st, whose objectives were respectively Bourlon Hill and the village of Fontaine beside it, were to advance east of the Canal du Nord which, though it contained no water, was a significant obstacle. Nugent's first job was to cover the 62nd Division's advance by using one brigade to break into the front-line trenches of the Hindenburg system west of the canal and move north along them, keeping pace with the 62nd on the other side. In his second role, as corps reserve, he was to be ready to deploy his other two brigades to assist the 62nd Division, either by continuing the advance northwards or by reinforcing the assault on Bourlon. Unlike the 62nd and 51st Divisions, the Ulster Division would have no tanks attached for the opening attack. Nugent left much of the detailed planning for 109 Brigade's break-in battle on the west bank to Ricardo and his gunner adviser, Lieutenant-Colonel Simpson of 173rd Brigade RFA (described by Falls as one of 'the most scientific and least conventional' junior British artillery commanders), while he and Place focused on possible operations east of the canal. The planning requirement here was quite different to Messines or Langemarck.[26]

[24] ON to CN, 4 Nov. 1917, in *Nugent*, p. 180.
[25] C. D. Baker-Carr, *From Chauffeur to Brigadier* (1930), p. 211; *OH*, 1917, iii, pp 316–21; IV Corps, 36 Div. war diary (TNA, WO95/2492).
[26] Falls, *Ulster Division*, p. 149; Nugent's personal copies of Cambrai operational papers (PRONI, D3835/E/10/7/67); Ulster Div. Narrative of Cambrai offensive (TNA, WO158/387).

The German trench raid

By 17 November preparations were well-advanced, with hundreds of tanks and guns having been concealed in Havrincourt Wood and the surrounding area. The 51st and 62nd Divisions had started moving into position, taking over trenches previously held by 107 and 108 Brigades opposite Havrincourt, with a screen of Ulster Division outposts to prevent the Germans discovering the changes. All seemed to be going well when, in the early hours of 18 November, an incident occurred that put the security of the British offensive at risk. At 5.30am a German raiding party from the *54th Division* swooped on a small post held by soldiers of the 1st Royal Irish Fusiliers and took them prisoner.[27] Nugent, when he heard, was dismayed:

> I am so furious, the Germans raided me last night and walked off with a Sergeant and 5 men, belonging to the 1st Battn R Irish Fusiliers, one of the regular battalions that has been recently sent to me. It was most important that the Germans should get no prisoners to question. I should like to shoot the whole party. Goodness knows how much the men taken prisoner knew, but the Germans will get everything out of them they do know, I am quite certain. We have not lost more than 3 or 4 men as a result of German raids since we came to France and this wretched regular battalion which ought to be an example has let us down.[28]

Nugent's ferocious reaction was driven, as his letter indicates, by fear the British attack plans would be compromised, a concern shared by the British high command. The hope was that any information the prisoners disclosed would be too limited and too late to enable the Germans to react. That did not stop Nugent's wrath descending on the Irish Fusiliers, and their CO, Shuckburgh Lucas-Clements, also from Cavan, was told that afternoon that he was to be replaced, though in the event his successor could not get up in time and Lucas-Clements commanded the battalion in the attack.[29]

One recent study, drawing on the record of the prisoners' interrogation, has argued that the information they gave, by causing some German units to be placed on higher alert in the Flesquieres sector, had a significant

---

[27] Jack Sheldon, *The German Army at Cambrai* (2009), pp 22–5.

[28] ON to CN, 18 Nov. 1917, in *Nugent*, p. 180.

[29] 1st R. Irish Fusiliers war diary (TNA WO95/2502). Lucas-Clements replaced Incledon-Webber, who left on promotion to brigadier, in September 1917. The episode clearly left no lasting resentment, as when Lucas-Clements married Rosamond Burrowes, daughter of one of Nugent's close friends, in Dublin in 1922 Nugent was asked to propose the health of the bride and groom (Nugent's diary, 7 June 1922, Nugent family papers).

impact on the battle and that 'this act of betrayal' was driven by poor morale and Irish disenchantment with both the war and British policy in Ireland.[30] According to the interrogation report, the prisoners referred to a possible attack in the Havrincourt area by the newly-arrived 51st (Highland) Division, a build-up of artillery and the presence in Havrincourt Wood of three camouflaged tanks. The party, comprising two Englishmen, two Ulster Protestants and two Irish Catholics, resented being left in an isolated position and the Irishmen amongst them were said to be 'thoroughly war-weary and speak badly of the English. They say if an uprising takes place in Ireland, they would take up arms against England without more ado'. The German intelligence officer concluded from these comments that 'the current military value of the 36th Division cannot be rated highly'.[31] The phenomenon of prisoners telling their captors what they thought they wanted to hear was common on both sides, and the outline of what the prisoners revealed has in fact long been known: the British official history in 1948 noted that the Germans had learned that a local attack in the Havrincourt area was likely in the next few days and that tanks might take part. As the prisoners were unaware of either the presence of large numbers of tanks or the artillery arrangements, and because operational-level surprise was clearly not compromised, demonstrated by the German disarray during the opening phase of the attack, most historians have with reason concluded that the information did not have a decisive effect.[32]

---

[30] John A. Taylor, *Deborah and the War of the Tanks* (2016), pp 145–53, 244–6, 263–4. The interrogation report, prepared by the German *2nd Army*, is in the military archives at Freiburg (ibid., p. 287).

[31] Taylor, *Deborah*, pp 146, 148–9. To describe statements made by frightened and disorientated men as a deliberate act of betrayal is excessively harsh. Taylor, whose analysis deserves attention, also suggests that the execution on 5th November of Pte. Hanna of the 1st R. Irish Fusiliers is a further indication of fragile morale in this unit. Hanna's was, however, a tragic case from which it is impossible to generalise: he deserted from the battalion only hours after joining and already had two suspended death sentences hanging over him (for deserting in Gallipoli and Salonika).

[32] *OH*, 1917, iii, pp 48–9; Sheldon, *German Army at Cambrai*, pp 24–5. That is not to say that the local defence at Flesquieres was not strengthened as a result of the prisoners' information or the Highland Division's task made harder; but the suggestion that this changed 'the course of the battle, and perhaps even the war' is hard to sustain (Taylor, *Deborah*, p. 246). The fundamental problem in this sector was not the last-minute reinforcement of the defence but operational difficulties on the British side, in terms of poor infantry-armour coordination during the initial attack and the breakdown of efforts during the afternoon of 20 November to launch a coordinated multi-divisional assault to pinch out the Flesquieres salient (*OH*, 1917, iii, pp 280–82).

On 19 November Nugent went around his brigades and spoke to the assembled officers about the next day's operations, before returning to his headquarters in Ytres, five miles behind the line.[33]

The British attack

The Cambrai offensive began at 6.20am on 20 November, when the assault divisions, supported by 378 fighting tanks, moved forward behind a rolling barrage laid down by over a thousand guns. The front-line defenders were taken completely by surprise and the first day generally went extremely well, with advances in places of up to five miles and over 4,000 prisoners taken.[34]

On the Ulster Division's front, at 8.35am, once the 62nd Division's advance east of the Canal du Nord had drawn level with 109 Brigade, the 10th Royal Inniskilling Fusiliers began their break-in operation at the Spoil Heap. Simpson's artillery bombardment proved highly effective, two 18-pdr brigades and a battery of 4-in. Stokes mortars firing thermit (incendiary) shells pounding the position before the assault went in, and resistance was slight. Seventy of the defenders, from the newly-arrived *20th Landwehr Division*, were captured and following up the Inniskillings and an attached company of the 14th Royal Irish Rifles advanced rapidly along the Hindenburg line, giving the Germans no chance to rally; the use of shoulder-slung Lewis guns, well-rehearsed drills for clearing dug-outs and the efficient leap-frogging of platoons through each other helped maintain momentum. Farnham's advance of 2,500 yards in two-and-three-quarter hours – his men reached the Demicourt-Graincourt road at 11.20am – was an impressive performance. The 9th Royal Inniskilling Fusiliers continued the advance against strengthening resistance for the next two hours, at which point the 11th Royal Inniskilling Fusiliers took over, halting at dusk 500 yards north of the Cambrai-Bapaume road, in touch with the 62nd Division on the right across the canal and the 56th on the left. Ricardo's men had advanced over 4,000 yards and taken more than 500 prisoners, the most successful action by a single Ulster Division brigade of the war.[35] Meanwhile, on the east bank of the canal, 107 and 108 Brigades had moved

33 107 Bde war diary (TNA, WO95/2502).
34 Gary Sheffield, *The Chief: Douglas Haig and the British Army* (2011), p. 251. For the Ulster Division at Cambrai, see Falls, *Ulster Division*, pp 143–80; Orr and Truesdale, *'Ulster Will Fight'*, ii, pp 330–53. The five assault divisions (from left to right) were the 62nd, 51st, 6th, 20th and 12th, with the 36th and 29th joining in later in the morning.
35 Falls, *Ulster Division*, pp 148–53; *OH*, 1917, iii, pp 61–2, 86–8.

up behind the 62nd Division and waited near Graincourt for orders to push on but the Yorkshiremen's advance had been held up short of Bourlon, and Nugent's brigades in the end were not committed.[36]

21 November

It was on the second day, 21 November, that the British plan began to go seriously wrong. Progress across the front slowed as the Germans rushed up reinforcements and despite heavy fighting the 62nd Division could not secure Bourlon, though the 51st Division took Fontaine. For a second day 107 and 108 Brigades waited for orders to advance that did not come, but west of the canal 109 Brigade soon became involved in a strenuous fight for the fortified village of Moeuvres. At dawn, the 9th Royal Inniskilling Fusiliers had resumed the advance until held up by heavy machine-gun fire. Overnight, reinforcements from the German *20th Division* had been deployed between Moeuvres and Bourlon, and during the day most of the *214th Division* also arrived and was fed immediately into the battle. When the 14th Royal Irish Rifles and 10th Royal Inniskilling Fusiliers renewed the attack at noon, therefore, they faced strong resistance but by late afternoon had nevertheless fought their way to the southern edge of Moeuvres. They could not stay there, though, in the face of intense machine-gun fire, and there were now the first signs of a problem that would be of increasing concern to Nugent as the battle continued: at 5.20pm an officer of the 14th Rifles reported that two companies had retired without orders but that he had 'reorganised them and taken them back … Men a bit disorganised but are holding on'.[37] A sense of brittleness about this unit would grow over the coming days. The total advance of 109 Brigade on the 21st was about a thousand yards.

During the day Nugent had gone forward to see what he could of the fighting and late that afternoon he was at last given full control of all three of his brigades.[38] Woollcombe ordered him to mount an attack next day (22 November) on both sides of the canal, in support of another push by the 62nd Division against Bourlon, H-hour being set for 11am. In preparation for it Nugent pulled 109 Brigade out for a rest and moved 108 Brigade over to the west bank of the canal to take their place. How he

---

[36] Bryn Hammond, *Cambrai: The Myth of the First Great Tank Battle* (2008),
  pp 151–62; Alexander Turner, *Cambrai 1917* (2007), pp 43–5; William Moore,
  A Wood Called Bourlon: The Cover-up After Cambrai (1988), pp 68–70;
  Capt. B. H. Liddell Hart, *The Tanks* (1959), i, pp 141–3; *OH*, 1917, iii,
  pp 57–9, 82–4.

[37] 14th R. Irish Rifles war diary (TNA, WO95/2511).

[38] ON to CN, 22 Nov. 1917, in *Nugent*, p. 183.

issued his orders for this new attack is instructive. At around 10pm on 21 November he gave telephone orders to his brigadiers, and the confirmatory written orders, containing important supplementary detail such as artillery timings, were signed off before midnight. The written orders still had to go forward, for part of their journey at least, by runner in the dark along congested trenches. In the case of Withycombe of 107 Brigade, whose headquarters were now near Graincourt, eight miles from divisional HQ and three miles beyond the old German front line, these did not arrive until 4.30am. Withycombe had already assembled his COs, however, and was able to hold his orders group immediately, so allowing the battalions time for their own battle preparations. Cole-Hamilton of the 15th Royal Irish Rifles, for example, was back at his command post at 7.15am giving orders to his company commanders, and an hour later his leading companies were moving into position.[39]

22 November

Although the cascade of orders within the division had worked well, neither brigade attack prospered on 22 November. That morning the Germans counter-attacked the 62nd and 51st Divisions heavily, retaking Fontaine, and the Ulster Division's attack became the only significant British offensive effort of the day. East of the canal 107 Brigade's lead battalion, the 15th Royal Irish Rifles, advanced 500 yards along the increasingly shallow Hindenburg support trenches before being held up at a block covered by machine-guns, and despite repeated efforts, including an attempt at dusk by the 10th Royal Irish Rifles to rush the position which cost them six officers, no further progress could be made. West of the canal 108 Brigade's attack started well, the 12th Royal Irish Rifles successfully capturing most of Moeuvres, but at 4pm they were hit by a powerful counter-attack, probably by the *214th Division*. Support arrangements within the brigade broke down, with urgent calls for artillery fire being answered too late and reinforcements from the 9th Royal Irish Fusiliers unable to get through the German barrage. By 6pm the Rifles had been forced back to the village's southern edge, which came as a nasty shock to Nugent: 'I thought all was well then and to my consternation the Germans counterattacked in the late afternoon and retook it. Too late in these short days to do anything to retake it'.[40] Earlier Haig had called in to Nugent's HQ on his way to see Byng and recorded their conversation in his diary:

[39] Nugent's Cambrai papers (PRONI, D3835/E/10/7/57); 107 Bde war diary and 15th R. Irish Rifles narrative of operations 20–27 Nov. 1917 (TNA, WO95/2502 and 2503).

[40] ON to CN, 23 Nov. 1917, in *Nugent*, p. 184; Falls, *Ulster Division*, pp 158–60; *OH*, 1917, iii, pp 122–3.

> At Ytres I saw Nugent Commanding 36th Division (Ulster). On the 20th he only used one brigade and their casualties had been very small. Enemy fell back quickly or surrendered. Today had been hard fighting at Moeuvres. He thought that Enemy had no infantry on their front only machine gun companies. Several of these machine gunners fought like fanatics and instead of surrendering blew out their brains.[41]

The weather remained cold and Nugent was increasingly worried about the impact on his men. His view after three days' fighting was that the offensive should be halted:

> I am rather afraid that we have got to the end of our effort. The success of the operation depended on our being able to exploit the surprise of the first day's attack. This is the 3rd day and we may be sure the Germans are rushing up reinforcements. The fact is it is too late in the year. Fortunately it is not cold for the latter end of November, but that is only comparatively speaking. It is cold and utterly wretched for men lying out all day and night.[42]

Haig disagreed. He and Byng concluded controversially on the 22nd that the offensive should continue, a decision influenced by the fact that the British could not remain where they were with Bourlon Hill still in German hands. IV Corps therefore prepared to resume its attack on Bourlon the next day, the plan for the morning of the 23rd involving an assault by the 40th Division, which had replaced the exhausted 62nd, and an attempt by the 51st Division to re-capture Fontaine. Woollcombe ordered Nugent to continue attacking on either side of the canal and in response to Nugent's repeated requests for additional assistance 107 Brigade was allocated 11 tanks. H-hour was set for 10.30am.

On the night of 22 November Nugent initiated a similar orders cycle to the previous day's. He again issued preliminary orders by phone, this time at 11pm. Withycombe again convened his orders group in the early hours, at 4am. The problem was that, while his infantry COs were there, the commanders of the tanks who would be supporting the brigade, from E Battalion of the the Tank Corps, were not: they were still with their vehicles crawling forward painfully towards the start-line. Not until 8.30am could they be collected and Withycombe issue his final orders. H-hour could not be postponed because it was tied into other operations and there followed

[41] Sheffield and Bourne, *Haig Diaries*, p. 349.
[42] ON to CN, 22 Nov. 1917, in *Nugent*, p. 183.

a desperate scramble to get orders out to the battalions and the tanks. One company commander had only 15 minutes to assemble his men and brief his officers before moving out, and there was no time for the tank crews and infantry to marry up properly.[43]

23 November

Unsurprisingly, 107 Brigade's attack ran into difficulties almost at once. Artillery support was weak, only a single field artillery brigade and four 6-in. howitzers being available. Six tanks were to take part in the initial phase (the capture of a position called Round Trench and the Hindenburg Support line), with the survivors joining the other five for the subsequent advance on the main objective, Quarry Wood, but in the event the tanks could make little impact. Two tanks accompanied the 15th Royal Irish Rifles, attacking on the right, for a short distance before one broke down and the other lost direction and disappeared; the battalion advanced only about a hundred yards before being pinned down. On the left the 8th Royal Irish Rifles got assistance from one tank in capturing Round Trench and Lock 5 nearby but could get no further. At least seven other tanks had been knocked out by artillery or had broken down before or shortly after crossing the start-line, and 107 Brigade's advance quickly ground to a halt.

West of the canal, 108 Brigade's attack at first went better. Here artillery support was stronger (three field brigades and nineteen heavy guns), and though the 12th Royal Irish Rifles and 9th Royal Irish Fusiliers made slow progress initially, the insertion of the 2nd Royal Irish Rifles led to the capture of most of Moeuvres for a second time. With the trenches on either side still in German hands, however, and the village being swept by fire from higher ground, the gains could not be held and by dusk 108 Brigade was again left clinging to the southern outskirts.[44] Nugent once more went forward in person – 'I can't get information as quick as I should like', he complained – and 108 Brigade's intelligence officer, Captain Godson, found him in a trench watching the attack on Moeuvres through binoculars. Godson recalled that Nugent 'was thinking of ordering another attack on Moeuvres & asked me my view. I said the troops had had enough & I could not think it would be successful'. German reinforcements opposite IV Corps now included the *21st Reserve Division*, and Nugent's sense was that the 23rd had been a critical day: 'We know the Germans have brought up large reinforcements and in my opinion what we don't get

[43] Nugent's Cambrai papers (PRONI, D3835/E/10/7/57); 107 Bde war diary (TNA, WO95/2502); Falls, *Ulster Division*, pp 163–5; *OH*, 1917, iii, pp 132–3; Hammond, *Cambrai*, pp 265–7.
[44] Falls, *Ulster Division*, pp 164–5; *OH*, 1917, iii, p. 132.

today we shan't get at all, unless we get Bourlon Hill. After 4 days' continuous fighting we are all rather 'out' and the situation is not clear. No news in this sort of fighting is often bad news'.[45]

24 November

On the following day, 24 November, the Ulster Division attempted one further attack, which failed to launch. The plan had been for 107 Brigade to mount a limited operation east of the canal to secure a better defensive position, supported by IV Corps's heavy artillery, but the guns had to be diverted to deal with renewed German counter-attacks at Bourlon. Nugent was visiting the brigades when the German attacks began:

> I went round our front as near as I could today but the Germans were shelling heavily and there was a good deal of dodging to do. I was passing behind some of my Artillery today which were in action and were being rather badly shelled. I saw a German shell land on one of my guns and demolish it, blew up all the ammunition that was beside it and knocked out 13 men. I saw one German attack which was beaten off.[46]

The attack he referred to was probably the virtual annihilation by the 15th Royal Irish Rifles and the divisional machine-guns of a party of Germans attempting to advance down the Hindenburg trenches, to observe which he must have been well forward.[47] His wish to see for himself was admirable but the limitations of 1917 communications meant that while doing so he was unable to exercise full command of the division. This central dilemma of Great War command gave rise to some interesting post-war observations by Cyril Falls, who as well as serving on Nugent's staff was later a liaison officer with the French:

> In general, British commanders and staffs went forward much more often than the French, and indeed too often during a battle. It was absurd that the divisional commander and the GSO1 should be absent at the same time on such occasions, but this was too often the case. At Cambrai … [a]t one stage of the battle I was the only representative of the General Staff in the office and the divisional commander was out.[48]

---

[45] ON to CN, 23 Nov. 1917, in *Nugent*, p. 184; Godson papers (IWM); *OH*, 1917, iii, p. 142.

[46] ON to CN, 22 Nov. 1917, in *Nugent*, p. 183.

[47] Falls, *Ulster Division*, p. 165.

[48] Falls, 'Contacts with Troops', p. 174.

107 Brigade's attack that afternoon did not take place. When the barrage, provided by the limited artillery available, began shortly before zero it was so obviously inadequate that the CO of the assault battalion, Lucas-Clements of the 1st Royal Irish Fusiliers, cancelled the attack. Given his precarious position following the raid of 18 November this was an act of considerable moral courage but there were no repercussions from Nugent. In fact, he was applying the same kind of resistance upwards himself:

> We have suffered all through by being the left Division of the attack and with a canal between us and the main objective which is Bourlon. We have had no Tanks and not enough artillery and we have had to attack continuously strong defences with heavy wire in front of them. I spoke strongly to Corps today about it and told them it was not fair to ask us to go on losing men and spoiling the men's morale by asking them to do what they know to be impossibilities. The Corps Comdr agreed and said he would not ask us to do any more attacks until he could give us artillery and Tanks.[49]

25–30 November

The troops were now very weary, Nugent observing that it was 'really dreadful going round to see the white drawn faces and red eyes of overtired men'. In the early hours of 26 November Frank Crozier, still a brigadier in the 40th Division, called to see him:

> I had a talk with my old Chief Sir Oliver Nugent, sitting on his bed, while he lay there telling me how the Ulster Division had done in the Cambrai battle. 'They have been a bit sticky', he said. 'Thiepval wiped the Division out. Messines did us a bit of good, but the Salient killed us', he lamented. 'It is not a question of morale, it is men, and we have not got them.'[50]

On the afternoon of 26 November news came that the division would be relieved that night. The infantry were pulled out – as usual the artillery, engineers and pioneers had to stay in the line – in the middle of a snowstorm, and to add to their exhaustion they found that some of their billets, in the Hermies area behind the original British front line, were occupied by other units and many ended up sleeping in the snow. Nugent handed over the sector to Major-General Pereira of the 2nd Division, who faced the unappealing prospect of attacking Moeuvres: 'The Division which relieves

---

[49] ON to CN, 24 Nov. 1917, in *Nugent*, p. 185.
[50] Brig.-Gen. F. P. Crozier, *Impressions and Recollections* (1930), p. 207.

us has to take it and they don't like the job' he told Kitty, 'I have been with their General this evening telling him all I could about it'.[51] He also commented on the progress of the offensive:

> Everything was a success up to a certain point, so long as the Tanks kept going, but once they had got to the limits of their power of moving we stopped … As soon as the Germans recovered from the surprise they rushed up machine-guns and the whole country in front of us is bristling with them. There is no possibility of advancing against machine-guns. They must be dealt with by Artillery, that means long delay, communications, getting up masses of ammunition and we have not got the guns here nor even roads to bring them by. The papers are full of what the Cavalry have done. It is a fact that the Cavalry have done absolutely nothing except block the roads and follow the Infantry. It makes us all so furious to read the frantic efforts made to boost the Cavalry which is as much out of date in this war as a naked man with a stone axe.

His view of the cavalry's role was widely shared but he would have cause to revise his opinion of the mounted arm, at least in part, during the March 1918 retreat. On the 28th the division spent the night near Ytres, where the troops were cheered by the news that they were to move to a quieter sector. The next day the infantry moved by train to an area west of Arras, 25 miles from Cambrai, with the transport following by road. The infantry's 'rest' lasted less than 24 hours, however, while for the transport it never began. At noon on 30 November came news that a massive German counter-attack had hit the British at Cambrai that morning, along with orders for the division to re-trace its steps urgently. By 2.30pm the battalions were already starting out – with no trains or motorised transport available, they had to get there by forced marches – while messengers met the transport, still in transit, and turned it back. By the night of 1 December, the division was back at Ytres, even wearier than when it left 48 hours earlier.

The German Counter-stroke

The German counter-stroke on 30 November, involving some 14 divisions, was a major operational-level attack designed to envelop the British salient in a pincer movement. The northern prong, comprising six divisions attacking southwards with its main effort between Bourlon and Moeuvres, was halted decisively in heavy fighting in which the Ulster Division's artillery, still deployed in support of the 2nd Division, played an important

---

[51] ON to CN, 27 Nov. 1917, in *Nugent*, p. 187.

part: the 153rd Brigade fired no fewer than 10,000 rounds that day, while 173rd Brigade on Demicourt ridge engaged over open sights German artillery batteries attempting to deploy on the slopes to the north.[52]

The story was different with the German eastern thrust, where eight divisions crashed into the British front between Epehy and Marcoing with devastating force, the defenders, with the exception of Lieutenant-General Snow's VII Corps, being taken badly by surprise. The Germans employed on a large scale for the first time against the British the storm-troop infiltration tactics they would use with such effect in March 1918, advancing rapidly behind a hurricane bombardment. The British 12th and 20th Divisions were sent staggering back with heavy losses, including hundreds of prisoners; on the flanks of the breakthrough the 55th Division to the south and the 29th to the north clung on with difficulty. By nightfall the Germans had advanced three miles and had even captured a significant section of the original British front line. The situation for the next 48 hours was critical as the British tried to shore up their defences. It was towards this threatened sector that the Ulster Division was hurrying, and it was not surprising that Haig, whom Nugent encountered on 30 November, was anxious: 'I met the C in C yesterday on my way back and he stopped me to talk. He again said some complimentary things about the Division, but he looked rather worried'.[53]

In fact, by the time the Ulster Division was committed to action, on the night of 4 December, the German counter-stroke was losing momentum and Crown Prince Rupprecht was contemplating closing it down. That was not known to the British, of course, and it made no difference to the strenuous fighting in which the division now became involved as both sides struggled for possession of Welsh Ridge, the high ground west of La Vacquerie dominating this part of the battlefield. On the night of 4/5 December 108 Brigade took over the Couillet valley, immediately north of Welsh Ridge, from the 6th Division, and on the afternoon of 5 December 109 Brigade began the relief of the 61st Division's 182 Brigade, holding the northern half of Welsh Ridge itself. The advance companies of the 9th Royal Inniskilling Fusiliers, 109 Brigade's lead unit, were still moving up when they found themselves in the middle of intense fighting as the German *9th Reserve Division* mounted a strong attack. Although the Inniskillings assisted 182 Brigade in halting it, the top of the ridge had been

---

[52] Falls, *Ulster Division*, pp 167–9; Sheldon, *German Army at Cambrai*, pp 188–223; Jonathan Boff, *Haig's Enemy: Crown Prince Rupprecht and Germany's War on the Western Front* (2018), pp 193–7.

[53] ON to CN, 1 Dec. 1917, in *Nugent*, p. 190.

lost, and by the time 109 Brigade completed the relief in the early hours of 6 December Nugent had already given Ricardo the task of driving the Germans back.[54]

Nugent assumed overall command of the Welsh Ridge sector at 6.30am on the 6th. His assessment of it was unpromising: 'I am holding a part of the Hindenburg Line but it is a bad line. It projects into the German lines and is overlooked from behind from Marcoing ... I have grave doubts about it'.[55] Ricardo now had two battalions on the ridge, the 10th Royal Inniskilling Fusiliers on the left and the 9th Royal Inniskilling Fusiliers on the right; the 14th Royal Irish Rifles were in support and the 11th Royal Inniskilling Fusiliers in reserve. Welsh Ridge had formed part of the Hindenburg defences, the original German front line and its support trenches crossing it just a couple of hundred yards apart. These trench complexes ran broadly at right angles to the Ulster Division's front and much of the fighting took the form of bombing attacks along them.

The main thrust of 109 Brigade's attack on 6 December was on its right, the old German front line. The 9th Royal Inniskilling Fusiliers' assault at first went well, forcing the Germans back over the crest and down the Hindenburg Line. Their fortunes then changed, as Nugent described to Kitty:

> The 9th Inniskillings finally drove the Germans out but in their zeal they followed them too far and the Germans got in behind them and they had to fight their way back and had many casualties, all the Company Commanders were either killed or wounded and in the confusion the men came back and the Germans have again got into our trenches.

During this fighting 2nd Lieutenant Emerson of the Inniskillings earned a posthumous Victoria Cross.[56] The German counter-punch caused consternation at 109 Brigade headquarters, which led Nugent to intervene personally:

> I saw from the ridge behind the one where our trenches are that there was a fight going on and I saw a number of men running about, so I carried on to General Ricardo's Hdqrs in the Hindenburg Line and found considerable excitement. The men were on the parapet and he himself was rather excited and thought the Germans were coming on in strength. However I knew that was not likely as

54 *OH*, 1917, iii, pp 268–9; Falls, *Ulster Division*, p. 172.
55 ON to CN, 5 Dec. 1917, in *Nugent*, p. 192.
56 ON to CN, 6 Dec. 1917, in *Nugent*, p. 193; Falls, *Ulster Division*, pp 173–4.

we had plenty of men and machine guns ready for that. They were just bombing their way up the trench we were in and the obvious answer was to organise a bombing party back again. I had to be rather sharp and terse in my remarks so as to get things calm again and the necessary steps taken to stop them coming any further.[57]

The situation on the ridge was also causing alarm at III Corps, under whose command the division now was, and that afternoon Nugent received a message from Lieutenant-General Pulteney:

> The corps commander directs that every possible means be taken to prevent any further advance of the enemy from the trench they have reoccupied. Machine-gun enfilade fire will be brought to bear on it in order to make it untenable by the enemy. The trench leading from it into our trench will be blocked with wire.

Nugent quite liked Pulteney, describing him as 'a cheery good fellow' – not an opinion that was universally shared, one of Pulteney's staff later describing him as 'the most completely ignorant general I served under during the war and that is saying a lot' – but this kind of detailed tactical advice was not required.[58] Nugent had already arranged for the 11th Royal Inniskilling Fusiliers under Lieutenant-Colonel Knott to take over from the 9th: 'Tomorrow morning we attack them again with I hope a proper system which there does not seem to have been before and I hope we shall finally eject them and keep them out'.[59]

At 6am on 7 December Knott's men mounted a skilful attack, supported by Stokes mortars, which drove the Germans back 300 yards, and rather than pursuing too far they consolidated their new position quickly, driving off two strong German counter-attacks. The ridge had been secured and Nugent was pleased – 'It is a great relief to us all', he noted, 'including the Corps and the Army ... as long as we hold it, the Germans cannot overlook us behind and we can move in some security and above all we overlook his communications for miles and he cannot form up for attack unknown to us'. A feature of the fighting had been the activity of the German air force, including von Richthofen's circus, in attacking ground targets; Nugent described how he 'lay in bed and quavered' during one bombing attack.

---

[57] ON to CN, 6 Dec. 1917, in *Nugent*, pp 193–4.
[58] Leask, *Putty*, pp 670–71; ON to CN, 7 Dec. 1917, in *Nugent*, p. 195; J. M. Bourne, *Who's Who in World War One* (2001), p. 239.
[59] ON to CN, 6 Dec. 1917, in *Nugent*, pp 193–4.

Like other senior officers he blamed the RFC for lack of fight – '[t]he class of pilot we have got nowadays or at present anyhow is not good enough. He has not got the nerve or the courage' – which was undeserved. While the RFC struggled at times during the battle to provide the necessary support to the ground troops they worked hard and suffered heavy casualties to redress the balance. The growing importance of the air dimension to ground operations was becoming ever more apparent.[60]

Morale

The division stayed in the line for a further week, daily awaiting another German push, and on 10 December Nugent reluctantly made a change in command:

> I have had to send General Ricardo home to my very great regret but in this recent fighting I saw he had lost his nerve and looked so old. One can't afford to run risks in this war and I sent for him and told him he must go home for a long rest. He was quite glad really and owned to being perished. I am very sorry to lose him.[61]

Ricardo had been at the front continuously since October 1915 as either a battalion or a brigade commander and there was no hint of criticism in Nugent's decision, it being widely accepted that even the best officers reached a point when they had to be rested. There were other problems in 109 Brigade, however, that had to be addressed urgently. It had always been Nugent's most dependable brigade, in the thick of the action at Thiepval, Messines, Langemarck and Cambrai, but signs of stress were showing through. The day after Ricardo's relief, on 11 December, there was a worrying incident in the 14th Royal Irish Rifles when 118 men reported sick en masse, and as a result a planned relief in the trenches could not take place. The battalion war diary concluded that 'it has at last been realised that until the men have had a complete rest they cannot be considered an efficient fighting unit'.[62] The health of the entire division was now poor and Nugent had been pressing for it to be relieved, but he regarded what occurred in the 14th Rifles as evidence of serious morale problems, and for him it was the last straw.[63] That day he wrote to the Adjutant General at

---

60 Falls, *Ulster Division*, pp 174–5; ON to CN, 6, 7 and 10 Dec. 1917, in *Nugent*, pp 194–5; *OH*, 1917, iii, pp 133, 265, 287.

61 ON to CN, 10 Dec. 1917, in *Nugent*, p. 195.

62 Walker, *Chocolate Soldiers*, pp 189–90; 14th Rifles war diary (TNA, WO95/2511).

63 Falls, *Ulster Division*, p. 176.

GHQ, asking what could be done to bring the three Inniskilling battalions of 109 Brigade up to strength – describing them as 'first rate fighting formations' – but also recommending the disbandment of the 14th Rifles:

> While Cheape was in command they certainly improved, but since he left they have been tried and found wanting. It is significant that their present CO told me two days ago that most of the English draft sent to them a year ago have become casualties. The Brigadier says he cannot trust them and I know that he is right. They are poor stuff, either as workers or fighters, and have been a constant source of anxiety during the past three weeks.[64]

Overall the division's morale had held up well at Cambrai. After Third Ypres spirits had undoubtedly fallen, accompanied, as in other formations, by a loss of confidence in the British high command, particularly Gough. This did not extend to Nugent or the division's senior leadership, however, and nor had the negative experience of Langemarck resulted in an increase in disciplinary problems or absence levels in the division: Nugent's soldiers were tired by late 1917 but there was no suggestion that they had lost faith in winning the war.[65] Nugent's reference in his conversation with Crozier to units being 'sticky' did, though, have a point. It was generally recognised that the division had done well at Cambrai, despite the tactical awkwardness of operating on both sides of the Canal du Nord and the inadequate artillery and armoured support available to it, but its resilience was unquestionably growing weaker. During the first five days of the battle each brigade's second and subsequent attacks, affected by strengthening German resistance and exposure to the winter weather, were understandably decreasingly effective and pressed with less determination. The 14th Royal Irish Rifles were an extreme case, but by mid-December the entire division badly needed a rest. On the nights of 14/15 and 15/16 December it was relieved by the 63rd Division, during a blizzard, and by the time the troops reached their billets they were at a low ebb physically. Battle casualties since 20 November had totalled 1,545, including around 350 dead or missing, but hundreds more were sick.[66]

[64] ON to AG GHQ, 11 Dec. 1917, in *Nugent*, p. 196.

[65] Bowman, *Irish Regiments*, pp 155–61; Alexander Watson, *Enduring the Great War: Combat, Morale and Collapse in the German and British Armies 1914–18* (2008), pp 153–5; Tom Thorpe, 'Military group cohesion in Territorial Force infantry battalions during the Great War and its relationship to their morale and military task performance' (PhD, King's College London, 2017).

[66] *OH*, 1917, iii, p. 382; Falls, *Ulster Division*, p. 176.

Aftermath

After the battle the success of the German counter-stroke became a matter of controversy. A court of inquiry put much of the blame on the regimental officers and men and largely exonerated the leadership of Third Army, but many, including Nugent, did not agree:[67]

> The German attack on the 30th took us completely by surprise … Naturally the papers try and put a camouflage over the business, but it was a bad business and reflects no credit on anyone on our side [and] we have had one of the worst rebuffs we have had in the whole war. It is no use trying to conceal facts which must come out. We were not prepared for a counterattack just where it was most likely to come but the poor show the men put up was not entirely due to fewness of numbers. They were absolutely worn out from cold and exposure and hard fighting and want of sleep. Men are not machines and they should never have been asked to do what they failed to do at this season of the year.[68]

A week later he reflected further:

> The fact is we had failed in the first 48 hours. We effected a surprise the first day and we profited to that extent but we couldn't use it and the reason why we couldn't was partly that the German machine gunners were better men than ours and held out with splendid courage. It was they who saved the situation for the Germans … As to the German attack on the 30th, the less written about it the better too. It isn't a story to be proud of, notwithstanding the silly rubbish written by the war correspondents of feats performed by supermen against hundreds of thousands of Boches who existed solely in their imaginations. The Ulster Division did well but they aren't supermen either and they didn't do better than other people.[69]

Nugent was nevertheless pleased with the division's performance – 'We have certainly done our share in this adventure', he told Kitty.[70] People at home had followed its progress closely, the Ulster press carrying detailed reports throughout the battle: the *Belfast Newsletter* on 26 November, for

[67] *OH*, 1917, iii, pp 297–305.
[68] ON to CN, 5 Dec. 1917, in *Nugent*, pp 192–3.
[69] ON to CN, 13 Dec. 1917, in *Nugent*, p. 197. His comment about the German machine-gunners was a reference to reports that British machine-gunners had not done well on 30 Nov.
[70] ON to CN, 15 Dec. 1917, in *Nugent*, p. 198.

example, announced that messages from the front gave 'thrilling pictures of the gallantry displayed by the Ulster Division in action'.[71] The division was also mentioned favourably in Haig's official despatch, and Nugent was gratified.

New Year's Honours

He was far from gratified, however, when the 1918 New Year's honours list was published on 2 January. In it nine of the 12 commanders of the assault divisions at Messines, including Hickie, were knighted or had existing knighthoods 'upgraded' for their part in the victory (the other two, with less than 12 months experience in command at the time of the battle, would be knighted in 1919). Nugent's name was glaringly absent, and he was deeply hurt. A mortified Hamilton Gordon wrote to him that day:

> The omission of your name from the list received this morning has caused me real distress, from which I shall take long to recover. I can think of no explanation but I can at least tell you how sorry I am and offer my sympathy … I may say that I gave the fullest expression to my appreciation of the good work and valuable services of yourself and your Division while under my command … I deeply regret that my recommendation was not acted on.[72]

The recommendation had been supported by Plumer, now in Italy, but was not forwarded to London. Only Haig personally could have blocked it. Tim Harington, when he found out, called it 'a most damnable shame' and thought that Plumer, had he been in France, would have protested.[73] Haig's reasons for singling Nugent out are unclear. While they had not got on at Staff College their meetings in 1916–17 had been amicable, Haig indeed thanking him personally for the Ulster Division's performances on the Somme, at Messines and at Cambrai. It seems likely that Nugent's failure to cooperate with GHQ's plan over the title annoyed Haig. It may be too that he was aware of, and angered by, what General Hutton later described as Nugent's 'too candid opinion of cavalry generals as leaders of infantry' and of his outspoken criticism of Gough in particular (though Nugent was scarcely alone in that).[74] Whatever the reason, Nugent's removal from the list seems mean-spirited, not something, whatever his failings, one usually associates with Haig.

[71] *Belfast Newsletter*, 26 Nov. 1917.
[72] Hamilton Gordon to ON, 2 Jan. 1918, in *Nugent*, p. 200.
[73] Harington to ON, 2 June 1918, in *Nugent*, p. 234.
[74] Hutton to ON, 30 July 1921, in *Nugent*, p. 272.

The strain on Nugent himself was beginning to tell. In early February Spender met Hessey (who, at Nugent's request, had replaced Ricardo), who 'talks of Nugent being very much older, and feeling bitter that he was not made a K in the last honours'; Spender thought Hessey, too, had aged and he heard that Place was 'tired out', though on a month's leave which should help.[75] Nugent had no opportunity to rest, however.

Re-structuring the infantry

In early 1918 the BEF underwent a major reorganisation of its infantry, driven by manpower shortages in France, with the number of battalions in each British infantry division reducing from 12 to nine. The reorganisation was complete by early March by when 134 British battalions had disappeared through disbandment or amalgamation. The changes, noted the official history, were the occasion of 'much heart-burning and many protests', and the Ulster Division was no exception.[76] Six of its service battalions were disbanded and replaced by three regular units (the 1st and 2nd Royal Inniskilling Fusiliers and 1st Royal Irish Rifles). As before many regulars were unenthusiastic, the 1st Rifles, for example, much regretting their transfer to 'the political division, as we know it'.[77] There were protests from home as well, with Belfast Corporation lobbying hard for the retention of the 14th Royal Irish Rifles. Nugent, however, was clear which units he wished to retain (the 9th Royal Inniskilling Fusiliers, 9th Royal Irish Fusiliers, and 12th and 15th Royal Irish Rifles).[78] His public position was that the choices were based on seniority and regional representativeness, but in the case of the Belfast battalions he had to deploy somewhat contorted arguments to justify selecting the 15th Rifles, which had risen in his estimation since 1916, ahead of the rest.[79] The surplus manpower from the restructuring was organised into the 21st, 22nd and 23rd Entrenching Battalions, intended as temporary labour units but which within weeks would find themselves in the front line.

---

[75] Spender to his wife, 2 Feb. 1918, in *Nugent*, p. 267n.

[76] *OH*, 1918, i, pp 53–5. Dominion formations were not affected.

[77] Capt. G. Whitfeld diary, 2 Feb. 1918 (IWM).

[78] ON to James Johnston, Lord Mayor of Belfast, 28 Feb. 1918, in *Nugent*, pp 207–08.

[79] The 15th R. Irish Rifles had in fact been initially raised as the 7th R Irish Rifles, but when it was realised that a unit with the same number was being raised as part of the 16th Division it was re-numbered as the 15th.

The changes were symbolic as well as practical, marking a further dilution of the division's original identity. 'The north of Ireland won't be able to talk much of the 'Ulster' Division after the reorganisation', Nugent remarked to Kitty, '[t]here will only be 4 battalions of them left'. In fact, the regular battalions all had northern recruiting areas and so retained the Ulster link, while the composition of the division's infantry, even as late as March 1918, was still over 50% Irish. The 36th Division now had, however, a more diverse range of backgrounds than two years earlier, a chaplain estimating the number of Catholics in it from all parts of the British Isles by early 1918 at between 3,000 and 4,000.[80] The reorganisation also left Nugent with six supernumerary COs: a vacancy opened up in the 2nd Royal Inniskilling Fusiliers to which he appointed Farnham, despite the fact that Farnham was neither a regular nor, originally, an Inniskilling (though he had proved himself at Cambrai); three others went to the entrenching battalions and two to posts outside the division.[81]

Changes in command

Changes were taking place at senior levels also. At Haig's headquarters long-standing staff officers like Kiggell and Charteris had left during the winter as a result of political pressure, while in London in February Robertson was replaced as CIGS by Henry Wilson. Nugent, who knew both men well, commented, 'I hope it may be for the good of the State. The Government and the State will never have a more loyal and devoted servant than Willie Robertson. Henry is of course a far more quick witted man but he couldn't be more thorough'.[82] Henry Rawlinson replaced Wilson as the British representative on the Supreme War Council at Versailles. While Nugent thought Rawlinson 'as clever as they make 'em', he also regarded him as 'rather a superficial person' and wondered whether he or Wilson would dominate: 'What one hopes naturally is that neither of these eminent soldiers thought of personal advancement at all, but only of using their brains to the best advantage of beating the Boche. I wonder'.[83]

[80] ON to CN, 29 Jan. 1918 (PRONI, D3835/E/16/12); Perry, 'Nationality', pp 79, 87; James Taylor, *The 1st Royal Irish Rifles in the Great War* (2002), p. 123.
[81] Battalion COs in March 1918 were – 107 Bde: 1st R. Irish Rifles (McCarthy-O'Leary), 2nd R. Irish Rifles (Cox), 15th R. Irish Rifles (Cole-Hamilton); 108 Bde: 12th R. Irish Rifles (McCallum), 1st R. Irish Fusiliers (Furnell), 9th R. Irish Fusiliers (Kelly); 109 Bde: 1st R. Inniskilling Fusiliers (Crawford), 2nd R. Inniskilling Fusiliers (Farnham), 9th R. Inniskilling Fusiliers (Peacocke).
[82] ON to CN, 18 Feb. 1918, in *Nugent*, p. 204.
[83] ON to CN, 20 Feb. 1918, in *Nugent*, pp 205–06; Jeffery, *Wilson*, pp 217–19.

More directly concerning for him were changes at corps and divisional level. For some time the lack of promotion had been on Nugent's mind; in November 1917 he had commented that 'a lot of the Corps Commanders ought to be relieved. I expect many Divisional Commanders think the same. It is high time there was some promotion'.[84] He recognised that timing had been against him: 'I think if I had the opportunity of coming out in the first months of the war I should have got a Corps when so many new ones were formed but it was natural that Corps Commanders should have been selected from those who had borne the burden of the fighting at the beginning'.[85] He was right: of 24 divisional commanders who served in the BEF in 1914 and survived, 19 (79%) became corps commanders, most during the army's major expansion in 1915–16; by contrast, of 165 British and Dominion officers appointed to divisional command in France and Flanders between 1915 and 1918, including Nugent, only 20 (12%) were promoted.[86] By the time promotion to corps level opened up again in 1918, his age and Haig's hostility were against him.

It was also clear by mid-February that GHQ had adopted a policy of appointing younger divisional commanders – 'I am, I fear,' Nugent told Kitty, 'looked upon as rather old to command a Division in France at the present time'. The changes would be substantial. Of the BEF's 38 New Army and Territorial divisional commanders in post in January 1918, 18 had been moved by May, along with eight of 18 corps commanders. Not all were sacked: two divisional commanders (Harper and Shute) were promoted, another (Feetham) was killed and at least three others were wounded or taken ill during the fighting in March and April. But 15 of these generals had been transferred to non-operational posts by the beginning of June, with comparable changes at brigade level.[87] The BEF would fight its Hundred Days campaign in 1918 under considerably revamped senior leadership. When Haig and his new chief of staff, Herbert Lawrence, visited the Ulster Division on 8 March Nugent sought reassurance, but while Haig was complimentary about the division's work Nugent got little comfort from Lawrence, who stressed the need for younger men to be promoted and older officers to make way. Nugent was very disappointed: 'I feel I am to be one of them. It is a very bitter draught to have to swallow and if I am kicked out it will not be treating me with fairness nor with any recognition of the work I have done. Well, there is no

---

84 ON to CN, 3 Nov. 1917, in *Nugent*, p. 269n.
85 ON to CN, 29 Dec. 1917, in *Nugent*, p. 199.
86 Robbins, *British Generalship*, pp 53–4.
87 Command changes calculated from Becke, *Order of Battle*.

redress and one must only bear it'.[88] On 20 March, just hours before the German offensive began, he noted that 'I have heard no more at present of my being one of the Div Comdrs to go home. 4 have already gone I know and several of the old Corps Comdrs. If I don't go this time I am bound to go with the next batch'.[89]

Events would, however, keep Nugent in his command for a while longer. A storm was about to descend on the BEF that would push the Ulster Division to the brink of destruction, bring the British close to defeat and propel Nugent into his greatest test, and perhaps finest hour, of the war.

---

[88] ON to CN, 8 Mar. 1918, in *Nugent*, p. 208.

[89] ON to CN, 20 Mar. 1918, in *Nugent*, p. 210. The four divisional commanders were Lukin (9th), Hickie (16th), Wanless O'Gowan (31st) and Wilkinson (50th). O'Gowan was replaced on the morning of 21 March, after the German offensive had begun. The changes at corps level may also have reflected dissatisfaction with the performance at Cambrai, since three commanders there – Woollcombe, Pulteney and Snow – had gone by March 1918.

9

Kaiserschlacht

The German spring offensive
and the crisis in command, March–May 1918

Introduction

Looming over the opening weeks of 1918 was the shadow of the massive offensive that Nugent, like most senior British officers on the western front, knew was coming as the Germans attempted to win the war before American strength became overwhelming. When it did, on Thursday 21 March, it was on a scale beyond anything the British army had experienced before. For Nugent it was a hugely demanding period as his division was battered almost to pieces and his ability to command at times stretched to breaking point. How he sought to lead his division illustrates some of the strengths and limitations of British operational command in this final year of the war. The effects were felt well beyond the battlefield. The offensive precipitated the conscription crisis in Ireland that further radicalised nationalist opinion and effectively ended any possibility of a political accommodation based on Home Rule within the United Kingdom; in one scholar's memorable description, 'the ramifications of a British military retreat from the Somme and the Lys in 1918 made inevitable a political retreat from the Liffey and the Lee in 1921'.[1]

New defence system

In mid-January the Ulster Division, now in XVIII Corps and part once more of the Fifth Army, took over a sector south-east of St Quentin previously held by the French. While Nugent and his staff found their French counterparts welcoming, the state of the defences was less satisfactory. The front-line trenches were in reasonable condition though in need of repair, but the position lacked depth. This was an especial problem given the defensive system, modelled on German methods, the British had introduced in December 1917.

---

[1] Jeffery, *Wilson*, p. 223.

The new doctrine required both defences sited in depth, to absorb the momentum of any attack, and sufficient counter-attack forces to drive the enemy back. Physically this involved the creation of three defensive zones – a Forward Zone, to disorganise and disrupt the attack, comprising company strongpoints with a number of larger redoubts behind them, rather than a continuously-held front line; a Battle Zone, one to two miles further back and similarly structured, where the main defensive battle would be fought; and a Rear Zone, holding units earmarked to counter-attack any enemy who reached the Battle Zone. Time was too short for the changes to be fully assimilated by the BEF before the German offensive was unleashed, and when it came the problems for the over-stretched Fifth Army were not only its excessive frontage, weak defences (along much of the front the Battle Zone was incomplete and the Rear Zone scarcely begun) and shortage of reserves, but also the fact that many officers and men had yet to adjust psychologically to the new defensive method.

Nugent as ever set to work vigorously, briefing his senior subordinates and visiting the brigades to address assemblies of officers and NCOs on the new concept, while he and his staff participated fully in a conference Lieutenant-General Sir Ivor Maxse, his corps commander, held for divisional, brigade and battalion commanders in February.[2] Nugent had, however, serious reservations about the system's workability. The Ulster Division's sector presented particular challenges. Its front straddled the Somme valley and was both very wide – some 6,000 yards – and divided by the Somme, and the St Quentin canal parallel to it, which separated the western part of the Battle Zone from the rest. When these two waterways reached St Simon, four miles behind the Battle Zone, they diverged at right angles, the Somme making a sharp turn to the west towards Ham, while the canal turned east, forming a major water obstacle immediately to the division's rear.[3] In addition, the boundary between the Ulster Division and the 14th Division on its right was also that between XVIII and III Corps, and it soon became clear that the two formations had different defensive plans, III Corps intending to hold its Forward Zone strongly while XVIII Corps planned to defend in greater depth. Nugent was concerned that if the Germans penetrated the 14th Division's Forward Zone and reached the tactically-vital high ground near Essigny, overlooking his right flank, his

[2] Notes for brigade conference, 1 Feb. 1918, and ON to CN, 15 Feb. 1918 (PRONI, D3835/E/7/11/12 and E/16/18); Maxse papers (IWM, 69/53/12).

[3] For the sake of clarity, in this account the canal/river line running south-west from St Quentin to St Simon is referred to as the St Quentin canal, the canal flowing east from St Simon as the Crozat canal, and the canalised Somme river flowing west from St Simon as the Somme.

own Battle Zone could become untenable: it would, he told Maxse (whom he admired), 'be waste of effort on our part to construct a line of redoubts which will be turned as soon as the front of the Division on our right is broken'. Maxse disagreed, insisting that a breakthrough against the 14th Division would provide 'no sufficient reason for the XVIII Corps to give way; quite on the contrary … I intend that you and all the Corps shall hold the passive defence line of redoubts, even if one or two of them are captured by the enemy'. The two corps' defences had still not been fully aligned when the German offensive opened, and on 21 March Nugent's forebodings proved well-founded.[4]

Final hours

On 20 March came confirmation that the German offensive was imminent, Nugent telling Kitty:

> Two Alsatian deserters came in last night and from their statements which are confirmed from other sources there seems no doubt that the day is very near. We expect to be attacked tonight or tomorrow and it is going to be a very big attack and will last for weeks. It is very grim sitting still and waiting … Bless you all my dearest. I wonder if I shall be able to write you tomorrow.[5]

That night a raid by the 61st Division, a few miles to the north, took prisoners who confirmed the attack would begin early the following morning.[6] Nugent at once alerted his brigadiers: Captain Rogers, with 108 Brigade, was 'playing bridge in the Mess, which was in a sort of dug-out on the side of a small hill, when the General [Griffith] was called to the telephone. He came back and said the Divisional Commander had informed him that from information received the attack was to be expected at about four o'clock the following morning'.[7] Rogers was sent forward to warn the battalion COs in person. The same cascade of information happened in the other brigades also. Captain Miller, commanding a company in the 2nd Royal Inniskilling Fusiliers' Forward Zone, received around midnight

> a chit from Farnham to the effect that it was a certainty that the attack would come on the 21st or 22nd, that there was to be no

[4] Maxse to ON, 10 Feb. 1918 (IWM, Maxse papers, 69/53/12); Tim Travers, *How The War Was Won: Command and Technology in the British Army on the Western Front 1917–18* (1992), p. 64; Simpson, *Directing Operations*, p. 140.

[5] ON to CN, 20 Mar. 1918, in *Nugent*, p. 210.

[6] Falls, *Ulster Division*, p. 92.

[7] Maj. V. B. Rogers, *An Autobiography* (1965), pp 36–7.

question of retreat … He wished me good luck, and I returned his wishes because I liked Farnham very much, and it seemed to me that this was likely to be the end of our acquaintance.[8]

Much has been made of deficiencies in British morale, doctrine and command resilience to explain the initial German success in March 1918. While these may have contributed, in the Fifth Army's sector, especially south of the Somme, the sheer power of the German offensive was explanation enough. On the opening day the Germans deployed 74 divisions against the 26 of the British Third and Fifth Armies, while their 6,608 guns fired over three million shells into the British defences in a matter of hours: 'It is doubtful', one historian has pointed out, 'whether any troops in the world could have stood their ground under that weight of fire and against that weight of numbers on an imperfectly fortified front, supported by an inadequate infrastructure'.[9] On 21 March Maxse's corps had three divisions in the line, including the Ulster Division, with another in reserve, against fourteen of von Hutier's *18th Army* (eight in the initial assault and six more in close support); Nugent's formation, sitting on an important German thrust line, would be engaged over the next eight days by nine different German divisions, forced to retreat over 30 miles, lose more than 6,000 men and only narrowly escape annihilation. For Nugent and his soldiers, the March fighting was continuous as well as chaotic, with one day blurring into the next. In retrospect, however, the battle can be divided into three phases: the fight for the division's main defensive position (21–22 March); the struggle for the Somme crossings (23–25 March); and the fighting on the Avre (26–28 March).[10]

The fight for the main defensive position (21–22 March)

The German opening bombardment, comprising both high explosive and gas, began at 4.40am on 21 March, and even at Nugent's headquarters at Ollezy, six miles behind the Battle Zone, the impact was awesome:

> The long expected has come at last. The German bombardment began at ¼ to 5 this morning and is still going on. In all my

[8] Capt. C. C. Miller memoir (IWM).
[9] Harris, *Douglas Haig*, pp 447–8; see also Simpson, *Directing Operations*, pp 131–54.
[10] The most comprehensive account of the Ulster Division in the March 1918 fighting is Michael James Nugent, *A Long Week in March: The 36th (Ulster) Division in the German Spring Offensive, March 1918* (2019). See also Falls, *Ulster Division*, pp 181–231; Orr and Truesdale, *'Ulster Will Fight'*, pp 364–85; Nicholas Perry, 'General Nugent and the Ulster Division in the March 1918 retreat', *Imperial War Museum Review*, 12 (1999), pp 4–17.

experience out here I have never known anything more terrific. It isn't a series of reports, but it is just one long roar … I cannot hope after this terrible bombardment that many of the front line troops can be left alive or at least unwounded.[11]

The effect of the shelling was compounded by the thick fog which had descended overnight, obscuring the defenders' pre-planned fields of fire and preventing effective artillery support, and for Nugent the implications were immediately apparent:

> It seems as if there were some strange devil who watches over the Germans. This morning dawned with so thick a fog that we can't see 200 yards. It is the first real fog there has been for months and it is disastrous that it should have come today. We are the people who suffer from it. This time it is the Germans who are attacking. They know where they want to go and we don't so it is all against us.

Almost immediately communications with the Forward Zone began to disintegrate. Within minutes contact with the 12th and 15th Royal Irish Rifles, the right and centre battalions, was lost; at 7.30am the last remaining line to the 2nd Royal Inniskilling Fusiliers was destroyed; and by 7.45am only one forward artillery battery and a single observation post were still in contact.[12] For news from his forward positions Nugent had to rely on either despatch riders and runners or officers sent forward to find out what was going on. Many messages never arrived and those that did were often hopelessly out of date. Movement in the rear area was also hampered by French refugees, and in Ollezy six military lorries had to be diverted to move civilians to the rear to keep routes clear.[13] At 8.15am Nugent still did not know whether the German assault had begun: 'All we can hear are the shells, we can see nothing and all the lines to the front are already cut and we have to depend on runners and byke [sic] orderlies, a very slow process when as in this case the Germans are shelling all the roads'. To his operational concerns was added personal anxiety for Farnham: 'I am so anxious about Arthur. I feel the responsibility of having given him a battalion, though if I hadn't someone else would have in some

---

[11] ON to CN, 21 Mar. 1918, in *Nugent*, pp 210–11.

[12] 36 Div. Account of Operations, 21–28 Mar., 36 Div. Signals war diary, 36 Div. artillery narrative, 109 Bde narrative, Mar. 1918 (TNA, WO95/2492, 2494, 2498 and 2509).

[13] Perceval-Maxwell to his wife, 2 Apr. 1918 ['Narrative'] (PRONI, D/1556/27/1/12). Perceval-Maxwell was attached to divisional HQ during the March fighting.

other Division. Well, dearest, we can only endure and fight on and try to live up to the watchword of the French at Verdun "Ils ne passeront pas".'

The main German infantry attack began at 9.40am, though almost certainly detachments were pushed forward earlier. During the day the Ulster Division was attacked by four German divisions. In the first wave were the *238th Division*, recruited in Hamburg and Hanover, attacking the 2nd Royal Inniskilling Fusiliers on the left; the *36th Division* from Prussia, coincidentally engaged against its numeric opposite number, assaulting the 15th Royal Irish Rifles and part of the 12th; and the *1st Bavarian Division*, from Munich, attacking the 12th Royal Irish Rifles and the left-hand battalion of the 14th Division. The *45th Reserve Division* reinforced them during the afternoon.[14] In addition a special assault group, built around one of the *36th Division's* reserve battalions but reinforced by a strong detachment of specially trained storm-troops and four A7V tanks, had been inserted between the *36th* and *1st Bavarians.*[15]

The Germans attacked the entire front of Nugent's Forward Zone but concentrated particularly on its flanks, moving along the Somme valley to the north and a re-entrant known as the Grugies valley from the south. Within two-and-a-half hours the Forward Zone had been largely overrun. In line with the new doctrine no attempt was made to defend the front trench, the forward companies instead manning their defensive posts, and the Germans swarmed between them concealed by the fog. On the right, the 12th Royal Irish Rifles' headquarters redoubt, Jeanne D'Arc, was lost early on: the acting CO, Major Hall, was captured in his dugout while scribbling a message to his reserve company and believed the Germans attacked the redoubt while their own barrage was still on it. One company did, however, hold out in a quarry until early afternoon before, surrounded and under attack by German tanks, it surrendered.[16] In the centre, Cole-Hamilton's 15th Royal Irish Rifles fought tenaciously for much of the day to hold Racecourse Redoubt, 2nd Lieutenant de Wind winning a posthumous Victoria Cross for repeated acts of courage, but by late afternoon Cole-Hamilton realised that his plan of hanging on until nightfall and then trying to escape was no longer feasible. Having consulted his senior officers, who 'agreed we could not hold the redoubt should the enemy assault again', he ordered all papers to be destroyed and then surrendered.[17] On the left the 2nd Royal Inniskilling Fusiliers lost their

---

[14] *OH*, 1918, i, pp 175–6n.

[15] Nicholas Perry, 'Journey's End: the fight for the Ulster Division's Forward Zone, 21st March 1918', *Irish Sword*, 95 (Summer 2004), p. 71.

[16] Maj. A. C. Hall (TNA, WO339/106543).

[17] Lt.-Col. C. Cole-Hamilton (TNA, WO339/8682).

forward positions quickly, though the front right company put up a sturdy resistance. Summoned to surrender in Boadicea Redoubt in the afternoon, Farnham faced the agonising choice of continuing a hopeless resistance or saving his men's lives by capitulating. He eventually decided, as the Germans 'brought up their minnies and field guns right up to us', to give up, telling Nugent after the war: 'Then I did what I believe I was right to do, but I have never got over it and don't think I ever will. I had a conference of officers and decided that any further effort to hold out was only useless waste of life, and that we would have to give in'.[18]

Farnham's decision has been cited in several works as an example of British defenders' low morale and lack of fight.[19] The impression of premature capitulation comes from accounts which suggest that Farnham was called on to surrender early in the afternoon and did so soon after, eleven officers and 241 men laying down their weapons; but in fact the German summons did not come until after 5pm and Boadicea Redoubt held out until nearly 6pm, about the time that Racecourse fell and long after the main German advance had rolled past.[20] Indeed, the contrasting experiences of these two British garrisons says as much about the behaviour of the attackers as the defenders – while the German *36th Division* chose to storm Racecourse, the *238th Division*, once their probing attacks had been repulsed, were prepared to stand off and offer the garrison of Boadicea the option of a negotiated surrender.[21]

Meanwhile, as the fog began lifting around midday, German units began probing the forward edge of the Battle Zone and by the time the mist had disappeared an hour later it had, as Nugent put it, 'done its foul work by hiding the Boches until they were close up to our main battle line'.[22] He snatched a few moments to complete his letter home and break some bad news:

> The latest is that the Germans have got all our forward lines along the whole front of attack as far as I can make out. From our 2nd position we can see the Germans on the ridge in front, where our front line was. There is no doubt it is all captured and Kitty dearest,

---

[18] Farnham to ON, 18 Mar. 1919 (PRONI, D3835/E/2/20).

[19] See, for example, Randal Gray, *Kaiserschlacht* (1991), p. 43; Samuels, *Command or Control*, p. 262; Richard Holmes, *The Western Front* (1999), p. 198.

[20] Samuels, for example, gives the time of the summons as 1.15pm, with Farnham surrendering shortly afterwards (*Command or Control*, p. 262), but Michael Nugent has demonstrated that it did not come until around 5.15pm (*A Long Week in March*, pp 143–6).

[21] Perry, 'Journey's End', pp 75–9.

[22] ON to CN, 22/24 Mar. 1918, in *Nugent*, p. 212.

Arthur was in front. He must be either dead or a prisoner. Poor
Arthur and poor Aileen [Lady Farnham]. It is terrible. I am afraid
there is no hope that he got away. He would not have left his men
and all his line has gone. We know that. Things have gone badly for
us. I am heartbroken about Arthur. Don't breathe a word yet to
anyone. Goodbye dearest. It is a very anxious time.[23]

The attack developed quickly. At 12.15pm reports reached him from the
right that the Germans had broken through the 14th Division's Forward
Zone and captured the high ground near Essigny. This, as the official
history put it, was 'a disaster of the first magnitude for the XVIII Corps to
the north'.[24] By 1.15pm the 1st Royal Irish Fusiliers, in 108 Brigade's Battle
Zone, were under assault from front and flank and Nugent ordered Griffith
to use his reserve battalion, the 9th Royal Irish Fusiliers, to shore up the
division's right flank. Soon afterwards, as the extent of the disaster suffered
by the 14th Division became clear, he had to deploy a second battalion, the
9th Royal Inniskilling Fusiliers from 109 Brigade, to extend his right
southwards. In the meantime the enemy had also gained a foothold in the
centre of his Battle Zone, at Contescourt: a platoon earmarked for its
defence had been destroyed by shell fire moving up and a counter-attack by
the 1st Royal Irish Rifles' reserve company was unsuccessful. Nugent, who
now had left only one reserve battalion, the 2nd Royal Irish Rifles, had to
use most of it, a company at a time, to contain the lodgement at
Contescourt.[25] The intention of using the Rear Zone battalions to mount
coordinated counter-attacks had been blown away by the weight of the
German attack. During the next few hours, however, no more ground was
lost and with the fog gone several German attacks were broken up by
artillery and machine-guns, the British defences at last able to operate as
originally intended. At 6.30pm Nugent made a further effort to recapture
Contescourt, using the remaining company of the 2nd Rifles, but the
attack was repulsed. Parties of Germans followed up their success
energetically, pushing into the division's rear, but fortunately the
continuing resistance of the defenders south of Contescourt prevented this
potentially dangerous thrust from being exploited.[26]

[23] ON to CN, 21 Mar. 1918, in *Nugent*, p. 211.

[24] *OH*, 1918, i, p. 184.

[25] 108 Bde narrative, 36 Div. Account, 36 Div. artillery narrative (TNA,
WO95/2504,2492 and 2494); Cyril Falls, *History of the First Seven Battalions of
the Royal Irish Rifles in the Great War* (1925), p. 139.

[26] 107 Bde narrative (TNA, WO95/2509); Falls, *Irish Rifles*, p. 140; Middlebrook,
Kaiser's Battle, p. 304.

At nightfall on 21 March, therefore, Nugent's Battle Zone was still holding but his right flank was precarious and the division had been severely damaged. Three of its nine infantry battalions had been destroyed (the 2nd Royal Inniskilling Fusiliers and 12th and 15th Royal Irish Rifles) and two had suffered significant losses (the 1st Royal Irish Rifles and 1st Royal Irish Fusiliers); four batteries of field guns had been captured, overrun in the fog behind the Forward Zone, along with two batteries of trench mortars; and 38 of the division's 64 heavy machine guns had been lost.[27] The commitment of a third of the division's infantry to the Forward Zone, where they could be neither supported nor withdrawn – defence in detail rather than in depth, as Falls put it – had here as elsewhere proved disastrous.[28] These losses were partly offset that night by the attachment from corps reserve of 61 Brigade and two artillery batteries of the 20th Division: at corps level too, reserves were being used to plug gaps rather than wrest the initiative from the Germans. Nugent sent a car to bring Brigadier-General Cochrane, 61 Brigade's commander, to his headquarters for a briefing, but even with these reinforcements he could scarcely look forward to the morning with confidence.

Gough, the Fifth Army commander, had however concluded that III Corps could no longer maintain its position and should fall back overnight across the Crozat canal to its rear. This in turn required the Ulster Division to swing back in conformity, pivoting on the 1st Royal Inniskilling Fusiliers still holding the Battle Zone west of the St Quentin canal and lining the canal at right-angles to its original position, facing east. Orders to this effect were received from XVIII Corps shortly before 8pm, and Nugent's headquarters had begun issuing telephone orders to the brigades by 8.20pm.[29] The withdrawal went well, the artillery pulling back first, followed at 10.30pm by the infantry: the darkness, a thickening mist and the fatigue of the attackers enabled the forward troops to get clear. This was a testing time for Nugent – 'It was a most anxious night. There is nothing so difficult as to withdraw troops in close contact with the enemy without letting the enemy know. It was 4am before I could lie down'.[30] The engineers in the meantime worked frantically to demolish 34 bridges across the canal, often delaying to the last minute to enable the rearguards to cross. One bridge was blown with the Germans already on it; at another the time fuse failed, and as the enemy attempted to rush across the sapper officer,

---

[27] 36 Bn MGC War Diary (TNA, WO95/2498).

[28] Falls, *Ulster Division*, p. 230.

[29] Falls, *Ulster Division*, pp 202; 107 Bde narrative. Some contingency planning for this possibility had been done.

[30] ON to CN, 22/24 Mar. 1918, in *Nugent*, pp 212–13.

2nd Lieutenant Knox, ran forward under fire and lit the instantaneous fuse, successfully destroying the bridge and surviving to win the Victoria Cross.[31] During the night Nugent relocated his headquarters across the Somme to the hamlet of Estouilles, just north of Ham, to be behind the centre of the division's new z-shaped position, which now had the 1st Inniskillings in the Battle Zone looking north; the rest of 109 Brigade along with 107 and 108 Brigades lining the St Quentin canal facing east; and 61 Brigade deployed at St Simon and along the Crozat canal, again looking north.

22 March

As dawn broke in dense mist once more on Friday, 22 March, Nugent was cheered by a piece of good news:

> I have heard about Arthur. A German officer sent a pigeon message by one of our pigeons captured in the redoubt Arthur's battalion or part of it was holding. He wrote 'Have captured the redoubt and have got the battalion commander as prisoner'. That would not have been much help as there were 3 redoubts and there were 3 battalion commanders in front, but I sent to our pigeon loft to ask the pigeoneer if he remembered which battalion the pigeon was sent to and he was able to say it went to Arthur's battalion. There is therefore no reason to doubt that Arthur is safe though a prisoner and if he had been wounded I expect the German would have mentioned it.[32]

The Germans soon resumed their attack, this time on the 1st Royal Inniskilling Fusiliers, still in the Battle Zone, who by mid-morning were almost surrounded in Ricardo Redoubt. At around midday, Nugent received orders to retreat again.

Maxse's decision on 22 March to withdraw XVIII Corps south of the Somme later became a matter of considerable controversy, Edmonds, the official historian, accusing him of an 'over-hasty withdrawal' and of ignoring Gough's intention to fight north of the river, on the forward edge of the Rear Zone (the so-called Green line), for as long as possible. Edmonds believed that Maxse took his decision well before it was operationally necessary and in so doing opened a gap with XIX Corps to the north which the Germans exploited. Maxse refuted this angrily, replying that he was 'shocked to see that the official historian has selected me for the role of a "scapegoat" in one of the greatest battles of the war'; he

---

[31] Report on demolition of bridges in XVIII Corps area (TNA, WO95/953); Falls, *Ulster Division*, p. 203.
[32] ON to CN, 22/24 Mar. 1918, in *Nugent*, p. 212.

maintained his withdrawal had been both unavoidable and well-managed.[33] Since no written copy of Maxse's orders that day survived, Nugent's interpretation of his orders helps throw light on Maxse's intentions.

According to the Ulster Division's after-action report, at 12.30pm Nugent informed his brigades that 'in consequence of pressure from the flanks, and in accordance with the decision of the Higher Command to hold the line of the Somme and the Canal de St Quentin, a further withdrawal was necessary'. At this point, however, there was no definitive order to fall back across the Somme: 107 Brigade was instructed to remain on the Green line, while 108 and 109 Brigades, though ordered back to Pithon, a village on the Somme, were not to cross the river. 109 Brigade, down to a single battalion (the 9th Royal Inniskilling Fusiliers), was further ordered to halt on the Green Line if it was found not to be strongly held by Maxse's remaining reserve, the rest of the 20th Division. At this point, therefore, the option of fighting north of the river was still open. Within an hour, however, the orders had changed. At 1.30pm Place, Nugent's GSO1, rang round the brigades again to say that the intention was now to fall back over the Somme. Edmonds was therefore correct in thinking Maxse made his decision early. The ensuing retreat was not, though, precipitate. 109 Brigade had stopped on the Green line, a decision taken by its brigade-major, Captain George Bruce, who when supervising the withdrawal judged the line to be too weakly held, an example of a relatively junior British officer exercising initiative. Nugent confirmed Bruce's decision when he met his three brigadiers (but not Cochrane) at Pithon at 2pm, and the retreat did not resume until 3.30pm when he ordered the division back across the Somme.[34]

There was no possibility of extricating the surrounded 1st Royal Inniskilling Fusiliers in the Battle Zone, but by holding out until late afternoon they assisted the rest of the division to get clear. Nugent recorded that evening:

> The 1st Battalion Inniskilling Fusiliers are the heroes of this Division. They are one of the regular battalions. Their duty was to hold a redoubt in the main line and they held it to the end. No man came back from it. They beat back 12 different attacks made we believe by the 1st Guard Division of the Prussians and at the last

---

[33] *OH*, 1918, i, pp 301–02; Maxse to Edmonds, 7 Oct. 1934 (TNA, CAB45/193). See also Tim Travers, *The Killing Ground* (1987), pp 232–3; Andrew Green, *Writing the Great War* (2003), pp 159, 165; Anthony Farrar-Hockley, *Goughie: The Life of General Sir Hubert Gough* (1975), pp 284–8.

[34] *OH*, 1918, ii, pp 275–6; Falls, *Ulster Division*, p. 204; Perceval-Maxwell, 'Narrative' (PRONI, D/1556/27/1/12, 2/4/18).

those who were watching from other places said the Germans just poured over in a wave, but none of the Inniskillings came away. They were ordered to hold their line and they held it to the end ... It is a great and gallant story.[35]

The German division was in fact the *5th Guards Division*; over 500 men of the Inniskillings were lost, about eighty being killed and the rest captured. By 11pm the Ulster Division was over the Somme, Nugent crossing just before the final brigade; it proved 'a rather exciting move too as the Germans were shelling a bridge we had to cross with a big gun. We had to get as close as we could to it, wait behind a house till the shell came and then gallop to get a safe distance before the next arrived'.[36] He later described how he sought to exercise control during this phase of the withdrawal:

> As a rule when I realised we should have to retreat soon, I sent everything and everybody of the Headquarters back several miles so as to get them out of the way and I stayed on with just 2 or 3 staff officers, a couple of cars, a lunch basket and kettle and remained until I had given every order that appeared possible to give and until we had actually begun to move back.[37]

At this stage, according to Perceval-Maxwell, divisional headquarters was 'in fairly good touch with what each Brigade was doing and also with what was happening on our immediate flanks'.[38] That was about to change.

The fight for the Somme crossings (23–25 March)

By the early hours of Saturday, 23 March, the division was lining the Somme and the Crozat canal along a five-mile front from Sommette-Eaucourt, just east of Ham, to a mile and a half north-west of Jussy. 108 Brigade (comprising, from left to right, the 21st Entrenching Battalion, attached from corps reserve; a composite 36th Division battalion composed of various details; and the 1st and 9th Royal Irish Fusiliers) held the left sector, 61 Brigade (7th DCLI on the left; 7th Somerset Light Infantry on the right; and 12th King's Regiment in support) held the right. The remnants of Nugent's other two brigades were just behind them, 109

35 ON to CN, 22/24 Mar. 1918, in *Nugent*, p.213. See Sir Frank Fox, *The Royal Inniskilling Fusiliers in the Great War* (1928), pp 138–9; Nugent, *A Long Week in March*, pp 155–7.
36 ON to CN, 22/24 Mar. 1918, in *Nugent*, p. 213.
37 ON to CN, 7 Apr. 1918, in *Nugent*, p. 224.
38 Perceval-Maxwell, 'Narrative' (PRONI, D/1556/27/1/12, 2/4/18).

Brigade (the 9th Royal Inniskilling Fusiliers and a few attachments) at Brouchy on the left, and 107 Brigade (the 1st and 2nd Royal Irish Rifles, the former very weak) at Cugny on the right. Divisional headquarters was in the village of Freniches, five miles south of the river.[39]

Nugent had so far commanded the division very effectively, conducting a second difficult withdrawal across a water obstacle within 24 hours. On 23 March, however, things started to unravel. The division had lost contact overnight with the formations on both flanks, the 30th Division on the left and the 14th on the right: under the pressure of the retreat, and because the line it was retiring to was longer than its original front, the Fifth Army was beginning to come apart literally at the seams. Every division during the March retreat blamed its neighbours for giving way, but often the Germans simply moved into the space created by over-stretched divisions contracting inwards.[40]

The Ulster Division was still settling into its new positions when, just before dawn, three German divisions, concealed for the third day running by thick fog, attacked across the Crozat canal against the 14th Division on its right, and 61 Brigade soon became caught up in this fighting. By late morning the outnumbered 14th had been forced back two miles, and Nugent just had time to form a defensive line with 107 Brigade before the German *10th Division* swung inwards; its attack was halted, with the help of some dismounted French cavalry, only after heavy fighting. Meanwhile, on Nugent's left, the German *23rd Division* had at first light forced the crossings at Ham, in the 30th Division's sector, and shortly afterwards attacked the 21st Entrenching Battalion in the flank, forcing it away from the river. This in turn enabled the *5th Guards Division* to cross the railway bridge at Pithon, which French engineers had been unable to destroy, and its two leading battalions captured the village of Aubigny before being forced out again in a dramatic counter-attack by the 9th Royal Inniskilling Fusiliers, led on horse-back by George Bruce. For the next few hours the situation remained stable.[41] At midday Nugent began another letter:

> Early this morning we got news that a Division on our right [sic – left] had given way and let the Boches across a river and marshes into Ham, a most serious disaster. We were holding the line of the river next to Ham and we are still holding it but it is a very

---

[39] Falls, *Ulster Division*, pp 204–06.
[40] Simpson, *Directing Operations*, p. 144.
[41] *OH*, 1918, i, pp 331–3, 339; Capt. V. E. Inglefield, *The History of the Twentieth (Light) Division* (1921), p. 240; Falls, *Ulster Division*, pp 210–11; 107 Bde narrative (TNA, WO95/2502).

precarious hold and the Germans have made a big dent in the line and may break in on us at any moment. It is very critical as we are certain the Germans will pour in reinforcements which may enable them to turn the whole of the river line. The French are coming up in support and some have already arrived but it will be touch and go … It has been far the worst battle of the war as far as we are concerned, but if in the end we beat the Germans, it will be worth it.'[42]

Throughout the morning Nugent maintained tactical control, issuing a stream of orders to the brigades, and by early afternoon the situation seemed to have improved, Nugent noting that '[t]he net result of today's operations is that we are holding our own'. This relative stability did not last long, however. At 3pm, on the right, elements of the German *10th* and *1st Bavarian Divisions* drove into Nugent's flank; 61 Brigade, in danger of being surrounded, fell back and lost most of the 7th Somerset Light Infantry in the process, while 108 Brigade had to retire in conformity and suffered heavily. At 4.30pm, on the left, the *5th Guards Division* also surged forward, capturing two key villages in the division's defensive perimeter, Aubigny (again) and Brouchy, while beside them other German forces advanced into the gap that had opened between the 36th and 30th Divisions. In the space of a couple of hours the Ulster Division's situation had deteriorated dramatically, its front, in the words of the official history, now representing 'a long narrow salient with a blunt top'. Matters were made worse when, at around 6pm, the Germans launched a further outflanking attack against 107 Brigade on the right. The outnumbered 1st and 2nd Royal Irish Rifles held up their advance for over four hours but at 10pm, the darkness illuminated by burning houses, two Prussian grenadier regiments at last captured the important village of Cugny.[43]

By the evening of 23 March, therefore, the division's plight was critical, with convergent attacks beating against its flanks: twice, fleeing soldiers from 109 and 61 Brigades had to be rallied by artillery officers through whose gun-lines they were retreating.[44] In the midst of this crisis, however, Nugent's communications broke down. He had remained at his headquarters at Freniches, dependant on unreliable telephone links, despatch riders and members of his staff to keep him informed. This last method was becoming increasingly risky: Falls described how the division's GSO2, Major Hodgson, 'was riding across a field when he was set upon

[42] ON to CN, 22/24 Mar. 1918, in *Nugent*, p. 214.
[43] *OH*, 1918, i, pp 342–3; Falls, *Ulster Division*, p. 211; idem, *Irish Rifles*, pp 141–2; Nugent, *A Long Week in March*, pp 168–73.
[44] 36 Div. artillery narrative (TNA, WO95/2494).

and harried like a hare by low-flying German aircraft … an intelligent and hard-working man was reduced to something like an automaton'.[45] Events were moving so fast that between 4pm and 7pm Nugent had little sense of how badly the battle was going. Indeed, he now took two decisions that suggested not only a commander out of touch but also, perhaps, one losing his nerve. He ordered his headquarters to retreat again, to the village of Beaulieu-sur-Fontaines, five miles to the rear, yet at almost the same time, shortly after 6pm, he informed his brigades that the situation had 'improved' and told them to hold their positions and, if possible, regain any ground lost.[46] This order issued at a time when all four of his brigades were either under attack or already in retreat, and the official history noted simply that '[f]ar from withdrawing the Ulster Division from the awkward salient which its front now formed, Major General Nugent ordered the 61st Brigade to hold on to the head of it at all costs'.[47] This picture of an out-of-touch headquarters, in over-hasty retreat and issuing unrealistic orders, fits well with the general critique of the British higher command during the March retreat.

Nugent's actions look rather different, however, when considered in the context of the arrival of the French.[48] Petain was now rushing troops forward to help the stricken Fifth Army, and while Nugent may have been temporarily unaware of the full extent of his own division's predicament, he knew that time had to be gained for the French to come up. By the afternoon of 23 March three French divisions had taken over most of III Corps's front on the right, and three more were due to be in position behind XVIII Corps the following day – indeed, the leading elements of one, the 10th Division (General Valdant), were already starting to form a defensive line immediately behind the Ulster Division. This explains Nugent's reference, in his 6pm order to the brigades, to an 'improving' situation, and also his determination to keep fighting on his existing line. It was the arrival of the French too that forced him to move headquarters (Perceval-Maxwell recalled that 'when the French arrived we were ordered off, and went back to another village'): Freniches now formed part of the French defences and Nugent had to vacate it, his choice of Beaulieu for his next location determined by the fact that the French intended to establish their own headquarters there.[49]

---

[45] Falls, 'Contact with troops', p. 176.
[46] 107 Bde narrative (TNA, WO95/2502).
[47] *OH*, 1918, i, p. 343.
[48] Elizabeth Greenhalgh, *The French Army and the First World War* (2014), pp 271–86.
[49] *OH*, 1918, i, p. 369; Perceval-Maxwell, 'Narrative' (PRONI, D/1556/27/1/12, 2/4/18).

He was still at Freniches, however, when Hessey came back in person at 7pm to brief him on the crisis at the front. Together they urgently devised a plan to try to restore the situation, which involved three hastily organised overnight counter-attacks to regain the villages of Aubigny, Brouchy and Eaucourt. Hessey hurried back to oversee the attacks while Nugent scoured his headquarters for further reinforcements.[50] In the early hours of 24 March he sent forward two companies of details: 'I have sent my last men up to support the defence. I have collected even the officers' servants and all sorts of odds and ends of men. Freddie Drummond [his ADC] has gone with them at his urgent request and I sent them off in lorries at 2am this morning'.[51]

The question arises of whether, in leaving Hessey to coordinate the counterattacks, Nugent was delegating command or abdicating it. Cochrane thought Nugent should have been more hands-on, writing after the war that at 'the end of each day Divisional Commanders should have gone and seen their Brigade Commanders, and arranged for some kind of concerted plan for the next day'.[52] His point was reasonable, and indeed Nugent on 22 March and again on the 26th did precisely that. His decision to remain at his headquarters on the evening of the 23rd was, however, driven by the need to keep in touch with Maxse, the French and flanking formations at a critical time. Using one of his brigadiers as effectively his deputy commander was something he had done on the Somme, when he left Withycombe in command in Thiepval Wood. He could have made no practical difference by going forward to direct attacks made by a total force of less than two weak battalions, while the almost non-existent communications at the front would have made it impossible for him to coordinate arrangements with the French. In the event only one of the three counter-attacks succeeded: 61 Brigade managed to re-occupy Eaucourt, but the party earmarked to attack Aubigny was ambushed en route and could not continue, and in consequence the 9th Royal Inniskilling Fusiliers' attack on Brouchy had to be cancelled.

24 March

On the morning of Sunday, 24 March, the Ulster Division's position rapidly became untenable. Ludendorff's decision the previous day to reinforce von Hutier's thrust against the junction of the British and French armies west of Ham has since been seen as a strategic error that placed the

[50] 107 Bde narrative (TNA, WO95/2502); Falls, *Ulster Division*, pp 213–14.
[51] ON to CN, 22/24 Mar. 1918, in *Nugent*, p. 214.
[52] Cochrane to Edmonds, 16 Apr. [1927], quoted in Travers, *How The War Was Won*, p. 55.

assaulting German armies on divergent paths, but the immediate consequences for the Ulster Division, about to be steam-rollered, were grave.[53] Nugent had ordered a withdrawal starting at 11am, but as soon as it began the German assault, by the *36th* and *1st Bavarian Divisions*, resumed. Severe losses were inflicted on 61 and 108 Brigades as they fell back across the open, while 107 Brigade on the right was also heavily attacked. The British and French were increasingly intermingled but employed different tactics, which added to the confusion – the French had orders to withdraw when put under pressure, and Nugent asked his French counterpart 'what the d...l his men were about'.[54] He had gone forward to visit the brigades but quickly encountered problems; at 12.10pm he saw Withycombe at 107 Brigade but found it impossible to get further:

> [I]t was a horrible scene of confusion. French and British retiring, guns and wagons, horses and men in most inextricable confusion, a roar of shelling and machine guns and the very heaviest kind of German shells bursting all round us. At one time when we got into a narrow road and hopelessly wedged in, I really thought I might have to abandon my car.[55]

He returned to his headquarters but without men could do nothing to influence events. Every minute's delay imposed on the Germans now counted: by dawn on the 24th two French divisions were in position behind XVIII Corps and the leading elements of two more were only six miles away, one (the 62nd) moving up directly behind the Ulster Division. Thanks to strenuous efforts by regimental and staff officers the front was stabilised at around midday, but early in the afternoon powerful German attacks resumed and at this point a major part of Nugent's line gave way – 'The salient held by the 36th Division', Falls wrote, 'suddenly caved. From all sides the semicircle fell back upon Villeselve'.[56] The 2nd Royal Irish Rifles on the right were cut off and destroyed. Nearby, Lieutenant-Colonel McCarthy-O'Leary of the 1st Royal Irish Rifles tried to reorganise retreating units passing through his position but they 'did not wait for orders and fell back in confusion'; similarly, 61 Brigade reported at 3pm the retreat of a '[g]reat mixture of troops very disorganised and difficult to

---

[53] See, for example, David T. Zabecki, *The German 1918 Offensives: A Case Study in the Operational Level of War* (2006), pp 143–7.

[54] Falls, *Ulster Division*, pp 213–14; ON to CN, 7 Apr. 1918, in *Nugent*, p. 225.

[55] ON to CN, 25 Mar. 1918, in *Nugent*, p. 216; 107 Bde narrative (TNA, WO95/2502).

[56] Falls, *Irish Rifles*, p. 102; *OH*, 1918, i, p. 405; Falls, *Ulster Division*, p. 214.

control and considerably demoralised … Our men withdrawing out of control is in some instances affecting the morale of the French'. In a sign of a breakdown in staff-work, Cochrane went to the village of Berlancourt 'to explain [the situation] to the 36th Division and arrived there at 4.17pm, but found that DivHQrs had moved and that there was no means of communication left'. In fact Nugent's headquarters had never been there, but the episode reinforced Cochrane's sense of isolation.[57]

108 Brigade's withdrawal was helped by a mounted charge near Villeselve by a 150-strong detachment of the 6th Cavalry Brigade (3rd Cavalry Division), which caught the German infantry in the open and cut down an estimated 70 as well as taking over a hundred prisoners. Nugent's strictures after Cambrai about cavalry having no role on a modern battlefield were partially disproved here, and following up the charge the 1st and 9th Royal Irish Fusiliers regained some ground.[58] Despite this local success the retreat soon resumed, in some cases covered by artillery firing over open sights. A defensive line was with difficulty re-established by the evening, helped by fresh French troops and with Hessey again playing a prominent part, as Nugent later described:

> General Hessey and his Brigade Major, George Bruce, were both magnificent. I can't describe adequately how splendid they were on a very critical occasion, the day the French first came up to reinforce us and then broke and the Division on my right also broke and some of our cavalry who were in front of us also came streaming back and it looked like a debacle. Hessey and Bruce rode right into the line, threatening to shoot any waverers and cheering and encouraging our men.[59]

His account of who had broken and when was inaccurate but the division's ordeal was, temporarily at least, coming to an end; late on the 24th it was ordered to pull back through the French 62nd Division.[60]

25 March

By the morning of Monday, 25 March Nugent's remaining troops were a few miles behind the line, getting some badly needed rest. For him it was 'all a ghastly nightmare':

[57] Taylor, *1st Irish Rifles*, p. 133; 36 Div. narrative, 61 Bde war diary (TNA WO95/2492 and 2125).
[58] Lt.-Col. J. B. Bickersteth, *History of the 6th Cavalry Brigade 1914–18* (n.d.), p. 85; Cunliffe, *Irish Fusiliers*, p. 349; Nugent, *A Long Week in March*, pp 183–90.
[59] ON to CN, 7 Apr. 1918, in *Nugent*, pp 224–5.
[60] Falls, *Ulster Division*, p. 217.

> I cannot credit that it is only 5 days ago that we were holding trenches just in front of St Quentin. Yesterday was a bad day for the French and British Armies. We lost much ground, a great deal of guns and ammunition have been captured. The French have been rushing up divisions to try to stop the rot, but there is a great deal of confusion and the Germans are giving us no rest. What is left of my Division had terribly heavy fighting yesterday and we had to fall back again in common with French and British.

He was intensely concerned about his men:

> My men have had no food, some of them for 2 and 3 days. They have had no sleep for 5 nights. They are absolutely beat. We are in support of the French but if they call on us before I am reorganised and before the men have had at any rate one good night's sleep, we shall be no help to them. This is truly Armageddon. Unless we can finally stop the German attack soon, I fear it will be the end.[61]

He also called on the French 62nd Division's commander, General Margot, under whose command he now was. He admired the French army and felt keenly their disdain for the British performance:

> I feel more than anything the attitude of the French towards us. They hardly pretend to be civil and I can hardly wonder. There is sure to be a devil of a row at home over our debacle. I think it may cause the downfall of the present Government and of either Henry Wilson or DH [Haig]. Certainly no one could have even in their worst moments anticipated so complete a catastrophe.

Nugent now began reorganising his troops. His artillery had been detached to support the French, who had been rushed up so quickly they had had to leave their own to follow on later. The remainder of the division marched back to Guerbigny, 15 miles to the rear, arriving after midnight on the 26th.[62] At this point 61 Brigade, now less than 500 strong, returned to the 20th Division and Falls expressed the Ulster Division's admiration for the 'wonderful endurance and devotion' of Cochrane's men; Cochrane's opinion of the Ulster Division's leadership was, as will be seen, far less positive.[63]

[61] ON to CN, 25 Mar. 1918, in *Nugent*, p. 215.
[62] Falls, *Ulster Division*, p. 218.
[63] Ibid., p. 219.

The Avre (26–28 March)

The division's rest was short-lived. German attacks continued throughout the 25th and a potentially disastrous gap opened between the British and French armies near Roye, to fill which there was available only what was left of the 30th and 36th Divisions. At 8am on Tuesday, 26 March Nugent was ordered by Maxse to occupy at once a line four miles long running north-south a few miles west of Roye, his right on the River Avre, linking up with the French, and his left to the north of the village of Andechy in contact with the 30th Division. He barely had time to gallop over the new position, see his brigadiers and give orders as to how it was to be occupied – 109 Brigade on the right and 108 Brigade the left, with 107 Brigade in reserve, each now scarcely a weak battalion strong – before the Germans arrived. Indeed, they reached Andechy before Nugent's men and 108 Brigade was unable to establish contact with the 30th Division. Instead, Griffith's men threw themselves into some old French trenches and prepared to resist the German assault. There was no time to lay line: communications depended entirely on despatch riders and visual signalling, and the division's GSO3, Cyril Falls, recalled spending most of 26 March riding along the front searching for information.[64]

For the rest of the morning attempts by the German *206th Division* to infiltrate forward were stopped by machine-gun fire. Its troops then started working round the division's open left flank, and at 1pm Nugent ordered 107 Brigade, comprising the remnants of seven different units, to occupy a blocking position behind and to the north of the rest of the division. Fighting continued throughout the afternoon; Nugent's line was heavily shelled, but without artillery he could make no reply. He and Hessey discussed the situation that evening. Nugent had intended to fall back to try to align with the 30th Division but, as he later recalled, Hessey persuaded him 'to hold on as long as it was possible to do so', and the result, he believed in retrospect, was the imposition of a further critical delay on the Germans.[65] It came, however, at heavy cost.

At 8pm a further enemy assault was launched, this time by the advanced guard, six battalions strong, of another fresh German formation, the *28th Division*, against the village of Erches in the centre of Nugent's line. Much criticism has been levelled at British commanders for positioning their headquarters too far back but there were risks in being too far forward also. Erches was captured and 108 Brigade's headquarters attacked: Griffith

---

[64] ON to CN, 28 Mar. 1918, in *Nugent*, p. 217; Falls, *Ulster Division*, pp 221–2; Falls, 'Contact with Troops', p. 176.

[65] ON speech to Ulster Division officers dinner, quoted in *Belfast Newsletter*, 13 Nov. 1920.

escaped but was slightly wounded in doing so, while Place, the division's GSO1, visiting the front by car, was captured along with the COs of the 1st and 9th Royal Irish Fusiliers to whom he had given a lift.[66] Nugent's forward headquarters was the next to be disrupted, at 9pm:

> I had just sat down to eat something when an orderly ran in to say the Germans were in the village [Guerbigny]. I had kept my car ready for emergencies and so I and the 2 staff officers with me rushed out, jumped into the car and started off down the road. As we came out of the gate on to the road, a German machine gun fired I suppose at us from a rise in the ground just within 200 yards of us.[67]

The car raced off with Perceval-Maxwell, a big man, perched on top of the equally-large GSO2 and with 'men hanging on all over the motor'.[68] They drove to a nearby French brigade whose commander assured them that the troops firing were his, who had mistaken the British for Germans. Nugent and his companions, on foot and preceded by a cyclist, returned tentatively to Guerbigny, the car travelling slowly behind, but had just settled in once more when again an officer ran in to report that the Germans were in the village, and 'this time he had a prisoner so there was no disputing it'. As Nugent described:

> [A]gain we bolted, the Germans actually close to us. I went back to [the] same village as [the] French Brigadier and insisted on his sending some men to guard the approaches through Guerbigny and clear the village. Eventually he sent 2 parties to hold the roads, but would do no more. I sat up all night sending out warnings, but all the despatch riders I sent out have disappeared and must have been taken. [69]

The German attack was eventually halted, though Erches remained in their hands, and the remainder of Nugent's line was still clinging on as dawn broke on Wednesday, 27 March. Touch had been maintained with the French on the right and regained with British troops on the left, but Nugent's task became hopeless when the French fell back again at first light and the advance by the German *28th* and *206th Divisions* resumed. At 10am he held a hurried conference with Hessey and told him to hold on with the fragments of 109 Brigade for as long as possible – in fact Hessey was forced

---

[66] Falls, *Ulster Division*, pp 222–3.
[67] ON to CN, 28 Mar. 1918, in *Nugent*, pp 217–18.
[68] Perceval-Maxwell, 'Narrative' (PRONI, D/1556/27/1/12, 2/4/18).
[69] ON to CN, 28 Mar. 1918, in *Nugent*, pp 217–18.

to retreat across the Avre soon after – while the other two brigades were ordered to pull back to the west. Most of the 1st and 9th Royal Irish Fusiliers (108 Brigade) in the centre, still holding on near Erches, could not get clear and were overrun after a hard fight, but further north 107 Brigade fell back a mile to a new line where it stayed for the rest of the day.[70]

During the morning Nugent's headquarters, shelled out of three locations in rapid succession, was temporarily put out of action, Nugent himself being struck by pieces of shrapnel but, as he put it, 'fortunately only frightened', and for a time he and Perceval-Maxwell were reduced to driving between villages trying unsuccessfully to find a working telephone to make contact with Maxse. They did, however, manage to re-form divisional headquarters and linked up with Hessey's detachment, now comprising survivors from both 108 and 109 Brigades and scarcely two companies strong. The men 'really couldn't keep their eyes open', recalled Perceval-Maxwell, and the officers too were out on their feet – 'it is impossible to describe the state of weariness they were in'. By now further French reinforcements were arriving and on the evening of 27 March what was left of the Ulster Division was again pulled out of the line. Nugent wrote: 'We have had desperate fighting on 26th and 27th, and I hope we have done what was required. At any rate the Division has fought almost to the last man. As far as I can make out there are not more than 500 men, exclusive of clerks and transport men, left'.[71] A final exertion remained. At 12.30pm on the 28th came word of an enemy advance and Nugent broke off his letter home with 'No time for more. The Germans have broken through again at Montdidier. I have to collect the fragments of the Division to help the French'. Fortunately, though deployed, the division was not engaged, the French having successfully halted the Germans. The weather had broken in torrential rain and Nugent 'spent the night on a mattress on the floor of a deserted house and Guy C[ampbell, his ADC] tried his hand at cooking an old hen he found, but it defeated me'. On 30 March the Ulster Division was finally withdrawn from the battle.[72]

Aftermath

The division's losses for the period from 21 March to 5 April were initially reported at 7,310, the heaviest of any of the 33 British infantry divisions involved in the retreat. The return of stragglers brought the figure down to

[70] 109 Bde narrative; Falls, *Ulster Division*, pp 226–7; Nugent, *A Long Week in March*, pp 194–210.

[71] Perceval-Maxwell, 'Narrative' (PRONI, D/1556/27/1/12, 2/4/18); ON to CN, 28 Mar. 1918, in *Nugent*, p. 216.

[72] ON to CN, 29 Mar. 1918, in *Nugent*, p. 219.

a still appalling 6,109, over 5,000 of whom were missing (the total excludes the serious losses suffered by 61 Brigade).[73] Although these figures include the relatively large numbers of prisoners lost on 21 March, the fatality rate was high, with perhaps 1,000 men of the division being killed.[74] Because of the focus on the opening day the intensity of the subsequent fighting is often overlooked, but nearly two-thirds of the Ulster Division's fatalities were sustained during the fighting for the Somme crossings and on the Avre.

After the war Cochrane made a number of criticisms of Nugent and his staff which have since been used as evidence of more general failings of the British command during the March retreat:

> On the evening of the 21st I saw the 36th Division Commander at Ollezy. I never saw him again during these operations, nor did I ever see one of his Staff Officers, nor did I receive any assistance of any kind from Divisional Headquarters. Also I did not see a Staff Officer of any other formation. Mine was, I regret to say, not an isolated experience. As soon as telegraphic and telephone communication with the Brigades ceased to exist, Divisional Headquarters in many cases became paralysed. They had become so welded to a set piece type of warfare that, when open warfare occurred, they failed to appreciate the situation, and were unable to function independent of a fixed headquarters.[75]

Cochrane's complaints were understandable, but they were certainly unfair. As noted earlier, the scale of the German offensive was unprecedented. The Ulster Division was engaged by four German divisions on the opening day; one on the second; four on the third; two on the fourth; none on the fifth, when it was in reserve; two on the sixth; and two on the seventh. It was not command failure but overwhelming odds that led to its near-destruction, nor was it psychological paralysis that prevented Nugent from exercising control on occasions, but the physical destruction of his communications. Much of his time was spent trying to find out what was happening on his flanks and behind him, in which he got limited help from his superiors who were generally as badly informed as he. Cochrane told Edmonds that 'the number of Staff Officers (12) Motor Cars (6) horses (30) and despatch riders (12) at the disposal of Divisional Headquarters ... provided ample facilities

[73] *OH*, 1918, ii, p. 491. Falls put the figure at 7,252 for the period 21–31 March, 80% of whom were missing (*Ulster Division*, p. 232).

[74] See Michael Nugent's detailed analysis of the division's casualties (*A Long Week in March*, pp 211–20).

[75] Travers, *How The War Was Won*, p. 55.

for finding out the situation at the front'.[76] They did not. Nugent used staff officers and despatch riders extensively; his messengers suffered heavy losses, his GSO1 was captured visiting the front and his GSO2 suffered shell-shock while doing so. Perceval-Maxwell recalled how it 'was very difficult to get in reports or news … Despatch rider after despatch rider went off and did not get back and hours passed without us getting any definite information. When we did get news it was generally bad and we heard the most alarming rumours, of course generally without a word of truth, though the truth was bad enough'.[77] Griffith of 108 Brigade, in a post-action report, reviewed the various methods of communication, from pigeons to power buzzers, used during the retreat and concluded that only the provision of extra staff officers for liaison purposes would have helped. Nugent's own conclusion, as he told Maxse, was 'the necessity of Brigadiers being close up to the fighting line and of the Div commander being within view or at least within 15 minutes reach by D[espatch] R[ider] from Brigadiers'.[78]

The remarkable feature of the March fighting is not that command arrangements occasionally failed but that the division managed to survive as a fighting entity at all. Significant delay and heavy casualties had been inflicted on a much superior enemy and, as the official history put it, despite its losses the Ulster Division 'had the satisfaction of knowing that it had done much to hold back the enemy on every day of the battle'.[79] Nugent and Hessey were the division's key personalities during the retreat, holding it together during eight days of intense fighting. Nugent's admiration for Hessey was fully reciprocated: Hessey wrote home that 'Oliver has been splendid and I and all of us would do anything for him'. Bob Perceval-Maxwell remarked of him, 'Poor fellow, no-one knows what was on his mind for those 7 or 8 days … All the time he was most awfully nice. I never knew what a good fellow he was before'.[80] Nugent himself observed on 1 April: 'One can hardly realise the 9 days of nightmare really existed. I seem to want to do nothing but sleep. Everything passed so quickly and the strain was so great and one was so strung up that now the tension suddenly has relaxed, it seems as if I had never really gone through the time'.[81] The following day he wrote 'I am very battered and mentally weary and so sad to think of all my men, dead wounded or prisoners and I

---

[76] Ibid., p. 55.

[77] Perceval-Maxwell, 'Narrative' (PRONI, D/1556/27/1/12, 2/4/18).

[78] Griffiths, 'Notes and Experiences on the Recent Fighting', 7 Apr. 1918 (PRONI, D3835/E/7/11/13); ON to Maxse, 14 Apr. 1918, in *Nugent*, p. 229.

[79] *OH*, 1918, ii, p. 18.

[80] Hessey papers; Perceval-Maxwell, 'Narrative' (PRONI, D/1556/27/1/12, 2/4/18).

[81] ON to CN, 1 Apr. 1918, in *Nugent*, p. 221.

feel it so much more that I know they were wasted unnecessarily'. Much of his bitterness was aimed, unfairly on this occasion, at Gough, of whose removal on 28 March he heard with relief.[82]

Rebuilding

On 30 March the division's survivors – less the artillery, which remained in action supporting the French for a further 24 hours – boarded trains near Amiens, their destination the Normandy coast near Abbeville.[83] Nugent hoped that 'we may be given time to reorganise and get some men and specialists trained', but in fact, with the British bracing themselves for a further massive German onslaught, he got scarcely 72 hours.[84] The final trains bringing his men up from Amiens arrived in Normandy on 1 April; by the evening of 4 April the last ones taking the division back into action had left Abbeville for the Ypres Salient, and on the afternoon of 6 April the division moved back into the line.

The first week of April 1918 illustrates the resilience of First World War formations. On 1 April Nugent noted that he did not know 'where our reserves and reinforcements are to come from as the Irish regiments are exhausted and there are no reserves left in Ireland'.[85] An immediate source of replacements was the entrenching battalions, whose soldiers were now re-absorbed urgently into the division most of them had belonged to only a couple of months before. The 15th Royal Irish Rifles, for example, was reconstituted on 2 April with six officers and 460 men from the 21st and 23rd Entrenching Battalions, while the 2nd Royal Irish Rifles received nine officers and 256 men at the same time; over the ensuing days the 1st and 2nd Royal Inniskilling Fusiliers obtained between them 23 officers and 120 men; and on 5 April the 12th Royal Irish Rifles, now in transit towards Ypres, got 8 officers and 330 men from the 22nd Entrenching Battalion, most of them formerly of the 11th/13th Royal Irish Rifles. These drafts were relatively easy to integrate. The next wave – reinforcements were now flooding into France, comprising mostly young conscripts – had to be hurriedly assimilated as the division took over the line, the 1st Royal Inniskilling Fusiliers receiving a draft of 300 men on 6 April while moving up to the trenches east of Ypres and the 12th Royal Irish Rifles a contingent of 337 on 8 April while in support.[86] The speed with which units were

---

[82] ON to CN, 2 Apr. 1918 (PRONI, D3835/E/2/608).

[83] Falls, *Ulster Division*, p. 232.

[84] ON to CN, 1 Apr. 1918, in *Nugent*, p. 221.

[85] Ibid.

[86] Battalion war diaries (TNA, WO95/2502, 2503 and 2509); Nugent, *A Long Week in March*, pp 212–13.

reconstituted was extraordinary despite the fact that, as Nugent noted, 'the difficulty of making them into a good fighting force within reasonable time is greater this time than any previous time because I have lost so many COs and Officers and NCOs'.[87]

He also had to deal with wholesale command changes. During March four battalion COs (and two 2ic's in command) had been captured, two more had been wounded and evacuated, and an experienced former CO, Philip Blair Oliphant, had been fatally wounded commanding the 22nd Entrenching Battalion. The strain on the survivors was evident. On 6 April John Peacocke of the 9th Royal Inniskilling Fusiliers, Nugent's longest-serving CO, was admitted to hospital, Nugent telling Kitty:

> John Peacocke has had a nervous breakdown and I am replacing him in command of his battn and he will probably go home at once for rest. He did most excellent work but was not really very fit when it began. One day 2 officers he was walking with were both killed by the same shell, one on either side of him, he was untouched but greatly shaken.[88]

Bob Perceval-Maxwell, now commanding the 15th Royal Irish Rifles, was also exhausted and Nugent was sympathetic:

> [H]e doesn't want to go and says quite frankly his nerves are not equal to taking the strain with a new battn of men from all parts, all strangers to him, so I told him to write to me officially and say so and I would try and get him a home job. After all, he isn't a soldier, he has been twice wounded and has 2 sons out here who have each been wounded and I don't blame him for wanting to get home. I am sorry he was ever sent out again.[89]

Perceval-Maxwell left on 25 April to assume command of a garrison battalion of the Royal Munster Fusiliers. Even more serious for Nugent was the loss of two of his brigadiers. Hessey's exertions had caused a recurrence of his hernia injury and he had to return temporarily to England. The timing was unfortunate because Nugent had recommended him strongly for promotion: 'I have recommended you for command of a Division', he told Hessey on 4 May, 'and I spoke to Sir H Plumer a couple of days ago asking him to star you on his list'.[90] (Hessey was not in the end promoted,

---

[87] ON to CN, 5 Apr. 18, in *Nugent*, p. 222.
[88] ON to CN, 7 Apr. 18, in *Nugent*, p. 224.
[89] ON to CN, 9 Apr. 18, in *Nugent*, pp 225–6. One of Perceval-Maxwell's sons was killed later in 1918.
[90] ON to Hessey, 4 May 1918 (Hessey papers).

probably because of his injury-enforced absences.) Also gone was Withycombe, drained by the intense fighting. 'I had to recommend Withycombe for a 6 months tour of duty at home', Nugent confided to Hessey, 'He has been too long in command of a Brigade and is stale'.[91] Only Griffith and Brock now remained of the officers at lieutenant-colonel rank and above who had fought at the Somme, and only Nugent himself of those who had arrived in France in October 1915.

Reputation

In addition to rebuilding his division, Nugent was also working to protect its reputation. A number of formations were not immediately made up to strength; there was, he told Kitty, 'a list of 5 or 6 in all to whom this may happen and they are notoriously Divisions which failed to do their duty'.[92] They included two with whom he had been closely associated, the 14th and 16th. He was bothered by the fact that the 36th Division had not been praised in Haig's initial despatch – 'I think it is very hard on the Division that the C in C has made no mention of them. I am afraid that the Divisions of the 5th Army will get very little acknowledgement'.[93] On his way from Normandy to Ypres he stayed overnight at GHQ and called on various acquaintances, including Ambrose Ricardo, now on the staff there; overall he found that 'everyone is very pleased with the Division and the way they fought and I find we are considered to have had the heaviest fighting almost of anyone', but he still wished 'the C in C had given us the satisfaction of recognising this by mentioning us as among the Divisions which had done well'.[94]

If Haig had not praised the division sufficiently the press at home had. The *Larne Times* of 6 April, for example, carried under dramatic headlines – 'Ulstermen's Glorious Stand. As Formidable In Defence As Attack. Thirty-Mile Retirement. Game To The Last' – a syndicated account of the March fighting. It not only described the division retiring 'with their faces to the enemy for more than thirty miles, giving battle all the way to protect their crumbling flank or to extricate hard-pressed neighbours', it also referred to Farnham's capture and news of it being conveyed by pigeon, the counter-attack at Aubigny led by Bruce on horseback, Freddie Drummond's role in bringing up reinforcements ('a staff officer who lost an arm at Hooge'), and the ambush of Place and his companions at Erches. The author, an American correspondent called Percival Phillips, had visited

---

[91] ON to Hessey, 26 Apr. 1918 (Hessey papers).
[92] ON to CN, 7 Apr. 1918, in *Nugent*, p. 223.
[93] ON to CN, 1 Apr. 1918, in *Nugent*, p. 221.
[94] ON to CN, 5 Apr. 1918, in *Nugent* p. 223.

the division during its brief stay in Normandy and seems to have interviewed Nugent in person, his account describing how the Ulstermen finished, 'as one general expressed it to me, "drunk with fatigue, yet absolutely game to the last"'.

The Battle of the Lys

On 8 April Nugent, in his HQ north of Ypres, noted his surroundings without satisfaction – 'Here I am back in this filthy Ypres sector in the very place where I had my Hdqrs at the time I left to command this Division … The Germans are further away, that is all, but the country to the front and rear is an indescribable waste of mud, shellholes and water, bleak and desolate beyond words'.[95] The Germans were about to get much closer. On 9 April the second stage of Ludendorff's offensive, Operation Georgette, began with a massive attack astride the River Lys, 15 miles to the south; Nugent heard the opening bombardment in his dug-out. The Germans achieved a major initial success, breaking through the unfortunate Portuguese corps ('I expect the Portuguese bravos legged it', commented Nugent unkindly, 'between them on one side and les braves Belges next door to me I feel very anxious').[96]

When the attack began 107 Brigade was in the line at Ypres with 109 Brigade in support, but 108 Brigade, in II Corps reserve, was rushed south to fight under command of the 19th Division in defence of Kemmel Hill. For the next week it took part in heavy fighting and suffered serious losses but helped delay the German advance long enough for reinforcements to arrive. Meanwhile the British at Ypres prepared to be attacked and Plumer withdrew his line closer to the city. Nugent's units covered the evacuation of artillery, ammunition and stores from the area east of Ypres, and on 16 April he told Kitty:

> Last night we withdrew from practically all the ground we captured with such heavy loss last summer in this part of Belgium. We are now back very close to where we were in 1915. I got all my Division back in safety and the Germans did not make any move to follow us until this afternoon. They are now shelling us, but that is not a new thing. We saw them this afternoon feeling their way forwards over the desolate plain in front of us.[97]

[95] ON to CN, 9 Apr. 1918, in *Nugent*, p. 225.
[96] ON to CN, 10 Apr. 1918, in *Nugent*, p. 226.
[97] ON to CN, 16 Apr. 1918, in *Nugent*, p. 230.

Skirmishing continued along the front as the Germans probed forward and Nugent was relieved when 108 Brigade, though weakened, re-joined on the 18th. He was also heartened to be back under Plumer's command:

> It is extraordinary the change of spirit and tone in the 2nd Army, compared with the 5th Army. Here everybody has such absolute confidence in Plumer. In the other, the mere fact of going to the 5th Army was like a death blow. It used to take all the heart out of troops. Service in the 5th Army was hated by Generals, regimental officers and men alike. The 5th Army never had a success and was responsible for the loss of more lives uselessly than all the other Armies put together. Gough had no qualification for commanding an Army, neither intellectual nor by training ... Please God for the sake of the British Army and the cause for which we are fighting he will never be employed out here again.[98]

That judgement was harsh as far as Gough's performance in March 1918 was concerned, but Nugent never forgave him for the Langemarck debacle. By the end of April the German offensive had been halted without the Ulster Division being heavily engaged, and while there were further attacks to come the worst for the allies was over.

Conscription crisis

The BEF's casualties in March had been huge and the government faced the prospect of extending conscription still further in Britain to make good the losses. Lloyd George concluded that for political and practical reasons Irish conscription was now essential, and at meetings on 27 and 28 March, while the Ulster Division was still fighting on the Avre, the cabinet endorsed his proposals. These involved conscripting 150,000 men in Ireland, part of an additional 550,000 to be raised throughout the UK. Some within government advised caution, including Lord Wimborne, the Lord Lieutenant, H. E. Duke, the Chief Secretary (who famously remarked of the forced enlistment of resentful Irishmen, '[w]e might as well recruit Germans'), the Inspector General of the Royal Irish Constabulary (RIC) and even Carson.[99] But Lloyd George believed that reaction in Ireland could be managed by linking conscription to early movement on Home

---

[98] ON to CN, 13/14 Apr. 1918, in *Nugent*, pp 227–8.

[99] Adrian Gregory, ''You might as well recruit Germans': British public opinion and the decision to conscript the Irish in 1918', in A. Gregory and S. Paseta (eds), *Ireland and the Great War* (2002), pp 113–32; Alan J. Ward, 'Lloyd George and the 1918 Irish conscription crisis', *Historical Journal*, 17:1 (1974), pp 107–29.

Rule, though without resolving how this could be done in a manner acceptable to both nationalists and Ulster unionists. He also had others, including John French and Henry Wilson, assuring him that opposition to conscription could be faced down.

The conscription bill's introduction on 9 April coincided with the opening of the German attack on the Lys and it completed its passage a week later, despite resistance from John Dillon and his colleagues in the Irish Parliamentary Party who recognised in it the political oblivion of their brand of moderate nationalism. The massive groundswell of opposition in Ireland included many Protestants, but it was in uniting all shades of nationalist opinion, the Catholic Church and the trade unions that the impact was felt most deeply. Anti-conscription demonstrations were held across much of Ireland; they included an 8,000-strong protest in Cavan town in early April followed shortly after by a bigger one, reportedly attended by 20,000 people, in Virginia, 12 miles from Mountnugent, where the crowd cheered a Sinn Fein speaker warning that an 'alien Government is trying to conscript Irishmen to save the British from their cousins, the Germans … This war was started without our consent and without consulting the people of this country, therefore we are in no way bound to carry it out'.[100] Nugent, like many of his class, had consistently underestimated the growing strength of Sinn Fein but there was no denying that reality now. On 18 April, the day 108 Brigade re-joined the division after its exertions at Kemmel, Samuel Young, the elderly Irish Party MP for East Cavan, died and the by-election on 20 June resulted in victory for Sinn Fein's Arthur Griffith. He did not take his seat, both because of the party's abstentionist policy and because he had been imprisoned some weeks earlier along with other Sinn Fein leaders, but it was clear that the nationalist electorate in Cavan, as elsewhere across the country, was determined to reject, not only conscription, but even Home Rule as hitherto envisaged and now wanted complete separation from Britain.

Replacement

No sooner had the military situation stabilised than GHQ resumed its programme of command changes. Between 26 April and 16 June, a corps commander, eight divisional commanders and a raft of brigadiers were transferred to non-combatant roles, Nugent amongst them. He was replaced on 6 May, his successor being Clifford Coffin, a sapper officer who had won the Victoria Cross at Third Ypres while commanding an infantry

[100] *Anglo-Celt*, 20 Apr. 1918.

brigade in the 8th Division, and whom Nugent regarded highly.[101] He had no time to visit the units under his command and may not have wanted to. Instead he issued a valedictory message to his COs:

> As I cannot come round and see all the Units of the Division to wish them good-bye, I must say what I can on paper. I want you to tell them how much I appreciate the splendid work they have done during the 2½ years that I have had the honour and pleasure of commanding the Division. They have never failed to reach a high standard of performance. They have shown at all times a high sense of duty and conscientious thoroughness in the discharge of it. I know they will do their duty as thoroughly in the future as they have done in the past. I should like to have had the opportunity to thank all your Officers personally for their work and to have told them how I appreciate it but I can only ask you to do it for me. I wish you all good luck in the future. I know you and your men will not fail.[102]

He received various messages of thanks and regret at his departure, one he appreciated particularly coming from Hessey:

> I am most awfully sorry you are leaving the Ulster Division: but I think from your point as to future prospects it is for the best as everyone in the division felt very keenly that you had been deliberately left out in the awards and honours lists for a long time past. I am sure I wish you the very best of good luck in India. And all of us who have been privileged to serve under you will always remember the devotion you gave to the division and the care you took of the interests of all in it.[103]

Others did not share Hessey's sorrow. Lily Spender in London heard the news from Lady Carson and hastened to tell Wilfrid: 'He is degomme – after a fashion! And has got a Corps in India! The C. in C. doesn't approve of him, but the Army C. [Plumer] does, so they compromised'.[104] Although not all the details were accurate it was a perceptive account of what had been going on behind the scenes. In late April Nugent had been warned he might be sent to India. He asked for a home posting but this was refused and after discussing the position with Plumer he decided to make the best of it, telling Hessey:

[101] Falls, *Ulster Division*, p. 244; Baguley, *Question of Ulster*, p. 408.
[102] Special order, 6 May 1918, in *Nugent*, p. 233.
[103] Hessey to ON, 12 May 1918, in *Nugent*, pp 233–4.
[104] Lily Spender to Spender, 3 June 1918, Baguley, *Question of Ulster*, p. 405.

The C.in.C India asked for me. I asked leave to decline but the W[ar] O[ffice] decided I must go. I think it is better I should. As long as Sir D.H[aig]. is C.in.C out here I shall receive no promotion. Plumer advised me to accept the promotion in India at any rate for the present. It is not pleasant being passed over by one's juniors and I am getting rather too senior out here for a Division. I am sorry but not so sorry as I should be if the Division contained anything like the old elements, but as you know it is almost entirely a new Division.[105]

The reference to promotion, picked up by Lily Spender, was interesting. His new command, the Meerut Division, was in terms of numbers comparable to a corps but it did not involve promotion. Whether there was a genuine misunderstanding or Nugent was simply putting a gloss on his removal is unclear.

Even as he left for the sub-continent the tide on the western front was turning. The British offensive at Amiens began on 8 August, five days after he took over the Meerut Division, and word of it soon reached India: he wrote to St George, now at Sandhurst, that '[t]he news from France is very good up to now. I think we have found a great soldier in Foch'.[106] The Ulster Division under his successor would go on to play an important role in the Hundred Days campaign, taking part, appropriately, in Second Army's recapture of Messines in September and deep advances in southern Belgium in October, winning another two Victoria Crosses in the process (and suffering 3,800 casualties that month, higher even than August 1917). By the time the division came out of the line for the last time, on 27 October, it was 25 miles east of Ypres and ten miles beyond Courtrai, progress unimaginable during the desperate fighting in March.[107]

[105] 4 May 1918 (Hessey papers). The C-in-C India was Sir Charles Monro, whom Nugent had known before the war.

[106] ON to St George, 14 Aug. 1918, in *Nugent*, p. 238.

[107] Falls, *Ulster Division*, pp 262–93.

10

Staying On

India, Ireland and the crisis of empire, June 1918–May 1926

Introduction

The end of hostilities in 1918 precipitated a 'crisis of empire' which dominated the closing years of Nugent's professional career and spilled over into his post-war world as a civilian.[1] The nationalist challenges to British authority in both India and Ireland had parallels with each other (and the political and military lessons of the Irish republican campaign would later influence both the strategy of the Indian nationalist movement and the colonial response to it), but Nugent experienced the two situations very differently.[2] In India from 1918 to 1920 he played an active part in the imperial power's coercive reaction – he of course saw it as maintaining law and order – to the most widespread challenge to British rule since 1857. In Ireland from 1920 to 1923, by contrast, although many of his former subordinates were directly involved in the conflict, he was a passive if concerned observer of the War of Independence and Irish Civil War and a resigned recipient of their political outcome: the political irrelevance of his once powerful class was again underlined. Instead he looked to commemoration and support for ex-servicemen as ways of providing practical assistance to former comrades, encouraging reconciliation on the island and, to a degree, expressing a continuing sense of a dual Irish-British identity in a manner appropriate to a citizen of a now independent country, the Irish Free State.

---

[1] See Keith Jeffery, *The British Army and the Crisis of Empire 1918–22* (1984).

[2] Deirdre McMahon, 'Ireland and the Empire-Commonwealth, 1900–1948', in Judith M. Brown and William Roger Louis (eds), *The Oxford History of the British Empire, Vol IV: The Twentieth Century* (1999), pp 145–6; Keith Jeffery, 'The road to Asia, and the Grafton Hotel, Dublin: Ireland in the 'British world', *Irish Historical Studies*, 36:142 (Nov. 2008), pp 243–56; Michael Silvestri, '"The Sinn Fein of India": Irish nationalism and the policing of revolutionary terrorism in Bengal', *Journal of British Studies*, 39:4 (Oct. 2000), pp 454–86; Kate O'Malley, 'Learning the tricks of the imperial secession trade: Irish and Indian nationalism in the '30s and '40s', *History Ireland*, 18:4 (July/Aug. 2010), pp 32–5.

India and the Meerut Division

The political situation in India in 1918 was very different from the relative tranquility of his previous tour in 1909. As in Ireland, pre-war tensions over the speed of progress towards self-government had been exacerbated by wartime pressures: India contributed significantly to the British war-effort, but by the second half of the war the costs, human and financial, were causing increasing unrest. The Montagu-Chelmsford report, published in June 1918 and proposing greater involvement of Indians in the government of their country, was rejected as inadequate by the Indian National Congress at the end of August – just as Nugent set out on his first round of inspections – and was criticised also by Muslim leaders, this being a period of rare, and from a British perspective dangerous, cooperation between Congress and the Muslim League.[3]

For the first few months, however, the situation was still calm on the surface and he was able to focus on getting to know his new command. While there was an Indian field formation, the 7th (Meerut) Division, which served in France, Mesopotamia and Palestine, the Meerut Division to which he had been appointed was an administrative district in the United Provinces (UP), part of India's Northern Command. It was large – it was, he told St George in August, '350 miles by 250 and there are something over 70,000 troops in it' – and included Delhi, now India's capital; it also adjoined the Punjab, which would be at the centre of the disturbances soon to break out.[4] In late 1918 it comprised a cavalry brigade and four geographically-based brigades (Agra, Bareilly, Delhi and Garwhal) along with a host of supply depots, training centres and other installations. Nugent had reporting to him a more junior major-general and 12 brigadiers and simply visiting his units was a major exercise. On 21 October he wrote:

> I have been travelling almost continuously since the 9th Sept spending 2 or 3 days in one place, a day in another and so forth. I don't know how many miles I have travelled but I suppose it must be nearly 1000. I have inspected almost 50,000 men and still have nearly 25,000 men to see. In Meerut alone there are nearly 15,000 men, cavalry, gunners and infantry. I have not seen them yet and there are still some outstations as well.[5]

---

[3] Derek Sayer, 'British reaction to the Amritsar Massacre 1919–1920', *Past and Present*, 131 (May 1991), pp 130–64.

[4] ON to St George, 14 Aug. 1918, in *Nugent*, p. 238.

[5] ON to St George, 21 Oct. 1918, in *Nugent*, p. 239. He was not the only new arrival. His neighbour commanding the UP's other major military district, the Lucknow Division, was Maj.-Gen. Sir Arthur Scott, who took up post two

He followed the progress of the war closely and at last, on 10 November 1918, he was able to write hopefully to Kitty:

> Dearest, Is it peace? This morning's Reuter says Foch has given the Germans till 11am tomorrow, 11th Nov, to make up their minds. I can hardly settle down to anything, waiting to know. I shan't probably hear till Monday night or Tuesday morning. I do not see how they can do anything else with revolution apparently on the point of breaking out all over Germany ... I can hardly picture to myself what peace will feel like again. The afternoon at F[arren] C[onnell] where you and I were sitting on the sofa at tea, when the telegram came seems so far away as to be almost another life. It was the end of an epoch, no doubt of that. Life will never again be the same and who knows what it will be like.[6]

The armistice was greeted by official India with parades and other celebrations, but Indian expectations about political reform had been heightened by the imperial victory their troops and resources had helped secure. The immediate cause of the violence of early 1919 was the enactment in March of the first of the so-called Rowlatt bills, which provided for the continuation of draconian wartime security measures and which were strongly opposed by much of the Indian political class.[7] Gandhi, already an influential leader, called for non-violent protests, in the form of shop closures and the suspension of routine services, to take place on 6 April. These protests and the authorities' response would culminate on 13 April in the Amritsar massacre, a watershed in the history of British India. It was in Delhi a fortnight earlier, however, that troops from Nugent's command became the first to fire on civilians, when a demonstration on 30 March got out of hand, a crowd attacked the railway station, and police and soldiers of the 1st (Garrison) Battalion Berkshire Regiment opened fire to disperse the rioters. Ten Indians were killed and a dozen wounded. Brigadier-General Drake-Brockman, the Delhi Brigade commander, deployed additional troops to patrol the streets and guard the civil lines, and though the city remained tense further clashes were avoided. The officers involved were convinced their actions had prevented trouble escalating and the Hunter Committee, established to investigate Amritsar

---

days after him and who had had a similar experience to his own, commanding the 12th Division with distinction on the western front from October 1915 to April 1918 before being replaced by a younger officer.
[6] ON to CN, 10 Nov. 1918 (PRONI, D3835/E/2/19/1A).
[7] Sayer, 'Amritsar Massacre', p. 135.

and the events leading up to it, accepted that view, despite sceptical questioning of Drake-Brockman and others by its Indian members.[8] Nugent, who had not been directly involved, was not called on to give evidence.

The main demonstrations on 6 April, including the two largest in Nugent's district, at Delhi and Meerut, passed off peacefully. Over the next few days, however, the situation spiralled out of control in the Punjab, the Indian army's main recruiting area, hard hit by over-recruitment and now facing the social and economic consequences of demobilisation and a post-war depression.[9] The catalyst was Gandhi's arrest on 9 April; serious rioting followed in several major cities, including Amritsar, where a number of European civilians were killed. The intensity of the disorder across north-west India convinced many British officials that they faced an insurrection, and press reports at home, based on official briefings, often referred to the Indian protestors as 'rebels'.[10] On 13 April Brigadier-General Dyer, who had been at Camberley with Nugent, ordered his troops to fire on a peaceful albeit illegal gathering in the Jallianwala Bagh in Amritsar, killing at least 379 people and wounding many more. He believed he had prevented a country-wide rising, but even within the badly-frightened British community in India that justification was not universally accepted; for most Indians the shootings represented simple mass murder, while public and political opinion in Britain was divided. Edward Carson was one politician who spoke up in defence of Dyer, but to many Irish nationalists the killings were evidence of British colonial brutality at a time when Irish armed resistance to British rule was building momentum.[11]

Nugent's surviving correspondence from his time in India in 1918–20 is limited and he kept no diary, so his personal views on what happened at Amritsar are unknown. He certainly believed that the unrest of March and April was politically motivated, telling Theffania, now at Oxford, on 29 April that 'a lot of rascally agitators incited the people of the Punjab to rebel'.[12] It was a busy period for him, liaising with the civil authorities and deploying units to support the police. While the UP was not as volatile as the Punjab its government, under Sir Harcourt Butler, acted energetically

[8] *Evidence taken before the Disorders Inquiry Committee* [Hunter Committee], Vol. I, *Delhi* (1920) (TNA, CAB27/92).

[9] Tan Tai Yong, *The Garrison State: The Military, Government and Society in Colonial Punjab, 1849–1947* (2005), pp 98–152.

[10] Nick Lloyd, *The Amritsar Massacre: The Untold Story of One Fateful Day* (2011), pp 123–8; *Irish Examiner*, 21 Apr. 1919.

[11] Lloyd, *Amritsar Massacre*, pp 69–107; Sayer, 'Amritsar Massacre', pp 135–43.

[12] ON to Theffania, 29 Apr. 1919 (Nugent family papers).

to pre-empt disorder, with the threat of military force explicit – 'I have put details of troops in all the places where trouble might occur', Nugent wrote, 'and I have warned the natives that they will get it hot and strong if they make trouble.'[13] In the event these precautionary steps were enough to prevent serious disturbances, which was fortunate because troops for internal security tasks were soon in short supply.[14] On 3 May 1919, less than three weeks after the Amritsar shootings, Afghan forces invaded north-west India. The Third Afghan War has been described as 'one of the most absurd and unnecessary wars that Britain (and India) has ever been involved in', and by early June the Afghans had been repulsed; battle casualties on the British side were low, but the army in India had had to commit prodigious resources, with at its height nearly 350,000 men and 158,000 animals deployed.[15] Although a peace agreement was signed in August 1919, a major tribal revolt in Waziristan dragged on into 1920, and while Nugent had no operational role in the campaign his district had to provide men for it, a significant and potentially dangerous diversion of troops. The risk of politically-motivated disorder remained acute for the rest of his time in India, with the Khilafat movement (a Muslim protest against the break-up of the Ottoman Empire) being followed by Gandhi's non-cooperation campaign, and a feature of this period in the UP was the extensive use, under Nugent's direction, of high-profile troop deployments known as 'flag marches' to boost the morale of the police and deter trouble.[16]

Despite the unrest, in late 1919, with Theffania at university and Alison away at school, Kitty travelled out to India to join her husband. St George had arrived in the sub-continent not long before her: commissioned earlier in the year and having only just missed the sword of honour at Sandhurst, he had been posted to the 3rd KRRC at Poona, and there was a cheerful family reunion in Bombay. By 1920, however, Nugent was increasingly concerned about the poor quality of British units in India, as an over-stretched army tried to meet too many world-wide commitments. On 30 June he wrote, 'The British Army out here is giving me great annoyance. They are very undisciplined and have much to learn before they can be

---

[13] Ibid.

[14] Gyanesh Kudaisya, '"In aid of civil power": the colonial army in northern India *c.* 1919–42', *Journal of Imperial & Commonwealth History*, 32:1 (Jan. 2004), pp 41–68; Martin Thomas, '"Paying the butcher's bill": policing British colonial protest after 1918', *Crime, History and Societies*, 15:2 (2011), pp 55–76.

[15] Brian Robson, *Crisis on the Frontier: The Third Afghan War and the Campaign in Waziristan 1919–20* (2004), pp 141–2.

[16] Kudaisya, 'Colonial army', p. 52.

called soldiers'.[17] His comments, it seems, were sparked by an incident then underway, not in his district but with a direct Irish connection, the mutiny of the 1st Connaught Rangers. On 28 June soldiers of a company of the Rangers in Jullundur, over 200 miles from Meerut, but only 50 from Amritsar, refused to do duty 'until all British soldiers had left Ireland' (they had been unsettled by disturbing reports of events at home, with tensions exacerbated by leadership problems within the battalion). The following day a detachment of the regiment at Solon followed suit, two men being killed in an attempt to seize weapons from the armoury. Within days both locations had been taken over by loyal troops and those involved arrested. The authorities were anxious about the signal this demonstration of the unreliability of British units might send to the Indian population and the Indian army, and harsh action followed: 61 soldiers were convicted by court-martial and 14 sentenced to death, though only one, 21-year-old James Daly, was executed, on 2 November 1920. The Viceroy, Lord Chelmsford, noted that the British would put themselves 'in a position of great difficulty in the future with regard to Indian troops if, in the case of British soldiers, we did not enforce the supreme penalty where conditions justified it'.[18] Although Nugent's views on the mutiny have not survived, that was an assessment he would probably have shared.

By the time of Daly's execution, however, Nugent was no longer in India. At the end of August his appointment, and with it his active army career, had come to an end and he and Kitty sailed for home. It had not been the quiet final posting he had expected, the foundations of British rule in the sub-continent having at times, particularly in early 1919, been severely shaken. Back in Ireland those foundations were in the process of being ripped out completely.

Ireland in 1920

The Nugents were returning to a country at war. There had been a gap of only ten weeks between the armistice in France on 11 November 1918 and the killing by the IRA of two police officers at Soloheadbeg in Tipperary on

---

[17] ON to Theffania, 30 June 1920 (Nugent family papers).
[18] Mario Draper, 'Mutiny under the Sun: The Connaught Rangers, India, 1920', *War In History*, 27:2 (2020), pp 202–23; Kevin Kenny, 'The Irish in the Empire', in Kevin Kenny (ed.), *Ireland and the British Empire* (2004), pp 109–11; Michael Silvestri, 'Nationalism, empire and memory: the Connaught Rangers mutiny, June 1920', *History Ireland*, 18:4 (July/Aug. 2010), pp 26–9. See also Sam Pollock, *Mutiny for the Cause: The Story of the Revolt of Ireland's "Devil's Own" in British India* (1969); Anthony Babington, *The Devil to Pay: The Mutiny of the Connaught Rangers, India, July 1920* (1991).

21 January 1919, generally regarded as the start of the Irish War of Independence.[19]

Nugent's comment to Kitty that the Great War had changed everything was particularly true for his own class, which entered the revolutionary period of 1919–23 having already suffered devastating losses in 1914–18. Over 70% of young men of military age from Irish landed families had served during the First World War and of these one in four had been killed, figures higher than for any other social group in Ireland and similar to those for other social elites in the United Kingdom (their enlistment and fatality rates were, for example, higher than for the same age group amongst Cambridge graduates and about the same as for Old Etonians).[20] In Cavan and the surrounding counties the list of dead included many whom Nugent knew personally, including Audley Pratt, whose family owned Cabra Castle near Kingscourt, killed at Langemarck; Alan Brooke's brother Victor of Colebrooke in Fermanagh and Norman Leslie of Castle Leslie in Monaghan, both killed in 1914; Lord Longford of Pakenham Hall in Westmeath, who died at Gallipoli in 1915; and Humphrey Fane Vernon, lost with Lord Kitchener on HMS *Hampshire* in 1916 and whose father had hosted the last Cavan Twelfth celebration before the war at his Belturbet estate. The war had brought tragedy to similar families in Britain – three of Kitty's nephews had been killed – but the imminent break-up of the United Kingdom as they had known it gave particular poignancy to the sacrifice of southern Irish families. As Lady Fingall of Killeen Castle in County Meath, where Nugent had often hunted as a young man, later wrote:

> I used to think and say, during the War, that if ever that list of Dead and Wounded could cease, I would never mind anything or grumble at anything again. But when the Armistice came at last, we seemed drained of all feeling. And one felt nothing. We took up our lives again, or tried to take them up. The world we had known had vanished. We hunted again, but ghosts rode with us. We sat at table, and there were absent faces. For us, I suppose, the Irish Troubles were a continuation of the War.[21]

---

[19] The title 'IRA' rather than 'Irish Volunteers' came increasingly into use in 1919–20 (Charles Townshend, *The Republic: The Fight for Irish Independence* (2013), p. 89).

[20] Of a sample of 1,074 young men from all 32 counties, aged between 15 and 30 in 1914 and whose families had owned substantial estates before the war, 756 (70%) had served in the armed forces of whom 192 (25%) were killed (Perry, 'Irish Landed Class', p. 328).

[21] Elizabeth, Countess Fingall, *Seventy Years Young* (1991), p. 386.

The Troubles, as Daisy Fingall suggested, were for those actively involved sometimes as lethal as the war; but even for the bulk of the population who were simply trying to get on with their lives, the risk of violence and the dislocation of everyday existence, whether caused by insurgents or state forces, were still a source of huge anxiety. In August 1920, while packing up in India, Nugent had written to Alison, only half in jest:

> I wonder what it will be like at home. I do not expect the people will be allowed to show any civility and I think everything is likely to be very unpleasant but I do not think they will shoot at us when we appear out of doors. I hope they won't. It would be such a nuisance to have to go out for a walk crawling on one's tummy.[22]

By the autumn of 1920 levels of violence were rising dramatically. Amongst the 1,300 or so fatalities in the War of Independence were 434 police and 150 soldiers, of whom around 90% were killed between June 1920 and July 1921. The bulk of the 750 or so civilian deaths, including IRA members, occurred in the same period.[23] Within weeks of Nugent's return some of the most notorious episodes of the Troubles had occurred, including Bloody Sunday (21 November), the Kilmichael ambush (28 November) and the burning of Cork (11/12 December).

A second feature of the violence, however, fortunately for Nugent and his family, was its uneven distribution. While the revolutionary war was at its most intense in County Cork and Dublin city other parts of the country remained relatively peaceful, Cavan amongst them. This was despite the county's strong Sinn Fein leanings (in the general election of December 1918 the party took both Cavan seats unopposed), its sizeable Protestant/unionist population and its proximity to what would become

[22] ON to Alison, 25 Aug. 1920, in *Nugent*, p. 235.
[23] The number of deaths in the revolutionary period is disputed: see Andy Bielenberg, 'Fatalities in the Irish Revolution', in John Crowley, Donal O Drisceoil and Mike Murphy (eds), *Atlas of the Irish Revolution*, pp 752–61; Charles Townshend, *The British Campaign in Ireland 1919–1921: The Development of Political and Military Policies* (1975), p. 214; S. J. Connolly (ed.), *The Oxford Companion to Irish History* (2004), p. 17. In the 18 months from January 1919 to the end of June 1920, 55 police and five military had been killed; in the next 13 months more than 350 police (including Black and Tans and Auxiliaries) and 145 soldiers died. The Black and Tans were temporary constables, mainly recruited in Britain, while the RIC's Auxiliary Division was a paramilitary force mainly composed of ex-British army officers – see D. M. Leeson, *The Black and Tans: British Police and Auxiliaries in the Irish War of Independence, 1920–1921* (2011).

Northern Ireland, all factors which might have been thought to tend towards violence. Republican groups in two adjoining counties, Longford and Monaghan, were very active: Farren Connell lay less than ten miles from the operating area of Sean McEoin's energetic north Longford IRA brigade, and 15 miles from County Monaghan where Eoin O'Duffy and Dan Hogan's units became, following the death of Hogan's brother on Bloody Sunday, more aggressive in their attacks on both Crown forces and loyalists. Levels of violence in particular areas were influenced by various factors, including demography, local traditions of activism, the quality of IRA leadership, the efficiency of the RIC and army and the quiescence or otherwise of loyalists. Cavan was not exempt – there were at least nine conflict-related fatalities, including three police officers, between January 1919 and December 1921 – but, like a number of adjoining counties (Meath, Westmeath, Leitrim) it escaped relatively lightly.[24] Nugent was lucky that the revolutionary struggle was never as bitter in south Cavan as it was, say, in west Cork, where one of his former COs, John Peacocke, was shot dead at his home in June 1920 (accused by republicans of being part of a loyalist 'murder gang', a charge denied by his friends), or local affection might not have been enough to safeguard him or his family.[25]

There were anxious moments nonetheless. Writing in the 1950s, Kitty recalled that the family was 'given indirectly to understand that as long as he [Nugent], or any of his family were in the house, it would not be burned down'. She attributed this to the fact that her husband 'was much respected and loved in the neighbourhood', but also to 'his quick wit and imperturbability [which] saved his family, the Household and Home in a 'Tight Corner" on a number of occasions'.[26] His property did not, even so, escape unscathed. In May 1920 a crowd of about a hundred men, some armed, had gathered in Mountnugent to demolish the unmanned police barracks, the RIC by now having withdrawn to the larger towns, before

[24] Peter Hart, 'The geography of revolution in Ireland', in *The IRA at War 1916–1923* (2003), pp 30–61; David Fitzpatrick, 'The geography of the War of Independence', in Crowley, O Drisceoil and Murphy (eds), *Atlas of the Irish Revolution*, pp 534–43; Marie Coleman, *County Longford and the Irish Revolution 1910–1923* (2006), pp 148–78; Dooley, *Monaghan*, pp 73–100; Tim Wilson, 'The strange death of loyalist Monaghan', 1912–1921', in Senia Paseta (ed.), *Uncertain Futures: Essays about the Irish Past for Roy Foster* (2016), pp 174–87; Brian Hughes, *Defying the IRA? Intimidation, Coercion, and Communities during the Irish Revolution* (2016), p. 102.

[25] For Peacocke's death, see Gerard Murphy, *The Year of Disappearances: Political Killings in Cork, 1921–22* (2011), pp 224–31.

[26] CN's 'biography' of ON, 27 Feb. 1954 (PRONI, D3835/E/4/5/E/1).

moving on to the court house where they broke in the doors and windows and burned all the documents they could find (in October 1920 Nugent, who owned both buildings, received £600 compensation for the damage).[27] This was part of a concerted IRA campaign that summer to destroy unoccupied barracks and other government buildings, and from mid-1920 republican courts increasingly replaced British ones throughout the county. From August 1920 also a republican 'Belfast boycott', involving the often forcibly-enforced boycott of northern goods in retaliation for sectarian attacks against Catholics in Belfast, had a significant economic impact; it lasted until early 1922 and forced families like the Nugents, accustomed to purchasing many items from Belfast, to adjust their spending habits or do without.

By mid-1920 the unionists of Cavan, Monaghan and Donegal had already been politically defeated, an outcome made harder because it came at the hands of their fellow Ulster unionists. The Government of Ireland Bill of February 1920 had proposed two Irish parliaments, one for the six north-eastern counties and one for the rest of the country. Farnham led a rearguard action in the UUC to try to get the entire province of Ulster included within the jurisdiction of the northern parliament, but the proposal was decisively rejected by the other delegates: Sir James Stronge of Armagh, who had visited the Ulster Division in France in January 1916, wrote that 'the three counties have been thrown to the wolves with very little compunction'.[28] By late 1920 most Cavan unionists, Nugent amongst them, recognised the inevitability of accepting the authority of the Dublin parliament once established. The nature of that parliament was not yet agreed, however, and that autumn the IRA's intensified campaign for independence was matched by an increase in the reprisals, official and unofficial, carried out by state forces (and particularly by beleaguered RIC officers, regulars as well as Auxiliaries and Black and Tans).[29]

By the autumn of 1920 it was also clear how unrealistic had been Nugent's wartime hopes that shared service at the front might help bridge political divisions at home. A bitter sectarian conflict had been developing since the summer in the six north-eastern counties, especially Belfast, which inevitably involved many of Nugent's former comrades.[30] The UUC had reactivated the UVF in July 1920 but this was largely overtaken by the

---

[27] *Londonderry Sentinel*, 15 May 1920; statement by Comdt. Sean Sheridan (Irish Military Archives, Bureau of Military History, WS1613); *Belfast Newsletter*, 22 Oct. 1920.

[28] Bardon, *History of Ulster*, pp 477–8.

[29] Leeson, *Black and Tans*, pp 157–90.

[30] Bardon, *History of Ulster*, p. 494.

establishment that October in the six-county area of the Ulster Special Constabulary (USC), an official but overwhelmingly Protestant force which by July 1921 would comprise over 3,300 full-time 'A' Specials and almost 16,000 part-time 'B' Specials. They included significant numbers of former Ulster Division soldiers, with ex-officers prominent in leadership positions – Hacket Pain was an RIC divisional commissioner in Ulster until ill-health forced his retirement (he died in 1924); former 36th COs or acting COs holding USC county or battalion commands included Goodwin (12th Royal Irish Rifles), Macrory (10th Royal Inniskilling Fusiliers), McCallum (8th Royal Irish Rifles) and Montgomery (9th Royal Irish Rifles); at least six former officers of the 9th Royal Irish Fusiliers served in USC units in Armagh; Ambrose Ricardo joined the USC in Tyrone, but resigned in a dispute with the county commander over the use of B Specials in his area, which he regarded as counter-productive.[31] Far from being reconciled, Irish ex-servicemen, probably in their thousands, were now serving in republican, loyalist and state forces and employing their military experience, and often a ruthlessness learned at the front, against both each other and the civilian population. Other ex-servicemen, though not directly involved in 'combatant' organisations, were deliberately targeted by the IRA, though the extent to which their previous military service was the sole reason is contested.[32]

One of Nugent's former subordinates held a particularly high-profile security post. In August 1920 Frank Crozier was appointed to command the Auxiliary Division of the RIC (ADRIC), then in the process being formed. The Auxiliaries, composed largely of demobilised British wartime officers, were intended to reinforce, though in fact their behaviour often undermined, the regular RIC, and Crozier was involved in several contentious events, including Bloody Sunday. He came to public

[31] Sir Arthur Hezlet, *The 'B' Specials: A History of the Ulster Special Constabulary* (1997 edn), pp 79, 87; Metcalfe, *Blacker's Boys*, pp 407–85 (officers' biographies). A third category, 'C' Specials, were seldom used. Paucity of sources makes it difficult to be precise about the number of ex-Ulster Division personnel in the USC (Bowman, *Carson's Army*, pp 195–6).

[32] See Paul Taylor, *Heroes or Traitors? Experiences of Southern Irish Soldiers Returning from the Great War 1919–1939* (2015), pp 13–15, for a discussion of ex-servicemen's participation in the IRA and RIC, including the Black and Tans and ADRIC. For the targeting of ex-servicemen, see Taylor, *Heroes or Traitors*, pp 75–88; Jane Leonard, 'Getting them at last': The I.R.A. and Ex-Servicemen', in David Fitzpatrick (ed), *Revolution? Ireland 1917–1923* (1990), pp 118–29; Peter Hart, *The IRA and Its Enemies: Violence and Community in Cork, 1916–1923* (1998), p. 314.

prominence in February 1921 when he resigned over the reversal by his superior General Tudor (mastermind of the artillery plan at Cambrai) of his decision to sack 21 cadets for robbing a shop near Trim, County Meath. Crozier's attempt to impose discipline was laudable if badly overdue – there were far more serious charges against the ADRIC during his time in command than mere robbery – but the dismissal process had certainly been arbitrary. Some commentators, perhaps seeking to blacken his reputation, later questioned the motives for his abrupt resignation and pointed to significant financial irregularities within the ADRIC uncovered after his departure.[33] Crozier's resignation attracted considerable publicity, however, and he continued the controversy in his autobiography, in which he quoted Nugent specifically as having a low opinion of the Auxiliaries and Black and Tans – 'they should never have been let loose in this country; they are not gentlemen'.[34] And there is no doubt that Nugent disapproved of these undisciplined non-regular police. He had at least one direct run-in with them, probably in early 1921 when the police and military were conducting large-scale sweeps in Cavan, when he intervened to secure the release of a young man from the Mountnugent area. According to Kitty this was 'the son of a poor widow taken off by the "Black and Tans" under the eyes of his mother in her own cottage', and that it was only through Nugent's 'ceaseless demands' that he was released unharmed.[35]

The truce and the Civil War

In June 1921 the new Northern Ireland parliament was opened by the King in Belfast and in July a truce was declared between the British and republican forces. The hopes of Nugent and others that peace had arrived were, however, premature. The treaty between the British government and the Irish delegation led by Michael Collins was signed in December 1921 and the Irish Free State came into existence in January 1922. The deep divide this created between pro- and anti-treaty supporters would erupt into civil war in June 1922, but the first half of the year was dominated by intensifying violence in Northern Ireland. In Belfast 236 people were killed in the first six months of 1922 and thousands more were forced to flee their homes; there were cross-border attacks and kidnappings along much of the new frontier; and in May the IRA launched a 'northern offensive' to try to destabilise the new state. Many Nugent had served with were directly affected. Amongst the police fatalities in May, for example, was Special

[33] Messenger, *Broken Sword*, pp 127–58; Leeson, *Black and Tans*, p. 121.
[34] F. P. Crozier, *Ireland for Ever* (1932), p. 71.
[35] CN's 'biography' (PRONI, D3835/E/4/5/E/1).

Constable William McKnight, shot in an ambush in Tyrone, who had won the Military Medal as a 36th Division sapper, while a few days later Shane's Castle, the family home of Hugh O'Neill, formerly on his staff, was burnt by the IRA.[36]

In south Cavan as in the rest of the country the sense of threat remained oppressive. In January 1922 armed and masked men held up one of Nugent's estate workers and his hay barn was set alight, while a few weeks later a terrified Protestant spinster, intimidated off her farm, arrived at Farren Connell late at night seeking shelter (Nugent heard that 'the blackguards who have hunted Miss Hepenstal out boasted that they would now clear Thompsons of Ross and then do the same to me').[37] These actions were not, it seems, the work of mainstream republican groups: when Nugent received a threatening letter purporting to come from the local IRA commander – who, with the strange intimacy characteristic of conflicts such as this, was also his neighbour - he was assured by him that it had not.[38] Nevertheless, as the Free State spiralled towards civil war and with violence continuing in the north, Nugent's diary became a catalogue of atrocities. In March 1922 he noted the '[s]hocking murder of whole RC family in Belfast', in April '[t]he shocking murder of Protestants in Co. Cork, presumably reprisals for murders of RCs in Belfast', in June the 'terrible murders of Protestants near Newry' and also the assassination of Henry Wilson in London, which 'has horrified the civilized world'.[39] In March IRA members commandeered his car and later in the year armed men raided the house for weapons; 'the indignity of living under conditions where one is at the mercy of such people is intolerable', he complained.[40]

When Free State troops attacked anti-treaty forces in the Four Courts in Dublin in June Nugent hoped, wrongly, that the assertion of the Provisional Government's authority against what he termed the IRA

---

[36] Bardon, *History of Ulster*, pp 491–2; Richard Abbott, *Police Casualties in Ireland 1919–1922* (2000), p. 287. The Royal Ulster Constabulary was created in April 1922. For the IRA's northern campaign, see Robert Lynch, *The Northern IRA and the Early Years of Partition 1920–22* (2006).

[37] Diary, 9 Jan., 17 and 27 May 1922 (Nugent family papers).

[38] Diary 1 May 1922 (Nugent family papers).

[39] Ibid., 25 Mar., 29 Apr., 19, 23 and 25 June 1922. For the specific incidents Nugent recorded see Tim Wilson, "The most terrible assassination that has yet stained the name of Belfast': the McMahon murders in context', *Irish Historical Studies,* 37:145 (May 2010), pp 83–106; Hart, *The IRA and Its Enemies*, pp 273–92; Robert Lynch, 'Explaining the Altnaveigh Massacre', *Eire-Ireland*, 45:3&4 (Fall/Winter 2010), pp184–210; Jeffery, *Wilson*, pp 281–7.

[40] Diary, 27 Mar., 29 Sep. 1922 (Nugent family papers).

'mutineers' would soon lead to a restoration of order. He gave credit to Griffith and Collins for their decision to act, recognising that 'they surely take their lives in their hands': two months later he recorded the death of Michael Collins in an ambush in Cork. He was in no doubt that if the Provisional Government fell he and his family would have to leave Ireland, writing at one point that 'I think this is probably our last year here. I do not think it likely there will be any place for me in the new order when and if it comes'.[41] The fighting was accompanied by a sense of anarchy that felt even more dangerous than the War of Independence, not least for former loyalists. Of 275 big houses destroyed between 1920 and 1923 almost 200 were burned in this period, mostly in Munster, and others, especially if unoccupied, were looted.[42] In April 1922 Nugent visited the wrecked home of the Maxwell family near Mountnugent and reflected, 'terribly sad to see Arley as it is and to think of what it once was and will never be again. How soon will it be before F[arren] C[onnell] is in like mess'.[43] News of the unsettled conditions in Cavan triggered an emotional reaction from St George, still in India, who in July 1922 implored the family to flee Ireland. In a rather over-wrought letter to his father – he had been unwell, had fallen foul of an unsympathetic colonel and feared being sent home as medically unfit – he warned that Farren Connell was no longer safe and that he might on his return be trapped in a place

> with which I associate all that I love most, but where I can now neither shoot, nor boat, nor drive a car, where I see all those whom but a few short years ago we numbered amongst our nearest friends, openly hostile in look and action, where I see you, Mummy, myself and my sisters relentlessly insulted and disrespected by those who should bow the knee near the very ground you tread.[44]

Nugent, however, was determined to stay if he could, and with the ending of the Civil War in May 1923 some degree of normality returned. For former unionists, though, 'normality' now had to be recalibrated.

---

[41] Diary, 15 Apr., 28 June, 22 Aug. (Nugent family papers).
[42] The number of fatalities in the Civil War is uncertain but may have been around 1,500: Bielenberg, 'Fatalities in the Irish Revolution', pp 759–61; for the destruction of big houses see Dooley, *Decline of the Big House*, pp 171–207.
[43] Diary, 26 Apr. 1922 (Nugent family papers).
[44] St George to ON, 12 July 1922 (PRONI, D3835/E/6/71).

Welfare and commemoration

Nugent had, as soon as he returned from India, turned his energies to supporting those who had survived the Great War and commemorating those killed in it. In the same way that he had seen shared service as a potential force for reconciliation, he now hoped that an inclusive approach to remembrance might serve the same purpose. He consciously set out to challenge both the narrowly-focused Ulster Protestant memorialisation of the Ulster Division being built into the 'foundation myth' of the new northern state, and the ambivalent and often hostile attitude towards 'British' commemoration in the rest of the country.

He took a close interest in the welfare of ex-servicemen. In 1915 in France he had established the Ulster Divisional Fund to assist former members of the division and their families, funded by the proceeds of divisional social activities, including canteens, concerts and the divisional cinema. He remained a trustee of the fund, which opened for applications in February 1919, and by the time it closed in October 1922 over 5,000 applications had been received, 2,876 grants made and more than £17,500 disbursed.[45] He was also strongly supportive of William Hickie's work on behalf of ex-servicemen in the south: from 1925 Hickie was chair of the British Legion's Southern Ireland branch (BLSI), and his declared objectives for the BLSI – 'to foster comradeship, to look after those in need, and remember the fallen' – exactly mirrored Nugent's own views.[46] He arranged for Hickie to address the Ulster Division officers' dinner in Belfast in November 1925, where Hickie was very well received, and in his own speech Nugent took the opportunity to give his former officers 'a heart to heart talk on helping the British Legion by joining it and working for it'.[47]

On returning to Ireland in 1920 he had also been invited onto the committee overseeing the building of the Ulster Tower at Thiepval, where he found himself somewhat uncomfortably working alongside James Craig, now Northern Ireland's prime minister. (On the other hand, his involvement in the project led to a reconciliation between him and Wilfrid Spender, so much so that he occasionally stayed with the Spenders when visiting Belfast.) The idea of an Ulster Division memorial had first been suggested by Carson in November 1918 and its completion, funded by public – including UVF – donations, was sponsored by the UUC and thereafter by the Northern Ireland government.[48] There was, therefore, no

[45] 'Account of the work of the Ulster Division Fund' (PRONI, D3835/E/2/21/34A).
[46] Taylor, *Heroes or Traitors*, p. 236.
[47] Diary, 6 Nov. 1925 (PRONI, D3835/E/3/16).
[48] Catherine Switzer, *Ulster, Ireland and the Somme: War Memorials and the Somme* (2013), pp 80–108.

doubt of the political intention behind it, but ironically, when it came to the opening ceremony on 19 November 1921 – attended by hundreds of people, many of them veterans who had travelled from Ulster – neither Craig nor Carson could be present, both laid low by illness. Henry Wilson as CIGS led for the army, General Weygand represented the French government and Charles Craig spoke on behalf of his brother. Nugent's own involvement included giving a lecture on the 1 July attack at a hotel in Amiens the evening before the ceremony, planting a tree during it and following Wilson in the post-event speeches in Albert. In his remarks Nugent paid glowing tribute to the soldiers of the Ulster Division and identified Messines and March 1918 along with the Somme as their finest performances, but he also deliberately broadened the focus – the Ulster Tower, he reminded those present, 'was to the honour of all Ulster soldiers, although the ground was specially sacred to the memory of the 36th Division', and he recalled that his men had fought 'alongside their fellow Irishmen from the South in the 16th Division with whom their relations were always most harmonious, sharing together the triumph of Messines and the bitter disappointment of 16 August at Ypres'.[49] His speech, according to reports, was warmly applauded.

The other major memorial to the 36th Division, along with the Tower, was the divisional history, written by Cyril Falls and published in 1922. Widely recognised as one of the best of its kind, it was intended to be accessible to a wide readership, and while its timing meant that it too played a role in reinforcing the division's place in the Ulster unionist pantheon, it was notable for its balance, objectivity and lack of hyperbole.[50] Carson, Craig and Nugent were patrons and Nugent took a close interest in its preparation, spending several weeks going through the draft in detail (and even declaring himself '[s]omewhat disappointed in Falls' writing').[51] Plumer provided the foreword and in it paid particular tribute to Nugent: 'All who served under him will always hold him in affectionate remembrance', Plumer wrote, adding, in a more pointed reference than many would have realised, that 'all Ulstermen should realize that they owe him a debt of gratitude'.[52]

Nugent was also in demand to unveil or open war memorials, including public monuments (Belfast's York Road railway station in November 1921; Lisburn in April 1923; Virginia, County Cavan, in August 1923;

[49] *Weekly Telegraph*, 26 Nov. 1921.
[50] Timothy Bowman, 'Ireland and the First World War', in Alvin Jackson (ed.), *The Oxford Handbook of Modern Irish History* (2014), pp 606, 612–14.
[51] Diary, 30 June 1922 (Nugent family papers).
[52] Falls, *Ulster Division*, p. x.

Ballymena in November 1924), memorials in churches (Kells, County Meath, in May 1924; Ballymacarrett in east Belfast in March 1926) and a memorial institute, with a free library, reading and recreation rooms, in Limavady (March 1922). Some of these were large events: thousands attended the unveiling of the Lisburn memorial, for example. Nugent's speeches contained common themes, including, as one might expect, gratitude for the sacrifice of the dead – as he pointed out in Ballymena, 'he knew many of those whose names were commemorated on the memorial' – sympathy for the bereaved, praise for those who had volunteered and acknowledgement of whichever local battalion had served in the division. Another consistent message, as with his speech at the opening of the Ulster Tower, was inclusiveness and reconciliation. In Limavady in 1922 he expressed the hope that if the new institute 'helped to bring men of different aspirations and views together to hear each other's opinions it would do infinitely more good than any memorial stone could do … [happiness] was not to be found in any land in which mutual understanding of each other was absent, or in any land where those who should be one people were divided by fears and suspicions of one another' (the point about 'one people' was, of course, a politically-loaded one). In Virginia in 1923 he looked forward to the day 'when the memory of all those of our country who gave their lives for Civilization as we interpret it and in obedience to what they believed to be their duty will be honoured and perpetuated in every town and village in Ireland'. In 1924 he reminded those gathered in Ballymena 'that the loyal services given by Ulstermen were not confined to one creed or one denomination, but by Ulstermen of all creeds and denominations'.[53]

The Lisburn event in 1923 prompted some revealing comments from James Craig, who also spoke at the ceremony. He welcomed Nugent as 'a distinguished citizen of Southern Ireland', and asked him to convey to the Free State the message that Ulster was happy to welcome from the south those who wanted to associate with them 'for the common welfare of the country', and the hope that the north 'would be able to send distinguished Ulstermen into the Free State to be treated with the courtesy that Lisburn had accorded the great soldier whom they had there as a guest'.[54] At one level the message was conciliatory (and complimentary), but even allowing for their difficult relationship his emphasis on Nugent's status as an outsider was an odd way to describe the British general who had commanded Ulstermen in action for longer than anyone else; it was also a reminder,

[53] *Northern Whig*, 3 Mar. 1922; *Nugent*, p. 237; *Belfast Newsletter*, 12 Nov. 1924.
[54] *Belfast Newsletter*, 30 Apr. 1923.

whether intentional or not, to former Cavan unionists who had tried hard to be part of Northern Ireland that they were now citizens of a different state.

Commemorations in the south in the 1920s were still well attended despite the violence of the 1919–23 period, and for the main armistice event at College Green in Dublin in November 1924, marking the tenth anniversary of the outbreak of war, the crowds were very large – perhaps 20,000 veterans paraded through the city, watched by 50,000 or more spectators.[55] Nugent was in Ballymena unveiling the war memorial there, but Kitty attended the Dublin ceremony on his behalf and afterwards Hickie wrote to thank her and apologise for the difficulty she had had in getting to the (temporary) cenotaph – the numbers had been far greater than expected, he confessed, which 'should make people think'.[56] In November 1925, when Nugent and Hickie attended the opening of the war memorial in Drogheda by Sir Bryan Mahon, 400 former servicemen paraded to the cenotaph watched in respectful silence by hundreds of people (though Nugent was not entirely impressed – 'A badly organized ceremony', he noted sniffily, 'B[ryan] M[ahon] dirty as usual, was depressing and inaudible').[57] But the main armistice event in Dublin a few days later, held in St Stephen's Green and again massively attended, did not go to plan. The display of poppies and union jacks the previous year had not gone unnoticed. At 11am, as Hickie, Mahon and Nugent prepared to move forward to lay their wreaths, republican protestors threw smoke-bombs into the crowd and panic ensued. There were scuffles between ex-servicemen and the demonstrators until the police intervened, and Nugent wrote bitterly that night 'Some blackguards let off smoke bombs at beginning of 2 mins silence which absolutely destroyed the solemnity and the silence as women screamed and there was a mild panic. What a horrible people and what a Christianity. I didn't see a single priest at the commemoration'.[58] Yet the real point was how relatively rare this incident, which was widely condemned, actually was. Even the advent of the De Valera government in the 1930s did not immediately change attitudes towards public commemoration in the south, and it was not until Ireland's neutrality in the Second World War (when armistice day parades in Dublin

55 Jeffery, *Ireland and the Great War*, p. 118; Taylor, *Heroes or Traitors*, pp 212–19.
56 Hickie to ON, 13 Nov. [1924] (PRONI, D3835/E/13/1).
57 Diary, 5 Nov. 1925 (PRONI, D3835/E/3/16).
58 Diary, 11 Nov. 1925 (PRONI, D3835/E/3/16).

were banned) that 'both the state and national consciousness [became] even more distant from a British association and First World War commemoration'.[59]

Knighthood

In January 1922, 11 months after Haig stepped down from active command, Nugent had at last been knighted for his war services (Henry Wilson, still CIGS, told General Hutton 'I was really and truly glad to be able to help Oliver to get his well-deserved honour and I hope it will be some comfort to a gallant soldier').[60] The family were delighted and so were many others. The letters of congratulation that flooded in, however, deplored the delay and the reason for it. Ricardo criticised 'the dirty work that kept you out of a reward that everyone recognised was your due'; Hickie had 'always felt your bad treatment just as keenly as if it had been my own for we had very similar tasks and difficulties'; Harington thought it 'monstrous … that you had not received it years ago and your many friends all thought the same'. Plumer himself summed it up: 'It should have been given you long ago. It is a case of "better late than never" – and that is all that can be said'.[61]

Staying on

The position of former unionists in the Free State was, as historians have pointed out, much more benign than the fate of other minority communities, particularly in eastern Europe, closely associated with a predecessor regime now displaced by a nationalist successor.[62] One manifestation of this relatively favourable treatment was the over-representation in the Irish Senate of former unionists, including Nugent's fellow divisional commanders Hickie and Mahon, Hickie becoming quite close to the new head of government, William Cosgrave. (It is striking, in

---

[59] Taylor, *Heroes or Traitors*, p. 218; Jeffery, *Ireland and the Great War*, pp 125–6. The De Valera government continued until the late 1930s to provide funding for the creation of the Islandbridge Memorial Garden.

[60] Wilson to Hutton, 10 Jan. 1922, in *Nugent*, p. 236.

[61] Letters to ON from Ricardo, 2 Jan. 1922; Hickie, 3 Jan. 1922; Harington, 8 Jan. 1922; Plumer, 11 Jan. 1922, in *Nugent*, pp 239–41.

[62] Tim Wilson, 'Ghost provinces, mislaid minorities: the experience of Southern Ireland and Prussian Poland compared, 1918–23', *Irish Studies in International Affairs*, 13 (2002), pp 61–86; idem, *Frontiers of Violence: Conflict and Identity in Ulster and Upper Silesia, 1918–1922* (2010), *passim*; Bardon, *History of Ulster*, pp 495–6.

fact, that amongst southern ex-loyalists it was often military figures, like Nugent, Hickie, Mahon and Bryan Cooper – not a regular soldier but a veteran of Gallipoli – who were prominent in seeking an accommodation with the independent Irish state, often with the objective of helping their wartime comrades.)[63] Yet, even so, newly-independent Ireland could be a cold house for former unionists, including the old landlord class. While there is considerable debate over the cause of the 33% fall in the Protestant population of the 26 counties between 1911 and 1926, and on the balance between structural factors (economic emigration, declining fertility levels, wartime losses, the withdrawal of British troops and civil servants) and political ones (intimidation, discrimination, alienation from the developing Catholic ethos of the Free State), political factors certainly contributed.[64] The effect on Nugent's immediate social network amongst the Cavan gentry, though a small sample, gives some indication of the impact on a once dominant group. Taking the Nugents with the 13 other landed families mentioned most often in his correspondence who were still resident in the county after the Great War, four of the 14 had left Ireland permanently by 1926; a fifth, the Farnhams, moved to England in 1922 but returned in 1927. Of their residences, two were burned and three were wrecked by looters while vacant, two subsequently being demolished.[65]

These figures do not suggest a former ascendancy class happy with their lot or feeling entirely secure in the new state, but nor do they suggest anything like a systematic effort to drive them out. Most of them remained until at least the 1930s, as did many of Nugent's close friends in neighbouring counties, like the Napers in Meath, the Pakenhams in

---

[63] I am grateful to Jane Leonard for pointing out the similarities between some of Nugent's views and those of Bryan Cooper, who was a member of the Dail in the 1920s and 1930s.

[64] Robin Bury, *Buried Lives: The Protestants of Southern Ireland* (2017), pp 13–33; Fitzpatrick, *Descendancy*, pp 159–80; Andy Bielenberg, 'Southern Irish Protestant experiences of the Irish Revolution', in Crowley, O Driscoil and Murphy (eds), *Atlas of the Irish Revolution*, pp 770–80. For Cavan landed families in the post-1918 period, see Cherry, 'The structure, demise and legacy of landlordism in County Cavan, *c.* 1870–*c.* 1970', pp 471–6.

[65] The families considered here, in addition to the Nugents, include two branches each of the Burrowes, Clements and Maxwells: Farnham (Farnham), Saunderson (Castle Saunderson), Pratt (Cabra), Clements (Ashfield, Rathkenny), Sanderson (Cloverhill), Venables (Redhills), Maxwell (Fortland, Arley), Burrowes (Lismore, Stradone), Fane Vernon (Erne Hill), Sankey (Fort Frederick). The Saundersons, Burrowes, Maxwells and Fane Vernons left. Of the houses, Redhills and Stradone were burned and Castle Saunderson, Arley and Fortland looted. I am grateful to Dr Cherry for his assistance on various points relating to these families.

Westmeath and the Godleys in Leitrim. Cavan's former landed families were fortunate that they had been less aggressively targeted than their counterparts in other areas of the country and that they were part of a still substantial Protestant community from which to draw support. There were, nevertheless, difficulties for Nugent and his family, some financial, others the result of the often petty sectarian under-currents that were part of Irish life in this period. When, for example, in 1925 the local Catholic clergy declared a boycott of a jumble sale to raise funds for the Protestant parish church he noted in his diary, 'I suppose the Priests cannot help themselves, but their Church is surely intolerant'.[66] He had obviously reflected some of his concerns to Plumer, who wrote in April 1925: 'You do not give a very cheerful account of your life in Ireland just now, nor of the prospects for the future. We can only hope things may improve. You are setting a fine example by staying on in your home and I am sure exercising influence for good on other people around you'.[67] Yet in many respects life went on as before. Nugent took up farming with characteristic single-mindedness and was elected to the agricultural committee of the Royal Dublin Society; he remained a member of the Kildare Street Club (where in 1925 he proposed that women be admitted as associate members); and he was a delegate to the Church of Ireland's General Synod.[68] In February 1924 he sat beside W. B. Yeats at a dinner in Dublin, though unfortunately Ireland's greatest poet did not strike him 'as particularly interesting'.[69] In the 1925 elections he and Kitty, like generations of Cavan Protestants after them, voted for the Cumann na nGaedheal (later Fine Gael) candidate as their first preference; '[t]here was a Republican', he scarcely needed to note in his diary, 'for whom we did not vote'.[70] By the mid-1920s Nugent and his family were well on their way to becoming integrated into the southern Irish state, and his journey from unionist landlord to Free State farmer was complete.

Nugent's health had been fragile since the war, and at the end of 1925 he underwent a major prostate operation that weakened him further. In late May 1926 he caught a chill which developed into pneumonia and on 31 May he died at Farren Connell. He was buried in the small parish church in Mountnugent three days later; amongst the large number of mourners, in addition to Kitty, the girls (St George was in India) and the wider family, were Arthur Farnham, Lord Westmeath, William Hickie and representatives of the Ulster Division. A memorial service was held at the

---

[66] Diary, 1 May 1925 (PRONI, D3835/E/3/16).
[67] Plumer to ON, 13 Apr. [1925], in *Nugent*, p. 236.
[68] CN's 'biography' (PRONI, D3835/E/4/5/E/1).
[69] Diary, 12 Feb. 1924 (Nugent family papers).
[70] Diary, 11 Mar. 1925 (PRONI, D3835/E/3/16).

same time in St Anne's Cathedral Belfast, attended by several hundred people including many former comrades. Reflecting the political difficulties he wrestled with, no senior political member of the Northern Ireland government came, but R. D. Blackmore, the cabinet secretary, and Wilfrid Spender, now head of the northern finance department, were present.

Another tragedy befell the family in 1929, with the death from tuberculosis of St George, who had left the army and been working in the Middle East. Oliver Nugent's commitment to Farren Connell was, however, carried on by the rest of the family. Kitty lived on in the house until her death in 1970, while Alison ran the farm (other than a period after the Second World War when she lived in America with her husband, Harry Hirschberg); in 1974 Farren Connell was taken over by her nephew, Myles Stoney, son of Theffania and her husband Oliver Stoney. When on 1 July 2006 Alison, aged 97, wore her father's medals at a ceremony at Islandbridge in Dublin marking the ninetieth anniversary of the Somme – the first large-scale official commemoration of the Great War since the creation of the Irish Republic in 1949, at which President McAleese laid a wreath – it was also 80 years since Oliver Nugent's death, 110 since he heard of Ida Wiseman's demise, and 120 since he decided to go to India to try to save Farren Connell.[71] The home he had fought so hard to protect was still in the family's possession well into the twenty-first century.

[71] *Irish Times*, 3 July 2006.

11

Conclusion

Oliver Nugent's lifetime, as has been seen, coincided with the terminal decline of the Irish landed class. In 1860, when he was born, Irish landlords owned 90% of Irish land, controlled local government and dominated Irish parliamentary representation; by the time of his death in 1926, the bulk of their estates had been transferred, under varying degrees of compulsion, to their former tenants, their political power broken and their social influence, especially in the newly-independent Irish Free State, greatly diminished. Yet his military career, paradoxically, also coincided with a period when Irish officers, many from landed backgrounds, played a crucial role in British military affairs. He was a member of an extended generation of Irish officers born between 1860 and the early 1890s who would fill key command and staff appointments in the two world wars. They included Wilson, Gough, Godley, Bulfin, Harington, Hickie, Kiggell, Mahon, Maude and Montgomery-Massingberd in the First World War (as well as sailors like Beattie, de Robeck and Pakenham), and Brooke, Alexander, Auchinleck, Dill, Montgomery, Pile, O'Connor and Dorman-Smith in the Second. Around two-thirds of these officers came from landed families or their cadet branches and had joined the army between 1880 and 1909, just as their political and economic power was being systematically dismantled by the British government. Yet that process was managed, whether deliberately or not, in such a way that their commitment to military service was preserved, to the great benefit of the British state in the first half of the twentieth century. Indeed, the apotheosis of the Irish landed class's connection with the army arguably came in June 1944, with Brooke as CIGS, Montgomery commanding the allied ground forces in Normandy, Alexander leading the allied forces in Italy and Auchinleck commander-in-chief in India.[1]

---

[1] Perry, 'Landed class', pp 314–15, 331. Also in June 1944 John Dill was Senior British Representative on the Combined Chiefs of Staff in Washington, though he did not come from a landed background. For a discussion of the post-1922 Irish connection with the British military, see Steven O'Connor, *Irish Officers in the British Forces, 1922–45* (2014).

Nugent's own contribution was significant, although perhaps less than his abilities deserved. He commanded the Ulster Division for 945 days in France and Flanders, the longest period on active service by an Irish divisional commander in either world war.[2] He was a demanding leader, driving his men hard but always doing his best, through careful planning and attention to detail, to keep as many of them alive as he could. That was not always possible: of the 32,000 casualties the division suffered during the war almost 26,000, nearly 80%, were incurred under his command, and it was a burden that bore increasingly heavily on him because he cared deeply for 'his beloved Ulstermen', as Kitty described them.[3] Professionally he was a highly capable officer and the division earned an enviable reputation under him. Handling the political dimension of his role was more problematic. By the outbreak of the Great War he was already more an Irish than an Ulster unionist and his views hardened in 1916 after the UUC's abandonment, as he saw it, of Cavan. He made little effort to understand the perspective of the Ulster unionist leadership, his regard for Edward Carson notwithstanding, and James Craig never featured amongst his 'beloved' Ulstermen. But while Nugent's strong opinions were sometimes an impediment to political-military cooperation, at the same time he ensured that political considerations, whether in relation to appointments or anything else, were never allowed to influence his operational decisions. He earned the respect of the best British commander on the western front, Plumer, and had his relations with Haig been better he could undoubtedly have gone further. His friend Maurice Crum, writing after the war, summed up his strengths and weaknesses with unblinking honesty: 'I see it is a strain of intolerance that has handicapped you – but you can't have all the virtues and no failings – so why should you complain – you have done great things and come through critical times, and never with anything but honour'.[4]

---

[2] Allan Adair commanded the Guards Armoured Division for longer during the Second World War but only 11 months, in north-west Europe, was on operations.

[3] CN's 'biography' (PRONI, D3835/E/4/5/E/1).

[4] Maj. F. M. Crum to ON, 2 Jan. 1922 (PRONI, D3835/E/2/21/39).

Annex A: Order of Battle

1st July 1916

GOC: Maj.-Gen. O. S. W. Nugent
GSO1: Lt.-Col. C. O. Place
AA&QMG: Lt.-Col. L. J. Comyn

CRA: Brig.-Gen. H. J. Brock
153 Bde RFA
154 Bde RFA
172 Bde RFA
173 Bde RFA

107 Bde (Brig.-Gen. W. M. Withycombe)
8th Royal Irish Rifles (East Belfast)
9th Royal Irish Rifles (West Belfast)
10th Royal Irish Rifles (South Belfast)
15th Royal Irish Rifles (North Belfast)

108 Bde (Brig.-Gen. C. R. J. Griffith)
11th Royal Irish Rifles (South Antrim)
12th Royal Irish Rifles (Central Antrim)
13th Royal Irish Rifles (Down)
9th Royal Irish Fusiliers (Armagh, Monaghan & Cavan)

109 Bde (Brig.-Gen. R. J. Shuter)
9th Royal Inniskilling Fusiliers (Tyrone)
10th Royal Inniskilling Fusiliers (Derry)
11th Royal Inniskilling Fusiliers (Donegal & Fermanagh)
14th Royal Irish Rifles (Young Citizens Volunteers)

Pioneers: 16th Royal Irish Rifles (2nd Co. Down)
RE: 121st, 122nd, 150th Fd Coys
RAMC: 108th, 109th, 110th Fd Ambulances
MGC: 107th, 108th, 109th Bde MG Coys

21st March 1918

GOC: Maj.-Gen. O. S. W. Nugent
GSO1: Lt.-Col. C. O. Place
AA&QMG: Lt.-Col. S. H. Green

CRA: Brig.-Gen. H. J. Brock
153 Bde RFA
173 Bde RFA

107 Bde (Brig.-Gen. W. M. Withycombe)
1st Royal Irish Rifles
2nd Royal Irish Rifles
15th Royal Irish Rifles

108 Bde (Brig.-Gen. C. R. J. Griffith)
12th Royal Irish Rifles
1st Royal Irish Fusiliers
9th Royal Irish Fusiliers

109 Bde (Brig.-Gen. W. F. Hessey)
1st Royal Inniskilling Fusiliers
2nd Royal Inniskilling Fusiliers
9th Royal Inniskilling Fusiliers

Pioneers: 16th Royal Irish Rifles
RE: 121st, 122nd, 150th Fd Coys
RAMC: 108th, 109th, 110th Fd Ambulances
MGC: 36th Bn

Bibliography

1. Manuscript sources

Imperial War Museum
Godson Papers
Maxse Papers

National Archives, Kew
CAB45
WO33
WO95
WO163

National Library of Scotland
Haldane Papers

Private Collections
Hessey Papers
Nugent Papers

Public Record Office of Northern Ireland
Farnham Papers
Farren Connell (Nugent) Papers
Herdman Papers
Montgomery Papers
Perceval-Maxwell Papers
Spender Papers

2. Official publications and works of reference

Becke, Major A. F., *Order of Battle, Divisions: Part 3A & B. New Army Divisions* (London, 1938 and 1945).

Burke, Sir Bernard (rev. A. C. Fox-Davies), *A Genealogical and Heraldic History of the Landed Gentry of Ireland* (London, 1912).

Edmonds, Brigadier-General Sir James (editor in chief), *History of the Great War: Military Operations, France and Belgium* (London, 1922–48) [particularly 1915 (ii), 1916 (i), 1917 (ii) and (iii), and 1918 (i) and (ii)].

Evidence taken before the Disorders Inquiry Committee [Hunter Committee], *vol. I, Delhi* (1920).

Maurice, Major-General Sir Frederick, *History of the War in South Africa*, vol. I (London, 1906).

3. Biographies, Autobiographies, Memoirs and Published Papers

Atwood, Rodney, *The Life of Field Marshal Lord Roberts* (London, 2015).

Atwood, Rodney, *General Lord Rawlinson: From Tragedy to Triumph* (London, 2018).

Baker-Carr, C. D., *From Chauffeur to Brigadier* (London, 1930).

Baguley, Margaret (ed.), *World War I and the Question of Ulster: The correspondence of Lilian and Wilfrid Spender* (Dublin, 2009).

Baron, Nick, *The King of Karelia: Colonel P. J. Woods and the British Intervention in North Russia 1918–19* (London, 2007).

Barrow, General Sir George, *The Fire of Life* (London, 1942).

Beckett, Ian (ed.), *The Army and the Curragh Incident 1914* (London, 1986).

Beckett, Ian, *Johnnie Gough, VC. A Biography of Brigadier-General Sir John Gough, VC, KCB* (London, 1989).

Beckett, Ian, and Steven J. Corvi, *Haig's Generals* (Barnsley, 2006).

Bew, Paul, *John Redmond* (Dundalk, 1996).

Boff, Jonathan, *Haig's Enemy: Crown Prince Rupprecht and Germany's War on the Western Front* (Oxford, 2018).

Bowen, Elizabeth, *Bowen's Court* (London, 1942).

Churchill, Sir Winston, *My Early Life* (1930, repr. London, 1949).

Colvin, Ian, *The Life of Lord Carson*, 3 vols (London, 1934).

Crozier, F. P., *A Brass Hat in No Man's Land* (London, 1930).

Crozier, F. P., *Impressions and Recollections* (London, 1930).

Crozier, F. P., *Ireland For Ever* (London, 1932).

Crozier, F. P., *The Men I Killed* (London, 1937).

Crum, Major F. M., *Memoirs of a Rifleman Scout* (1950, repr. Barnsley, 2014).

Denman, Terence, *A Lonely Grave: The Life and Death of William Redmond* (Dublin, 1995).

Falls, Cyril, 'Contact with Troops: Commanders and Staff in the First World War', *Army Quarterly* 88:2 (1964), pp 173–80.

Farrar-Hockley, Anthony, *Goughie: The Life of General Sir Hubert Gough* (London, 1975).

Feilding, Rowland, *War Letters to a Wife: France & Flanders 1915–1919* (London, 1929).

Fingall, Elizabeth, Countess of, *Seventy Years Young* (1937, repr. Dublin, 1991).

Fleming, N. C., *The Marquess of Londonderry: Aristocracy, Power and Politics in Britain and Ireland* (London, 2005).

Godley, Alexander, *Life of an Irish Soldier* (London, 1939).

Godley, Ann (ed.), *Letters of Arthur, Lord Kilbracken GCB and General Sir Alexander Godley, GCB, KCMG, 1898–1932* (priv. publ., *c.* 1940).

Gough, Hubert, *The Fifth Army* (London, 1931).

Gwynn, Denis, *Life of John Redmond* (London, 1932).

Haldane, General Sir Aylmer, *A Soldier's Saga* (Edinburgh, 1948).

Hankey, Donald, *A Student in Arms* (New York, 1917).

Harris, J. P., *Douglas Haig and the First World War* (Cambridge, 2008).

Hyatt, A. M. J., *General Sir Arthur Currie: A Military Biography* (Toronto, 1987).

Jackson, Alvin, *Sir Edward Carson* (Dublin, 1993).

Jackson, Alvin, *Colonel Edward Saunderson: Land and Loyalty in Victorian Ireland* (Oxford, 1995).

James, Lawrence, *Imperial Warrior: The Life and Times of Field-Marshal Viscount Allenby, 1861–1936* (London, 1993).

Jeffery, Keith (ed.), *The Military Correspondence of Field Marshal Sir Henry Wilson 1918–1922* (London, 1985).

Jeffery, Keith, *Field Marshal Sir Henry Wilson: A Political Soldier* (Oxford, 2006).

Kochanski, Halik, *Sir Garnet Wolseley: Victorian Hero* (London, 1999).

Leask, Anthony, *Putty. From Tel-el-Kebir to Cambrai: The Life and Letters of Lieutenant General Sir William Pulteney* (Solihull, 2015).

Lucy, John, *There's a Devil in the Drum* (London, 1938).

MacFarland, Elaine, *'A Slashing Man of Action': The Life of Lieutenant-General Sir Aylmer Hunter-Weston MP* (Oxford, 2014).

Macready, Nevil, *Annals of an Active Life*, 2 vols (London, 1924).

Macrory, Patrick, *Days That Are Gone* (Limavady, 1983).

Maxwell, R. M. (ed.), *Villiers-Stuart Goes To War* (Edinburgh, 1990).

Messenger, Charles, *Broken Sword: The Tumultuous Life of General Frank Crozier 1879–1937* (Barnsley, 2013).

Norman, Terry (ed.), *Armageddon Road. A VC's Diary 1914–1916: Billy Congreve* (1982, repr. Barnsley, 2014).

Perry, Nicholas (ed.), *Major-General Oliver Nugent and the Ulster Division 1915–1918* (Stroud, 2007).

Powell, Geoffrey, *Plumer: The Soldiers' General. A Biography of Field-Marshal Viscount Plumer of Messines* (London, 1990).

Powell, John, *Haig's Tower of Strength: General Sir Edwin Bulfin – Ireland's Forgotten General* (Barnsley, 2018).

Prior, Robin and Trevor Wilson, *Command on the Western Front: The Military Career of Sir Henry Rawlinson 1914–18* (Oxford, 1992).

Reitz, Denys, *Trekking On* (London, 1933).

Richards, Frank, *Old Soldier Sahib* (London, 1936).

Robertson, Norah, *Crowned Harp* (Dublin, 1960).

Robertson, Field-Marshal Sir William Robertson, *From Private to Field-Marshal* (London, 1921).

Rogers, Major V. B., *An Autobiography* (priv. publ., 1965).

Serle, Geoffrey, *John Monash* (Melbourne, 1982).

Sheffield, Gary, *The Chief: Douglas Haig and the British Army* (London, 2011).

Sheffield, Gary, and John Bourne (eds), *Douglas Haig: War Diaries and Letters 1914–1918* (London, 2005).

Spiers, Edward M., *Haldane: An Army Reformer* (Edinburgh, 1980).

Thompson, Bill (ed.), *Morland – Great War Corps Commander* (Kibworth Beauchamp, 2015).

4. Unit and Formation Histories

6th Connaught Rangers Research Project, *The 6th Connaught Rangers: Belfast Nationalists and the Great War* (Belfast, 2011).

Berkeley, Reginald, *The History of the Rifle Brigade in the War of 1914–1918*, vol. 1 (London, 1927).

Bickersteth, Lieutenant-Colonel J. B., *History of the 6th Cavalry Brigade 1914–18* (London, n.d.).

Bond, Lieutenant-Colonel R. C., *The King's Own Yorkshire Light Infantry in the Great War* (London, 1929).

Burrowes, A. R., *The 1st Battalion the Faugh-a-Ballaghs in the Great War* (Aldershot, n.d.).

Canning, W. J., *Ballyshannon, Belcoo, Bertincourt: The History of the 11th Battalion the Inniskilling Fusiliers (Donegal & Fermanagh Volunteers) in World War One* (Antrim, 1996).

Canning, W. J., *A Wheen of Medals: The History of the 9th (Service) Bn The Royal Inniskilling Fusiliers (The Tyrones) in World War One* (Antrim, 2006).

Connelly, Mark, *Steady the Buffs! A Regiment, a Region, and the Great War* (Oxford, 2006).

Cunliffe, Marcus, *The Royal Irish Fusiliers 1793–1950* (London, 1952).

Denman, Terence, *Ireland's Unknown Soldiers: The 16th (Irish) Division in the Great War 1914–18* (Dublin, 1992).

Doherty, Richard, *The North Irish Horse: A Hundred Years of Service* (Staplehurst, 2002).

Falls, Cyril, *The History of the 36th (Ulster) Division* (Belfast, 1922).

Falls, Cyril, *The History of the First Seven Battalions the Royal Irish Rifles in the Great War* (Aldershot, 1925).

Farndale, General Sir Martin, *History of the Royal Regiment of Artillery: Western Front 1914–18* (London, 1986).

Fox, Frank, *The Royal Inniskilling Fusiliers in the World War* (London, 1928).

Fuller, Steven, *1st Bedfordshires. Part One: Mons to the Somme* (Hitchin, 2011).

Hare, Steuart, *The Annals of the King's Royal Rifle Corps*, vol. 4 (London, 1929) and vol. 5 (London 1932).

Inglefield, Captain V. E., *The History of the Twentieth (Light) Division* (London, 1921).

Liddell Hart, Captain B. H., *The Tanks*, 2 vols (London, 1959).

McCance, Captain S., *History of the Royal Munster Fusiliers*, vol. II (Aldershot, 1927).

Metcalfe, Nick, *Blacker's Boys. 9th (Service) Battalion, Princess Victoria's (Royal Irish Fusiliers) (County Armagh) and 9th (North Irish Horse) Battalion, Princess Victoria's (Royal Irish Fusiliers) 1914–1919* (Woodstock, 2012).

Mitchell, Gardiner, *"Three Cheers for the Derrys!": A History of the 10th Royal Inniskilling Fusiliers in the 1914–18 War* (Londonderry, 1991).

Moore, Stephen, *The Chocolate Soldiers: The Story of the Young Citizen Volunteers and 14th Royal Irish Rifles during the Great War* (Newtownards, 2016).

Orr, David, and David Truesdale, *'Ulster Will Fight …', Volume 2: The 36th (Ulster) Division from Formation to the Armistice* (Belfast, 2016).

[Samuels], API & DG, *With the Ulster Division in France: A Story of the 11th Battalion Royal Irish Rifles (South Antrim Volunteers) from Bordon to Thiepval* (Belfast, n.d. [*c.* 1918]).

Sandford, Stephen, *Neither Unionist Nor Nationalist: The 10th (Irish) Division in the Great War* (Sallins, 2015).

Smith, Leonard V., *Between Mutiny and Obedience: The Case of the French Fifth Infantry Division during World War 1* (Princeton, 1994).

Stevenson, Robert, *To Win the Battle: The 1st Australian Division in the Great War, 1914–1918* (Melbourne, 2013).

Tardif, Philip, *The North Irish Horse in the Great War* (Barnsley, 2015).

Taylor, James, *The 1st Royal Irish Rifles in the Great War* (Dublin, 2002).

Taylor, James, *The 2nd Royal Irish Rifles in the Great War* (Dublin, 2005).

The King's Royal Rifle Corps Chronicle (1927).

White, Stuart, *The Terrors: 16th (Pioneer) Battalion Royal Irish Rifles* (Belfast, 1996).

5. Secondary Works

Abbott, Richard, *Police Casualties in Ireland 1919–1922* (Cork, 2000).

Ashworth, Tony, *Trench Warfare 1914–18: The Live and Let Live System* (London, 1980).

Babington, Anthony, *The Devil to Pay: The Mutiny of the Connaught Rangers, India, July 1920* (London, 1991).

Bardon, Jonathan, *A History of Ulster* (Belfast, 1992).

Barker, Ralph, *A Brief History of the Royal Flying Corps in World War 1* (1995, repr. London, 2002).

Barnett, Correlli, *Britain and Her Army, 1509–1970* (London, 1970).

Bartlett, Thomas, and Keith Jeffery (eds), *A Military History of Ireland* (Cambridge, 1996).

Bartlett, Thomas, 'The Connaught Rangers Mutiny, India, July 1920', *History Ireland*, 6:1 (Spring 1998), pp 5–7.

Beach, Jim, 'Issued by the General Staff: doctrine writing at British GHQ, 1917–18', *War in History* 19:4 (2012), pp 464–91.

Beaumont, Joan, *Broken Nation: Australians in the Great War* (Crows Nest, NSW, 2013).

Beckett, Ian, *The Amateur Military Tradition 1558–1945* (Manchester, 1991).

Beckett, Ian, *The Great War 1914–1918* (Harlow, 2001).

Beckett, Ian, *A British Profession of Arms: The Politics of Command in the Late Victorian Army* (Oklahoma, 2018).

Beckett, Ian, Timothy Bowman and Mark Connelly, *The British Army and the First World War* (Cambridge, 2017).

Beckett, Ian, and Keith Simpson (eds), *A Nation in Arms: A Social Study of the British Army in the First World War* (Manchester, 1995).

Bence-Jones, Mark, *Twilight of the Ascendancy* (London, 1987).

Bennett, Will, *Absent-Minded Beggars: Yeomanry and Volunteers in the Boer War* (Barnsley, 1999).

Bew, Paul, *Ideology and the Irish Question* (Oxford, 1994).

Boff, Jonathan, *Winning and Losing on the Western Front: The British Third Army and the Defeat of Germany in 1918* (Cambridge, 2012).

Bond, Brian, *The Victorian Army and the Staff College, 1854–1914* (London, 1972).

Bond, Brian (ed.), *'Look to your Front': Studies in the First World War* (Spellmount, 1999).

Bourne, J. M., *Britain and the Great War 1914–1918* (London, 1989).

Bourne, J. M., *Who's Who in World War One* (London, 2001).

Bowen, Elizabeth, *Bowen's Court* (New York, 1942).

Bowman, Timothy, *Irish Regiments in the Great War: Discipline and Morale* (Manchester, 2003).

Bowman, Timothy, *Carson's Army: The Ulster Volunteer Force, 1910–22* (Manchester, 2007).

Bowman, Timothy, 'The Ulster Volunteer Force and the formation of the 36th (Ulster) Division', *Irish Historical Studies*, 32:128 (2001), pp 498–518.

Bowman, Timothy, and Mark Connelly, *The Edwardian Army: Recruiting, Training, and Deploying the British Army, 1902–1914* (Oxford, 2012).

Brown, Judith M., & Wm Roger Louis (eds), *The Oxford History of the British Empire, Vol. IV: The Twentieth Century* (Oxford, 1999).

Burke, Tom, *The 16th (Irish) and 36th (Ulster) Divisions at The Battle of Wijtschate-Messines Ridge, 7 June 1917* (Dublin, 2007).

Bury, Robin, *Buried Lives: The Protestants of Southern Ireland* (Dublin, 2017)

Butler, William, *The Irish Amateur Tradition in the British Army 1854–1992* (Manchester, 2016).

Callan, Patrick, 'Recruiting for the British Army in Ireland during the First World War', *Irish Sword*, XVII, 17:66 (1987), pp 42–56.

Chandler, David, and Ian Beckett (eds), *The Oxford Illustrated History of the British Army* (Oxford 1994).

Cherry, Jonathan, and Brendan Scott (eds), *Cavan: History and Society* (Dublin, 2014).

Coleman, Marie, *County Longford and the Irish Revolution 1910–1923* (Dublin, 2003).

Connolly, S. J., *The Oxford Companion to Irish History* (Oxford, 2004).

Conway, Stephen, *The British Isles and the War of American Independence* (Oxford, 2000).

Conway, Stephen, *War, State, and Society in Mid-Eighteenth-Century Britain and Ireland* (Oxford, 2006).

Cook, Tim, 'The Politics of Surrender: Canadian Soldiers and the Killing of Prisoners', *Journal of Military History*, 70:3 (2006), pp 637–65.

Corns, Cathryn, and John Hughes-Wilson, *Blindfold and Alone: British Military Executions in the Great War* (London, 2001).

Crowley, John, Donal O Drisceoil and Mike Murphy, *Atlas of the Irish Revolution* (Cork, 2017).

Delaney, Douglas E., and Serge Marc Durflinger (eds), *Capturing Hill 70: Canada's Forgotten Battle of the First World War* (Toronto, 2016).

Dooley, Terence, *The Decline of the Big House in Ireland* (Dublin, 2001).

Dooley, Terence, *The Irish Revolution 1912–23: Monaghan* (Dublin, 2017).

Dooley, Terence, 'The Organisation of Unionist Opposition to Home Rule in Counties Monaghan, Cavan and Donegal, 1885–1914', in *Clogher Record*, 16:1 (1997), pp 46–70.

Draper, Mario, 'Mutiny Under the Sun: The Connaught Rangers, India, 1920', *War in History*, 27:2 (2020), pp 203–23.

Duffy, Christopher, *Through German Eyes: The British and the Somme 1916* (London, 2006).

English, Richard, *Irish Freedom: The History of Nationalism in Ireland* (London, 2006).

Falls, Cyril, *The First World War* (London, 1960).

Farrar-Hockley, Anthony, *The Somme* (London, 1964).

Fergusson, Sir James, *The Curragh Incident* (London, 1964).

Fitzpatrick, David, *Politics and Irish Life 1913–1921* (Dublin, 1977).

Fitzpatrick, David, *Descendancy: Irish Protestant Histories since 1795* (Cambridge, 2014).

Fitzpatrick, David, 'The Logic of Collective Sacrifice: Ireland and the British Army 1914–1918', *Historical Journal*, 38:4 (1995), pp 1,017–30.

Fitzpatrick, David (ed.), *Ireland and the First World War* (Dublin, 1988).

Fitzpatrick, David (ed.), *Revolution? Ireland 1917–1923* (Dublin, 1990).

Foster, R. F., *Modern Ireland 1600–1972* (London, 1988).

Fox, Aimee, *Learning to Fight: Military Innovation and Change in the British Army, 1914–1918* (Cambridge, 2018).

Gillespie, Raymond (ed.), *Cavan: Essays in the History of an Irish County* (Dublin, 1995).

Gooch, John (ed.), *The Boer War: Direction, Experience and Image* (London, 2000).

Gray, Randal, *Kaiserschlacht* (London, 1991).

Grayson, Richard, *Belfast Boys: How Unionists and Nationalists Fought and Died Together in the First World War* (London, 2009).

Grayson, Richard, *Dublin's Great Wars: The First World War, the Easter Rising and the Irish Revolution* (Cambridge, 2018).

Grayson, Richard, 'Ireland's New Memory of the First World War: Forgotten Aspects of the Battle of Messines, June 1917', *British Journal for Military History*, 1:1 (Oct. 2014), pp 48–65.

Green, Andrew, *Writing the Great War: Sir James Edmonds and the Official Histories 1915–1948* (London, 2003).

Greenhalgh, Elizabeth, *The French Army and the First World War* (Cambridge, 2014).

Gregory, Adrian, and Senia Paseta (eds) *Ireland and the Great War: 'A War to Unite Us All'* (Manchester, 2002).

Griffith, Paddy, *Battle Tactics of the Western Front: The British Army's Art of Attack, 1916–18* (London, 1994).

Griffith, Paddy (ed.), *British Fighting Methods in the Great War* (London, 1996).

Hammond, Bryn, *Cambrai: The Myth of the First Great Tank Battle* (London, 2008).

Hart, Peter, *Somme Success: The Royal Flying Corps and the Battle of the Somme 1916* (Barnsley, 2001).

Hart, Peter, *The IRA and its Enemies: Violence and Community in Cork, 1916–1923* (Oxford, 1998).

Hart, Peter, *The IRA at War 1916–1923* (Oxford, 2003).

Harvey, Trevor, *An Army of Brigadiers: British Brigade Commanders at the Battle of Arras 1917* (Solihull, 2017).

Hayes, Geoffrey, Andrew Iarocci and Mike Berchthold (eds), *Vimy Ridge: A Canadian Reassessment* (Waterloo, Ontario, 2007).

Heinl, Robert Jr, *The Dictionary of Military and Naval Quotations* (Annapolis, 1966).

Hennessey, Thomas, *Dividing Ireland: World War 1 and Partition* (Abingdon, 1998).

Hezlet, Sir Arthur, *The 'B' Specials: A history of the Ulster Special Constabulary* (1972, repr. Belfast 1997).

Hodgkinson, Peter, *British Infantry Battalion Commanders in the First World War* (Farnham, 2015).

Holmes, Richard, *The Western Front* (London, 1999).

Holmes, Richard, *Tommy: The British Soldier on the Western Front 1914–1918* (London, 2004).

Horne, John (ed.), *Our War: Ireland and the Great War* (Dublin, 2008).

Houlding, J. A., *Fit for Service: The Training of the British Army, 1715–1795* (Oxford, 1981).

Hughes, Brian, *Defying the IRA? Intimidation, Coercion, and Communities During the Irish Revolution* (Liverpool, 2016).

Hughes, Colin, *Mametz: Lloyd George's Welsh Army at the Battle of the Somme* (Gerrards Cross, 1982).

Hughes, Matthew, and Matthew Seligmann (eds), *Leadership in Conflict 1914–1918* (Barnsley, 2000).

Jackson, Alvin (ed.), *The Oxford Handbook of Modern Irish History* (Oxford, 2014).

Jeffery, Keith, *The British army and the crisis of empire 1918–22* (Manchester, 1984).

Jeffery, Keith, *Ireland and the Great War* (Cambridge, 2000).

Jeffery, Keith, *1916: A Global History* (London, 2015).

Jeffrey, Keith (ed.), *'An Irish Empire'? Aspects of Ireland and the British Empire* (Manchester, 1996).

Jeffery, Keith, 'The Road to Asia, and the Grafton Hotel, Dublin: Ireland in the 'British World', *Irish Historical Studies*, 36:142 (Nov. 2008), pp 454–86.

Johnson, Matthew, 'Leading from the Front: The 'Service Members' in Parliament, the Armed Forces, and British Politics during the Great War', *English Historical Review*, 130: 544 (June 2013), pp 613–45.

Jones, Simon, *Underground Warfare 1914–1918* (Barnsley, 2010).

Jones, Spencer (ed.), *Courage Without Glory: The British Army on the Western Front 1915* (Solihull, 2015).

Judd, Denis and Keith Surridge, *The Boer War: A History* (London, 2002).

Kenny, Kevin (ed.), *Ireland and the British Empire* (Oxford, 2004).

Kershaw, Ian, *Making Friends with Hitler: Lord Londonderry and Britain's Road to War* (London, 2004).

King, Anthony, *Command: The Twenty-First Century General* (Cambridge, 2019).

Krause, Jonathen (ed.), *The Greater War: Other Combatants and Other Fronts, 1914–1918* (Basingstoke, 2014).

Kudaisya, Gyanesh, ''In Aid of Civil Power': The Colonial Army in Northern Ireland c1919–42', *Journal of Imperial and Commonwealth History*, 32:1 (Jan. 2004), pp 41–68.

Lee, John, *The Gas Attacks at Ypres 1915* (Barnsley, 2009).

Leeson, D. M., *The Black and Tans: British Police and Auxiliaries in the Irish War of Independence, 1920–1921* (Oxford, 2011).

Lloyd, Nick, *The Amritsar Massacre: The Untold Story of One Fateful Day* (London, 2011).

Lloyd, Nick, *Passchendaele: A New History* (London, 2017).

Lynch, Robert, *The Northern IRA and the Early Years of Partition 1920–22* (Newbridge, 2006).

Lynch, Robert, 'Explaining the Altnaveigh Massacre', *Eire-Ireland*, 45:3&4 (Fall/Winter 2010), pp 184–210.

MacDonald, Catriona M M and E W McFarland (eds), *Scotland and the Great War* (Edinburgh, 2014).

MacDonald, Lyn, *1915: The Death of Innocence* (London, 1993).

McCarthy, Chris, *The Somme: The Day-by-Day Account* (London, 1993).

McCarthy, Chris, *Passchendaele: The Day-by-Day Account* (London, 1995).

McCarthy, Pat, *The Redmonds and Waterford: A Political Dynasty 1891–1952* (Dublin, 2018).

McDowell, R. B., *Crisis and Decline: The Fate of the Southern Unionists* (Dublin, 1997).

McGreevy, Ronan, *Wherever the Firing Line Extends: Ireland and the Western Front* (Dublin, 2016).

McMahon, Deirdre (ed.), 'The Irish Settlement Meeting of the Unionist Party, 7 July 1916', *Analecta Hibernica*, 41 (2009), pp 203–70.

Mercer, Eric, 'For king, country and a shilling a day: Belfast recruiting patterns in the Great War', *History Ireland*, 11:4 (2003), pp 29–33.

Middlebrook, Martin, *The First Day on the Somme* (London, 1971).

Middlebrook, Martin, *The Kaiser's Battle* (London, 1978).

Mitchinson, K W, *Defending Albion: Britain's Home Army 1908–1919* (London, 2005).

Moore, William, *A Wood Called Bourlon: The Cover-up after Cambrai* (London, 1988).

Moreman, Tim, *The Army of India and the Development of Frontier Warfare, 1849–1947* (London, 1998).

Murphy, Gerard, *The Year of Disappearances: Political Killings in Cork 1921–1922* (Dublin, 2011).

Nasson, Bill, *The South African War 1899–1902* (London, 1999).

Nenadic, Stana, 'The Impact of the Military Profession on Highland Gentry Families, *c.* 1730–1830', *Scottish Historical Review*, 85:1 (2006), pp 75–99.

Nevill, Captain H. L., *North-West Frontier: British and Indian Army Campaigns on the North-West Frontier of India 1849–1908* (London, 1912).

Nugent, Brian, *A Guide to the 18th-Century Land Records in the Irish Registry of Deeds* (Corstown, 2012).

Nugent, Michael James, *A Long Week in March: The 36th (Ulster) Division in the German Spring Offensive, March 1918* (Warwick, 2019).

O'Connor, Steven, *Irish Officers in the British Forces, 1922–45* (Basingstoke, 2014).

O'Malley, Kate, 'Learning the Tricks of the Imperial Secession Trade: Irish and Indian Nationalism in the '30s and '40s', *History Ireland*, 18:4 (July/Aug. 2010), pp 32–5.

Orr Philip, *The Road to the Somme* (Belfast, 1987).

Pakenham, Thomas, *The Boer War* (London, 1979).

Paseta, Senia (ed.), *Uncertain Futures: Essays about the Irish Past for Roy Foster* (Oxford, 2016).

Passingham, Ian, *Pillars of Fire: The Battle of Messines Ridge, June 1917* (Stroud, 1998).

Pennell, Catriona, *A Kingdom United: Popular Responses to the Outbreak of the First World War in Britain and Ireland* (Oxford, 2012).

Perry, Nicholas, 'Nationality in the Irish Infantry Regiments in the First World War', *War and Society*, 12:1 (1994), pp 65–95.

Perry, Nicholas, 'General Nugent and the Ulster Division in the March 1918 Retreat', *Imperial War Museum Review*, 12 (1999), 4–17.

Perry, Nicholas, 'Journey's End: The Fight for the Ulster Division's Forward Zone, 21st March 1918', *Irish Sword*, 14:95 (2004), pp 65–80.

Perry, Nicholas, 'The Landed Irish Class and the British Army, 1850–1950', *War in History*, 18:3 (2011), pp 304–32.

Philpott, William, *Bloody Victory: The Sacrifice on the Somme and the Making of the Twentieth Century* (London, 2009).

Pollock, Sam, *Mutiny for the Cause: The Story of the Revolt of Ireland's "Devil's Own" in British India* (London, 1969).

Porter, Andrew (ed.), *The Oxford History of the British Empire, Volume III: The Nineteenth Century* (Oxford, 1999).

Prior, Robin and Trevor Wilson, *The Somme* (London, 2005).

Prior, Robin and Trevor Wilson, *Passchendaele: The Untold Story* (London, 1996).

Pugsley, Chris, *On the Fringe of Hell: New Zealanders and Military Discipline in the First World War* (Auckland, 1991).

Pugsley, Chris, *The ANZAC Experience: New Zealand, Australia and Empire in the First World War* (Auckland, 2004).

Putkowski, Julian, and Julian Sykes, *Shot at Dawn: Executions in World War One by authority of the British Army Act* (1989, repr. Barnsley, 2003).

Rawling Bill, *Surviving Trench Warfare: Technology and the Canadian Corps 1914–1918* (Toronto, 1992).

Reid, Colin, 'Stephen Gwynn and the Failure of Constitutional Nationalism in Ireland, 1919–21', *Historical Journal*, 53:3 (2010), pp 723–45.

Robbins, Simon, *British Generalship on the Western Front 1914–18* (London, 2005).

Robson, Bryan, *Crisis on the Frontier: The Third Afghan War and the Campaign in Waziristan 1919–20* (London, 2004).

Roe, Andrew, *Waging War in Waziristan: The British Struggle in the Land of Bin Laden, 1849–1947* (Lawrence, Kansas, 2010).

Samuels, Martin, *Command or Control: Command, Training and Tactics in the British and German Armies 1888–1918* (London, 1995).

Sayer, Derek, 'British Reaction to the Amritsar Massacre, 1919–1920', *Past and Present*, 131 (May 1991), pp 130–164.

Schofield, Victoria, *Every Rock, Every Hill: The Plain Tale of the North-West Frontier and Afghanistan* (London, 1984).

Seligmann, Matthew S. (ed.), *Military Intelligence from Germany 1906–14* (Stroud, 2004).

Sheffield, Gary, *Forgotten Victory. The First World War: Myths and Realities* (London, 2001).

Sheffield, Gary, *The Somme* (London, 2003).

Sheffield, Gary (ed.), *Leadership and Command: The Anglo-American Military Experience Since 1861* (London, 1997).

Sheffield, Gary, and Dan Todman (eds), *Command and Control on the Western Front* (Staplehurst, 2004).

Sheldon, Jack, *The German Army on the Somme 1914–1916* (Barnsley, 2006).

Sheldon, Jack, *The German Army at Passchendaele* (Barnsley, 2007).

Sheldon, Jack, *The German Army at Cambrai* (Barnsley, 2009).

Silvestri, Michael, '"The Sinn Fein of India": Irish Nationalism and the Policing of Revolutionary Terrorism in Bengal', *Journal of British Studies*, 39:4 (Oct. 2000), pp 454–86.

Silvestri, Michael, 'Nationalism, Empire and Memory: The Connaught Rangers Mutiny, June 1920', *History Ireland*, 18:4 (Aug. 2010), pp 26–9.

Simkins, Peter, *Kitchener's Army* (Manchester, 1988).

Simkins, Peter, *From the Somme to Victory: The British Army's Experience on the Western Front 1916–1918* (Barnsley, 2014).

Simon, Brian and Ian Bradley (eds), *The Victorian Public School* (Dublin, 1975).

Simpson, Andy, *Directing Operations: British Corps Command on the Western Front 1914–18* (Stroud, 2006).

Spiers, Edward, *The Late Victorian Army 1868–1902* (Manchester, 1992).

Stanley, Peter, *White Mutiny: British Military Culture in India 1825–1875* (London, 1998).

Stewart, A. T. Q., *The Ulster Crisis* (London, 1967).

Strachan, Hew, *The Politics of the British Army* (Oxford, 1997).

Strohn, Matthias (ed.), *The Battle of the Somme* (Oxford, 2016).

Stubbs, John, 'The Unionists and Ireland, 1914–18', *Historical Journal*, 33:4 (1990), pp 867–93.

Switzer, Catherine, *Ulster, Ireland and the Somme: War Memorials and the Somme* (Dublin, 2013).

Taylor, John A., *Deborah and the War of the Tanks* (Barnsley, 2016).

Taylor, Paul, *Heroes or Traitors? Experiences of Southern Irish Soldiers Returning from the Great War 1919–1939* (Liverpool, 2015).

Thomas, Martin, ''Paying the Butcher's Bill': Policing British Colonial Protest after 1918', *Crime, History and Societies*, 15:2 (2011), pp 55–76.

Townshend, Charles, *The British Campaign in Ireland 1919–1921: The Development of Political and Military Policies* (Oxford, 1975).

Townshend, Charles, *The Republic: The Fight for Irish Independence* (London, 2013).

Travers, Tim, *The Killing Ground: The British Army, the Western Front and the Emergence of Modern Warfare* (London, 1987).

Travers, Tim, *How the War was Won: Command and Technology in the British Army on the Western Front 1917–18* (London, 1992).

Tripodi, Christan, *Edge of Empire: The Political Officer and British Tribal Control on the North-West Frontier 1849–1947* (Farnham, 2011).

Turner, Alexander, *Cambrai 1917* (Oxford, 2007).

Turner, Alexander, *Messines* (Oxford, 2010).

Turner John, *British Politics and the Great War* (London, 1992).

Tyerman, Christopher, *A History of Harrow School 1324–1991* (Oxford, 2000).

Vaughan W. E., *Landlords and Tenants in Mid-Victorian Ireland* (Oxford, 1994).

Ward, Alan J., 'Lloyd George and the 1918 Irish conscription crisis', *Historical Journal*, 17:1 (1974), pp 107–29.

Watson, Alexander, *Enduring the Great War: Combat, Morale and Collapse in the German and British Armies 1914–18* (Cambridge, 2008).

Westlake, Ray, *The Territorials 1908–1914* (Barnsley, 2011).

Wilson, Tim, *Frontiers of Violence: Conflict and Identity in Ulster and Upper Silesia, 1918–1922* (Oxford, 2010).

Wilson, Tim, 'Ghost Provinces, Mislaid Minorities: The Experience of Southern Ireland and Prussian Poland Compared, 1918–23', *Irish Studies in International Affairs*, 13 (2002), pp 61–86.

Wilson, Tim, '"The most terrible assassination that has yet stained the name of Belfast": the McMahon murders in context', *Irish Historical Studies*, 37:145 (May 2010), pp 83–106.

Yong, Tan Tai, *The Garrison State: The Military, Government and Society in Colonial Punjab, 1849–1947* (New Delhi, 2005).

Zabecki, David T., *The German 1918 Offensives: A Case Study in the Operational Level of War* (Abingdon, 2006).

5. Theses

Cowan, Anthony, 'Genius for War? German Operational Command on the Western Front in Early 1917', PhD, King's College London (2016).

Harris, P M, 'The Men Who Planned the War: A Study of the Staff of the British Army on the Western Front 1914–1918', PhD, King's College London (2013).

Taylor, Michael, 'The History of 119 Infantry Brigade in the Great War with Special Reference to the Command of Brigadier-General Frank Percy Crozier', PhD, University of Birmingham (2016)

Thorpe, Tom, 'Military Group Cohesion in Territorial Force Infantry Battalions During the Great War and its Relationship to Their Morale and Military Task Performance', PhD, King's College London (2017).

Index

In the case of officers, both the rank held at the individual's first appearance in the text and that finally achieved are shown.

Abbeville, 251
Abercorn, Duchess of, 102
Ackroyd, George (Pte), 73
Afghan War, Third, 263
Afzul, Sher, 19
Ahern, William, 48–9
Albert, 202, 274
Aldershot, 3, 54, 80, 82, 85, 157, 201
Alexander, Harold (Field-Marshal Lord), 281
Allenby, Edmund (Capt, Field-Marshal Lord), 25, 61–4, 66, 74, 79, 89, 141, 145
Allenby, Lady, 89
Amiens, 86, 137, 251, 258, 274
Amritsar, 261–3, 264
Ancre, River, 86, 106–07, 111, 113–14, 116, 120–22, 128, 130–31, 169
Andechy, 246
Anglo-Celt, 45–9
Annandale, A. J. (2nd Lt), 100
Arras, 171, 172, 215
Asquith, Herbert, 42–3, 46, 66, 75, 157
Aubers Ridge, 57
Aubigny, 239–40, 242, 253
Auchinleck, Claude (Field-Marshal Sir), 281
Authuille Wood, 125, 132
Avre, River, 230, 246, 248, 249, 255

Bailleul, 57
Baker-Carr, C. D. (Col, Brig-Gen), 205
Ballymena, 275, 276
Ballymena Observer, 181
Barrow, George (Capt, Gen Sir), 23–5
Battery Valley, 124, 129
Bayley, P. F. (Capt), 70
Beattie, David (Admiral of the Fleet Lord), 281
Beaucourt (village and Redoubt), 113–14, 116, 122, 124
Beaulieu-sur-Fontaines, 241
Belfast, 46, 53, 82–3, 87, 90, 101–02, 105, 145, 158, 159, 160, 165, 167, 182, 200, 223, 268, 270–71, 273–5, 280
Belfast Corporation, 90, 223
Belfast Newsletter, 104, 158, 181, 221–2
Bell, Eric (Capt) VC, 129
Bellewaarde Ridge, 61–3
Belturbet, 47, 265
Berlancourt, 244

Bermuda, 35
Bernard, Herbert (Col), 89, 122, 154
Bernaville, 86
Biggar, Joe, 10
Birdwood, William (Gen Sir), 151
Birrell, Augustine, 105
Black Mountain, 15, 18
Blacker, Stewart (Lt-Col), 108, 136, 140, 144, 153–4, 156
Blackmore, R. D., 280
Blair Oliphant, Philip (Lt-Col), 190, 252
Blood, Bindon (Col, Gen Sir), 14, 21, 22
Blood, Charlotte, 14
Bloody Sunday (1920), 266, 267, 269
Bluff, The, 74
Boadicea Redoubt, 233
Boelke, Oswald (Capt), 116
Bombay, 12, 263
Bonar Law, Andrew, 75, 159
Bordon, 82
Boulogne, 57, 193
Bourlon (village, Hill), 204–05, 209, 211, 213–15
Bowen, Elizabeth, 2
Bowen, Francis (Lt-Col), 90, 154
Braithwaite, Walter (Capt, Gen Sir), 25, 205
Briody, Father, 10
British and Dominion armies
> *Army*
>> First, 61
>> Second, 55, 57, 74, 79, 142, 145–9, 169, 173–4, 176, 182, 186, 192, 255, 258
>> Third, 88–9, 127, 141, 195, 204–05, 221, 230
>> Fourth, 106, 111–12, 114, 118
>> Fifth, 182–3, 185–6, 192–3, 195, 227–8, 230, 235, 239, 241, 253, 255
> *Corps*
>> II, 57, 60, 185–6, 254
>> III, 88, 204, 218, 228, 235, 241
>> IV, 195, 204–05, 211–13
>> V, 61–2, 66, 142
>> VI, 66, 70, 77, 195
>> VII, 89, 216
>> VIII, 141
>> IX, 142, 145, 147, 163, 171, 173–4
>> X, 110–17, 123–6, 131–4, 173

XIII, 89
XIV, 89
XVIII, 227–9, 234–6, 241, 243
XIX, 182, 183, 186, 189, 191, 194, 236
II ANZAC, 167, 173, 178
Canadian, 151, 163

Division
2nd, 214–15
3rd, 59, 61–4, 68
3rd Cavalry, 244
4th, 86, 93, 97–9, 198
5th, 58
6th, 65, 75–6, 216
8th, 95, 257
9th, 57, 203
10th, 149
11th, 173, 176, 179
12th, 57, 216
14th, 12, 54, 55–80, 86, 228–9, 234,
239, 253
15th, 183–4, 193
16th (Irish), 83–4, 86, 99, 101, 112,
135, 145, 149, 160–61, 163–8,
173, 178, 181–2, 183, 184, 186,
188–9, 191–5, 198, 253, 274
17th, 95
19th, 112, 147, 173–4, 254
20th, 144, 216, 235, 237, 245
25th, 173, 198
29th, 113, 123, 199, 216
30th, 239–40, 246
32nd, 95, 107, 110–16, 121–7,
130–32, 174
36th (Ulster), vii–viii, 25, 34, 57, 58,
79–80, 81–4, 268, 273–4, 279, 282
composition and identity, 81–4,
143–5, 149–53, 157–62, 181,
223–4
organisation, 82, 106, 171–2,
197–9, 251–2
selection of senior officers, 86–94,
119, 153–7, 199–202, 252–3
discipline and morale, 95–101,
206–07, 219–20
relations with 16th (Irish)
Division, 163–8, 180–82,
193–5, 274
tactical training/development,
84–5, 94–5, 117–19, 168–71,
195–6, 227–8
operational planning, 110–17,
173–5, 183–4, 186–7, 204–05,
228–9
trench raids, 106–07, 146–8,
175–6, 203–04

offensive operations, (the Somme)
121–33; (Messines) 176–80;
(Third Ypres) 184–93;
(Cambrai) 208–14
defensive operations, (Cambrai)
215–19; (Spring 1918)
229–51, 254–5
casualties, 136, 140, 180, 193,
230, 248–9, 282
37th, 118, 155, 169
38th, 84, 142
39th, 142
40th, 157, 159, 211, 214
46th, 58
48th, 86
49th, 110, 113, 117, 124–5, 130–33
51st, 150, 205, 206–07, 209–11
55th, 183–4, 193, 216
56th, 205, 208
61st, 193, 216, 229
62nd, 205, 206, 208–11
63rd, 220
Wessex, 40
3rd Australian, 151
1st Canadian, 88
1st New Zealand, 95

Brigade
Guards
Hampshire (TF), 39–42, 55
3rd Cavalry, 48
6th Cavalry, 244
8, 154
12, 98–9
15 Reserve, 105, 170
41, 54, 55–80
42, 61–4
43, 67, 72–3, 76–7
49, 194
61, 235, 238–43, 245, 249
107, 83, 86–7, 89–90, 94, 97–100,
116–17, 122–4, 127, 129–30, 132,
137, 142–3, 170, 176, 180, 184–5,
187, 198–9, 206, 208–14, 237,
239–40, 243, 246, 248, 254
108, 83, 86, 90, 93, 94, 98, 116–17,
121, 130, 137, 144, 180, 185–9,
194, 198, 203, 206, 208–10, 212,
216, 229, 234, 237, 238, 240,
243–4, 246, 248, 250, 254–5, 256
109, 83, 86, 90, 94, 98, 116–17, 121,
130, 132, 137, 176, 180, 185–9,
205, 208–09, 216–20, 234, 237,
238–40, 246–7, 254
119, 157
146, 125, 127, 130–32

147, 125, 132
148, 125, 131–2
182, 216
1st Tank, 205
Royal Artillery:
   113th Army Bde RFA, 172
   153rd Bde RFA, 84, 172, 216
   154th Bde RFA, 84, 172
   172nd Bde RFA, 84, 172
   173rd Bde RFA, 84, 172, 205, 216
   1st/1st Territorial London, 84
Royal Engineers, 120, 127
Cavalry and infantry units:
   10th Hussars, 44
   18th Hussars, 28
   13th Imperial Yeomanry, 32
   29th Regt, 3
   104th Reg, 5
   Bedfordshire Regt, 1st Bn, 19, 93
   Berkshire Regt, 1st (Garrison)Bn, 261
   Black Watch, 7th Bn, 156
   Connaught Rangers:
      1st Bn, 264
      6th Bn, 165, 166–7, 181
   Dorset Regt, 2nd Bn, 107
   Duke of Cornwall's Light Infantry:
      6th Bn, 72
      7th Bn, 238
   Durham Light Infantry:
      2nd Bn, 52
      10th Bn, 67
   Essex Regt, 2nd Bn, 98
   Gordon Highlanders, 1st Bn, 20
   Hampshire Regt:
      4th Bn, 40
      5th Bn, 40
      6th Bn, 40, 42
      7th Bn, 40
   King's Own (Royal Lancaster Regt),
      1st Bn, 99
   King's Own Scottish Borderers,
      2nd Bn, 20
   King's Own Yorkshire Light Infantry:
      2nd Bn, 87
      1/4th Bn, 132
      1/5th Bn, 132
   King's Regt, 12th Bn
   King's Royal Rifle Corps (KRRC):
      1st Bn, 7–9, 14–23, 26–30
      2nd Bn, 38
      3rd Bn, 35, 263
      4th Bn, 11–14, 35, 37–9, 56
      7th Bn, 56, 65, 70–73
      8th Bn, 56, 58–9, 70–73
   King's Shropshire Light Infantry,
      5th Bn, 63

Lancashire Fusiliers, 2nd Bn, 37, 98
Oxfordshire & Buckinghamshire Light
   Infantry, 5th Bn, 64
North Irish Horse, 44, 141, 198, 203
North Staffordshire Regiment,
   1st Bn, 65
Princess Patricia's Canadian Light
   Infantry, 154
Rifle Brigade:
   7th Bn, 56, 61, 70–73
   8th Bn, 56, 65, 70–73, 75, 76–7
   9th Bn, 70–73
Royal Dublin Fusiliers, 2nd Bn, 28, 164
Royal Inniskilling Fusiliers:
   1st Bn, 223, 235–8, 251
   2nd Bn, 223–4, 229, 231–3, 235,
      251
   7th Bn, 188, 194
   9th Bn, 106–07, 116, 120–23,
      127, 154, 176, 178, 185, 188,
      208–09, 216–18, 223, 234,
      237, 239, 242, 252
   10th Bn, 82, 94, 95, 106–07,
      116, 119, 120–22, 154–5,
      176, 178, 185–6, 201–02,
      208–09, 217
   11th Bn, 94–5, 116, 119, 121,
      123, 147–8, 154, 176, 186–8,
      201, 208, 217–18
Royal Irish Fusiliers:
   1st Bn, 28, 198, 200–01,
      206–07, 214, 234–5,
      238, 244, 247–8
   7th/8th Bn, 194
   9th Bn, 82, 108–09, 116, 120,
      122, 133, 136, 140, 144,
      152–4, 166, 175–6, 186, 188,
      194, 198, 201, 203–04, 210,
      212, 223, 238, 244, 247–8
Royal Irish Regt, 2nd Bn, 194
Royal Irish Rifles:
   1st Bn, 223, 234–5, 239, 243
   2nd Bn, 144, 198, 199–200, 212,
      234, 239, 243, 251
   7th Bn, 198–9
   8th Bn (8th/9th Bn), 87, 89, 90,
      98, 116, 122, 154, 176, 184,
      198, 201, 212
   9th Bn, 82, 87, 89, 90, 97–8,
      99–100, 116, 122, 129, 132,
      147, 154, 157, 165, 176, 178,
      184, 186, 198–201, 234
   10th Bn, 87, 89, 97–8, 116, 118,
      122, 136, 154, 176, 178, 184,
      210

11th Bn (11/13th Bn), 83, 98–9, 116, 120–22, 154, 176, 179, 185, 188, 198, 251

12th Bn, 83, 90, 94, 97, 107, 116, 122, 133, 144, 154, 176, 179, 185–6, 210, 212, 223, 231–2, 235, 251

13th Bn, 86, 116, 120, 122, 154, 166, 175, 186, 188–9, 198

14th Bn (Young Citizens' Volunteers), 83, 90, 97–9, 116, 118, 120–21, 123, 137, 154–6, 159, 165, 169–70, 176, 178, 186, 188–9, 193, 199, 201, 208–09, 217, 219–20, 223

15th Bn, 87, 89, 90, 98, 99–100, 107, 116, 121–3, 154, 176, 178, 184, 201, 210, 212–13, 223, 231–3, 235, 251, 252

16th Bn, 128, 171

Royal Munster Fusiliers:
1st Bn, 178
2nd Bn, 5–7

Somerset Light Infantry, 7th Bn, 238

West Yorkshire Regt:
1/5th Bn, 131
1/7th Bn, 130–31, 133
1/8th Bn, 131

York & Lancaster Regt:
1/4th Bn, 132
1/5th Bn, 125

Entrenching Battalions:
21st, 223, 238–9, 251
22nd, 223, 251–2
23rd, 223, 251

Royal Flying Corps, 69, 115, 218

Tank Corps, 202, 205, 211

British Legion, 273

Brock, Henry (Brig-Gen), 93, 115, 253

Brooke, Alan (Field-Marshal Lord Alanbrooke), 265, 281

Brooke family, 7

Brooke, Victor (Maj), 265

Brouchy, 240, 242

Browne, Percy (Lt), 32

Bruce, George (Capt, Maj), 153, 156, 237, 239, 244, 253

Brush, George (Lt-Col), 119, 154

Bulfin, Edward (Gen Sir), 42, 281

Bull, George (Lt-Col, Brig-Gen), 90, 154

Bull Ring, 147

Bullecourt, 183

Buller, Redvers (Gen Sir), 22, 23–4, 27, 32

Burnand, N. G. (Lt-Col), 154

Burrowes family, 35

Butler, Harcourt (Sir), 262

Butler, Montagu, 4

Byng, Julian (Gen Sir), 41, 195, 204, 210–11

Calais, 66

Camberley, Staff College, 22, 25–6, 33, 54, 61, 91–2, 112, 161, 222, 262

Cambrai, 182, 197, 198, 204–22

Cambridge, Duke of, 22, 37

Campbell, Guy (Maj), 202, 248

Capper, Thomas (Capt, Maj-Gen Sir), 25

Carleton, F. R. C. (Lt-Col), 31

Carson, Edward, vii, 46, 49, 50, 52, 84, 92, 101–02, 103–05, 108–09, 137–9, 141, 144, 149–50, 181–2, 195, 202–03, 255, 262, 273–4, 282

Carson, Lady, 92, 158, 160, 165, 257

Cather, Geoffrey (Lt) VC, 133

Cavan, County, 1, 8–9, 26, 34–6, 42–50, 67, 81, 83, 105–06, 108–09, 139–40, 256, 265, 266–8, 270–72, 278–80, 282

Cavan, Lord (Lt-Gen), 89

Cavan militia, 5

Cavan Volunteer Force (CVF, Cavan Volunteers), 34, 43–50, 55, 82, 187

Ceannt, Eamonn, 107

Chakrata, 13, 38

Charteris, John (Brig-Gen), 224

Cheape, Gerald (Lt-Col, Brig-Gen), 155–6, 189, 199, 220

Chichester, Robert (Lt-Col), 90

Childers, Hugh, 5

Chitral campaign, 19–21, 23

Churchill, Winston, 5, 22, 32, 75

Chute, Pierce (Lt-Col), 89

Clairfaye Farm, 117

Clery, Francis (Maj-Gen Sir), 32

Cochrane, J. K. (Brig-Gen), 235, 237, 242, 244–5, 249

Cockburn, George (Brig-Gen), 56, 76–7

Cocks, Archibald, 52

Coffin, Clifford (Maj-Gen) VC, 256

Colbert, Con, 107

Colchester, 35, 37

Cole-Hamilton, Claud (Lt-Col), 185, 201, 210, 232

Collins, Michael, 270, 272

Colvin, Amy, 14

Colvin, Auckland (Sir), 14

j298

Comyn, Lewis (Lt-Col, Col), 92–3, 115, 165, 202

Congreve, Billy (Maj) VC, 68

Congreve, Walter (Maj-Gen, Lt-Gen Sir) VC, 75–6, 89

Contescourt, 234
Cooper, Bryan (Maj), 278
Cork city, 11, 107, 198, 266
Cork, County, 266-7, 271-2
Cosgrave, William, 277
Couchman, George (Brig–Gen), 83, 86–7
Couillet valley, 216
Couper, Victor (Maj-Gen Sir), 56, 59, 61–3, 64, 66, 70–74, 76–7, 79
Courtrai, 258
Cowans, John (Lt-Gen, Gen Sir), 41, 88
Craig, Charles, 83, 138, 274
Craig, James, vii, 31, 81, 83–4, 101, 108–09, 138–9, 141, 158–60, 181, 273–5, 282
Cramer, Charles (Lt-Col), 16
Croydon, 84
Crozat canal, 235–6, 238–9
Crozier, Frank Percy (Lt-Col, Brig-Gen), 90, 95, 97–8, 100–01, 122, 132, 154, 157, 159, 200, 214, 220, 269–70
Crozier, James (Pte), 99–100
Crum, Maurice (Lt, Maj), 30, 56, 59, 72, 282
Cugny, 239–40
Cumann na nGaedheal, 279
Curragh, The, 34, 48, 89
Currie, Arthur (Gen Sir), 151, 168

Daly, Dr, 30
Daly, James (Pte), 264
Dawson, R. (Maj-Gen), 142
De Falbe, V. W. (Lt-Col), 65
De Robeck, John (Adm Sir), 281
De Valera, Eamon, 182, 276
De Wind, Edmund (2nd Lt) VC, 232
Defence of the Realm Act (DORA), 51–2
Delhi, 260–62
Demicourt, 216
Desborough, Lord, 75
Devlin, Joe, 108
Dill, John (Field-Marshal Sir), 281
Dillon, John, 256
Donegal, County, 43, 83, 108, 140, 268
Dorman-Smith, Eric (Brig), 281
Douglas, Charles (Gen Sir), 41
Doullens, 172
Drake-Brockman, D H (Brig-Gen), 261–2
Dranoutre, 175
Drogheda, 276
Drummond, Freddie (Capt), 202, 242, 253
Du Toit, Lt, 30
Dublin, 7, 34, 42, 49, 105, 158, 163, 266, 268, 271, 276, 279, 280
Dudgeon, Frederick (Maj-Gen), 205
Duke, H. E., 255

Dundee, Natal, 27–30
Durban, 26–7
Durband, 14, 15,
Dyer, Reginald (Capt, Brig-Gen), 25, 262

Easter Rising, 103, 105–06
Eaucourt, 242
economics of soldiering, 7–12, 36
Edmonds, James (Capt, Brig-Gen Sir), 25, 126, 236–7, 249
Elles, Edmond (Maj-Gen, Lt-Gen Sir), 15–16
Elwes, Henry (Lt-Col), 201
Emerson, James (2nd Lt) VC, 217
Epehy, 216
Erches, 246–8, 253
Essigny, 228, 234
Estouilles, 236
Eton, 4, 5

Falls, Cyril (Lt, Capt), 81, 93, 95, 112, 120, 136–7, 142, 146, 148, 180, 184, 186, 205, 213, 235, 240, 243, 245, 246, 274
Fane Vernon, Humphrey (Sub-Lt), 265
Farnham family, 43, 278
Farnham Lady, 91, 234
Farnham, Lord (10th Baron), 9
Farnham, Lord (Arthur Maxwell, 11th Baron), 35, 43–5, 47, 83, 91, 94–5, 98, 108, 141, 165, 192, 200–01, 208, 224, 229–34, 236, 253, 268, 279
Farrar-Hockley, Anthony (Gen Sir), 126
Farren Connell, 1–4, 8, 9–12, 18, 23, 24, 26, 35–6, 42, 49, 51, 67–8, 106, 261, 267, 271–2, 279–80
Feetham, Edward (Maj-Gen), 225
Feilding, Rowland (Lt-Col), 167, 181
Fergusson, Charles (Lt-Gen Sir), 58, 59
Ferrier, James (Maj-Gen), 54
Festubert, 57
Fingall, Lady, 265–6
Flesselles, 86
Flesquieres, 206
Foch, Ferdinand (Marshal), 74, 258, 261
Fontaine, 205, 209–11
Ford-Hutchinson, George (Lt-Col), 89–90
Fortescue, Sandie (Brig-Gen), 56
Fowler, John (Capt, Lt-Gen Sir), 25
French army:
  - 10th Div, 241
  - 62nd Div, 243–5
  - 20th Artillery Regt, 117
French, John (Field-Marshal Lord Ypres), 5, 37, 78, 256

Freniches, 239–42
Frezenberg, 183
Furse, William (Capt, Lt-Gen Sir), 25

Gaffikin, George (Maj), 129
Galbraith, Dr, 30
Gallipoli (Dardanelles), 19, 57, 67, 265, 278
Gandhi, Mahatma, 261–3
Gardner, Pte, 20
General Synod (Church of Ireland), 279
George V (the King), 37, 49, 77, 85, 103, 137, 145, 270
German army
    18th Army, 230
    XIV Reserve Corps, 131
    1st Bavarian Div, 232, 240, 243
    3rd Bavarian Div, 178
    5th Bavarian Div, 187, 189
    5th Guards Div, 238–40
    9th Reserve Div, 216
    10th Div, 239–40
    12th Reserve Div, 189
    20th Div, 209
    20th Landwehr Div, 208
    21st Reserve Div, 212
    23rd Div, 239
    26th Reserve Div, 128, 131
    28th Div, 246–7
    36th Div, 232–3, 243
    40th (Saxon) Div, 176
    45th Reserve Div, 232
    53rd Reserve Div, 70
    54th Div, 206
    206th Div, 246–7
    214th Div, 209–10
    238th Div, 232–3
Ginchy, 149
Givenchy, 61, 63
Godley, Alexander (Lt-Gen Sir), 167
Godley family, 35, 279
Godson, E. A. (Capt), 189, 212
Goodman, H. R. (Lt-Col), 200–01
Goodwin, William (Lt-Col), 269
Gordon, Francis (Lt-Col), 90, 154, 200
Goring-Jones, M. D.(Brig-Gen), 130–31
Gough, Hubert (Brig-Gen, Gen Sir), 48, 139, 142, 169, 182–7, 189–92, 196, 220, 222, 235–6, 251, 255, 281
Graincourt, 209–10
Grandcourt, 124, 128–9
Green, S. H. (Maj, Lt-Col), 202
Green, 'Verdant' (Lt-Col), 56, 59, 69
Greenly, Walter (Brig-Gen, Maj-Gen), 89
Grenfell, Billy (2nd Lt), 75

Grenfell, Julian (Capt), 75
Griffith, Arthur, 256, 272
Griffith, Charles (Brig-Gen), 93–4, 189, 229, 234, 246–7, 250, 253
Grimsby, 50, 52
Guerbigny, 245, 247
Guillemont, 149
Gunning, Mrs, 27
Gunning, Robert (Lt-Col), 26, 28–9
Gwynn, Stephen, 165–7
Gwynne, Howell, 138

Hacket Pain, William (Brig-Gen), 83, 93, 119, 152, 170, 269
Haig, Douglas (Capt, Field-Marshal Lord), vii, 24–5, 53, 74, 99–100, 111, 115, 119, 135, 151, 160–62, 172–5, 180, 182–3, 185, 191, 193, 204, 210–11, 216, 222, 224–5, 245, 253, 257–8, 277, 282
Haking, Richard (Capt, Lt-Gen Sir), 25
Haldane, Aylmer (Capt, Gen Sir), 31, 62–3, 66, 68, 74–6
Haldane, Richard, 37–8
Halifax, Nova Scotia, 4
Hall, A. H. (Maj), 232
Ham, 228, 236, 238–9, 242
Hamilton, Ian (Col, Gen Sir), 19, 32, 41
Hamilton Gordon, Alexander (Lt-Gen Sir), 145, 161, 173, 175, 179, 182, 196, 222
Hankey, Donald (Cpl, 2nd Lt), 72–3
Hannay, Canon, 4
Hare, Steuart (Capt, Maj-Gen Sir), 42
Harington, Charles ('Tim') (Maj-Gen, Gen Sir), 79, 145, 173–4, 196, 222, 277, 281
Harper, George (Maj-Gen, Lt-Gen Sir), 205, 225
Harrow school, 4–5
Hartlepool, 53
Havrincourt, 203–04, 206–07
Hawker, Lanoe (Maj) VC, 69
Hazara, 14
Head, Maj, 44
Headfort, Lord, 11
Hedauville, 115
Henderson, G. F. R. (Col), 25–6
Heneker, William (Maj-Gen, Gen Sir), 95
Henry, Robin (Lt), 202
Hepenstal, Miss, 271
Heriot-Maitland, George (Lt-Col), 56
Hessey, William (Lt-Col, Brig-Gen), vii, 119, 156, 223, 242, 244, 246–8, 250, 252–3, 257
Heuston, Sean, 107
Hickie, William (Maj-Gen Sir), 84, 112, 152, 160, 163, 166, 175, 189–92, 222, 273, 276, 277–8, 279, 281

Hickman, Thomas (Brig-Gen), 83, 119
Hirschberg, Harry, 280
Hodgson, G. C. S. (Maj), 240–41
Hogan, Dan, 267
Home Rule, 10–11, 42–9, 79, 101, 108–09,
    139–40, 164–6, 168, 227, 255–6
Hooge, 67, 68–77, 127, 185, 186, 202, 253
Hull, 50–53, 54
Hull Daily Mail, 53
Hunter Committee, 261–2
Hunter-Weston, Aylmer (Capt, Gen Sir), 25,
    141
Hutton, Edward (Lt-Gen Sir), 74, 77–8, 95–6,
    97, 222, 277

Incledon-Webber, Adrian (Lt-Col, Brig-Gen),
    200–01
Indian army
    Meerut Division (United
        Provinces), 258, 260–64
    7th (Meerut) Division, 260
    Brigades
        Agra, 260
        Bareilly, 260
        Delhi, 260–61
        Garwhal, 260
    Regiments
        2nd Bengal European, 5
        37th Dogras, 19
        Guides Infantry, 20
        5th Gurkha Rifles, 17
        1st Punjab Infantry, 17
        2nd Punjab Infantry, 17
        3rd Sikhs, 17
        15th Sikhs, 19
Indian National Congress, 260
Indus, River, 14
Irish Civil War, 36, 259, 270–72
Irish Convention, 163, 168
Irish Free State, 259, 270–71, 275, 277–80, 281
Irish landed class and the British army, 2–3, 7–9,
    36, 265, 281–2
Irish Parliamentary Party, 42, 256
Irish (National) Volunteers, 43, 45, 49–50, 83,
    104
Irish Republican Army (IRA), 264, 266–71
Irish War of Independence, 36, 259, 265–70, 272
Irish Women's Association, 102
Irles, 128
Islandbridge, 280

Jackson, L. C. (Lt-Col), 112
James, Walter (Capt), 22–3

Jeanne D'Arc Redoubt, 232
Jeudwine, Hugh (Maj-Gen, Gen Sir), 184
Joffre, Joseph (Marshal), 104, 111
Johnston, R. H., 47
Jullundur, 264
Jussy, 238

Keir, John (Lt-Gen Sir), 41, 70–71, 73–4, 77,
    79, 145
Kells, Co. Meath, 275
Kelly, James (Col), 19
Kelly, Philip (Lt-Col), 201
Kemmel Hill, 58, 175, 177, 254, 256
Kent, Thomas, 107
Ker-Smiley, Peter (Maj), 83, 91, 99
Khilafat movement, 263
Kiggell, Launcelot (Maj-Gen, Lt-Gen Sir), 41,
    119, 224, 281
Kildare Street Club, 279
Kilmichael ambush, 266
Kilmorey, Lord, 11
King, William (Lt-Col), 175
Kinloch, Alexander (Lt-Col, Brig-Gen), 13, 19,
    21
Kitchener, Lord (Field-Marshal), 54, 66, 75, 78,
    85, 86, 265
Knott, John (Maj, Lt-Col), 187, 201, 218
Knox, Cecil (2nd Lt) VC, 236
Knox, John (Maj, Lt-Col), 201
Kohat, 15–16

La Vacquerie, 216
Ladysmith, 26–7
Land Act 1903 (Wyndham Act), 35–6
Land League, 10
Langemarck, 196, 201, 205, 219–20, 255, 265
Lansdowne, Lord, 14
Larne Times, 253–4
Lawrence, Herbert (Lt-Gen Sir), 225
Lees, Elliott (Sir), 26, 32
Lees, Thomas (Sir), 67
Lees, Thomas Evans, 26
Leigh, Mr, 17
Leitrim, Lady, 102
Leitrim, Lord, 83, 102, 108
Lennox Hill, 27–8
Leslie family, 43
Leslie, Norman (Capt), 265
Limavady, 275
Lindley, 31
Lisburn, 274–6
Litton, Richard, 3

Lloyd, E. H. (Lt-Col), 154
Lloyd George, David, vii, 84, 108–09, 141,
    149–50, 152, 157, 255
Lockhart, William (Maj-Gen, Gen Sir), 16–18,
    22
Londonderry family, 7
Londonderry, Lady, Edith, 88
Londonderry, Lady, Theresa, 88
Londonderry, Lord, 88
Longford, Lord (Brig-Gen), 31, 265
Loos, 57, 98
Lord, John, 9
Low, Robert (Gen Sir), 19–21
Lucas-Clements, Shuckburgh (Lt-Col), 206, 214
Lucy, John (Capt), 198
Ludendorff, Gen, 242, 254
Lyle, Hugh (Lt-Col), 89–90
Lynch, Peter, 49
Lynden-Bell, Arthur (Capt, Lt-Gen Sir), 25
Lys, River, 227, 254, 256

M'Fadzean, William (Pte) VC, 120
MacDonnell, Lady, 102
MacDonnell, Lord, 46–7
Macdonogh, George (Capt, Lt-Gen Sir), 25
Mackenzie, Colin (Capt, Maj-Gen Sir), 25
Maclachlan, Ronnie (Lt-Col), 56, 65, 71, 75
Macready, Nevil (Gen Sir), 105, 149–50, 152
Macrory, Francis (Maj, Lt-Col), 94, 120, 154–5,
    185, 201–02, 269
Madden family, 43
Mahon, Bryan (Gen Sir), 5, 276, 277–8, 281
Malakand Pass, 19–21, 22
Malcolm, Neil (Maj-Gen Sir), 187, 196
Mallin, Michael, 107
Malta, 3, 5–7, 10
Manchester Guardian, 45–7
Marcoing, 204, 216–17
Margot, Gen, 245
Markham, Charles (Lt, Brig-Gen), 12, 56, 63
Marlborough, Duke of, 32
Martinsart, 120
Maude, Stanley (Gen Sir), 281
Maxse, Ivor (Lt-Gen Sir), 228–9, 230, 236–7,
    242, 246, 248, 250
Maxwell family, 35, 272
McAleese, President, 280
McCall, Henry (Lt-Col), 20–21
McCallum, J. D. M. (Maj), 201, 269
McCalmont, Hugh (Lt-Col, Brig-Gen), 83, 90
McCarthy-O'Leary, H. W. D. (Lt-Col), 243
McCracken, James (Pte), 99–100
McEoin, Sean, 267
McKnight, William (S/Con), 270–71

McNeill, Ronald, 202
Meerut, 13, 38, 260, 262, 264
Menin Road, 64, 71–2
Mersey Camp, 184
Mesnil Ridge, 120, 132
Messines, viii, 58, 144, 154, 163–6, 171–82,
    186–7, 191, 193, 194, 196, 197, 198,
    199–200, 205, 214, 219, 222, 258, 274
Meyer, Lucas, 27–8
Meynell, Godfrey (Lt-Col), 91
Middlebrook, Martin, 126
Miller, C. C. (Capt), 229
Milne, Sir George (Capt, Gen Sir), 25
Möller, Col, 28–9, 31
Monaghan, County, 43, 108–09, 140, 265,
    267–8
Monash, John (Maj-Gen, Gen Sir), 151
Monro, Charles (Gen Sir), 89
Montdidier, vii, 248
Montgomery (-Massingberd), Archibald
    (Maj-Gen, Field-Marshal Sir), 111, 281
Montgomery, Bernard (Field-Marshal Lord), 281
Montgomery, W. A. (Capt, Maj), 201, 269
Mont Noir, 153
Morland, Thomas (Lt-Gen Sir), 110–16, 119,
    123–7, 130–32, 139, 141
Morning Post, 138
Moeuvres, 209–12, 214–15
Mountnugent, 1, 10, 43, 45, 49, 256, 267–8,
    270, 272, 279
Mount Sorrel, 74
Mouquet Farm, 113
Mouquet Switch Line, 126–7, 131
Murray, Archibald (Capt, Gen Sir), 25, 54,
    77–8, 80
Murray, James Woulfe (Gen Sir), 54
Muslim League, 260

Naper family, 35, 278
Neills, steward, 105–06
Neuve Chapelle, 53–4, 57
Nivelle, Robert (Gen), 172
Northern Ireland, 267, 270, 273, 276, 280
Northern Whig, 45
Nowshera, 19
Nugent (Hirschberg), Alison, 38, 263, 265, 280
Nugent, Catherine (Kitty, née Lees), 26, 29,
    30–31, 32, 35, 36, 38, 39, 42, 47, 52, 66–7,
    82, 102, 105–06, 233–4, 263–4, 265, 267,
    276, 279–80, 282
Nugent, Christopher Edmond, 3, 4
Nugent, Cyril, 9
Nugent, Edmond, 3–4, 9–10
Nugent (née Litton), Emily, 3

Nugent, Oliver
early years, 1–5
Royal Munster Fusiliers, 5–7
KRRC, (1st Bn) 7–12, 14–23, 26–33;
(3rd Bn) 35; (4th Bn)12–14, 37–9
North-West Frontier, 14–23
Staff College, 25–6
Boer War, 26–33
family, 26, 35, 38, 105–06, 263, 279–80
political views, 10–11, 34, 42–9, 81,
101–02, 108–09, 157–9, 167–8, 259,
268, 277–9
Cavan Volunteers, 43–50
Hull, 50–54
41 Brigade, 55–80
36th (Ulster) Division:
leadership style, 95–6, 156–7
command on operations
(Somme) 121–3, 126–7, 129–32,
133–4; (Messines) 177, 179;
(Third Ypres) 185–6, 189–90;
(Cambrai) 209–11, 213, 217–18;
(spring 1918 offensive) 234–5,
237–8, 239, 240–42, 243, 246–8,
249–52
relations with military superiors,
(Gough) 185, 192, 222, 251, 255;
(Haig) vii, 25, 135, 161–2,
174–5, 222, 225, 282;
(Plumer) vii, 52, 145, 174,
255, 257, 274, 282
Meerut Division, 259–64
Irish War of Independence/Civil War,
264–72
Great War Commemoration, 273–7
knighthood, 277
life in the Irish Free State, 277–80
Nugent, St George (1825–84), 3, 9
Nugent, St George (1859–65), 3
Nugent, St George (1899–1929), 3, 26, 31, 105,
258, 260, 263, 272, 279, 280
Nugent (Stoney), Theffania, 35, 262–3, 280
Nunburnholme, Lord, 53

O'Connor, Richard (Gen Sir), 281
O'Duffy, Eoin, 267
O'Neill, Hugh (Capt), 83, 271
Ollezy, 230–31, 249
Orange Free State, 26
Orange Order, 47, 96, 104, 145
Ormerod, George (Lt-Col), 89
Ovillers, 128
Oxford University, 56, 93, 262

Paget, Arthur (Gen Sir), 48
Pakenham family, 7, 35, 278
Pakenham Hall, 35, 265
Pakenham, H. A. (Lt-Col), 102, 154
Pakenham, William (Adm Sir), 281
Palmer, Pte, 20–21
Parke, Aubrey ('Pip') (2nd Lt), 66–7, 77
Parke, Evie, 52
Parke, Lawrence ('Ponto') (Lt-Col), 32, 40
Parke, Walter (Lt), 52
Parnell, Charles Stewart, 10
Passchendaele, 192, 204
Pathan (Pashtun) tribes:
Afridis, 17
Asazai, 15
Hassanzai, 15
Isazai, 18
Orakzai, 16–17
Swatis, 20–21
Peacocke, John (Maj, Lt-Col), 106, 127, 131,
156, 190, 252, 267
Pearse, Patrick, 107
Pelly, Raymond (Lt-Col, Brig-Gen), 90, 154
Perceval, Edward (Maj-Gen), 110, 112, 124–5,
127, 130–33
Perceval-Maxwell, Bob (Maj, Lt-Col), 86, 166,
189–90, 238, 241, 247–8, 250, 252
Pereira, Cecil (Maj-Gen Sir), 214–15
Peshawar, 12, 13, 16
Petain, Philippe (Gen), 172, 241
Philipps, Ivor (Maj-Gen), 142
Phillips, Percival, 253–4
Piccadilly Farm, 60–61
Pilcher, Thomas (Maj-Gen), 142
Pile, Frederick (Gen Sir), 281
Pithon, 237, 239
Place, Otley (Lt-Col), 112–13, 115, 123, 125,
153, 155, 205, 223, 237, 247, 253
Plumer, Herbert (Gen Sir), vii, 50, 52, 55, 57–8,
66, 74, 78–9, 145, 154, 161, 170, 173–6,
180, 183, 192, 196, 222, 252, 254–5,
257–8, 274, 277, 279, 282
Poona, 263
Pope Benedict XV, 97
Poperinghe, 67
Powell, Herbert (Maj-Gen), 82, 86, 93, 139
Pozieres, 110–11
Pratt, Audley (Capt, Lt-Col), 44, 148, 187, 190,
200, 265
Pratt, Mervyn (Capt), 44
Pretoria, 30–32, 56
Pulteney, William (Lt-Gen Sir), 88–9, 204, 218
Punjab, 14, 15, 260, 262

Quigg, Robert (Pte) VC, 133
Quin, Stewart, 200

Racecourse Redoubt, 232–3
Railway Sap, 107
Railway Wood, 64
Rawalpindi, 14, 15, 18–19
Rawlinson, Henry (Maj-Gen, Gen Sir), 41,
    53–4, 106, 111 15, 119, 142–3, 224
Recruitment (including conscription), vii,
    103–05, 135, 144–5, 149–53, 255–6
Redmond, John, 42, 46, 49, 101–02, 105, 108,
    149–50, 152, 163–4, 167
Redmond, William, 167–8, 181–2
Reitz, Denys (Lt-Col), 198–9
Rennie, George (Lt-Col), 56
Ricardo, Ambrose (Lt-Col, Brig-Gen), 94, 102,
    106–07, 108–09, 132, 154–7, 169, 171,
    187, 189, 196, 202, 205, 208, 217, 219,
    223, 253, 269, 277
Ricardo Redoubt, 236
Richards, Frank, 89–90
Richardson, A. C. (Capt), 92
Richardson, George (Sir), 139–40
Richardson, Lady, 102
Robb, Frederick (Maj-Gen Sir), 54
Roberts, Freddie (Lt), 19
Roberts, Frederick (Field-Marshal Lord), 19, 22,
    23, 26, 31–2
Roberts, Lady, 19, 23
Robertson, George (Surgeon-Maj), 19
Robertson, Philip (Maj-Gen Sir), 95
Robertson, William (Capt, Field-Marshal Sir),
    23–5, 104–05, 224
Rogers, V. B. (Capt, Maj), 229
Rowley, F. J. M. (Brig-Gen), 170
Royal Dublin Society, 279
Royal Irish Constabulary (RIC), 255, 267–9
    Auxiliary Division RIC (Auxiliaries),
    268–70
Roye, 246
Rubempre, 137
Rupprecht, Crown Prince, 216
Russell, Alick (Lt-Col), 91–2, 112
Russell, Andrew (Maj-Gen Sir), 95
Rycroft, William (Maj-Gen Sir), 110, 112,
    114–15, 121, 125, 127, 142

St Anne's Cathedral, Belfast, 280
St Eloi, 59, 74
St Julien, 183, 186, 193
St Omer, 57
St Pierre Divion, 113–14, 116, 122

St Simon, 228, 236
St Quentin, 227, 245
St Quentin canal, 228, 235–7
Samana ridge, 16
Sanctuary Wood, 69–72
Sanders, George (Cpl) VC, 133
Sandhurst, 258, 263
Saunderson family, 35, 43, 47
Saunderson, Edward (Col), 11
Saunderson, Somerset, 44, 140–41, 167, 202
Savage, William (Lt-Col), 154
Saxe-Weimar, Edward (Prince), 11
Schwaben Redoubt, 110, 113–14, 116, 121–4,
    126–31, 134
Seaford, 82
Serre, 111, 128
Sheridan, R. B., 45
Shute, Cameron (Maj-Gen Sir), 95, 175, 225
Shuter, Reginald (Brig-Gen), 119, 157
Simpson, H. C. (Lt-Col), 205, 208
Singleton, H. (Maj, Lt-Col), 153
Sinn Fein, 48, 50, 182, 256, 266
Smith, Joseph, 52–3
Smith, W. G. F. (Lt), 65
Smith-Dorrien, Horace (Gen Sir), 37, 41, 53, 78
Smyth, Ross (Lt-Col), 120
Snow, Thomas (Lt-Gen Sir), 89, 216
Soloheadbeg, 264–5
Solon, 264
Somerville, H. (Maj, Lt-Col), 92
Somerville, Stafford (Lt-Col), 154, 188, 190
Somme, battle of, viii, 110–34, 135, 142, 144,
    146, 149, 153, 154, 161, 164, 168, 171–2,
    173–4, 182–3, 197, 199, 200, 202, 222,
    227, 242, 253, 274, 280
Somme (1918), 227–8, 230, 232, 236–44, 249
Sommette-Eaucourt, 238
Spanbroek, 148
Spender, Lilian (Lily), 102, 137–8, 158, 165,
    181, 194, 257–8
Spender, Rex (Lt), 194
Spender, Wilfrid (Capt, Lt-Col), 83, 87, 89, 90,
    92, 94, 95, 97–8, 101–02, 107, 108–09,
    119, 136–41, 156–7, 158, 164–5, 181,
    193–5, 223, 257, 273, 280
Stamfordham, Lord, 145
Stewart-Moore, John (Lt), 90
Stoney, Myles, 280
Stoney, Oliver, 280
Strickland, Father, 97
Stronge, James (Sir), 268
Stuart-Wortley, Dick Montagu (Lt, Maj-Gen),
    29, 39, 174–5
Stuart-Wortley, Edward Montagu (Maj-Gen),
    141–2

Stuff Redoubt, 124, 129
Symons, William Penn (Maj-Gen Sir), 27–8

Talana Hill, 27–30, 31, 39, 174, 198
Tatlow, Garnett, 11–12
Templeton, James (Pte), 99–100
Territorial Force, 37, 39–42
The Times, 138
Thiepval, 111, 113–16, 121, 123, 125–7,
    129–32, 142, 156, 171, 200, 214, 219, 273
Thiepval Wood, 106–07, 113, 115, 120, 122,
    125–6, 128–31, 133, 154, 242
Thompson family, 271
Townshend, Charles (Gen Sir), 41
Transvaal, 26, 30, 32
Trim, 270
Tudor, Hugh (Maj-Gen Sir), 270

Udny, Richard, 17
Ulster Covenant, 42–3, 108
Ulster Declaration, 42
Ulster Divisional Fund, 273
Ulster Divisional History, 274
Ulster Special Constabulary (USC), 269
Ulster Tower, 273–4, 275
Ulster Unionist Council (UUC), 43, 83,
    108–09, 140, 200, 268, 273, 282
Ulster Volunteer Force (UVF), viii, 34, 43–7,
    50, 52, 81–4, 87, 93, 96–7, 104, 139, 157,
    198, 268, 273
Ulster Women's Unionist Council Gift Fund,
    102
United Provinces, 260, 262–3

Valdant, H. (Maj-Gen), 241
Vignacourt, 97
Villeselve, 243–4
Vimy Ridge, 171, 180
Virginia, Co. Cavan, 256, 274–5
Vivian, Odo (Maj, Lt-Col), 189, 201
Von Hutier, Gen, 230, 242
Von Laffert, Gen, 178
Von Lossberg, Gen, 183

Von Richthofen, Manfred (Capt), 116, 218
Von Soden, Gen, 128

Walters, chauffeur, 51
Waring, Holt (Maj), 166
Watts, Herbert (Lt-Gen Sir), 182, 184, 186,
    189–91, 193, 196
Waziristan, 263
Welsh Ridge, 216–18
Westmeath, Lord, 279
Weygand, Maxime (Gen), 274
White, George (Gen Sir), 19, 22, 24, 27, 31
Wigan Copse, 203–04
William Redan, 107
Williamson, Samuel (Pte), 100
Wilson, Henry (Lt-Gen, Field-Marshal Sir), 1, 5,
    57, 224, 245, 256, 271, 274, 277, 281
Wimborne, 26
Wimborne, Lord, 255
Wiseman, Ida, 9–10, 24, 280
Wisques, 169
Withycombe, William (Brig-Gen), 87, 93–4, 99,
    130, 132–3, 170, 184, 200, 210–11, 242–3,
    253
Wolseley, Garnet (Field-Marshal Lord), 22
Woodroffe, Sidney (2nd Lt) VC, 75
Woods, Philip (Maj, Lt-Col), 132–3, 199–200
Woollcombe, Charles (Lt-Gen Sir), 41, 204–05,
    209, 211
Wytschaete, 173, 178, 179

Yeats, W. B., 279
York, 50
Yorkshire Bank, 203
Young, Samuel, 256
Ypres (city, Salient, Second and Third Battles),
    viii, 12, 55, 57–80, 87, 93, 163, 164, 171,
    172, 182–96, 197, 199, 202, 220, 251,
    253–4, 256, 258, 274
Ytres, 208, 211, 215
Yule, James (Brig-Gen), 28

Zouave Wood, 70–76